GAME ON

GAME ON

THE ALL-AMERICAN RACE TO MAKE CHAMPIONS OF OUR CHILDREN

TOM FARREY

 Printed in the United States of America. For information, contact ESPN Books, 19 East 34th Street, 7th Floor, New York, New York 10016.

ISBN: 978-1-933060-46-0

ESPN books are available for special promotions and premiums. For details contact Michael Rentas, Assistant Director, Inventory Operations, Hyperion, 77 West 66th Street, 11th floor, New York, New York 10023, or call 212-456-0133.

FIRST EDITION

10 9 8 7 6 5 4 3 2 1

For

Cole

Anna

Kellen

and every child of their generation

CONTENTS

INTRODUCTION

A RACE TO THE BOTTOM

During the television broadcast of the 2005 British Open, the sports apparel giant Nike introduced a 30-second commercial celebrating the personal story of its lead endorser, Tiger Woods, who would go on to win his 10th major championship. You may recall the ad: Skillfully editing home video of Tiger as a child into scenes from one of the world's most prestigious tournaments, the producers imagined him mastering the Old Course at St. Andrews while still in elementary school. It opens with Tiger hunkered over the ball, his tiny head swallowed by a red-and-white mesh hat. With an elegant, rounded swing, Tiger sends the ball down the middle of the fairway. In the teeming gallery, beneath a row of international flags fluttering in the wind, adults reach for their binoculars. Tiger holes a chip shot and does a joyous little dance-walk, right hand clutching his club like Fred Astaire with a cane. "A piece of history being served up for us by Tiger Woods at this moment," the announcer purrs. The masses pour onto the Old Course in pursuit of the boy king, the ancient castle-like clubhouse behind him. His nurturing mother, Kultida, snaps photos from the gallery. His visionary father, Earl, claps at a respectful distance. Layered over these scenes is the guitar-driven sound of a Rod

Stewart melody. As Tiger drains a long putt and looks to the heavens with delight, Stewart reaches the chorus.

I wish that I knew
What I know now
When I was younger

On the July day the spot airs, I am in San Diego, interviewing children who finished preschool and kindergarten only a month earlier. None of the 54 boys and girls present needs slick video production to envision playing for elite titles at their age. In fact, that's precisely what they are doing, competing in the recently added 6-and-under division of the Callaway Junior World Golf Championships. In private, tournament organizers call it the Diaper Division, as the kids are still too young to fill out and tally up a scorecard—most haven't learned math yet. Still, the three-day event has the feel of an international spectacle. Most of the golfers are from the U.S., but there are also representatives from South Africa, China, the Philippines, Guam, and England. (The last in the person of a tow headed boy named Tiger. Tiger Adams, that is.) A Mexican child brought a teaching pro as his caddy and a cheering section that trails him around the 18-hole course. The winner, a Japanese boy who offers a Tiger fist pump after each birdie, is followed the entire time by a television crew from home.

Welcome to youth sports in the 21st century.

It is a world unrecognizable to many Americans who grew up in simpler times, which were actually just a few years ago. It is a world desperately organized around the principle of identifying and promoting—and often exploiting—the next generation of athlete-entertainers, an ethos that reaches beyond the sport of golf and can be found, in some form, in virtually every community in which child's play is organized.

When Woods was a boy, the lowest age division offered at the Junior Worlds was 10 and under. At age 6, even with the beautiful swing that got him on *The Mike Douglas Show* as a toddler, he wasn't about to beat older, stronger kids. There were no glass trophies to hoist, no glory to be had, few press clips to show off to schoolmates. It was the same for kids in most other sports. Elite competition only began around the start of middle school, most visibly with the Little League World Series. And even that event had a freak-show quality to it, with victory often going to the team with the most adult-sized pitcher. One of the more memorable sports moments of the early '80s occurred in 1982, when a Kirkland, Washington, team led by boy-man Cody Webster ended Taiwan's winning streak at the Little League World Series. Webster stopped growing shortly after that, and later drew zero interest from major league baseball clubs.

World titles for tots are just one manifestation of the new thinking, which holds that it's never too early to train children as competitors. There are 12-year-olds driving racecars. Eleven-year-olds are turning pro in skateboarding. Ten-year-olds get recruited by college basketball programs. Nine-year-olds hire professional coaches. Eight-year-olds play 75 baseball games a year. Seven-year-olds vie for power-lifting medals. Six-year-olds have personal trainers. Five-year-olds play soccer year-round. Four-year-old tumblers compete at the AAU Junior Olympics. Three-year-olds enter their third year of swim lessons. Two-year-olds have custom golf clubs.

Just for kicks, to get a sense of where all this might be headed, I flew to Australia with a cheek swab from my 1-year-old son, Kellen, to get his DNA tested by a company that uses genetic analysis to recommend specific sports. Guess what? My baby boy has the right stuff for a certain Winter Olympic event.

We should not be shocked by any of these developments. Children of this generation do many things earlier than their parents and grandparents did. Preschool is now a standard part of the educational experience. Kids read earlier, play poker earlier, watch violent movies earlier, even go through puberty earlier. Barbie was marketed originally to girls between the ages of 6 and 10; now her popularity peaks with kids half that age, and by 8 or so many girls are wearing sexualized clothes. JonBenét Ramsey—who, thanks to her untimely death and subsequent celebrity, was frozen forever in the national consciousness as a 6-year-old beauty queen in pancake makeup—is simply a metaphor for our times.

Even so, for the largest number of kids, sports are their primary organized activity outside of school. The race to the bottom in youth sports, where there's no such thing as too young, represents one of the most profound—and unexamined—trends of recent decades. In the years after World War II, when the ideal of a sheltered childhood was finally achieved by the American middle class, kids spent many weekend days playing in the sandlot with other neighborhood kids. They picked teams, made up rules, and quit at the first sight of an ice-cream truck. When I was growing up in the 1970s in Hollywood, Florida, we spent countless after-school hours playing touch football in the street, throwing the ball over the cars that drove by. Now it's rare to see kids of any age playing sports in any location without the company of a coach.

As a father of three, I have a personal stake in how the push to incubate child athletes has transformed the entire landscape of youth sports. As I write this sentence, at the outset of my reporting, my oldest son, 8-year-old Cole, plays "travel" soccer—a form of competition that has descended on most communities in the past decade and which attempts to build standout players through high doses of exposure to the sport. It begs for a four-season commitment, with two practices and two games each week during the fall, a slightly reduced schedule in the spring, plus an indoor winter league and summer clinic that are optional but recommended. His coaches' requests are actually quite reasonable in light of what's asked of children on other travel teams in the area. Still, we have turned our weekends over to soccer, driving as much as an hour away to other small Connecticut towns, some of which my wife Christine and I have never heard of. We let Cole try out for this team reluctantly, anticipating the loss of family dinners together but ultimately figuring that if he doesn't catch the bullet train now, he might lose the chance to play soccer in high school. The other kids just would be too tactically advanced. Allowing Cole to join the team was the result of, oddly, a conservative impulse—the preserving of an option, the chance to have a chance.

I wish I could tell you that we were acting irrationally. But it isn't the case. All the players on our town's current high school team participated in travel soccer programs. No one just takes up the sport in ninth grade and makes the cut anymore, unless they're an incredible raw athlete. Now, we're effectively holding our varsity tryouts in the grade school years.

Our daughter, 7-year-old Anna, is in her third season of rec-league soccer, the form I began playing at age 10 in the 1970s. Compared to Cole's travel soccer commitment, hers entails half the practices and games, all of which are held at the town field. The emphasis is more on fun than on winning. But some of these second graders are in their *ninth* season of soccer, having signed up each fall, winter, and spring since kindergarten (three seasons a year). A couple of the dad-coaches are getting anxious to play for something, with travel ball still a year away. Some of these games can get intense, with the coaches and a dozen parents yelling instructions at any given time. The most physically mature girls dominate. As Anna floats on the outside of the beehive—the smallest and most timid girl on the field—I know that she's wondering if sports are for her. My fear is that she's asking herself that question too early, before she has had a chance to grow into her body. I wonder why we as parents and as a society would want to have any 7-year-old kid ask that question, given the benefits of playing sports and the hazards of physical inactivity.

This is a book written with great respect for the needs of children like Anna, who are in danger of being socialized away from athletics prematurely. Youth sport is the most important institution in all of sports, because it is where the magic begins. It's where we learn to love sports, picking up fitness habits and rooting interests that can last a lifetime. But it's an institution at a historic crossroads, one in which performance often matters more than participation does. It's less and less accessible to the late bloomer, the genetically ordinary, the economically disadvantaged, the child of a one-parent household, the physically or mentally disabled, and the kid who needs exercise more than any other—the clinically obese.

Team sports are played mostly by people under age 18, whether in a league or casual format. And for all the flash and fury of elite youth sports in recent years, most team games have lost participants since the mid-1990s. Among the organizations that have recognized this trend is the Sporting Goods Manufacturers Association, the trade group whose members equip child athletes. "Organized team sports in schools and leagues have grown in recent years, largely because of a strong infusion of female players," the SGMA wrote in its 2005 "State of the Industry" report. "But organized team sports tend to emphasize elite players and competition, freezing out millions of children who might like to play for fun." A national study conducted for SGMA that year estimated that 26 million boys and girls ages 6 to 17 participated in at least one organized team sport, while 10 million participated only in a non-organized team sport and 12 million did not participate in a team sport at all. "However, it must be emphasized that while participation in organized team sports is increasing, it is by no means keeping up with population growth," the report noted. "As a piece of the total pie, organized team sports participation is also shrinking." (See chart below.)

These are not encouraging developments for an industry that depends on a wide pipeline of new fans and sports consumers. Over the previous decade, the SGMA report noted, participation among children and adults in nearly all of the 100 sports and activities measured either dropped or grew more slowly than the overall population. The trend applies even to golf. Despite the construction of many new courses, between 1998—just after Woods won his first Masters title—and 2004

Participation in Team Sports

Kids ages 6 to 17 who participated in either organized or casual play at least once during the year, in millions.

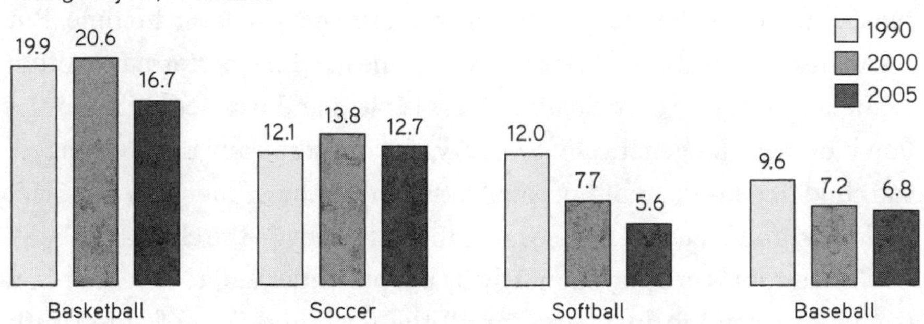

Source: Sporting Goods Manufacturers Association/American Sports Data

golf lost an estimated four million more participants than it gained. A subsequent survey, conducted in 2006 for the SGMA by a different company using a separate questionnaire and methodology, suggested that participation levels in golf have been flat, not falling. Either way, the game's appeal has not grown in the Tiger Woods era, contrary to popular myth.

"The overall picture is one of an increasingly sedentary population," the SGMA concluded. "This is not only bad for business, it's bad for the country."

It's hard to overstate the influence Woods has had on youth sports culture. Everyone knows his story: The number one golfer has been in training since his number one birthday, by which time his father had already given him a metal putter. "Go ahead," reads one of the ubiquitous airport ads for another of Woods' sponsors, a consulting firm. "Be a Tiger." In the photo, Woods is hitting bravely into a thick fog. It's a metaphor that resonates with today's parents, sold on the notion that champions can be manufactured through faith and early preparation. The power of Tiger's story has erased in the public mind the cautionary tale of Todd Marinovich, who just a few years before was served up as evidence of what happens when a parent works too hard to create a star athlete. His father, Marv, groomed him to be a pro quarterback; Todd rebelled, joined a rock band after college, and washed out of the NFL prematurely in a haze of drugs.

Even the lesson of Michael Jordan's success is no match for Woods. The most accomplished athlete of our era only began to focus his energies on basketball in 11th grade, when he finally made his high school team. His experience is not uncommon. Retired NFL tight end Kellen Winslow began playing football in 12th grade. Current tight end Tony Gonzalez was also a basketball player in college. Tim Duncan was a competitive swimmer for much of his youth. Even in tennis, a sport long known for obsessive parents, a study shows that most top American pros walked a multiple-sport path, the way Andy Roddick, who played basketball through high school, did. The world's top tennis player, Roger Federer, played soccer into his early teenage years. Each of these athletes can cite the mental and physical benefits of learning other sports while young. Baseball Hall of Famer Tony Gwynn told me that his uncanny ability to hit to the opposite field came from the hand-eye coordination he developed as a point guard; he felt like he was able to practically dig the ball out of the catcher's mitt. And he suggests he never got burned out on baseball because he switched his full attention to the sport late, only in college.

Our doctors should be specialists, not our children. Kids now are often encouraged to focus on one sport, as if being asked to order from the children's menu at Ruby Tuesday. Not uncommon is the notion expressed by Randy Lee, coach of the McDonough (Ga.) Dawgs, a team of second-graders that won an American Amateur Baseball Congress national title. "If you don't start early, you're left behind," he told me. "And with the cost of college these days, it sure would be nice to get a scholarship." Coaches and parents like Lee, whose son plays for the Dawgs, know how truly remote a financial payoff might be, that the great majority of high school athletes never go on to play college ball, and that only the rarest of gems make it to the pros. For them, all the more reason to improve your odds by turbo-charging kids with private instruction and lots of early competition.

Tiger Woods has slapped a Good Housekeeping Seal of Approval on these efforts, as a model athlete and the kind of son any parent could be proud of.

But the forces that have shifted the paradigm of youth sports go well beyond the success of one golfer. In fact, the foundation was laid at the beginning of the 20th century, when the educators and wealthy industrialists who first organized children's games built a winner-take-all structure into boys' (and, later, girls') competitions. The rise of Little League after World War II invited parents onto playing fields as untrained volunteer coaches, where they dressed up their kids to look like miniature big leaguers. And politics have also played a part; among the social programs that were slashed in the 1980s by Ronald Reagan were those funding urban parks and recreation centers that supported inexpensive, broad-based athletic participation. Public dollars began to shift in the direction of professional leagues, through the construction of expensive stadiums that would jack player salaries—and up the incentive for child athletes to seek careers in those sports. The NCAA member universities put extra shine on the dangling carrot, quadrupling the amount of so-called "scholarship money" doled out to their athlete-entertainers. Elite travel teams—sometimes known as "premier" or "select" or "club" teams—were created as a means to gain access to scarce resources. They exploded in popularity in the late 1990s, after Little League, the leading youth sports organization, backed away from its "dual participation" rule which prohibited kids from playing with other, non-Little League teams during the same season. The stage was set for endless slates of games and year-round play.

"A whole new industry was born," says Little League CEO Steve Keener.

Another key event, largely overlooked, was the ironically named Amateur Sports Act of 1978, passed by Congress at the height of the Cold War. The law put the U.S. Olympic Committee in charge of grassroots sports in this country and the sanctioning of sport-specific national governing bodies (NGBs), such as U.S. Soccer. But it gave no money to the USOC so that it could fulfill its mandate, and the USOC has made little effort since then to push coaches' education and athlete-development research down to the youth level. The law also unwittingly made a desperate actor of the Amateur Athletic Union. Stripped of its historic role of picking Olympic teams, the once aristocratic AAU reinvented itself as a toll booth with a down-home touch. In the process it became a youth sports colossus, starting with basketball in which sneaker money is at stake. The AAU now oversees and collects big fees at more than 250 national championship events in 35 sports. The age divisions get lower every year. At the AAU Junior Olympics in New Orleans a couple of months before Hurricane Katrina, a preschooler with ribbons in her hair showed me the gold medal in tumbling she was taking back home to Chicago. Her winning routine, a series of somersaults, took a total of 11 seconds. Or about as long as it took to process her family's credit card payment at registration.

When the president of the AAU looks at kid sports, he sees customers, not amateurs. "You know what I say a true amateur is?" President

Bobby Dodd tells me. "I say the true amateur is that 3- to 5-year-old that is pickin' clover one minute and then runnin' over and sittin' on mom's lap, and then comin' over and bouncin' the basketball and maybe makin' a pass. Hasn't been given a pair of sneakers. Hasn't been recruited to go play on the elementary team. That's the only true amateur."

Youth sport in the United States isn't supposed to be a free-for-all. Laws provide mechanisms to clamp down on excesses. But preserving an ethic that fosters participation into the teenage years just hasn't been a priority, and this book will explore the consequences of that neglect. On the one hand, we have first-graders who can shoot threes, third-graders who can jack 200-foot home runs, and the occasional ninth-grade golfer good enough to turn pro. On the other hand, thousands of kids are getting frozen out or are opting out of the manic youth sport struggle by the end of middle school—a time when 30 percent of all American kids are obese or at risk of becoming so.

Participation levels in team sports peak at age 11, then decline rapidly at around 15. That's when teenagers reach high school, with its limited number of available teams. That arrangement works fine at small public schools and private schools with the resources to offer a broad range of sports. But the larger, often urban, public schools can sometimes accommodate on their teams no more than one-fifth of the students. For the rest, options are limited. Even physical education classes are disappearing, thanks in part to the misperception that private, non-school club sports will fill the void. Playing sports has become a case of the haves and the have-nots, just like other phases of American life. The current generation of parents, among the first to have come up through large public schools, recognizes the obstacles facing their children, so they join the youth sports arms race if they can afford to.

In this book, the fundamental questions that I ask are: Has the success of a few come at the cost of many? And: How much success are we truly seeing? For all the resources lavished on a limited set of early achievers, the downstream results on the international stage in the first generation of pro athletes to emerge from the new paradigm have been underwhelming to say the least. The U.S. topped the medal count at the Athens Olympics in 2004, but on a per-capita basis 38 countries were more efficient at delivering champions. Beyond Tiger, the PGA Tour is increasingly populated by foreigners, and the biennial Ryder Cup has been won by the U.S. team just once since 1993. In men's soccer, which introduced the travel team concept to youth sports more than two decades ago, the U.S. couldn't get out of the first round in the 2006 World Cup. Our men's hockey team was a non-factor at the 2006 Turin Olympics, and the women settled for bronze. We're getting thumped even in sports that we invented. The U.S. failed to medal in the inaugural World Baseball Classic, finishing behind Japan, Cuba, South Korea, and the Dominican Republic. For the men's basketball team, a gold medal at the Beijing Olympics would represent its first major title in eight years. The women are coming off a semifinals loss at the 2006 World Championships.

I'm not sure, but I think we still rule in football (American rules, that is).

And in competitive hot-dog eating, now that Kobayashi has been dethroned.

There are bright spots, but you get the general idea. We Americans think of ourselves as architects of the greatest sporting nation ever created. Our athletes are worldwide brands—LeBron James, Alex Rodriguez, Peyton Manning, the Williams sisters, and especially Tiger. Our investment in elite sports can be seen from the window of any airplane, as it flies over taxpayer-financed stadiums sparkling like ten-carat diamonds amid urban and college-town landscapes across America. Our flag flies more often than any other in Olympic medal ceremonies. Our professional leagues are followed globally. Our university games are watched nationally. On Friday nights, the lights of high school football dominate locally. But beneath that thin, shiny layer of elite spectator sports is a system that is troubled, if not failing. On the grassroots level, at the base of the feeder system, too many kids are funneled into too few sports. At too early an age. With too little emphasis on basic motor development, too much focus on the final score, and too much early specialization. Under the aegis of youth sports organizations that give too little consideration to available scientific and educational research, and under the guidance of coaches with too little training in what is and is not age appropriate. No wonder so many kids wind up having Tommy John surgery.

It's easy to blame parents for the problems of youth sports. Occasionally, we read a report about a volunteer coach bribing his pitcher to bean an autistic teammate or a Pop Warner game ending in a 100-person melee or some parent killing another over a sideline grievance. We shake our heads sadly and ask, *Why can't these people behave?* That's what I did when I began reporting on this subject. Then I signed up for a daily e-mail bulletin by University of Missouri law professor Doug Abrams, who collects youth sports news articles. Trust me when I say that while much of what happens in youth sports is healthy and good and productive, just about every day in America there is an incident that will make your head spin. I realized quickly that there are just too many parents going haywire for there not to be something structurally askew with the whole setup.

This book explores the topic primarily through the lives of the pacesetters, the kids and parents with the most ambitious athletic dreams. Each chapter features a new set of characters, and connects their worlds to the historic, economic, behavioral, social, religious, and other influences that have shaped and reshaped youth sports. I must say, I came to like nearly everyone that I met. The stereotype of the abusive parent pushing the reluctant kid usually doesn't apply. Most want their kids to be champions in life, not just sports. And when parents go to extremes in prepping their kid for athletic stardom, it never springs from a lack of love. On the contrary, they usually are trying to do right by their child in the best way they know how, within the circumstances and sport system presented to them. John Reese, who expects to spend $90,000 on his son J-Mychal's basketball development through his high school years, summed up the dilemma pretty well. "If a kid comes to you and says he wants to be a doctor, do you tell him he's not smart enough?" he said. "Or that it's too expensive? Do you shoot that dream down? Or do you try to help him attain it?" Keep that in mind as you read their stories.

The book is organized in a manner that reflects the race to the bottom in youth sports. Each chapter explores a theme relevant to would-be athletes of that age—Chapter 1, a visit to a Los Angeles sperm bank to get a glimpse of the search for athletic genes, corresponds to the first year of life, while Chapter 14, about a community torn by a sex scandal in the nation's top-ranked football program, takes us up through the start of high school. As I traveled across the continent and halfway around the world to study this topic, one revelation built upon another. While the people in each chapter come from distinct places and play different sports, parallels in their stories emerge, allowing lives to be stitched together in the manner of an American Dream quilt. I have also sprinkled in, here and there, a few elements of my own journey as the father of two children already in youth sports, with a third soon to enter that realm.

Each week, millions of children play some form of organized athletics. The aggregate attendance at these events dwarfs that at pro and perhaps even college sports, with fans (parents) no less emotionally invested in the result. Youth sport is a cherished American institution, though not for universal reasons. Some see it as a playground for all, others a proving ground for the athletic elite. I've written this book out of a gut sense that these two philosophies need not conflict with each other, that they are compatible, even. That if sports are made to be fun, and measures are taken to keep as many children involved as possible, as late as possible, then more winners will emerge at the top. I'm less convinced Rod Stewart is right, that kids should know what adults know.

Making champs of children starts with kids just being kids.

And with good jock seed, of course.

AGE 1

BONUS BABIES

Los Angeles, California

I have come to L.A. looking for sperm.

Strong sperm. Swift sperm. Athletic sperm!

Such a thing does exist, I am told.

"Wanna see?" says Diana Schillinger, lab manager at California Cryobank, a reproductive tissue depository that can be found on the west side of this sprawling city, just a couple miles from the beaches of Santa Monica. With her shoulder-length brown hair, reading glasses, and approachable manner, Schillinger exudes the vibe of a content suburban mom, and right now she is eager to show off the "future people" in her care. She motions to a techie who is hunkered over a microscope offering a glimpse of the world I wish to enter. More sanitary than sartorial in a blue disposable lab coat and hairnet, the techie slides his stool out of the way, making room for me to peer into the eyepiece.

I see eyelashes. No, oops, wait a minute ... there they are. Sperm. Sperm everywhere. Hundreds, maybe thousands, of sperm. Some move back and forth at a manic pace. Some just meander, like surfers waiting for the right wave. Others are inert. Maybe it's been too long since high school biology class, but I find it amazing that so much life—so much visibly different life—could occupy the tiniest dot on a thin plate of lit-up glass. I feel like Horton the elephant discovering the colony of Whos.

"Good sperm are the ones that are not just moving, but moving in a forward progression," Schillinger says. "You don't want them to zigzag. You want the one that's going to get to the egg and fertilize it first."

She smiles at the irony. "It's like an Olympic race."

I see what she means. The most commanding sperm move like Michael Phelps, their S-shape tails whipping through the neighborhood pond as if it is what they were born to do, all power and elegance. Schillinger cannot tell me who provided the sample, whether or not it came from one of the UCLA athletes who get paid to give weekly. Donor anonymity is a must in her business. But the best sperm at least *move* athletically, almost in a straight line, staying in their lane, efficiently crossing the grid of squares in the viewing field that helps the techie estimate the number of active, or motile, sperm. Whenever he sees one, he clicks a counter.

This sample has 150, the techie announces, impressed. It will now advance to the next stage in the process, where it will be "washed" in a centrifuge, an act of purification that removes the slacker sperm and ensures that clients paying $350 a vial get only the very best candidates—the all-stars, if you will—of baby creation.

Each vial will include about 10 million sperm. One to two vials will be used in each insemination. Usually, it takes a healthy woman six to eight inseminations to get pregnant. All said, about 100 million sperm will fight for the right to make one baby.

A hundred million, and only one winner.

No wonder so many of us believe our children can be special athletes. Just to get born, with or without the aid of a cryobank, they already have beaten enormous odds. At the moment of their first breath, they are Darwin's champions. And the sperm that wins this hellacious battle for conception gets to its destination, the egg, not by thinking its way through the fluid, but through coordination, fitness, and outstanding physical effort. Life begins with an act of elite athleticism.

And yet, is that all there is? Could it be that some children are born with the genetic stuff to go on to actually *become* elite athletes? And others just aren't?

• • •

It's the first and most important question to ask, as the answer each of us chooses to believe inevitably shapes the philosophy of youth sports with which we are most comfortable. If you believe, as Scandinavian societies are prone to, that rarefied talents are largely inborn, then you might promote a sport-for-all system that invests in the infrastructure of the grassroots and assumes that the natural elite will bubble up from the masses. But if you believe, as many Americans do, that rarefied talent is largely an expression of free will, then you would promote an ethos that rewards early initiative and commitment above all else.

Ryan Nece has wrestled with the nature vs. nurture question for a long time.

The former UCLA linebacker, now an NFL veteran in his sixth year, was made the old-fashioned way. Back in the late 1970s, his father, Ronnie Lott, passed his mother, Cathy Nece, in a hallway at Eisenhower High School in Rialto, California—a working-class suburb about an hour's drive east of the California Cryobank. Ronnie and Cathy smiled at each other. He was a sophomore, the rising star on the school's football and basketball teams; she was a senior, the high-spirited daughter of a local restaurateur. They began dating. Four years later, after Lott's sophomore year at USC, Cathy gave birth to a chunky, eight-pound boy with long, curly hair. Ryan entered the world on Feb. 24, 1979, so mellow and happy that he made no effort to swipe away the newborn skullcap a nurse placed on his head.

At the time, Lott was laser-focused on getting his career going, so Nece raised Ryan on her own. Growing up, Ryan talked to his dad now and then and flew up on occasion to attend 49ers games as Lott built his reputation as the greatest defensive back in NFL history. But Cathy was the dominant figure in Ryan's life, and the boyhood she gave him was decidedly free of organized sports. He rode ATVs in the sand dunes of the desert east of San Bernardino; camped in the Grand Canyon; fished amid snowcapped peaks at Mammoth Lake, where his maternal grandpa taught him the values of patience and a steady pole; took family car trips down to Baja California, where he stood next to the Sea of Cortez and tried to imagine the creatures that lived in the deepest blue water. He has fond memories of those years. "I got to be a boy," he tells me, sitting at the dining room table in his mother's cul-de-sac home in the shadow of the San Bernardino Mountains. "I got to be adventurous in other ways, not just adventurous on the playing field."

When Ryan was 5, his mother signed him up for T-ball. She gave him a lefthander's mitt.

"Is he lefthanded?" the coach asked.

"No," Cathy Nece said, perplexed.

That's how little she knew about baseball, that righties don't catch with their right hand. It would be the first and last time she enrolled him in youth sports. She wasn't hostile to the idea; she just wasn't going to push or even suggest it. When Ryan finally joined a team again, in fifth grade, it was of his own volition. He announced to her one day that he wanted to sign up for Little League in order to play with his friends. Some of them already had six years of organized baseball experience at that point. They knew how to turn double plays, work the count, and hit to the opposite field. Ryan's best friend, Teddy, had the coolest glove and bat on the market, a batting cage in his backyard, and a father who worked the umps from the stands when he thought a call should have gone his son's way. He seemed determined to get his boy a college scholarship.

His first year in baseball, Ryan was voted an All-Star. Playing for the league's worst team, he made acrobatic catches in centerfield and stole home to seal its lone victory. The next season he hit a home run in his first at-bat, earning the right to be honorary mayor for the day. Success came quickly in other sports, too. On his middle school teams, he was a terror at the net in volleyball, and he was the best athlete on the basketball court. In track, he proved to be the fastest 12-year-old in Southern California. Lott was there that day at the University of Riverside, one of the first times he saw Ryan compete at an elite level.

Ryan remembers his dad being shocked at the result. *Whoa. That's my kid?*

Lott tells me he can't remember that day—"Too long ago," he says. But the sense of total surprise would not have been out of character for him or anyone else of that era. It was 1991, a decade before most of the human genome would be sequenced, offering fresh insights on the nature vs. nurture debate. Lott certainly considered willpower to be at the core of his own achievements, which were many: a national championship with USC, four Super Bowl titles with the 49ers, and 10 Pro Bowl appearances. He was known as a ferocious tackler, the rare safety who actually scared running backs. The son of a military man, his technique was to imagine a point five yards behind the ballcarrier and drive right through the obstacle to that target, separating the poor sucker from his snot and, perhaps, the ball. He likened the impact on his own body to repeatedly getting hit with a bat, a sacrifice he was willing to make. Lott was a self-made man in the American tradition of Abraham Lincoln, John D. Rockefeller, and Sam Walton, each of whom rose from modest origins to the top of his profession.

For him to see Ryan dominate athletically, instantly, would have been to think ... *what?* That his son's success was his? That his Hall of Fame career was somehow biologically aided, maybe even ordained? Perish the thought. Even today, Lott prefers not to talk about the role of genes in athletic achievement or the endowment he may have passed on to his son.

"That's not fair to him or to me," Lott says. "As a parent, I just don't think that's something I would even think about." He has that kind of mental discipline.

But the son is a man of his time too: the first decade of the 20th century, when these questions not only are entertained but sometimes get answered in the same breath. At the dining room table, Nece crosses his large hands, lays them on the table, and bears down to make a point. He flashes a look that is unmistakably, eerily Ronnie Lott. It's that calm, hard-eyed stare of an eagle locked on his target, which in this case is me.

"You know what?" Nece says. "Growing up with my dad not being around much, it was odd. People who remembered him were always like, 'Man, there are so many things you do that are just like your dad. Your mannerisms: the way you talk, the way you hold your hands.' And I wondered, Is that innate? Is that something that is just in me?" Nece pauses, finding his resolve. "I now really believe that it is."

Despite his late start in organized sports, Nece has gone further and done more than any of the thousands of athletes to come out of his town.

That group includes his best friend Teddy, who peaked at 5-foot-8 and never made it past junior college baseball. An agile 6-foot-3 and 225 pounds, Nece has the necessary size and speed, and the sort of ball-hawking instincts that remind coaches of his father.

Competing at the highest level of the game only confirmed his suspicion. At the Tampa Bay Buccaneers' 2005 training camp, seven players were sons of NFL veterans. Nece was among five who made the team: fellow linebacker Barrett Ruud (son of Tom, who played the position for the Bills and Bengals), tight end Alex Smith (former Broncos defensive end Edwin), and quarterbacks Brian Griese (Bob, the Dolphins Hall of Famer) and Chris Simms (another QB, Phil, of the Giants). The Bucs' locker room had so many NFL aristocrats, it may as well have been the House of Lords.

In his head, Nece worked through the usual explanations for how someone like him might have ended up in the pro sports penthouse ...

Environment? Sure, but not in the same sports-centric way as some of his fellow aristocrats. Unlike Simms and Griese, Nece did not grow up in a home immersed in football. There was no sitting around the TV during *Monday Night Football*, dissecting the Cover 2 defense with Dad. His dad was in the Bay Area on Mondays, mending his weekend wounds. When Lott and Nece did speak on the phone, father never encouraged son to adopt the sport. Lott, despite the warrior persona, preferred that his boy play tennis and avoid the brutality of the game that had reshaped his own body.

Nepotism? Nah. Nece had his own last name, and, much as local newspaper headlines tried to play up the connection ("Nece Makes a Lott of Tackles"), his own identity. He fought hard for that independence, rarely mentioning his father in conversations. For awhile in high school, his mom would not allow sportswriters to interview her son unless they agreed not to ask about Lott. Nece was so determined to make it on his own and not piggyback on his dad's fame that he picked UCLA over USC on signing day and the Bucs over the 49ers as a rookie free agent.

Desperation? Hardly. It cannot be said that he simply wanted it more, needed it more. Nece had a classic middle-class childhood that included two parents (with stepfather Bill Thomas), a stay-at-home mom, and a backyard playscape. He was given a solid education and would go on to graduate from UCLA with 3.2 GPA in a tough major, business economics. He was a kid with options in life and a sense of himself that extended well beyond the gridiron to the campfires and fishing holes of his youth.

"I understand there are bigger things out there than just myself and the game," Nece says. "That's one of the tough things I've had to learn coming into the NFL, that balance can kind of take away from your edge. You gotta be focused and in that zone to keep your job. Some guys I'm competing against are supporting a wife, two kids, their mom, their wife's mom and dad, and they all live in the same house. He's the only one bringing home a check, and if he doesn't get this check, he goes back to his hometown and has to get a job at Wal-Mart. And he still has to provide for everybody. *That's* the guy whose job I'm trying to take. So if I'm thinking about going back to the Grand Canyon, I'm probably going to lose that battle."

And for that—mustering a siege mentality—Lott has been extremely valuable.

Gotta put yourself in a foxhole, Ryan, he told him in rookie training camp.

Foxhole? the suburban son asked.

Foxhole, Lott emphasized. *Do whatever it takes to hold your position.*

Nece has done just that, and he's now among the one-third of NFL players who have lasted as long as five years in the league. These days, he often calls Lott for advice. Their relationship has grown since he made the league, in '02. But the connection has always been there, as athletes. The speed. The anticipation. The coachability. Nece's all-around, adaptable athleticism reveals itself when he steps onto a basketball court, where Lott once dreamed of becoming the next Magic Johnson, before he switched his ambitions to football in high school, when he topped out at 6-1. "I was telling my mom today that sometimes I forget how good an athlete I am," Nece says. "Then I go play some pickup basketball, and I'm just running around and scoring at will. I'm like, These guys are supposed to be basketball players?"

Without intending to follow his father's path, Nece ended up in football and even found his way to the safety position. That's what he was recruited as out of high school, moving to linebacker at UCLA when several players went down to injury. He had to bulk up, but there was no need to ask him to toughen up. As a senior, he played half a game on a broken leg. It was a sacrifice that elicited the inevitable comparisons to his father, who famously kept playing at the end of the 1985 season despite a mangled left little finger, part of which was later amputated. "Genes are genes," Nece explains.

Though his childhood was far from perfect, Nece considers himself fortunate. He had the best of both worlds. Distilled to its essence: nature from dad, nurture from mom. He was given all the tools and none of the expectations.

"So many parents think their child is going to be great," Nece says, "but they've never seen greatness. They've never been around greatness. And there's a huge difference ... " He pauses for a moment, perhaps realizing that parsing good from great could be perceived as his thinking that he, too, is great, and that is just not his style. He's an average linebacker by NFL standards who was raised not to brag. But he has also seen parents, like Teddy's father, try to manufacture elite athletes from scratch, so he continues. "The great ones will be able to compete whether they get the early training or not. No matter when they hop on the track, they'll be able to acclimate to the environment. Then proceed to dominate.

"The cream rises to the top, basically."

• • •

Let's run the numbers from the bottom up.

Less than half of all American children will play high school sports.

Of those, only 1 in 28 will go on to play any sport in college, at any level.

Of those, 1 in 75 will get drafted by one of the major professional leagues—football, baseball, hockey, soccer, and men's and women's basketball—where the vast majority of full-time jobs can be found.

Of those drafted, most will not make the team or, in the case of baseball, advance to the majors. An even smaller fraction will last more than a few years at the highest level, where pensions are acquired, the real money is made, and the full benefits of America's affection for sports stardom await. Throw in the occasional golfer, tennis player, auto racer, bass fisher, and rodeo cowboy, and perhaps 300—maximum—of the four million babies born each year ultimately will pull a paycheck long enough to plausibly say they had a career in pro sports. (Factor in the growing number of foreigners flowing into U.S. pro sports, and the job prospects will get even worse in the coming years. But that's a whole 'nother subject. See Age 13.)

So from the moment of conception, the odds of a child's eventually making a living as an athlete are roughly one in 13,333. Or one in 1.3 trillion, if you're going back to the origin and counting all the eligible sperm.

Like Lott, I want to believe that children can do whatever they want with their lives if they just apply themselves. That's certainly what I tell my kids, as no message seems more worth heeding than the Calvin Coolidge mantra that my father, a realtor, found and printed out when he was breaking into the business: *Nothing in the world can take the place of persistence. Talent will not; nothing is more common than unsuccessful men with talent. Genius will not; unrewarded genius is almost a proverb. Education alone will not; the world is full of educated derelicts. Persistence and determination alone are omnipotent.*

Thomas Jefferson is my favorite American. I take inspiration from his "self-evident truths" that "all men are created equal," as codified in the Constitution. I'd like to think it's more than a statement of political rights. And I *really* like the contemporary finding that humans share something like 99.8 percent of the same DNA. I find sublime what it implies, that we are far more alike than we are unalike.

Still, they are everywhere now, the athletic aristocrats, challenging those romantic notions about the egalitarian basis of elite sports. If Nece and his mother were less polite and had the television on while we ruminated on that March morning, we could have seen the Florida Gators, led by the lanky Joakim Noah, working their way through the men's NCAA Tournament toward the Final Four. Noah's mother is a former Miss Sweden and while no one would suggest that he got her beauty genes—he claims UCLA cheerleaders yelled "Ugly! Ugly!" to taunt him—he appears to have tapped some of the best DNA of his father, the dreadlocked tennis Hall of Famer Yannick Noah. Joakim's sidekicks included Al Horford, son of former NBA center Tito Horford, and Taurean Green, son of former NBA forward Sidney Green. The trio returned in 2007 and won a second-straight national championship. That year, members of the Jockocracy would populate every one of the Final Four teams: Georgetown featured Patrick Ewing Jr. (and was coached by John Thompson III); UCLA had Darren Collison, son of 1984 Olympic sprinter June Collison; and Ohio State was led by Mike Conley Jr., whose father was the 1992 Olympic gold medalist in the triple jump.

In fact, three sons of former pros are arguably the most remarkable current athletes in our biggest sports. Kobe Bryant, son of former NBA first-rounder Joe "Jellybean" Bryant, is a highlight machine with three championship rings who shoots and scores as if it were his imperial privilege. No quarterback, with the possible exception of Tom Brady, has put up better numbers than the Colts' Peyton Manning, brother of fellow Super Bowl MVP Eli of the Giants and son of Saints legend Archie. Then, of course, there is home run king Barry Bonds—an extraordinary talent who, even before allegedly embracing anabolic steroids (ah, the greed!), was certain to surpass father Bobby and reach Cooperstown.

Not a day goes by when some athletic blue blood doesn't make headlines. It could be Rafael Nadal, nephew of a Spanish soccer pro, holding up another French Open trophy. Or the latest trade rumors involving Wally Szczerbiak, son of a former ABA player. Or Brent Barry, the latest NBA son of Hall of Famer Rick, hitting a big shot for the San Antonio Spurs. Or Jalen Rose passing his father, ex-All-Star Jimmy Walker, on the all-time scoring list. Or the Indiana Pacers' Mike Dunleavy Jr. baffling the Los Angeles Clippers, coached by his NBA alum dad. In the NFL, as with the NHL, hiring the sons of former pros is now tradition. On any given Sunday in 2006, highlights were likely to have been generated by Kellen Winslow (son of Hall of Fame tight end Kellen), Matt and Tim Hasselbeck (ex-Patriots tight end Don), Lofa Tatupu (longtime vet Mosi), Stanley Wilson III (Stanley Jr., drug-bust goat of Super Bowl XXIII), Sam Adams (Patriots lineman Sam), Dan Klecko (Jets defensive lineman Joe), Andre Carter (Denver nose tackle Rubin), Chris McAlister (Eagles running back James), Jabar Gaffney (Jets receiver Derrick), Ted Washington (Oilers linebacker Ted Sr.), Jay Foreman (Vikings tailback Chuck), Marion Barber Jr. (Jets running back Marion), Marques Tuiasosopo (Seahawks lineman Manu), Bobby Carpenter (Giants running back Rob), or Daylon McCutcheon (Rams tailback Lawrence). The roll call was even longer in Major League Baseball that year, as 30 children of alums were on rosters, including the sons of Cecil Fielder, Gary Matthews, Tony Gwynn, Jesse Barfield, and Ken Griffey Sr. On and on, the list goes. Pick a sport, any sport. And I wouldn't want to bore you with all the "sons of" and "daughters of" who reached the highest level in college sports.

Why the royal flush now? One theory is that, well, athlete sperm are finding athlete eggs more often. The feminist movement opened up sports opportunities for girls in the 1970s, in turn creating opportunities for male and female athletes to meet. More than a few paired up in the ensuing generation, enhancing the chances of perpetuating the Jockocracy. We now so eagerly await the athletic talent that might result from such matches that the son of Andre Agassi and Steffi Graf shot a tongue-in-cheek commercial in which a pint-size Jaden (actually, it's an actor) spanks tennis winner after winner. When Pete Sampras' son Christian was born, in 2002, bookies gave the baby a 2,000-1 shot to beat Jaden in a Wimbledon final.

When I was a kid in the 1970s, it was the coaches' sons we heard about. They were players like Pete Maravich, who was encouraged to dribble out the window of the family car while it was moving as a way to develop his handle. Those kids came along at a time when the rules and culture of pro sports still prized players whose chief attributes were fundamentals and hustle. So with a halfway decent piece of clay, a coach might be able to fashion a pro out of his son. But those were the last of a breed that had begun to die out in the 1950s. Escalating salaries were ramping up the rewards for athletic success, and racial barriers were falling, encouraging talented teenagers to aim for a career in pro sports. The coaches' sons we hear about now usually go into coaching. They are grinders, like the Patriots' Bill Belichick, who for all his football intelligence could barely play at the Division III college level. Or Nece's boss, Jon Gruden. Even with that finely tuned gridiron snarl, Gruden never had the stuff to play in the league. The modern game is just too athletic.

Of course, for every Peyton Manning there's a Jeffrey Jordan, the eldest son of Michael. He walked on to the University of Illinois basketball team after not drawing scholarship offers from large conference teams. But an athlete not living up to the reputation of his or her famous father does not suggest that the genetic contribution is negligible, says Robert Malina, a leading sports scientist and the former director of the Institute for the Study of Youth Sports at Michigan State University. "It just shows that genes are a lot more complicated than we think they are," he says. "Remember, a youngster can inherit his or her athletic ability from the mother, not the father. It's a fifty-fifty proposition. Half of the genes come from Mom, half from Dad."

MYTH NO. 1

The best athletes are those who work the hardest.

THE TRUTH

The elite often have innate, natural advantages.

Each human being has about 20,000 genes, with one copy coming from each parent. Flip a genetic switch here and there, and you might get a Barry Bonds; flip them another way, and you might end up with a Bobby Bonds Jr., Barry's big brother who never made it past Triple-A in the minor leagues. Most children of pro athletes don't even get that close to the top level.

Malina is among the foremost gurus in these matters. He co-authored, with Claude Bouchard and Louis Pérusse, the first comprehensive reference book on the role of genes in athletic performance, the soberly titled *Genetics of Fitness and Physical Performance*. It was written for exercise scientists and anthropologists like himself, with mind-mashing sentences such as: "Heritabilities for the dashes vary somewhat with distance: 20m, 0.83; 30m, 0.62, 0.81; 60m, 0.45, 0.72, 0.80, 0.91 (57)." When it was published, in 1997, no one outside of his academic field paid much attention.

I'm paying attention now, and not just because *SportsCenter* has become Aristocrat Hour. As a father, I've become curious about the gifts—or perhaps lack thereof—that my wife and I may have handed our three children.

Here's what we know: Physical traits, and ultimately human performance, are the result of interplay between the forces of nature (genetics) and nurture (environment). Some are controlled more by genetics than others are. Height is the characteristic most strongly influenced by genetics, accounting for at least 70 percent of our ultimate height, with nutrition covering much of the rest. Also largely fixed is bone structure, which sets the biomechanical parameters for the functioning of arms and legs. To a lesser but still significant degree, muscle fiber type—i.e., slow-twitch (endurance) vs. fast-twitch (power)—is dominated by genes. And parents who are mesomorphic, or naturally muscular, are more likely to pass on that body type than are parents who are naturally skinny or fat.

Advantage: Shaquille O'Neal. Disadvantage: Spike Lee.

In terms of performance, one study found that three-quarters of a child's ability to pull weights with his or her arms is due to the genes passed down from the biological parents rather than from training. Genes appear to deserve credit for about two-thirds of a child's vertical-jumping ability as well as a male child's aerobic capacity (it's almost 90 percent in female children). In motor development, tests for sprinting, jumping, and throwing suggest that anywhere from 14 to 91 percent of performance is related to genes; the skills are too complicated and malleable to evaluate with much precision. We do know that balance and flexibility—critical for gymnasts and hockey goalies—are somewhat inherited.

Many of these findings are based on studies of twins separated at birth, not high-performance athletes. And the switches that control genetic advantages, for height or otherwise, express themselves later in some children than in others, so it's not always obvious early on who might be gifted. Still, Malina says, "To reach elite levels, you've got to have 'it,' whatever 'it' is, and I would argue that 'it' is most likely genetic. Elite athletes are special. They are at the extreme end of the curve in any number of characteristics. Now, how they put it all together to come up with a winning performance is another story. Genetic factors are significantly involved in a variety of characteristics deemed important for sports performance, but translating these to actual performance is quite complex.

"The biggest differences among athletes are in the head."

Here, in the neurons, is where Nece believes he most set himself apart from peers on school teams. He is a quick learner, capable of imitating physical behavior with relative ease. His instinct is to find the best player on the field or on the court, study the movements he most admires, and adopt them. He marries that ability with an impulse to win that borders on the manic. "In dodgeball, I was always the last guy left," he says. "I was always the guy competing." His mother preferred to instill compassion in her son and made him pick the weakest kids for his team when he was playing neighborhood ball. He hated that but learned to take it as a challenge. He battled hard in the classroom, too: When a fellow third-grader turned in his timed math test with minutes to spare, Nece swore that he wouldn't be beat again, even though there was no extra credit for being first to the teacher's desk. "It was a race from then on," he says.

Trying to understand the hardwiring of an athlete's brain, I reach out to Gregory Stock, who works on the campus where Nece went to college. Stock is director of UCLA's Program on Medicine, Technology, and Society, where his job is to think through the latest advances in genetic science. Privately, I am hoping the biophysicist will suggest that Nece's competitiveness, now recast into the kill-or-be-killed ethic of his father, is an acquired feature—perhaps the result of, say, watching too many Ah-nold flicks as a boy. Stock cannot provide total comfort. "The genes of a top performer aren't just the physical ones," he says. "There are all sorts of genes in play that regulate behavior, such as the willingness to move past pain. Basically, all the attributes linked to personality are strongly influenced by genetics, anywhere from a quarter to three quarters [inherited], depending on the trait. Aggression has a strong genetic component."

Got it. The meek may inherit the earth, just not a Super Bowl ring.

So now I'm starting to wonder: When it comes to creating elite athletes, could most of the work actually be done before anyone—even the delivery room doctor—gets their hands on the kid? To test this notion, I dial up another member of the UCLA family, Bill Walton, whose training is in hoops, not heritability. As the hippie center of the champion

Bruins basketball teams of the early 1970s, now an ABC/ESPN analyst known for his eclectic ramblings, perhaps he can balance the discussion.

I reach Walton at his San Diego home, the one with the tepee in the backyard.

"My dad was the most unathletic person I ever saw," he says. "I saw him run one time at the church picnic, and I fell over laughing. But here was a guy who taught me everything about life—about family, love, trust, confidence, and, most of all, hard work. This was a guy who held three jobs at the same time, who gave up his life so our dreams as a family could come true. When I decided my dream was to be a basketball player, I wasn't going to let anything stand in the way. I had 32 operations, most of them on my feet and ankles, during my playing days." Walton played until he could not take another step. "My career was ruined by genetic structural defects in my feet."

God giveth, God taketh away. I love Walton's humanistic bent, but as his big voice bellows through the phone line, I find it hard to ignore the fact that he is still a member of the lucky sperm club. Walton in his playing days was 6-foot-11, which means his access to a hoop set 10 feet in the air was greater than that of all but the tiniest sliver of the population. (His son, NBA aristocrat Luke, is 6-8.) Only three percent of grown men in the U.S. are taller than 6-foot-3. Hardly anyone is shorter than that in the NBA, where the average player is 6-7 and only 10 or so players each year are less than six feet tall. Poor Jeffrey Jordan: At 6-1, he has almost no chance of following dear old dad into the league.

Sports commentators frequently refer to NBA players as the best athletes in the world. That's not true. They're the best athletes in the world among the tiny subset of humans who are ridiculously tall. The (relatively) short guys who survive this mighty struggle for roster spots are usually freaky in their own unique way. Allen Iverson, 6-foot-and-not-a-damn-inch-more, is breathtakingly quick. Dunk champion and everyman hero Spud Webb—who was 5-6 in sneakers at best and whose 12-year career ended in 1998—had a vertical leap of 42 inches. A jump of one-third of an athlete's height is considered impressive; Webb's was an astounding 64 percent. Two-time MVP Steve Nash is a frail-looking 6-3, but he possesses a spatial awareness that allows him to anticipate movements of teammates and defenders perhaps better than anyone else.

Members of Jockocracy need not flow from famous moms and dads. The father of former NFL quarterback Jeff Hostetler was a Mennonite farmer who was forbidden from playing sports, yet Norman's son won a Super Bowl, and 16 of his 19 grown grandchildren have gone on to play college sports. Another example: Michael Phelps' father was a state trooper, his mother a middle-school teacher. But he won the genetic lottery anyway. Arguably the greatest swimmer ever, with six gold and two bronze medals at the Athens Olympics, he has the ideal body for the sport. He is tall with an extralong torso, extralong arms, and size 14 feet that act as flippers. His feet are so flexible, he can lie on his back with legs outstretched and make the tips of his toes touch the floor. Most of all, he has a talent that coaches say cannot be taught, a fishlike instinct for finding the right positions in which to glide through the water.

The three-ring circus of elite sports is full of odd specimens benefiting from innate traits. Soccer star Mia Hamm was legendary for her stamina. No wonder: A test at the Gatorade Sports Science Institute found that she produced half as much sweat as the normal athlete. The institute's director told *The Wall Street Journal* that this allowed Hamm to play for longer stretches without having to drink fluids. Other researchers have found that Andy Roddick, whose 155-mile-an-hour serve is the fastest on record, can arch his back in a manner that effectively allows him to rotate his right arm 44 percent farther than the average tennis pro. D'Brickashaw Ferguson was the first lineman taken in the 2006 NFL draft, in part because the New York Jets were enamored with his 7-foot-3 wingspan, ideal for keeping pass rushers at bay. Dara Torres, who came into 2008 with the goal of making her fifth Olympics at 41, has a high amount of fast-twitch muscle fiber for a swimmer, and, due to lactic acid levels that offer pain tolerance, she can push those musles hard. Retired Tour de France champ Lance Armstrong may or may not have taken performance-enhancing drugs, but his oversize heart beat more than 200 times a minute, allowing the pumping of an extraordinary amount of blood and oxygen to his legs.

For years people assumed that Eero Mäntyranta, the great Finnish cross-country skier, was doping when he won two gold medals at the 1964 Olympics. After all, others trained much harder. Only later was it discovered that he had a rare genetic mutation that allowed his body to produce 50 percent more red blood cells than a normal person. Those cells carry extra oxygen to his muscles. It's the same advantage drug cheats try to get by taking EPO, the banned substance that has been linked to Tour de France riders.

These cases offer an instructive lesson.

"We share 98.5 percent of our DNA with a chimpanzee," Stock says. "We share 50 percent with a head of cabbage." Meaning: We need to think critically about the notion that human beings share 99.8 percent of all DNA with each other. No matter how much genetic matter people have in common, the difference, not the similarity, is what counts in elite sports competition. While no one gets to the pinnacle of any profession without hard work—and that's certainly true of sports, as well—genetic serendipity often provides the edge that separates a pro athlete from the masses.

Likewise, one innate disadvantage can sideline a promising star who otherwise has all the tools to make it at the highest level. One of the planet's most brilliant soccer players is Lionel Messi, who at age 13 was much shorter than the other boys in his Argentine hometown because his pituitary gland wasn't producing much growth hormone. A Spanish club, FC Barcelona, got wind of his situation and offered to pay for medical treatment if he joined the club. Messi moved overseas, got $800-a-month HGH injections, and shot up to 5-6—just large enough to play world-class soccer. FC Barcelona literally grew a superstar. Or at least rescued one from oblivion.

Seventeen years ago, when Ronnie Lott saw his son light up the track as a 12-year-old, any public discussion of biological diversity and athletes was a topic best avoided, especially in the media. CBS football prognosticator Jimmy "The Greek" Snyder and Los Angeles Dodgers executive Al Campanis had just gotten fired for clumsily delivered, undoubtedly racist comments about the success of black athletes and the lack of black managers, respectively. It was a time when African-American athletes were coming to dominate the NFL and whites were disappearing from NBA rosters, so the discussion about the state of sports in America was often framed in racial terms. While indeed there are some documented differences among ethnic groups, race-based science has always been too blunt a tool in understanding variations in individual performance. In fact, scientists now realize that two people of different races can share more genetic similarities than two people of the same race.

Nece's story isn't about race. His father is black, his mother white. His success can no more be analyzed by racial criteria than can that of Tiger Woods, who is one-quarter African, one-quarter Chinese, one-quarter Thai, one-eighth Caucasian, and one-eighth Native American—or "Cablinasian," as he once called himself. Like Woods, Nece renders pointless the metric of race, which scientists now understand as primarily a cultural grouping anyway.

Much closer to the mark, Nece merely picked his parents well.

• • •

Most elite athletes know they are gifted. In a 2001 study of U.S. Olympic champions whose names were not disclosed, 70 percent said they believed that nature played a role in their success. In my informal survey of 65 athletes in a variety of sports at Stanford University and the University of Michigan, all but two said that "innate athletic talent" was important in reaching the NCAA Division I level. LeBron James, who didn't play organized sports until age 9, and Kellen Winslow Jr. each went so far as to tattoo the phrase "The Chosen One" onto their bodies. They know how truly remote the chances of stardom are for most children from the moment of conception—that the making of an athlete begins with, even depends upon, great raw material. Which you just can't buy.

Unless you go to the California Cryobank.

In a second-floor office above the lab, CEO Gary Weinhouse reaches over his neat desk and hands me an informational packet about the world's largest sperm bank, which claims to have assisted in an estimated 25,000 births since 1977. Inside is a donor catalog listing each of the couple of hundred sperm samples that are for sale. Donors are organized by

ID number, and their entries include basic data such as hair and eye color, blood type, skin tone, years of education, and college major. On the company website is even more extensive scouting data plus baby photos, audio interviews, personality analyses, and handwritten donor essays. Personally, I have no interest in becoming a Cryobank client; my wife and I already must play zone defense just to contain our three kids created by more traditional means. But I must say, I am impressed with the options available to would-be parents with custom needs and a jones for sports. This is like the popular Madden NFL video game, which allows for the selection of parents in building a virtual player. Except that this is real.

The catalog includes about 10 athletes from UCLA and other colleges. Basketball players. Football players. ("Not me," Nece later tells me.) There's even an All-America swimmer. Among the offerings: Donor No. 3448, a tight end for an unspecified college football team. On the audio CD of his interview, the 6-3, 230-pounder says with palpable pride, "My distinguishing physical characteristics are thick calves and strong legs." I learn that the blond, blue-eyed health science major enjoys classical music and chemistry lab, but that, of course, "Sports is basically my life." He says his father played football at a "big-name school," and his sister "is athletic too." Like him, she surfs and plays volleyball. The Keirsey Temperament Sorter pegs his character type as that of Performer—a category used to describe "born entertainers" who "love the excitement of playing to an audience and will quickly become the center of attention wherever they are."

His sperm, at $315 a vial, appears to be selling like hotcakes. On his website bio is a customer advisory, with key words bolded for emphasis:

> This donor has retired from California Cryobank's donor program and **has a limited number of vials available**.

It's not easy to sell out an individual's seed. The Cryobank allows as many as 25 babies to be born from one donor's sperm. That's more than twice as many children as former NBA stud Shawn Kemp famously fathered via less clinical means with a half-dozen different women, and nearly three times as many as current NFL running back Travis Henry produced with nine women. Athletes are some of the most enthusiastic participants at the Cryobank, not the type of guys who "retire" themselves prematurely. It's easy money, $900 a month for three, um, donations a week at the Cryobank's satellite facility just off the UCLA campus. Some athletes go about their business discreetly, but others bring a lot of ego to the exercise, emerging from their provocatively wallpapered rooms with a swagger, slapping down their sample cup, and demanding to know if they just set a new record for specimen volume (the high mark is 20 vials, the average is four). They'll say disappointedly, "Only *seven*?"

"The only difficulty we've found with the athletes is their game schedule, which throws a wrench in *our* schedule," Weinhouse says. "Also, we need to be sure that they're abstaining for 48 hours for best specimen quality, and that's something not every athlete is crazy about." The Cryobank has had to kick out some guys for a lack of discipline.

And who's buying all this athlete discharge? A lot of people. There was one lesbian couple, former college athletes themselves who wanted their kid to be tall and coordinated. But usually it's infertile heterosexual couples in which the husband recognizes the upside: that he can give his child superior athletic genes. "I'd say somewhere between 40 percent and two-thirds of the infertile couples look to prioritize athletic traits," Weinhouse says. In fact, after ethnicity—many clients simply want a baby who looks like they do—attributes such as height and body shape are the most frequently requested. These traits even trump intellectual indicators such as SAT score and degree major. "It may not necessarily be that someone is looking to create a college scholarship athlete, but they want their child to be athletic," he says. Fit, young, and sporting a goatee, Weinhouse is the father of two children under the age of 3. He sympathizes. "They don't want their child to be picked on. They want him or her to make the team and not have to sit on the bench."

It all speaks to the growing appreciation for the role genes play in athletic success.

But much of America still relates more closely to what would appear to be the manufactured excellence of Tiger Woods.

AGE 2

FREAK OF NURTURE

Paonia, Colorado

In the United States of America, we believe in our kids.

We believe in 'em like Earl Woods believed in his youngest son, which is to say, we see their potential greatness and think it our duty to bring that greatness forth.

Fifty books a day. That's how many Michael Stanifer reads to his daughter, Molly, who sits on his lap and listens to story after story about friendly ladybugs, persistent trains, and a mischievous gorilla who won't say good night. It's 9 a.m. on a tranquil summer morning in the high desert of southwestern Colorado, and they've already worked through eight of the books in the plastic crate next to the couch. "Want to read another one?" Michael says in gentle voice. "Bring it over here." By immersing his toddler in books, he is sure he can create a habit for life. You don't have to be a child development specialist to surmise that Molly, whose dark brown eyes take in every page, will benefit from such enrichment.

But why stop there? Now that he's a stay-at-home dad, so committed to being a father that he put his high school teaching career on hold, the case for sports training before potty training seems more alluring than ever: His TV screen is constantly lit up with Tiger Woods' grinning mug as he hoists some trophy or the other. This week, Earl's boy will go on to win the 2006 PGA Championship, his 12th major. Michael is old enough to remember Tiger at age 2 chipping and putting with Bob Hope on *The Mike Douglas Show*. He wondered then what might come of the tyke, if maybe he'd become the next Jack Nicklaus. And damn if three decades later Tiger isn't chasing down the all-time greats! That Tiger sobs at the memory of his recently deceased father, who handed him a putter at nine months, makes his story all the more compelling. "I thought it was so neat when Tiger said if he could play golf with any one person, it would be his dad," Michael says. "As a parent, you understand that."

So, after coffee and a quick breakfast, Michael packs several milk bottles into an insulated cooler and slides his 26-pound girl into the child car seat in his black SUV, the one with the bumper sticker that reads "Men Who Change Diapers Change the World." The golf clubs—his and hers—are already in the trunk from the last time they headed out to his favorite course, which he plays several times a week, year round. He is mad about this game he discovered, like Earl, his early 40s. He is sold on the life lessons and spiritual connection to nature that it can encourage. Built tall and rugged in a manner reminiscent of a Western frontiersman, he loves sending that little white ball into the thin air and blue skies that surround the nearby Grand Mesa. He's whittled his handicap down to 7. But these outings are as much about introducing Molly, just shy of her second birthday, to a pursuit he hopes she adopts for life.

Hey, he jokes, maybe she'll even get good enough for a college scholarship.

"Golf is one of the most difficult sports to get good at," Michael had told me on the phone a week earlier, before inviting me to his postage-stamp Ponderosa, the family home in a small neighborhood carved out of the untamed hills of cowboy country. "The sooner you start them, the better they are."

Getting to Paonia wasn't easy. It's a six-hour drive from Denver, past all the ski resorts, not far from the Utah border, smack dab in the middle of nowhere—if masses of humans are your notion of somewhere, that is. To get here, you must negotiate two-lane roads that follow twisting rivers and hug the sides of cliffs, where sign after sign warns that deer could jump into your path at any time. In places, the canyon walls get so steep that even your satellite radio signal cuts out. At the end of the trek is a reclusive largely Mormon coal-mining town of 1,500 with no bars, one pizza joint, and one doctor—Michael's wife and Molly's mother, Devon. But I just had to come.

Because if the gospel of Earl Woods can be found all the way out here, amid the mountain lions and the scrub brush, then it's official: The Word is everywhere.

• • •

In April 1997, Eldrick "Tiger" Woods became the youngest Masters champion ever at 21 years, 3 months, and 14 days. At the end of his record 12-stroke victory that day, waiting just beyond the final green, was his old man, Earl, who gave his son a bear hug so smothering that the red of Tiger's shirt could barely be seen beneath the black of Earl's. Tiger slipped on the green jacket, and together they flew to Chicago for an appearance on *Oprah*, where the queen of daytime television told the young prince of the links, "You are my hero and America's hero because of the hope that you've inspired in everybody." She asked Earl, now a public figure, how he'd groomed his prodigy. He shared a few of his strategies. The syndicated show went out to 205 domestic and 132 international markets.

Soon afterward, *Training a Tiger: A Father's Guide to Raising a Winner in Both Golf and Life*, a new book by Earl Woods and *Golf Digest* writer Pete McDaniel, zoomed into the top 10 of the *New York Times* best-seller list. McDaniel says he doesn't know how many copies were sold in the ensuing months, just that it was plenty. Earl, who had cut the deal with HarperCollins and brought on McDaniel as a hired gun, used to joke that he got rich before his son did. He continued to promote the book, eager to dispense his winning advice on the lecture circuit and wherever Tiger gave youth clinics.

In the first chapter, Earl wrote, *It all begins with the parent's desire to make the child's life better, to enhance his or her probability of success in life. What the parent has to do is say, "I want my child to have it better than I. I want my child to have more opportunities, and more support.*

I want my child to be better prepared to handle life than I was. I want my child to be more successful. I want my child to be rewarded for effort." The conceit, simple but ambitious, was that the destinies of children could be directed, maybe even forged, by you, their moms and dads.

How? Through programming. When Tiger came home from the hospital at five days old, Earl writes, he cranked up the jazz music and *established my personal imprint on his mind*, because he regarded jazz as the most creative and complex form of music. He sat Tiger in a high chair in the garage so the infant could watch Dad hit balls into a net. Soon Tiger was imitating his swing, trailing him around on the course with his own, cut-down set of clubs. Earl's advice to parents: *Start the learning process when the child is young enough so that the performance of the game is totally ingrained.* There was no such thing as too young, in his way of thinking. *It can start with a plastic ball and club placed in your child's crib. Babies learn rapidly. They will associate the club with the ball and make hitting the ball a game.*

Earl Woods lacked any credentials to make such statements outside of being the father of four, one of whom became a superstar athlete. He wasn't formally schooled in pediatrics, kinesiology, neurology, psychology, or any other clinical -ology. He was a soldier by training, a Vietnam vet who had gone on to hold managerial positions as a civilian. Certainly, Tiger's ultracompetitive mother, Kultida, as much as nurturing Earl, was another key factor in the boy's success. ("No matter how close a friend you are, you must kill that person" was her advice to her son on how to approach golf rivals.) But Earl was on to something too that researchers had begun to figure out: Human beings learn at an astonishing rate when very young, perhaps faster than at any other time in their lives. And Earl's was a message the broader society was ready to act upon.

Beginning in the mid-1980s, parents started becoming aware of the developmental importance of the first five years of a child's life. As Steven Mintz observes in 2004's *Huck's Raft: A History of American Childhood*, the new child-rearing manuals conveyed a sense of urgency that had been absent in previous books. Educationally oriented preschools proliferated, with curricula designed to enhance the cognitive, motor, language, and social skills of children. A raft of developmental toys, mobiles, books, tapes, and videos flooded the marketplace, facilitating a shift in parenting philosophies. The "prepared" childhood was emerging, replacing the ideal of a "protected" childhood that had been promoted in the decades after World War II, when parents were encouraged not to pressure kids, to let them develop on their own, among their neighborhood peers.

Out: the goal of creating "normal" children, ones who could fit in easily in the expanding middle class.

In: the mission of creating "special" kids, ones best prepared to rise above the masses.

Tiger Woods seems the very picture of prefabricated excellence. The fact that he started golf training around the time that he learned to play peek-a-boo has been emphasized by Earl, who told stories of applying military technique—Standard Operating Procedure—to establish a preshot routine with toddler Tiger. By 18 months, Tiger knew not only "one, two, buckle my shoe" but had seen enough golf to know when 3 was a par and 4 was a bogey. The wisdom of Earl's ways was visually reinforced by that ubiquitous clip from *The Mike Douglas Show*. It was as if—like some Pinewood Derby project—Earl and Tiger had been given a block of wood and four wheels, and had carved their way to victory.

The nation's forefathers would have recognized Earl's methods. Though play was considered frivolous and sport a distraction from religious purpose, the Puritans were convinced that molding the very young was the surest way to achieve their survival in the New World. During the 16th and 17th centuries, their leaders produced many books on the topic for fathers, who at the time were the parent considered most responsible for child-rearing. "Parents," wrote one minister, "ought to begin to nurture their children, as soone [sic] as they are capable of any instruction." To encourage infants to walk, girls and boys were dressed in long robes, which made crawling difficult. They learned to read as early as possible.

When people would ask Tiger how he got so good, Earl wrote in his book, *he would smile and say, "Practice, practice, practice, oooh!"*

Or as Thomas Edison once said, genius is one percent inspiration and 99 percent perspiration. Commitment has long been recognized as a means to achievement. But soon after Tiger turned pro, a harder set of numbers emerged to describe what it took to acquire elite performance in a sport: 10 years or 10,000 hours. Researchers fascinated with the acquisition of expertise had long ago established that it took at least a decade for most of the top chess players to reach the international level. (Bobby Fischer, with nine years' experience, was a bit of an anomaly.) By the early '90s, musicians had been added to the list, with the best pianists having logged by age 20 at least 10,000 hours of "dedicated practice"—which is not the same thing as goofing around at the keyboard. It involves setting specific goals and focusing on technique as much as outcome. Golfers have not been surveyed. Still, in a 2001 book, the psychologist and Florida State professor K. Anders Ericsson, one of the world's leading researchers on expertise, suggested that the sport's top performers could be expected to fall into the above category as well. Ericsson touted the benefits of early, supervised learning in golf while noting that the top nine golfers voted best of the 20th century had a mean starting age of 8.8 years. He predicted that children would begin practicing their games at younger ages as the value of such effort becomes more established. His reference and inspiration: Earl Woods' little 190-page bible. "Tiger turned out pretty well, huh?" Ericsson says.

Stanford man. Bearer of green jackets. World's richest athlete. Yup, pretty well.

Of course, those who make history—and those riding shotgun—get to write it. Earl could have declared that the key to raising a Tiger was to feed him raw meat, and the next morning some parents somewhere might have sprinkled ground chuck on their kid's oatmeal. Earl's finished product, his golden son who overcame the racial and class biases of golf, was that alluring. McDaniel, Earl's co-author, told me many parents have come up to him at events and shared that they followed Earl's advice about piping the right music into the nursery. It wasn't just minorities who were inspired. At a Tiger youth clinic in Chicago, a conservatively dressed white man in his early 30s told McDaniel that he had cut down a set of clubs for his 18-month-old and also slipped the book under the boy's pillow, hoping its lessons would be absorbed somehow, perhaps by osmosis. "A lot of parents say they hadn't even considered golf for their child until *Training a Tiger* came out," McDaniel says.

The hardcover sells for $18. Makes you wonder how much California Cryobank could get for Tiger's sperm. People forget: He's a member of the jockocracy, too. Earl, a catcher with a cannon arm, was a pretty good athlete himself. He had to be to become the first black baseball player in the history of the old Big 8 Conference. The first time on a golf course, Earl shot a 91; he soon pared his handicap down to a four.

• • •

"This is what Tiger has done for the sport," Tony Kewalramani says with a sweeping wave at the scene before him. "All this ... Tiger."

The teaching pro from Los Angeles is standing on the grass behind the clubhouse of Colina Park Golf Course in San Diego. Smartly outfitted in crisp slacks and a shirt that are just a bit darker than his prematurely silver hair, Kewalramani, 42, peers through sunglasses at the international collection of boys and girls chasing balls up and down the groomed hills of this par-3 course that a few years ago was reconfigured just for kids. Their daddy-caddies have brought them here to vie for the brilliant cut-glass trophy of an oversize ball that goes to the winner of the 6-and-under division of the Callaway Junior World Golf Championships.

Fifty-five boys and 10 girls have signed up for the three-day, 54-hole event—or more accurately, their parents have signed them up. After all, kids entering kindergarten and first grade don't read up on tournaments like these and beg their parents to sign them up; most can't even read yet. And they certainly don't pay the thousands of dollars in travel bills that it costs some families to get here; most aren't even old enough to receive an allowance. Organizers for the Junior Worlds privately call this the "diaper division." When Woods won six times at the Junior Worlds at various levels, the lowest division was 10-and-under, which he won at age 8. Now, due to parent demand, titles are dispensed even to tots. An 8-and-under division was added in 2000, 6-and-under in 2004.

Brandon Kewalramani, Tony's son, is a veteran. The previous year, at age 5, he placed seventh in the field. He expects more from himself this summer. He has been "playing" since he was 1, when he would watch his dad swing the club and ask to do the same. He would hold Tony's hand and whack the ball with a plastic stick. Now the 45-pound, 44-inch-tall boy has a full, elegant swing most adults would envy.

"I like baseball, too, but I don't play a lot," he says. Brandon has the mature, dark brown eyes of a boy twice his age. "It'll ruin my swing. I'm focused on golf."

It's easy to be. Since teaching top junior golfers is Dad's job—Tony tutored Michelle Wie on her short game when she was 13—Brandon spends four hours a day on his home course, honing his strokes. Putting, chipping, driving, and imagining what it will take to become just like you-know-who. He wants to go to Stanford, even though Dad helps coach the UCLA team. Great, Tony tells him, but know that every other kid in the sport wants to follow that path too.

No kidding. Everywhere on the greens today, Tiger fist pumps are common. Many kids wear the icon's branded Nike gear. An African-American boy from Dallas smiles for a photo by shrieking, "Tiger!" A 5-year-old blond kid from England with a fuzzy orange tiger clubhead cover is actually named Tiger—Tiger Adams—though his parents insist that's just coincidence. In the group behind Brandon, who enters the final day in third place, is a pint-size San Diegan who argues with his father over where to aim his shot. On the tee box, the daddy-caddy hands his son a club and tells him to hit to the right of the pin, away from the bunker and water on the left.

"No, Tiger line," says the boy, who wants to shoot straight for the flag. To him, Tiger represents adventure, gusto, going for it.

The middle is safer, suggests the dad, a corporate manager who prefers the discipline in Tiger's game.

"Tiger line," the boy protests.

No, really, the middle, the dad quietly insists.

The little lefty swings hard. As the ball falls into the rough, near the bunker, dad sighs. The boy, though, doesn't seem the least bit bothered with his triple bgey. He smiles and squeals triumphantly, "I went Tiger line!"

This essential conflict in elite youth sports—between work and play—is on full display over the weekend. More than a few daddy-caddies are guilty of overcoaching, which is officially discouraged. Several of them receive warnings from Rick Johnson, the lanky young assistant pro at Colina Park who patrols play with a walkie-talkie and a watchful gaze from beneath a baseball cap pulled down low. "It's almost like a video game," he says. "It's as if the parents are going up against Tiger Woods on PlayStation, and they're inputting the club, telling the kid where to aim, even selecting the power level. They're providing all the mental processing and golf knowledge. The kid's just hitting it."

Walking 18 holes a day for three straight days under the blazing summer sun is a lot to ask of many children this age, even when bribed with M&Ms and GameCubes for "working hard." They lose concentration, get silly ... and in some cases get chastised, or worse, by frustrated parents. Most of the parents I saw controlled themselves, but there was abuse, too. On the final hole, Brandon was teeing off when an audible thud came from the rear, behind the tee box, where one of his playing partners had retreated after sticking his shot in a lake.

"You see that?" Tony was asked by the third father in the group.

"No, but I heard it."

"His dad just socked him in the head."

Johnson missed that one. But he learned about it later. The intensity displayed by some parents in this crucible, made possible only because of the rise of Tiger, gives him pause. "Part of me worries about what's going to happen when the kid goes home," he says. "Part of me worries what's going to happen in a week. Part of me worries about what's going to happen to the psyche of the kid in the long run." Then in the next breath, Johnson shifts gears, and shifts again, back and forth, the arguments in his head capturing the deeper societal debate about how best to raise children. "Who's to say who's right and wrong?" he says. "I mean, we always look at our school systems and go, 'We're too easy on our kids.' Yet we get mad at parents who push their kids too hard. So it's like, what are we shooting for? Are we trying to create the best students, the best golfers, the best basketball players? Or do we want kids to be self-motivated? And ..."

His voice rises, philosophy now colliding with psychology.

"Is self-motivation really possible at this age?"

Tony Kewalramani can appreciate the dilemma. Last year at the Junior Worlds, Brandon shot well on the first day but withered on the second, chunking and spraying balls all over the course. Tony, normally very calm and thoughtful, ripped into his son. "What's wrong? What are you doing?" Tony was thinking about all the hard work they had put into Brandon's game. Perhaps the outburst came from a good place; Tony emigrated from India 25 years ago to pursue the American Dream. He knows that golf, the unofficial sport of establishment America, can be a means to a better life. And Brandon appeared to have some talent, maybe even, hmm, don't say it *too* loudly ... Tiger talent? But that afternoon in San Diego had been miserable for both of them. The following day, the starter on the first tee gave his group a lecture reemphasizing the need to behave on the course.

Turning to Tony, who was crouched on one knee beside him, Brandon said, "Dad, are you listening? He's talking about you."

Tony squirmed, while pretending not to notice. The starter continued. "Dad, you're listening, *right*?" Three times Brandon asked his father some form of this question. Just enough to change their relationship completely.

"Now we're best friends," Tony says. He'd be lying if he didn't think there was a chance that Brandon could someday play on the PGA Tour. But he thinks of them as true partners in this *golf journey*, as Earl Woods called it, Brandon dictating his goals and when he wants to play, and Tony encouraging him to measure his progress against himself, not others. "I don't want Brandon to be the next Tiger Woods," he says. "I want him to be the best he can be. If I start saying he's the next Tiger Woods, I might as well flush my head in the toilet."

At these Junior Worlds, Brandon would place third—the only American in the top five—earning him a trophy that he would raise at a ceremony attended by a couple hundred onlookers, mostly his rivals and their parents.

Tony Kewalramani regrets some of his past behavior, but not having marinated his son in golf at an age once thought ridiculously premature. Just look at Brandon's swing, easy as habit. Just look at his scores, displayed on a leaderboard lit up by the summer sunset: 56-60-57, for a total of 173, just 11 strokes over par. Anyone who's played golf can appreciate how impressive those scores are, even on a par-3 course. The men's golf team at San Diego State had played Colina Park two weeks earlier, and their average round was only a couple strokes better.

The value of early exposure to the game—at least this game—seems undeniable watching the diaper division sort itself out. Most of the top boys in the tournament have been playing for years, and most hit more greens here than they missed. They usually got out of bunkers in one and kept their putts to two. The winner, a Japanese boy two strokes better than Brandon, even put backspin on his ball at times. The only thing miniature about the golf here was the size of the participants, whose daddy-caddies kept the scorecards because the kids are too young to do the math.

"Earl had a vision," Tony says admiringly, "a 20-year vision. He realized he had found an open space in the industry of golf—which is that if you start to work with children early, you can do some incredible things. No one was doing that when Tiger came up."

• • •

The other morning, I sat down on our living room couch to read the newspaper. Kellen, our toddler, plopped down next to me, grabbed the sports section and attempted to do the same, even assuming my body language. His toenails were bright red because he had seen his big sister getting hers painted and had wanted the same treatment. He was dressed to his ankles in one of big brother's old soccer jerseys because those are all he ever wants to wear. He tags along to his siblings' games all the time, often in his sister's old cleats because he found them in some closet and insisted, "Why not? I like soccer, too." At his sister's game—Anna plays for the "Brazil" rec-league team—I made the error of blinking and had to chase him down at midfield because he'd decided to join her *jogo bonito*.

As anyone who has spent time with 2-year-olds knows, they are manic mimics. They learn by copying behavior. Sometimes, they even get it right.

This urge to imitate extends to movement skills, which begins to explain how a kindergartener can score as well as a college golfer on a par-3 course. And why Molly Stanifer's dad isn't nutty to think that handing her a club might eventually bear fruit.

The human body takes about two decades to reach its ultimate size, but 95 percent of the brain and central nervous system gets formed by age 7, and most of that growth is in the first four years. During that time, cells are being created and connected in ways that support the basic components of neuromuscular coordination. By 18 months, the cell content of the cerebellum—part of the brain that affects movement—has already reached adult levels. It's far from mature from a cognitive standpoint, but the physical infrastructure is all in place. At the same time, a coating of dense fat called myelin is starting to wrap itself around nerve endings; the thicker the insulation, the better the transmission of nerve signals to the muscles. (See chart below.)

Nature may determine the outer limits of motor skills, but their development is a plastic process affected by habitual physical activity and the practice of specific movements. At age 2, Molly and Kellen might not be able to do much more than strike a ball with a plastic club. But each time they whack it, signals are sent to their neural systems—the

Rate of Systems Development

Bodily systems growth through childhood as a percentage of total development attained at age 20.

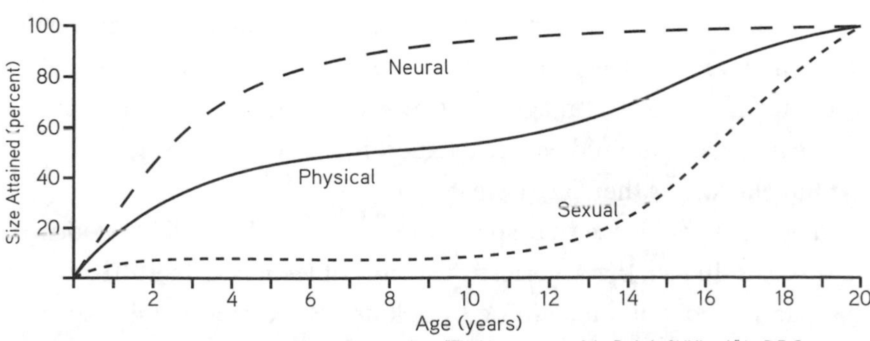

Source: Redrawn from "The Measurement of the Body in Childhood," by R.E. Scammon, in The Measurement of Man, *J.A. Harris et al., eds., 1930, University of Minnesota Press*

brain, nerves, and eyes—and with repetition, the signals suggest that the capacity of performing this activity needs to be developed. That, essentially, golf is a survival skill. Infants can barely grasp and shake an object, much less be trained. But in general, the sooner those signals are sent to the neural system of a child, the better chance he or she will have of later nailing a technique. A similar neurological process controls the learning of language, which is why parents are encouraged to expose kids to foreign tongues as early as age 1.

The first few years of life aren't the only opportunity to acquire basic motor skills. Those skills continue to develop, and another big window opens up between 10 and 12. But it shrinks considerably after the early teenage years, and the best that most people can do after that is fine-tune. The late neurologist Harold Klawans attributed the failure of Michael Jordan's foray into professional baseball to a lack of practice in the years when his synapses were being formed. Though he enjoyed baseball as a kid, his adult desire to switch from the NBA to the major leagues was scuttled by his inability to react to breaking balls. "The brain has to learn how to recognize the spin and speed and direction of the ball as it leaves the pitcher's hand, and then to swing the bat at just the right speed and in precisely the proper location to hit the ball solidly as it crosses the plate," Klawans wrote. "This is a tall order for anyone's brain. And the sad fact was that at age 31, [Jordan's] brain was just too old to acquire that skill."

These concepts aren't foreign to Molly's mother, who is medically trained in child development. She also was an accomplished athlete herself. In high school, she was one of the nation's top three cross-country skiers, a member of the world junior team. She went on to compete on the Division I level in college. She believes that her success was enabled by the fact that she was on skis at age 3. "I think if you're seeing the movements at an early age, you could be a real expert by 10 or 12," she says.

But she knows there are caveats, too.

There's no evidence that sport immersion works with *most* kids in *most* sports. In fact, the American Academy of Pediatrics in 2001 advised that parents hold off on training little kids. "Basic motor skills, such as throwing, catching, kicking, and hitting a ball, do not develop sooner simply as a result of introducing them to children at an earlier age. Teaching or expecting these skills to develop before children are developmentally ready is more likely to cause frustration than long-term success in the sport." Plus, the AAP warned, "even with coaches available to teach rules and skills of a sport, children may not be ready to learn or understand what is being taught."

Some humans just have a special gift for imitation, an aptitude that could be related to what scientists call "mirror neurons" in the brain that lock down motor acts through visual observation of others' behavior. Finishing two spots behind Kewalramani at the Junior Worlds was a moon-faced Chinese boy in pressed white slacks whose family had spent about $10,000 traveling to the U.S. for the summer kid-golf circuit. Watching Tian Lang Guan, I could see why his parents were so eager to invest in his future. His swing is—or, rather, his swings are—straight off the PGA Tour.

"Ernie Els!" the gaunt, bespectacled father barked in accented English, ordering the son to show me the South African's motion.

The boy put his head down and replicated Els' swing.

"Vijay Singh!" the father commanded.

The boy nailed that trademark swing too, which, like all the rest, he had learned to mimic from watching golf videos back home.

"Tiger Woods!"

On and on went the copycat cuts, each executed with precision. The session ended only when the boy, hands tired from playing all day, inadvertently let go of his five-iron on the follow-through. The club helicoptered 30 yards in the air, nearly clipping the head of a frightened kid in a nearby playground. "Sorry!" Tian's embarrassed father called out.

Although golf is a difficult game to master, it's actually among the easiest sports to learn in the first few years of life. Not only is the ball stationary, but the target is too. Golf requires little in the way of balance, jumping ability, or spatial awareness—traits that mature later in children. There's no need for speed, quickness, agility, or aerobic fitness. The absence of these characteristics makes the game—no offense, golfers—less a sport than an act of rote ball striking. Size, strength, and power each offer advantages, but not much on a course in which the longest hole is 140 yards. To tame Colina Park, a golfer needs good vision and a simple, consistent swing. The rest is mental, much of which was supplied by the puppeteering daddy-caddies.

Obviously, the more a golfer practices, the more he or she learns to manage situations on their own. According to Ericsson, the chief value of 10,000 hours of focused effort to an athlete is the development of long-term working memory, which helps a golfer anticipate the complex trajectory of a ball, the undulations of a green, and variable conditions such as wind direction. Laboratory research also shows that experienced golfers are better able to control their breathing and heart rate during the swing than their less-skilled peers are.

Tiger always had a knack for learning quickly and by imitation. He was whacking balls with his putter into the garage net at 10 months, mirroring the deliberate setup and stance of his father. Earl also had the foresight to teach him the game from the green out, an ingenious move that was ahead of its time. He started with the putter, added the wedge, and so on, until finally introducing the most powerful club in the bag, the driver. Golfers historically have been taught the game in the opposite manner, from the tee box forward. Earl's method was more consistent with the science of motor learning, which suggests that complex skills are most efficiently mastered by first gaining proficiency on simpler maneuvers.

Technique itself is merely a function of perfecting sensory-motor habits, learned activities that are practiced to the point of automation. The motor centers are taught how to act in a relaxed and economical way, so that ultimately a movement flows from the unconscious. The action just occurs on its own, once the go-ahead to do it is given. All that drilling also helps the muscles and joints recognize minute deviations in proper form.

"If kids are taught developmentally and start with what's simple and build from there, they can learn skills early," says Crystal Branta, a Michigan State professor of motor development whose research was cited by the AAP in its recommendation. "There are some phenomenal kids who have the cognitive capacity to understand what's being taught and the emotional ability to be in that arena. Some of them will have just the right blend of tools."

So, maybe Earl was right: It is possible to groom a golfer from the crib up.

A better question: Should we?

MYTH NO. 2

Early, focused skills training makes a Tiger roar.

THE TRUTH

In golf, sometimes; in most sports, no.

• • •

Near the end of his life, Pablo Picasso went through a phase in which he painted an awful lot like a child. His color schemes lacked chromatic harmony, with reds set against purples, bright orange against pale yellow. Critics noted that his brushwork became "artless," in the manner of a preschooler whose motor coordination was still developing. His construction of reality became incomplete and unstable. Gone was the cubism and surrealism of previous eras, in which he tried to interpret reality by distorting facades and human forms in a thought-out manner. And long gone was his earliest work, the more literal renderings of subjects he was encouraged to paint as a young boy by his ambitious father, an art teacher. When Picasso was asked why he chose to produce such unsophisticated work, he explained, "When I was these children's age, I drew like Raphael. It has taken me my entire life to learn how to draw like they do." He yearned for what he had missed out on 60 years earlier. "It takes a long time to become young," he said.

The world can thank Don José for directing his son so expertly, so early on. And it might someday thank Doug Rue for engineering the golf development of his son, Jackson. But for right now, Jackson just wants to be a kid before his childhood expires.

I'd heard about Jackson Rue from the tournament organizers at the Junior Worlds, who wondered what had come of the former prodigy. By age 6, he already had six holes-in-one, some captured on videotape. Soon, he had his own website and press clippings. Jackson was young Picasso with a putter, with better scores at the Junior Worlds than Tiger Woods had at age 8. And then he vanished from the junior golf scene.

I check his website, which remains active. The front page reads, simply:

> Jackson Rue is now 11 years old and has already enjoyed more success at golf tournaments than most people could imagine. Lately, Jackson has taken a break from golf and explored some other sports including: hockey, tennis, racquetball and pool. He has really been enjoying hockey!

This is all true, as I find out when I visit with Jackson and Doug in Coquitlam, B.C., a town just above the Washington State border on the outskirts of Vancouver. Jackson indeed has taken to Canada's national game. But the exclamation mark on the website message was written by Doug, and, as he makes clear, it's laced not with joy but with frustration.

"The hockey is mindless, and it's going nowhere," Doug says. "I'm just trying to be a caring dad and be patient. When he tells me he's ready to come back to golf, I'll be there quicker than you can shake a stick."

The father has been nothing if not devoted to Jackson's golf talent. He spent so much time on the course with Jackson that the small manufacturing business he owned went bankrupt, partly out of neglect. He traveled the continent with him—Virginia, Miami, Illinois, the whole summer junior circuit—chasing the biggest trophies. He got him access to some of the best teaching pros, in Washington, Pebble Beach, and other places. He read Earl's book. He even wrote a letter to Arnold Palmer, trying to set up a meeting between the past and future kings of the links.

But after a few years of this, Jackson said *enough*. Enough to the eight-hour training sessions. Enough to the inevitable expectations. Enough to sacrifices. "I was burned out," he told me. "I just wanted to be with my friends."

We're on a public course near his hometown. Doug has invited me up here to play with Jackson because I'm from ESPN, and he thinks that will get Jackson excited about competing again. The boy hasn't picked up a club in months and hasn't signed up for a tournament in two years. He's gotten taller, added a few pounds around the waist. But it's clear he still has the gift. He's long off the tee and has great hands around the greens. He even looks like a pint-size John Daly, with full cheeks, blond hair, and thick legs.

"Can I try that, Dad?" he asks, after Doug botches a flop shot. He's intrigued by the challenge.

He sticks the shot, winding up just a couple feet from the pin.

"He used to be able to chip better than his instructors," Doug whispers.

Jackson is happy to be out here today with Dad and the ESPN guy. He still likes this game. But it's obvious to me that he isn't coming back to it anytime soon. He needs it to be a game again, not a future profession. And that's not going to happen until his dad, much as he loves Jackson, gives up the dream. In fact, Jackson isn't going to take any game seriously—hockey, billiards, tennis—unless he can do it on his terms.

"He turned out to be the top badminton kid in his school, then I got him a net and he decided he didn't want to play anymore," Doug says, dispirited. "I'm sure good stuff will come down the road, but it's hard on me."

It's been hard on his marriage, too. He and Jackson's mother separated, in part because of the strain caused by Doug's enthusiasm for advancing the golf career of their only child. "People tell me that I'm overreacting," Doug says. "That Jackson has God-given talent. That he could take three to six years off and be right there again." But it feels like a golden opportunity is disappearing.

A couple of years later, I call Doug again to find out how Jackson is doing. "He's doing fine," says Doug, still waiting for Jackson, now 14, to return to sports—any sport. "He's quite content and happy. I don't know how or why, but he is."

One problem with the deliberate training of very young children is not what it does to them, but what it can do to the adults around them. Early success can be intoxicating—and disorienting, knowing that potential greatness is in your care. If he's this good now, parents may think, imagine how good he could be when he gets older. Worlds shrink, and the needs of a child become subordinate to the perceived needs of his athletic career.

"Childhood should be a smorgasbord, instead of being pushed into a sport at an early age," says Robert Malina, the youth sports researcher and expert on growth and maturation. "Otherwise, you're violating a kid's rights."

There's always a risk in attempting to coax athletic excellence from an early age. Andre Agassi's father dangled a ball strung to a racket above him on the day he was born. Jennifer Capriati did sit-ups as a toddler. Jeff Gordon raced quarter midgets at age 5 and testifies to the value of that experience. ("Starting young isn't an advantage," the NASCAR champion told ESPN's *Outside the Lines*. "It's probably the *only* reason I'm here today.") But athletes only know their own journey. And the news media highlights their stories because they are each, by definition, unique. "How many kids were trained like Tiger and never made it? We don't know," Malina says. "How many lives were ruined in the process?"

Even the success stories come with wrinkles.

Michelle Wie was supposed to be Tiger's heiress to the golf throne, at least on the women's side. From the time she first gripped a club at age 4, she figured that's what she would do with the rest of her life. Her parents groomed her to be a destroyer, and at age 10 she became the youngest player ever to qualify for the U.S. Amateur Public Links Championship. At 15, she turned pro, got rich on endorsement deals that capitalized on her youth—and started playing in PGA men's tournaments. That's how much confidence Mom and Dad had in her skills. But two years later, it was clear she had moved too fast, too soon. She was noncompetitive in the men's events, hadn't won a women's event, couldn't keep a regular caddy, and dropped out of tournaments for wrist injuries and mysterious ailments. She revealed herself as over-programmed athletically and underdeveloped emotionally. Meanwhile, another Honolulu golfer seized the world's attention—Tadd Fujikawa, who in 2006 became, at age 15, the youngest person ever to qualify for the U.S. Open. At 5-1, a foot shorter than Wie, he would reach the pros with relatively little size or experience; he had started playing golf only at age 8 and until age 12 was primarily focused on winning judo titles.

As for Tiger Woods, Malina sees the same thing as do the various corporations that pay him north of $75 million a year to link their image to his: a performance machine. And that's what troubles him. "Tiger is like the athletes from the old Eastern Bloc," Malina says. "He's programmed the same way Olga Korbut and Nadia Comaneci were, to respond to certain situations in certain ways. I don't think he has much of a real personality. Earl probably did something right with Tiger as a child. But we'll never know the full picture, because we'll never know what he's like as a person. Remember, we know very little about Tiger Woods."

A megacorporation unto himself, Tiger has perhaps the most carefully managed story line in the history of sports. We've seen the photos and home video that have been released publicly of Tiger as a happy child. We've seen the Nike commercials of him dancing as a boy on the green after sinking a putt. We've heard the cardboard declarations ("I always smile when I think back to my childhood") made at press conferences and in carefully vetted interviews. But in the dozens of books written about and by him, and in the thousands of magazine and newspaper profiles that have been published, he has not shared much of himself, guarding his psyche and privacy with the same discipline that he brings to his game. ("I am a control freak," he told *Sports Illustrated.*) One of the few times that he let his guard down was in a men's fashion magazine early in his professional career, when he was quoted telling off-color jokes; it came off as an awkward attempt to show people that he's just a regular guy, not a robot. Golf writers who have followed his career still frequently ask, "Who is Tiger Woods?"

Perhaps it has taken Tiger a while to figure out the answer. His defining identity is as a golfer and, more recently, a father—a role he clearly enjoys. His first child, daughter Sam Alexis, was born just hours after he won the 2007 U.S. Open, and when the season concluded, he left the clubs in the garage for seven weeks. He emerged with a genuine smile on his face. (And yes, Sam has watched him hit balls at the range and held a club in her tiny hands, but so far Tiger hasn't engaged in any Earl-like talk of embarking on a mystical golfing journey with his baby girl.)

It's a welcome sight. Rudy Duran, Tiger's coach from age 5 to age 10, in April 2006 told *The New York Times*, "There was no question in my mind that if he came home and said he wanted to play the piano, there would have been no anxiety by his parents." But the success Tiger had experienced by that age—every kid wants to make their parents proud—virtually assured that golf wasn't going to get shelved. And implicit in Duran's statement is the notion that golf wasn't Tiger's idea in the first place. Earl always insisted otherwise.

At the very least, Earl masterfully managed his son's interest in the sport. When Tiger was 2, he would ring his father at work and ask to join him on the course that afternoon; Earl would fake hesitation, so that when he finally consented, Tiger would think he'd pulled one over on Pops. Another of his tricks was to never let Tiger hit as many balls as he wanted to at the range so that his son would always want to come back. Later, during practice sessions, Earl used what he called "prisoner-of-war interrogation techniques"—dropping bags or barking comments on Tiger's downswing—in order to build mental toughness. Earl may have been an amateur shrink, but the techniques he used are supported by research on how to motivate and focus athletes. "He naturally and accurately at the earliest time possible integrated psychological-skills training with physical-skills training," says Colleen Hacker, a psychologist who's worked with the U.S. women's national soccer team. "This is what people like me try to do when we come into an athlete's life—except by then they're 25 years old."

Earl did his job well. Arguably, too well for the rest of us.

In 2001, the same year the AAP issued its recommendation against early training, Earl recognized that he had spawned a generation of parents who had set unrealistic goals for their kids. "And I tried to head it off," he told *Golf Digest*. "I make it very, very clear [in the book] that my purpose in raising Tiger was not to raise a golfer. I wanted to raise a good person." Still, he continued to promote the idea that Tiger's highly tailored childhood was the catalyst of his success, relating tales of course-management lessons at age 4. Tiger was a confirmed golfer by the end of kindergarten, whether that was Earl's goal or not. Tiger dabbled in baseball and cross-country later but quit those sports in middle school because they interfered with golf.

Exclusive focus on one sport is now a major theme in youth sports and one of its greatest sources of controversy. Motor-skills expert Crystal Branta says that from a physical developmental point of view, the priority should be on learning general athletic movements—running, jumping, hopping, skipping, and so forth—that can serve as a foundation for entry into multiple sports once children's bodies mature. Otherwise, their options shrink. "It's like learning the alphabet," she says. "The more letters you know, the more words and sentences you can put together. If you only learn how to play golf, you'll know how to walk and swing a club, but you won't know how to catch a ball. If you get tired of golf, or don't get better at it, you won't have other sports to fall back on."

For all the abuses of some of the former Eastern Bloc sports systems—most famously, enforced drug use—its sports scientists knew it was generally better not to have athletes specialize in one sport until they were 15 or 16, and sometimes later. They forced most of their child athletes to play multiple sports and in track and field encouraged participation in the decathlon, with the expectation that their best event or sport would reveal itself in due time and, in the interim, they would pick up transferable skills (much as Fujikawa surely benefited from the balance and concentration skills he learned in judo).

By contrast, early specialization can cause mental exhaustion and, as a child gets older, overuse injuries. With orthopedists seeing a rise in joint injuries involving preteen athletes over the past decade, the AAP now formally opposes specialization before a child reaches puberty, usually 11 for girls and 12 for boys. But it's just advice, easily ignored.

"In brutal honesty, Tiger's impact has been nothing but negative," says Brian Grasso, executive director of the International Youth Conditioning Association, a Chicago-based group that certifies trainers, physical therapists, and coaches who work with child athletes across sports. "If we look at the larger picture of what's happening in kids' lives, we are not helping them by overtraining them. These are not miniature future professional athletes."

No, some are just miniature athletes with professionals shaping their future.

David Leadbetter is the father of modern golf instruction, the Buddha of the links, one of the most exclusive private coaches in the world. From beneath his trademark straw hat he has analyzed the swings of such headliners as Els, Nick Faldo, Greg Norman, Andy Bean, Ian Poulter, David Frost, and Wie. Oh, and a 2-year-old from California whose family flew across the country to have the guru watch their toddler hit balls at Leadbetter's Florida academy. "And the boy could hit it," he recalls with a chuckle. "Swung it back in John Daly fashion and hit it."

We've seen that sight before. And the result left a well-meaning father in B.C. out in the cold.

• • •

Despite its name, Devil's Thumb Golf Club feels a lot closer to heaven than to hell. The sun shines 300 days a year up here, a mile and a half above sea level in the shadow of the Grand Mesa of western Colorado. The grass seems greener, nourished as it is from pure mountain water devoid of the alkali and salt in the river water that lower courses survive on. Here, in nature's temple, is where Michael Stanifer feels the impulse to nurture.

"Molly, here's your putter," he says and then drops a plastic ball on the practice green. She slaps it a few feet in the direction of an antelope grazing in an adjacent fairway. Yes, Molly's still in diapers. But Michael's "jaded," as he calls it, because "I know the science part of it." That's what he was teaching in a high school, before he took a leave. As a former athlete, he can also appreciate the value of developing motor skills. He used to be able to chuck a baseball more than 90 miles an hour as a teenager, but he never got past semipro ball because he was busy taking care of a disabled brother and helping his family pay its bills by rebuilding houses. "Your child is your hope," he says. "You see the endless possibilities. You've had your chances; you've made your choices. When you have a kid, anything's possible."

Devon wants the world for Molly too. Or at least as much as elite sports gave her, which was a lot. Friends. Travel. A sense of accomplishment that made her teen years less turbulent. She kept accomplishing, right on through med school. A native of Boulder, she's thinks Paonia might be too small to provide the same breaks. "I've thought about being in a place where there are more opportunities for her to do sports at a high level," she says. "Getting her good coaches so the sky's the limit."

It's all so tempting. So natural. So loving, really.

And yet ... something tugs at their Supermom and Superdad capes, keeping them from infusing Molly's young life with too much athletic purpose. Maybe it's that Michael and Devon can each think of cases where precocious talent became something of a curse. Devon once coached a 10-year-old ski prodigy with serious Olympic potential who quit before high school because her parents pushed her too hard. "There must be something Earl Woods did to foster his son's interest in sports," she says. "But it seems that so many others can't do it."

Maybe it's that when Devon went to college in Norway for a year, she learned that the best adult athletes typically are those who played a variety of sports in their teenage years, rather than specialized early in one. Until then, she hadn't thought about the transferable value of basic coordination, balance, and other foundational skills.

Or maybe, just maybe, it's those blond curls on the back of Molly's head, uncut since birth. Curls that dance in the breeze, serving to remind those around her of her age. It's a magical age, really, when you think about it—full of wonder and discovery and momentary passions. Slide your spirit into her strawberry-themed leather moccasins, and you're young again. Who could want more than that?

Whatever digs at Michael and Devon, they check themselves. A couple of weeks ago, Michael cut down a metal putter for Molly, who had been showing more interest in his equipment than in her plastic set. But she quickly dropped the club—too heavy. Molly is back to the plastic set, which, Michael has decided, is fine with him.

"She's already great," he says, tousling her curls, "just as she is."

He's introduced his favorite sport to Molly and will let her take it from there. He and Devon can afford to be patient with her athletic development, thanks to where they live. Paonia may not be Boulder, but it's infinitely more conducive to an active lifestyle than many towns. It's certainly not as challenged as one old industrial enclave back East.

AGE 3

FIRST CUT

New Britain, Connecticut

"All right guys, ready to run?" chirps Lisa, the Start Smart Soccer instructor.

It's early on a Saturday morning in New Britain, a hard-luck suburb of Hartford, and with Lisa's call-out, 16 boys and girls begin jogging across the dew-covered grass at a field in the center of town. Parents smile and chuckle at the horde of preschoolers, who don't follow Lisa along the white chalk line so much as scatter behind her like the fall leaves that blanket the grass on the far sideline. When she reaches midfield, she tries to organize them into a row so she can get them to begin stretching.

"Bend over to the ground ... " she says, quickly getting interrupted.

"I saw the movie *Cars*," one boy blurts out, all non sequitur, because that is what 3-year-olds do.

"I saw the movie *The Incredibles*," the boy next to him announces.

It takes the better part of a minute to get them to focus again on the task at hand.

Friendly but firm, Lisa is good with the kids. But she's no Earl Woods. As the hour-long session progresses, it becomes apparent that there is only so much structure a coach can bring to the activity of preschoolers, who mostly just want to explore. Some of them dribble in the right direction. Others don't. Some keep picking the ball up with their hands. Some need to be steered through the cone drills. Nathan, a bespectacled boy in a Red Sox sweatshirt, leans against the leg of his 25-year-old father, Mark Dziczek, pouting in frustration.

"I don't want to do that," he says during a trapping drill.

"You wanna go home?" Mark asks, not really meaning it.

"I wanna go over there," Nathan says, pointing toward the sideline.

"But you wanna play soccer, right?" Mark says. "You gotta learn. You gotta practice."

Start Smart is a program of the National Alliance for Youth Sports (NAYS), a Florida-based nonprofit whose bread and butter is a voluntary coach certification program that community leagues can sign up for. Over the past decade, Start Smart has been a lucrative addition to NAYS' suite of products. It's marketed as a developmentally appropriate tool to help parents get their kids, beginning at age 3, ready for organized youth sports through the performing of "motor skill tasks that gradually build confidence in children while they are having fun at the same time." Often sold through local parks and recreation departments, Start Smart programs are also offered in baseball, basketball, golf, and football.

Given that most children don't develop mature movement patterns until age 6 or so—and given the difficulty of simply holding the attention of preschoolers—some youth experts question how truly smart it is to offer programs that attempt to teach sport-specific skills to kids half that age. "You shouldn't have a pedigree of knowledge coming into T-ball," says Brian Grasso, the International Youth Conditioning Association official. "Teaching skills and tactics is what youth sports is for, or at least should be." They'd rather see kids playing with balls without adult direction, chasing dogs in the backyard, laughing, and building basic athleticism.

But when raising a kid in Forgotten America, you grab whatever's available.

• • •

Half a continent away from the Grand Mesa of Colorado, and culturally even further removed than that, New Britain is neither new nor particularly British. Settled in 1687, it is now home to the largest Polish population in Connecticut, as well as a growing number of immigrants from Puerto Rico, Mexico, Somalia, Laos, Vietnam, the Ukraine, and many other places on the globe. They come here because they can afford to live here. Once known as the Hardware Capital of the World, New Britain's manufacturing base has been decimated. As jobs got shipped to cheaper labor markets and wealthier families fled to nearby leafier towns, the price of homes sank. The tax base shriveled. Crime and delinquency rose. And today, among seventh and eighth graders in this city of 72,000, one in four has a close friend who has been arrested in the past year.

The place still has its charms: a museum of American art, a Double-A farm club, ethnic eateries. A hilltop field at Stanley Quarter Park on a brilliant autumn morning belongs in that group as well. But I am urged not to get too carried away.

"You go two streets over, you got projects," Mark Dziczek says. "You go two streets over anywhere in New Britain, you got projects."

It would be nice to think that at age 3, the odds wouldn't already be stacked against Nathan being athletic. But they are. By sixth grade, only 20 percent of the kids at his area middle school pass the state's physical fitness test, which measures children in four ways, adjusted for age: push-ups (to pass, sixth-grade boys have to be able to do 11, girls 8), partial sit-ups (25 and 24), a flexibility exercise called sit-and-reach (25 and 26), and a mile run (9:15 for boys, 10:30 for girls). None of these standards are considered to be especially challenging by the state, rather it considers them the minimum level of fitness to maintain health.

By eighth grade, the kids passing the test drops to 13 percent.

Mark harbors no illusions about Nathan and elite sports. He simply wants to get him through high school in decent physical shape because, "I know there will be benefits." Some of those are listed in cursive on a weathered "The Benefits Are Endless" sign hanging from the brick parks-and-rec building next to the soccer field: "Meet Friends, Build Memories, Teach Vital Life Skills." Others are more clinical and can be found on the Centers for Disease Control website: Engaging in physical activity on most days of the week reduces the risk of developing diabetes, high blood pressure, cardiovascular disease, colon cancer, and feelings of depression and anxiety. It helps control weight and builds healthy bones. It can improve function of the endocrine and immune systems.

Those who exercise as teenagers are more likely to do so as adults. Physically fit men have fewer overnight hospital stays and visit their doctors less frequently than others. Not only are those who are in shape more likely to live long, they also live better. It's been shown that thinner people make more money than heavier ones, perhaps because employers discriminate against the obese when deciding who gets promotions or choice training opportunities. The rich can afford better health care. And the healthy pay lower insurance premiums. Health and wealth are in cahoots.

Exercise increases the quantity of nerve synapses, blood vessels, and, ultimately, the size of the brain. Celebrated jocks with an eye on pro careers sometimes struggle to meet minimum entrance requirements at colleges, but don't be misled by such anecdotal evidence: Elite high school athletes on the whole get better grades than other students. A 2005 study by the federal government found that athletes are more likely than nonathletes to attend college and get degrees, and that team captains and MVPs achieve at even higher rates once out of high school. Historically at least, many have risen to leadership positions in the business world. A 1987 survey of 75 Fortune 500 companies indicated that 95 percent of their highest-ranking executives played high school sports (just 54 percent were involved in student government, and 43 percent in the National Honor Society).

But if Nathan is going to go the route of the fit and not the fat, the obstacles are many.

The challenge begins at home, which for him is a modest three-bedroom Cape on one-fifth of an acre in a neighborhood built out in the 1960s. By the standards of most kids in New Britain, he's well-off. Across the street is an unnamed, unoccupied patch of grass the size of a basketball court. Mark, a machinist, and his wife Melissa, a receptionist, cobbled together the money to buy their weathered house partly because of that odd chunk of community space on the other side of the road. When Mark gets home each weekday at 4 p.m.—taking the parenting baton from Melissa, who works the "second shift" (4:30 to 10:30 p.m.), as they say in New Britain—he heads outside with Nathan and his other son,

1-year-old Tyler. They have home run derbies and fly kites in that little oasis, during the warm months at least. But there are limits to the boys' freedom. They cannot roam beyond that lot, which is ringed by streets. And Mark feels he must be there with them to keep them from chasing a ball in front of a car. Or worse, getting taken by some creep.

Anxiety about child predators is everywhere now in both urban and suburban America, restricting children's access to free play. The fear era pretty much was launched in the South Florida town where I was raised, when a Hollywood boy several years younger than me, Adam Walsh, was abducted in 1981 after his mother left him alone momentarily while shopping in the same Sears store where I, too, checked out the latest video games. You may recognize the heartbreaking photo of Adam at 6, baseball bat above his right shoulder, his smile missing a couple of front teeth. His disappearance—and the eventual recovery of his severed head in a canal—sparked a national movement. It helped to spur the formation of the National Center for Missing and Exploited Children, and his father, John, became host of the popular TV show *America's Most Wanted*. Adam's story still resonates with parents—and with elected officials on both sides of the aisle. In a rare show of 2006 bipartisanship, Congress passed the Adam Walsh Child Protection and Safety Act, creating a national database of sexual offenders that can be accessed via the Internet.

To be sure, the protective instincts of parents are now being exploited for political and commercial gain. A year before the law passed I spent the afternoon with a family in an upper middle-class suburb of Issaquah, Wash., 20 minutes east of Seattle. It's a destination community for professionals, with architecturally interesting rooflines, manicured gardens, and a Starbucks at the bottom of the hill. The protected neighborhood has one way in and one way out, and stay-at-home moms keep an eye on unfamiliar cars. But the 3-year-old boy of the house was not allowed to play out in the front yard. Why? Because his mom watches plenty of local TV news, which habitually trumpets the locations of pedophiles; fear always drives ratings. Though she hadn't heard of any registered offenders within a couple miles of their home, she was nervous. So her son spent much of his time inside finding adventure ... at the end of his right index finger. He would log on to the Internet and, with the click of a mouse, make JoJo the clown jump rope. Or he'd pop in his Bob the Builder CD and make something cool with Bob's very own hands. The mother worried that her son wasn't going to develop the physical and social skills she did as a girl when she rode her bike all over the West Seattle neighborhood in which she grew up in the 1970s. It was a different era: Since then, unstructured play and outdoor activities for children between the ages of 3 and 11 has declined by nearly 40 percent.

It's not altogether clear whether we are living in a more dangerous society now or whether we are merely more aware of its potential dangers. Either way, the era of the 24/7 parent is upon us; the sociologist Jay Coakley observes that this is the first generation in the history of the world in which parents are held accountable for the whereabouts and actions of their children every minute of every day. If we're not watching over them at an organized event or at our house, we are supposed to know the adult who is. This is easier for some families to achieve than for others. My kids are fortunate in that we found a home in a semirural, middle-class neighborhood with decent-size lots. It's not a gated community, nor are we invulnerable to crime, but we feel it's safe enough to leave them alone for hours at a time. Our children spend their after-school time in the backyards of the four families on our side of the hill, throwing baseballs, riding bikes, and digging at worms in the dirt. When I started researching this chapter, I checked our area in the sexual offender database, and there wasn't much cause for alarm.

I can understand how Mark feels more threatened. When I plugged Nathan's address into the database, the names of 93 registered sexual offenders were listed as living within a couple miles of his home. Thirty-three of them had been convicted of offenses specifically against children; one lived a couple blocks away, and another a few doors beyond him. The vast majority of assaults are perpetrated by someone the victim knows, like a relative, but Mark isn't taking chances.

"You can't trust anybody," he says.

So when he isn't across the street, Mark stands outside his front door, drawing on a cigarette, watching his boys ride tricycles and draw chalk designs on their short, cracked driveway. The dozens of butts at his feet mark the many hours he has logged at this post over the months, being a good dad. But he can't stand out there all day. He worries about keeping the kids active, "especially with the whole obesity thing in the U.S." Nathan, whose round face and glasses make him look a bit like the blond kid in *Jerry Maguire*, is already a touch chubby—nothing too alarming, but down the road fitness could become an issue.

It takes a village to raise a fit kid these days. But the village cannot be relied upon.

There's only so much help Nathan will get from ... public schools. When structured well and taught daily, physical education introduces kids to new sports and emphasizes skills for a lifetime of fitness. But in New Britain, P.E. classes in elementary school are held just twice a week, for 30 minutes. In middle school, classes nudge up to 80 minutes a week. At the town high school, freshmen and sophomores are required to take one semester of P.E. and one semester of health each year, and nothing after that. Those numbers are consistent with the national pattern, in which only half of all high school students attend P.E. classes one or more days a week—and those who attend a daily class has dropped to 33 percent (from 42 percent in 1991).

Nathan won't get much help from ... the federal government. The signature educational initiative of the Bush Administration was the No Child Left Behind Act, which holds school administrators accountable for student test scores in academic subjects. It's easy to cut P.E. when your job is on the line, as has occurred in New Britain because schools consistently have not met federal standards. Nationwide, 14 percent of schools reduced physical education time to make more room for math and reading instruction. Just as No Child Left Behind was coming online, the Department of Education began annually to disperse grants that helped 200 schools and other entities revamp their P.E. curricula, which too often have offered more standing around than sweating hard. The program, funded by the Carol M. White Physical Education for Progress Bill, has helped deliver measurable results through the use of "fun fitness" activities such as rock climbing and inline skating. But New Britain schools have never been among those that received any of the roughly $70 million a year that get dispersed. For much of the country, physical education effectively is becoming privatized, outsourced to athletic training firms and nonschool programs that require payments from parents who can afford them.

MYTH NO. 3
America is the world's athletic superpower.

THE TRUTH
We're the fattest nation—and it all starts in preschool.

He won't get much help from ... New Britain. Nathan loves swimming; he was introduced to it last year. But the town has closed two of its five pools since then, in order to shave $60,000 a year off the budget. "It's one of those life skills," the city's recreation manager argued in opposition before city leaders, to no avail. After eight years of pressure on the mayor's budget, the cuts are getting pretty ugly. In 2006, the town terminated an all-day summer rec program for 125 middle-school children, a group that's especially vulnerable to rising obesity rates. In New Britain, most kids of that age already play sports or exercise less than two hours a week.

He won't get so much help from ... the corporate sports establishment. Mark is a fan of the Boston Red Sox and New England Patriots, whose merchandise he and Nathan wear on their heads and torsos. Both clubs have sponsored community outreach efforts that address the need to get kids active and healthy, including public-service campaigns created by Major League Baseball and the NFL in which the teams participate. But when Nathan gets old enough to care about their games and join his father in front of the television, he'll also find programming rich in commercials for fast-food chains and soft drink companies. The Patriots' sponsors include McDonalds and Pepsi; the Red Sox have deals with Coca-Cola and Dunkin' Donuts. Television in general is rife with messages by such sponsors—one study found that the average preteen absorbs 7,600 food commercials a year. Games are populated with ads for junk food that has been largely removed from Connecticut schools by state mandate. Capitalism moves to a different beat: profit.

No surprise there. But the structure of organized sports will limit Nathan's chances of burning off those calories. In most countries around the world, opportunities are offered primarily through local clubs that are funded with membership fees and, in many cases, some form of government subsidy. These clubs usually have facilities. People join the clubs as kids and sometimes play there the rest of their lives on teams made up of older men and women who gather for recreational games. In the U.S., children during their early years play in leagues organized by local clubs—whether it is T-ball or Pop Warner football or youth soccer—but those opportunities disappear as high school approaches. Many community-based recreation leagues, which usually find room for any kid who signs up, do not offer programs for kids older than 13 or 14. The idea is that from that point on schools take over, a mostly viable arrangement in smaller middle schools and secondary schools where coaches need bodies to fill out teams. (School-based sports also work in places like South Africa where one high school might field as many as 15 rugby teams.) But in larger schools, the traditional one-team, one-school structure leaves many kids with no access to roster spots. At New Britain High School, even with 23 teams for boys and girls at the freshman, jayvee, and varsity levels in 11 different sports, only 500 of the school's 3,400 students are athletes—15 percent.

The percentage of sophomores at the school who passed the state fitness test: 19.

Coincidence?

Teens can get some exercise working physical, part-time jobs, of course. And anyone can go run around on their own—it's a free country. But it isn't happening much. In the absence of feasible alternatives, making a New Britain High School team would appear to be the most direct and realistic pathway to fitness. For decades, intramural sports were an option for the less talented, less fit, and late-maturing kids—precisely the sort of children who most need to stay active. But intramurals in New Britain were eliminated in the early 2000s. School administrators wanted to keep the weight room open in the afternoons for anyone who wanted to use it; the money for that got killed too. Leonard Corto, the former high school football coach, now athletic director for all New Britain schools, has noticed that students have gotten flabbier since intramurals and P.E. took the hits. “There’s definitely been an effect,” he tells me. “Even our athletes aren’t as in shape as they once were.”

Hard Hittin’ New Britain, as the Golden Hurricanes are known, has won four state football titles since the early ’90s. On Friday nights in autumn, the marching band—with its powerful drumming section and accompaniment of clarinets, trombones, and trumpets—can be heard from miles away. When opposing fans see the flash from the costumes of the Majorettes, Cane-ettes, and Color Guard, and hear about the 110 football players whom the school sponsors, it’s easy to assume New Britain is a jock school. At least a couple of players each year get Division I football scholarships. One of them, Tebucky Jones, went on to make a small fortune as an NFL cornerback.

But it’s just the tip of the iceberg that everyone sees. Mark Dziczek knows what lies beneath the surface. Having grown up in New Britain, he’s lived it. A workout freak in high school, he was in that minority who got to take advantage of the sports program that his parents and every other taxpayer in town helped pay for. (Maintaining the school’s athletic fields alone costs the city rec department $250,000 a year.) He made the baseball team and was briefly on the football team, then quit because he couldn’t get playing time. Small and not all that fast, he lacked the natural gifts of a Jones or a Ryan Nece. And by waiting until high school to take up football, his technique was less polished than that of his more experienced teammates. By the late ’90s, enthusiasm alone had expired as a ticket to playing time in sports at a school this large.

So that’s why he’s in Stanley Quarter Park on a Saturday morning, paying $50 for six hour-long soccer lessons of questionable value, nudging his son to learn athletic skills before the boy is perhaps ready.

“See, dad?” Nathan says, picking up the ball during a dribbling drill and pointing to the number 3 marked on a black hexagon. It’s not just the size of the ball.

“Yeah, that’s your age,” Mark says.

Time to learn how to hunt. For playing time.

• • •

On the eve of the 1996 Atlanta Olympics, the U.S. Department of Health and Human Services released the most comprehensive review ever of the physical activity of Americans—an inch-thick work that Secretary Donna Shalala likened to the Surgeon General's historic 1964 report on smoking that laid the groundwork for the tobacco-free zones that are now part of corporate and civic life. Shalala's report found that only half of young people were vigorously active on a regular basis. Those habits got worse as children moved through adolescence and into adulthood. More than 60 percent of grown-ups weren't getting sufficient exercise, and 25 percent weren't getting any exercise at all.

At the same time, Americans were ingesting an increasing number of calories, which sedentary people have a tougher time burning off. They can become obese, which is defined as having a very high amount of body fat in relation to lean body mass, or a Body Mass Index (BMI) of 30 or higher. By '96 a crisis was already in the making. At the time, 30 states had obesity prevalence rates of between 15 and 19 percent. Shalala declared the situation to be a dangerous trend that needed to be turned around quickly, for the health of the nation and its citizens. She called for a "massive national commitment" to get people exercising for at least 30 to 45 minutes a day, a new "physical activity movement" that would start with school-based interventions promoting fitness habits for life.

Since then, the state-by-state picture has changed dramatically, unfortunately not in the way Shalala hoped. (See chart on next page.)

Obesity is a term that gets argued about a lot by experts. The most skeptical ones say that the entire concept of obesity is an arbitrary notion created by a small group of scientists and doctors who in some cases are funded by the weight-loss industry. But you would have to be chemically seduced by your supersize value meal to look at the progression on the following page and not choke on your fries. And actually, these are conservative estimates based on self-reports in telephone interviews. The truth is not so easily fudged during doctors' exams, which show that one-third of the adult population is obese, and another third—which isn't represented in this chart—is categorically overweight, or close to being obese.

Obesity in the U.S.

Percentage of the adult population in each state with a BMI of 30 or higher

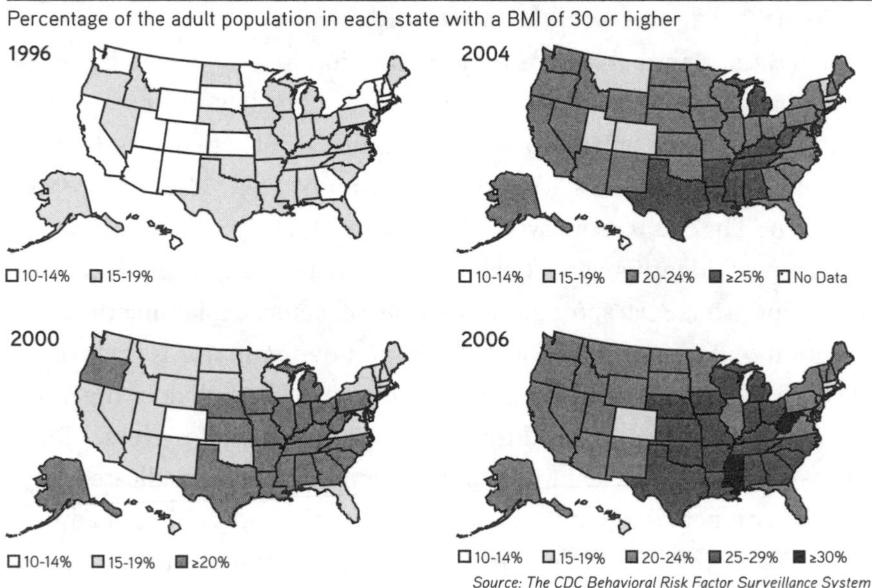

Source: The CDC Behavioral Risk Factor Surveillance System

The current generation of children is the first in a century predicted to live shorter lives than their parents. A large part of that can be attributed to issues related to obesity. The number of overweight kids has more than tripled since 1980, according to the CDC. Among those between ages 6 and 19, more than nine million kids—18 percent—are considered obese. The figure is projected to hit 20 percent by 2010.

Every nation in the developed world has seen a dramatic rise in corpulence over the past quarter century. But none of those countries approach the obesity rate of the U.S, where the average adult has added 25 pounds. We have bigger caskets and car seats. Airplanes need more fuel to ferry us around. We are a nation that has responded to the call of Sir Mix-A-Lot, who liked big butts (and he could not lie). The heavyset rapper should be the first choice to sing the national anthem at the debut game at any new pro sports stadium with wider seats—which is to say, *every* new pro sports stadium. Fan comfort is among the rationales that has driven the boom in stadium construction over the past two decades. More than 80 clubs have received new or renovated homes since 1990, with the public picking up two-thirds of the $20 billion tab.

Meanwhile, ordinary Americans are far less involved in playing sports than they were in 1990. The Sporting Goods Manufacturers Association (SGMA) partners with survey organizations to collect reams of data and issue annual reports on participation in every sport. Baseball, basketball, softball, gymnastics, inline skating, volleyball, badminton, and racquetball all appear to have lost millions of participants. "This is not only bad for business, it's bad for the country," SGMA executive vice president Thomas J. Cove wrote in his introductory statement for the 2005 report, identifying the declines as by far the biggest challenge facing his industry. Each sport has its own set of factors explaining the deterioration of its grassroots, but the common denominator is that casual play is in decline. Among team sports, only in basketball does the number of pickup players exceed the number of organized players. "Team sports participation is being consolidated among its most dedicated players who compete in organized settings under the supervision of adults," the SGMA report concluded. "At the same time, millions of youngsters have stopped playing the games just for the fun of it."

Today, kids start playing sports earlier than ever before. And when they quit or get cut, they're often gone from the game for good. From the grassroots up, more than ever the sports structure is configured in a manner designed to identify and promote the next generation of athlete-entertainers—whether for the pro leagues, colleges, or just the Friday night lights of New Britain. These talented children become the focus of the youth sports system, which leaves few options for the teenager of low or average ability. One report published in the *President's Council on Physical Fitness and Sports Research Digest* estimated that restrictions on team membership in high school eliminated half of all participants from the pre-high school level. "The organizational structure of sports in the United States—and not a lack of interest on the part of potential enrollees—is primarily responsible for the reduction in participation at age 14 and beyond," wrote the authors, Michigan State researchers Vern Seefeldt and Martha Ewing.

There are no headlines or nightly news clips for great performances in intramurals, which have largely disappeared from the national landscape. And physical education in many schools has been either neglected or used as little more than a stepping stone to varsity glory. New Britain has one of the better weight rooms in Connecticut, thanks to fundraising by the former football coach, Jack Cochran. But the way the district paid much of his salary was by making him a P.E. teacher, a job he neglected. He often arrived late to class, left early, or just stopped showing up for weeks at a time. Cochran acknowledged to the *Hartford Courant* that he sometimes shirked the duties of that job in order to fulfill his responsibilites as a coach. "I couldn't be in two places at once," he said.

Should a child like Nathan not develop fitness habits for life, Americans as a whole will pay the price. The U.S. spends more than 15 percent of its Gross Domestic Product (GDP) on health care, a greater share than any other developed country in the world. In 2003, an average of $5,671 was spent on each citizen. The largest share—46 percent—was picked up by the government, whether federal, state, or local. Unless changes are made, experts say, costs will only escalate in the coming years. The U.S. government forecasts that by 2015 health care expenditures will reach $4 trillion, gobbling nearly 20 percent of the nation's GDP. Obesity and related conditions, such as diabetes and heart disease, are among the key drivers in the rising costs. According to one estimate, obese children rack up health care costs of $750 million a year, three times as much as kids who are fit.

Tom McMillen has benefited as much as any American from the way we organize athletics. He was the No. 1 high school basketball player in the country in 1970, and became a star at the University of Maryland. That path led to his becoming a member of the Olympic team, a Rhodes Scholar, an NBA center, and a congressman. After that, during the Clinton Administration, he was co-chair of the President's Council on Physical Fitness, a barely funded, strictly advisory committee that works with the Department of Health and Human Services to recommend programs to encourage sports participation. The group has no power, but it did provide McMillen a front-row seat to the relationship between elite-level and community sports.

"The whole sports structure in America needs a relook, as we are really the only country in world without a Ministry of Sport or a Ministry of

Youth—different countries call them different things," McMillen tells me. "There really isn't a champion for grassroots sports. We've developed a nation where there are a lot of resources at the top, for stadiums, for elite athletes. But there's little at the bottom and no governing mechanism to focus on it. So the results are not surprising that we have the fattest children in world, and health costs are staggering.

"We've run our pathway to pro sports through the schools, so it becomes a corrupting force in our schools. At the same time, we're not focusing on what we should be doing with the nation, which is broad-based participation. Kids are dropping out because they can't make the school team. And P.E. has gotten cut. So what are kids resorting to? Screen time—TV, video games. That's the damage. That's the product of running elite sports through the school system. It's not just a sports issue anymore. It's a health issue."

For Nathan, the fight for fitness, for his sake but also for ours, starts soon. Heart disease and obesity can begin in early childhood. If a child is obese by age 4, he or she has a 20 percent chance of being obese as an adult; if obese as an adolescent, 80 percent. Statistics also show that the fitness habits of a child's parents play a key role, as the odds increase if even one parent is obese. With 198 pounds on his 5-foot-8 frame, Mark is on the cusp of joining that category in terms of BMI. "Me and my wife are not in great shape, but we're not in terrible shape," he says, tugging on his Patriots hat. He has the athletic physique to readily drop pounds—if, between his job and family duties, he could just find the time to work out again.

For now, the cigarettes will have to keep his weight under control.

• • •

You'd never suspect that the republic was separating into fitness haves and have-nots if all you did was walk around one of the sporting goods megastores that has opened over the past decade. You might even think all the headlines about obesity describe a fake crisis. The floor space devoted to individual sports is nearly as large as the entire sporting goods stores of a generation ago. Swooshes are everywhere. Glossy, larger-than-life, cardboard cutouts of LeBron and Tiger in action give palaces like my local Dick's Sporting Goods a dynamic vibe.

Then you start asking questions, and a different picture emerges.

One day after returning from the Callaway Junior Worlds, I was in the golf section at Dick's, shopping for a set of clubs for my 8-year-old son, Cole. (His first.) The man next to me was doing the same for his son. How old? I asked. "Two," he said with a sheepish smile. I headed down the escalator to the shoe section, with its wall of more than a hundred offerings located beneath a gigantic, multiscreen television tuned to a basketball game. Lit up under the center of the display were the running shoes, by far the largest subsection—which struck me as odd, since I rarely see people jogging on the area roads. I was trying to imagine who bought all those sneakers.

"About 40 percent of our running shoes are sold to, you know, the larger individual," the salesman explained delicately. "They like the extra cushioning."

Maybe I would too, if I was overweight and just wanted to walk from point A to point B comfortably.

The trends are the same with other categories of sneaker—some of which are now sold in wider widths. For the wider set. One industry analyst tells me that perhaps only one-quarter of all basketball shoes sold today are actually used for basketball.

Americans have long thought of themselves as the world's most active people. For decades, Europeans have been picking out U.S. tourists on their streets by our choice of footwear—we look ready for a game to break out at any moment. But our athletic ethos is now more about style than about lifestyle. It's the image we have of ourselves, or at least of who we would like to be (Melo, Lance, Peyton, Tebucky, etc.). Nationally, according to the SGMA, only 30 percent of all sports apparel and athletic footwear sold is actually used for sports or fitness; the rest is purchased for reasons such as fashion or comfort. Among children, the imbalance is even more distinct: Only one quarter of the $8 billion spent on their sports apparel is used for sports or exercise.

From this subset of the population, we must build our world champions. Tough assignment, given the way we teach some games.

AGE 4

LES RED, WHITE, AND BLUES

Clairefontaine-en-Yvelines, France

The Americans, Seriously.

So declared the headline in a *New York Times* magazine piece a few weeks before the 2006 World Cup was held in Germany. And Lord, didn't many of us want to believe it. Anyone who had ever been called unpatriotic for appreciating a well-struck in-swinger, anyone who grew up going to North American Soccer League games as a kid (as I did in Fort Lauderdale), anyone who wanted to see U.S. soccer succeed at the highest level because the game is the global language and cultural fluency matters in the midst of an unpopular, isolating war—all of us, in our hearts, hoped that maybe this was our time. The U.S. had made the quarterfinals in '02 and now was ranked No. 5 in the world, behind only Brazil, the Czech Republic, the Netherlands, and Mexico. Sure, there are always raised eyebrows about FIFA's rankings, whispers and screams that wins against weak teams are given too much weight. But the vibe from national team coach Bruce Arena was one of smoldering confidence, even Long Island cockiness, projecting the sense that while he didn't want to overpromise and underdeliver, a run deep into the monthlong tournament in Germany would not surprise him and shouldn't surprise us. The Americans, he suggested, would marshal their traditional strengths—fitness, competitiveness, physical play—to neutralize opponents. Arena said, "One day, when we get it right and become the best, it's because we did it our way, no one else's way." Nike, chief sponsor of the national team, suggested that perhaps that moment was at hand, insisting in print ads that soccer was now as American as fireworks on the Fourth of July. The ad noted that the sport's 17 million U.S. participants—a grassroots juggernaut—was greater than the total population of Holland. "By sheer numbers alone," the ad read, "we are going to sweep over most of the globe."

Then the games began.

In the opener, a 3-0 washout to the Czechs, the Americans looked like college kids chasing old pros around the pitch. It was 1998 all over again, with the U.S. failing to muster any kind of offensive attack. Passes were made without precision. Balls skipped off the feet of wide-open teammates. Analysts questioned Arena's tactics, while Arena in turn blasted his designated star Landon Donovan for a supposed lack of aggressiveness. DaMarcus Beasley, the speedster, was a nonfactor, too often passing back. Goalkeeper Kasey Keller punted into areas of the field populated only by Czechs. In the next game, the U.S. gutted out a 1-1 tie with eventual champion Italy when the Azzuri accidentally knocked the ball into their own net. Nevertheless, the Americans through two games had generated just one shot on goal, fewer than any other team. With a 2-1 loss a few days later to Ghana, an African republic the size of Oregon, the Americans disappeared from the World Cup. Just as dispiriting, there were few, if any, highlight clips to savor, no moments of brilliance to make a fence-sitting sports fan back home fall in love with the team. Once again, theories were advanced for why we just can't get it right—and why in 30 years of purposeful effort the U.S. has yet to deliver one world-class player. The venerable if soccer-snarky Frank Deford crowed that the game just isn't in our DNA. Others proposed that soccer doesn't sort out winners and losers clearly enough to endear itself to athletically gifted American boys who grow up hearing that ties are like kissing your sister. Some pundits wondered if the supposed psychic disconnect flows from the nation long ago having declared its independence from England, the birthplace of soccer.

Sure. Maybe that's it.

Or maybe it's just that a country reaps what it sows.

• • •

I know we're supposed to loathe the French. But they once went to war against the English, too. On our side. And let's face it, they do soccer pretty well. Maybe there's a thing or two we can learn in frog land.

Two weeks before the World Cup is set to begin, I take a plane to Paris, then a train to a small village an hour southwest of the city, then an automobile deep into the heart of the Rambouillet Forest. As my cabbie turns his Renault onto the entrance road of the national training center for the French Football Federation, it hardly seems like we have arrived at the world's foremost soccer academy. The place is perfectly tranquil, save for the chirping of birds and the gentle rustling of leaves. Rhododendron bushes with pink and white flowers line the playing fields that lead to an old castle at the center of the grounds, making the training center feel like an arboretum. There are few signs of grand athletic ambition anywhere until the cabbie reaches the castle and—*pow!*—we are blinded by the gleam of a humongous, golden, gaudy replica of a World Cup trophy whose design and scale seem more fit for the lobby of some Las Vegas theme hotel. France won the right to hoist the monument during the 1998 World Cup with a 3-0 victory on home soil against Brazil in the championship game.

A few minutes later, I am in the second-floor office of André Mérelle, the sage I have come to see. As the federation's director of youth development, he oversees the grooming of the next generation of would-be French stars. The wall to the right of his cluttered desk is lined with group photos of boys from the past decade who have been selected for focused training as teenagers. Each year 1,500 13-year-olds around France are identified by scouts as having the most promise, with 650 of them earning tryouts at Clairefontaine, as the training center is commonly called. They come in waves of 50, until a final 24 are offered scholarships to live there and train on weekdays after school.

"Take a look," Mérelle says, firing up a DVD on his laptop. "This is what we do."

The video is of the last day of tryouts, the final cut. From its bird's-eye angle, the camera pans across a row of boys lined up shoulder to shoulder in blue jerseys. Immediately, one of the first characteristics that reveals itself is their ethnicity: The first eight or nine are of African descent and very few after that are of European stock. When I ask Mérelle about this, he takes my notepad and draws a picture of a doughnut with a small hole in the middle. The hole, he says, represents Paris. The doughnut represents its sprawling suburbs where most immigrant families live. Wealth dominates the inner city, so here the poor—mostly first- and second-generation transplants from former colonies such as Senegal, Cameroon, and Algeria—get pushed out to the 'burbs, with their high-rise concrete blocks and nearby manufacturing jobs.

"This is where we get the gifted players," Mérelle says, shading in with his pen the eastern side of the doughnut. He draws an X at the bottom. "Henry is from here," he says.

That would be Thierry Henry, now one of the world's top strikers. To the basic American sports fan, the face might look familiar. He's the other guy with Tiger Woods and Roger Federer in those ubiquitous Gillette razor ads. He's also the "close friend" that Tony Parker enthused about in the press conference after his San Antonio Spurs wrapped up the 2007 NBA title, in which the flashy point guard became the first Euro to be named MVP of the championship series. Henry, on break between seasons, wore Parker's No. 9 jersey while watching the final game in the stands and posed with Parker later, holding the Spurs' fourth trophy of the past decade.

Soccer aficionados don't need any introduction to Henry, as they know the résumé. Two-time MVP of England's Premier League, where he played before moving to FC Barcelona. Arsenal's all-time leading scorer. Those familiar with the sport marvel at his prodigious talent: the combination of size, explosion, and invention. Though 6-foot-2, he is masterful with the ball, with a dribbling style that is not fixed. Defenders are forced to give him space to operate. But left alone, he can be deadly, too, knifing in from the wing to launch a powerful shot controlled for speed, spin, and placement. He's good with his noggin, too. In a

2006 World Cup semifinal match, Henry elevated near the goalmouth to deflect a pass into the roof of the net for the winning margin in a 1-0 victory against Brazil. He looked like Randy Moss rising for six in the end zone.

When Henry arrived at Clairefontaine at age 13, he was given access to some of the top coaches in the country. They worked with him to develop the choices he makes when he receives the ball, how to read the game flow, and the mastery of skills such as juggling, kicking with both feet, crossing, heading, and shooting with precision over power. By contrast, there was little emphasis on building strength, speed, and other physical traits that typify the U.S. game. If Henry tried something new with the ball and failed, he was not punished. Experimentation was encouraged as much as good form was, and no matches were played during the two years he was in residence here. That de-pressurized environment allowed him to develop and refine his talents, which he then put to use in weekend games with his home-area club team. By 17 he was starting at the highest professional level in France, and by 20 he was the leading scorer for the French team when it won the '98 World Cup.

Every prospect accepted into Clairefontaine receives the same type of intense technical and psychological polishing. It's two hours a day, five days a week of skills, skills, skills. Since Henry left the academy, more than 80 players who came to train here have gone on to play professionally, including two fellow starters (Louis Saha and William Gallas) on the '06 World Cup team.

Investing in 13-year-olds is a highly speculative business. At that age, a boy who went through puberty early might dominate a late bloomer who actually has superior talent—and more upside. To understand their growth potential, X-rays are taken of the left wrists of the final 50 prospects to pinpoint their "bone age," which often differs greatly from their actual age.

Mérelle, hunkered over his laptop, points to a tall boy in the lineup.

"This one is 17," he says of the boy's bone age. "This one is 11 ... This one is 13 ... "

He smiles, marveling at the biological differences. "Incredible, huh?"

Elsewhere, early bloomers gain access to elite teams simply because they're bigger, stronger, and faster than their age peers. One study of Portuguese prospects found that soccer "systematically excludes late maturing boys," who often drop out of the game as a result. Even a few months of physical maturity can make a difference in access to select teams, and thus, to top coaches. The phenomenon is called the Relative Age Effect. Children born in the last three months of a selection year—just before the cut-off date in assigning kids to age-specific teams—are significantly underrepresented at the youth levels when compared with those born in the first three months. The downstream effect of that discriminatory process can be seen at the pro level, where players born in the first three months of a given year are far more common. The pattern of skewed birth date distributions has been documented in other sports as well.

The careful identification and development procedures at Clairefontaine inevitably get much of the credit for delivering world-class athletes. But a high-end soccer laboratory isn't primarily what sets France apart—there is a similar, if less sophisticated, under-17 residency camp in Florida affiliated with U.S. Soccer that has helped groom such players as Donovan and Beasley. Indeed, the true strength of the French system stems from what happens with players at the local level, even before they get selected for special training at national and regional centers. As Mérelle says, with equal parts emphasis and acknowledgment, "Henry was already good in front of the goal when he came to us."

It all starts with falling in love. Which isn't just a French thing.

• • •

In 1985, the University of Chicago educational psychologist Benjamin Bloom studied the development histories of 150 elite athletes, musicians, artists, and academics going back to their early childhood. He found striking similarities in their paths to excellence. He wrote that "no matter what the initial characteristics of the individual, unless there is a long and intensive process of encouragement, nurturance, education, and training, the individuals will not attain extreme levels of capability in the particular fields." They worked hard. They benefited from the guidance of high-quality mentors. They were given opportunities to achieve mastery.

But before any of that could happen, at the entry phase the sport or activity had to capture their imagination. A wild romance was born somehow. The same development was later found in a survey of U.S. Olympians, whose affection for their sport would serve as fuel for self-improvement throughout their careers.

How to spark such passion? The impulse of many modern parents—even those with the most modest of hopes for their child athlete—is to attempt to arrange the marriage through early, persistent doses of organized team sports. In many U.S. communities, the process is set into motion around age 4.

Let's head back to Connecticut for a minute. Just across the interstate west of New Britain is the more affluent, middle-class-and-up Farmington Valley. Here parents deluged with marketing messages about providing children with the "very best" enrichment programs often have the resources for a series of sign-ups, sports-related or otherwise. Stay-at-home moms ferry their tots from Gymboree classes to sing-along music sessions to infant swimming lessons, hoping to give their Little Einsteins every developmental advantage. (Set aside for a minute the fact that Albert Einstein himself didn't talk until age 3.) The Saturday-morning soccer program for preschoolers at the area YMCA—with its chalked fields, regulation-size balls, and structured drills—is just another manifestation of that thinking.

For the final 30 minutes of the hourlong session, the blue team matches up against the orange team in a "noncompetitive"—that's what the catalog says, at least—match. Play is dominated by the two or three most physically advanced kids, who kick the ball hard and give chase, the pack forming behind them in the shape of a teardrop. Some of them keep dribbling right past the end line toward the neighboring graveyard, until a parent corrals and redirects the flock back onto the miniature pitch. Some of the kids seem engaged. Most seem bewildered or even bored. A girl standing in the goalmouth makes like an airplane, altogether uninterested in stopping a ball from slowly rolling into the net. A boy in cleats pouts as his father tries to nudge him off the sideline, frustrated at his son's lack of aggression. "He just needs to get more of that killer instinct," the father says to me. The boy had spent much of the game hugging his dad's leg, uncomfortable with the idea of stealing the ball from other kids. "He's used to sharing. He tells me, 'It's their turn to kick it, Daddy.'" Hey, on children's TV, that's what Franklin the turtle might do.

When the referee tweets his whistle at the end of the nongame, the parents whose children happen to be enjoying the action let out a collective deflated "*Awww.*"

The preschool exercise at the Y serves as a portal into a system that regards competition as the preeminent training tool. Starting next year, when these kids are in kindergarten, they will be able to start in the town's recreational leagues, with their once-a-weekend games and sideline orange slices. But with fall and spring outdoor sessions, many kids will be playing dual seasons. At age 8, travel ball begins, with its select groups of boys and girls playing outside the structure of the rec league and representing their towns in tournaments and games around the state. By age 9, some teams will be playing as many as four games a weekend during the fall and spring. They play on Mother's Day, Father's Day, Memorial Day, Labor Day, and Columbus Day; there are few holidays from organized soccer. A couple of years later, some of those kids also will get invited to join private, often for-profit "premier" clubs that draw talent from a wider area. By the end of elementary school, the very best child athletes could be playing 100 outdoor and indoor games a year—twice as many as the best French *teenagers*.

This is not the way great players are made, Mérelle says.

"Everyone wants to win games. That's good," he says. "But *how* do you win? If you're too focused on winning games, you don't learn to play well. You get too nervous, because you're always afraid to make errors."

The French system recognizes the value of unstructured play. And that innovation and passion bloom when children are given the time and space to create games on their own. Without uniforms. Or league standings. Or game clocks. Or emotionally invested adults. It's an inspired place in which improvisation rules, rewards are intrinsic, playing personalities are developed—and a child learns to see things that don't reveal themselves as readily in formal games.

At *ESPN The Magazine*, we arranged a conversation between Henry and Phoenix Suns point guard Steve Nash, who has twice been voted NBA MVP. The French soccer star was well aware of the talents of Nash, who compensates for his relative lack of height (6-3) with brilliant playmaking and an ability to create space where none seemed to exist a split second earlier. Henry—who once gave Nash a tour of Clairefontaine ("one of the best days of my life," Nash says)—told Nash that he and Parker were among his favorite athletes to watch.

"Tony has the same view you have on the court—that soccer player's view," Henry said.

"I'm excited to hear you say that," said Nash, who had the advantage in both nature (he's the son of a former soccer pro) and nurture (he grew up playing lots of soccer, hockey, lacrosse, and basketball, both organized and pickup) working for him.

"You see more than what is in front of you," Henry said. "I hear people watch you and say, 'What a pass!' And I'm like, What do you mean? Because for me, it was obvious."

Sports scientists have a name for this seemingly supernatural talent: field sense. It's the ability to anticipate the movements of people and objects in motion, and it takes many forms. It could be the act of finding the open man just before the player breaks free. Or flicking a puck into the corner of a net guarded by a goalie who fatefully leans a quarter-inch the wrong way. Or predicting the trajectory of a Beckham bender in a soccer game. And while some people may have more of an innate capacity to develop the skill than others, researchers now believe that it's a talent that can be trained for—through, ironically, free-form play.

One of the leading scientists in this area is Australian skills-acquisition expert Damien Farrow, who, in interviewing elite athletes, discovered the value of loosely organized games in the development of flexible thinking and acute spatial awareness. "We should be modeling our programs on that," Farrow has said. "And what do we do instead? We put children in regimented, very structured programs, where their perceptual abilities are corralled and limited."

In Brazil, the legendary home to *jogo bonito* (Portuguese for the beautiful game), unstructured play is the standard when young. Poverty is widespread, so children kick balls and makeshift balls in alleys, on beaches, on small, enclosed courts, anywhere, with friends and neighbors and parents and grandparents. This is how most of the Brazilian greats, from Pelé to Ronaldinho, were introduced to the sport. Organized games are delayed until age 8 or 9. The result? Brazil has such an abundance of talent that soccer observers say the South American nation could probably field four separate teams all of which would be competitive in the World Cup.

France, like the U.S., is happily burdened by wealth in most areas. Parents can enroll their children in soccer clubs at just about any age and often do starting around age 6. So to protect the development of child athletes from the natural impulse of adults to have kids compete immediately—"We suffer from that here too," Mérelle says—the French push coaching education, perhaps more vigorously than any soccer federation in the world. Nearly 20,000 coaches from the youth level up have received certificates for completing classes at the federation's Paris training center. Training isn't mandatory at the lowest levels, but it's common. And information gets pushed down the pipeline 340 days a year to the thousands of local clubs that work with kids. A youth coach would have to be a recluse not to know the federation believes players must be allowed the freedom to express themselves with the ball. That ball control while moving is the basis of the French game. That the focus must be on attacking skills. That 7-year-olds shouldn't play in formats any larger than five-on-five, to maximize touches and keep everyone involved. That no child should get slotted into one position until well into his teenage years. That individual technique is far more important to teach through age 16 than tactics are. That coaches need to be quality demonstrators, so that kids can visually lock down the fundamentals. That yelling at players should not be tolerated. And, above all, that training must be fun.

French children typically play no more than one game a week, and the seasons aren't endless. Even as high as the 13-and-under level, most club teams play 30 or 35 games a year, max. Such restraint leaves ample time, energy, and motivation for kids to kick a ball around in the neighborhood, the sort of unsupervised environment where imaginations soar most effortlessly. It's been this way for decades. Henry, when not being coached on a well-worn pitch, spent many hours booting a ball against concrete walls in his suburban ghetto. Zinédine Zidane, the three-time World Player of the Year who retired after the '06 World Cup, received instruction as a teenager in one of the French federation's regional training facilities—but no one, including Zizou, would suggest that the origins of his sorcery began there. His exquisite feel for the ball was developed years earlier in the crowded, government-built projects of Marseille, messing around on the gravel of his town's central square and in the living room of his family's apartment where, through his trial and error, all the lights got smashed out.

The highlights these players would go on to deliver are the kind that creates soccer devotees.

"Remember when I came to France for your game against Ukraine?" Nash asked Henry in their conversation. "At one point, Zizou played it to you, and you played it back. You hit it hard, and it was heading between his knee and his waist. He let the ball hit him, but the way he rotated his hips, it stopped on the grass. Didn't bounce, didn't do anything. He was like a martial artist. I can't even explain it."

"I know what you're talking about," Henry responded. "To receive the ball that way you need to relax the right part of your body."

Relax. A foreign word to those caught up in the maelstrom of American youth sports.

• • •

Some sports require early incubation of athletic talent in order to reach the highest competitive levels. Female gymnastics is among that small group. Bodies with womanly curves are harder to control on the various bars and beams, so the race to build Olympic champions is a race to beat the full onset of puberty. Potential champions must be identified and trained in a focused way from a very early age. Some prospects specialize in gymnastics before they even enter school. Other sports, such as golf and tennis in which swings are critical, can offer rewards for those who lay down specific motor patterns at an early age (though pre-K lessons aren't a prerequisite for making the U.S. Open someday).

MYTH NO. 4
Organized competition breeds success.

THE TRUTH
Unstructured play is often more valuable.

A more patient, deliberate approach can be taken in the vast majority of sports. Over the past decade, one of the models that has begun to take hold in Europe and other developed nations—though less so in the U.S.—was authored by Dr. Istvan Balyi, a former Hungarian sports scientist who since 1974 has worked in Canada. His framework, Long-Term Athlete Development (LTAD), is based on his experience with elite athletes and suggests that there are five age-appropriate stages that should be respected when attempting to make champs of children. LTAD bears many similarities to features found in the French soccer system.

Here's how Balyi describes the phases, in excerpts from his writing:

> **Stage 1—FUNdamentals**
> *Age:* Males 6-9/Females 6-8 years
> *Objective:* Build overall motor skills ... Speed, power, and endurance are developed using FUN games. Appropriate and correct running, jumping, and throwing techniques are taught ... If children and parents have a preferred sport, participation once or twice per week is recommended, but participation in other sports three or four times per week is essential for future excellence. If the children later decide to leave the competitive stream, the skills they have acquired during the FUNdamental phase will still benefit them when they engage in recreational activities, which will enhance their quality of life and health.

Stage 2—Learning to Train
Age: Males 9-12/Females 8-11 years
Objective: Build overall sports skills ... During this time children are developmentally ready to acquire general sports skills that are the cornerstones of all athletic development. This is the "window of accelerated adaptation to motor coordination" ... If fundamental motor skill training is not developed between [these ages], a significant window of opportunity has been lost, compromising the ability of the young athlete to reach their full potential ... A 70 percent practice to 30 percent competition ratio is recommended.

Stage 3—Training to Train
Age: Males 12-16/Females 11-15 years
Objectives: Build the aerobic base, build strength toward the end of the phase, and further develop sport-specific skills ... Special emphasis is also required for flexibility training due to the sudden growth of bones, tendons, ligaments, and muscles ... During competitions, athletes play to win and to do their best, but the major focus of training is on learning the basics as opposed to competing ... A 60 percent training to 40 percent competition ratio is recommended by experts, and the 40 percent [figure] includes competition and competition-specific training. However, these percentages vary according to sport and individual specific needs. Athletes undertaking this type of preparation will be better prepared for competition in both the short and long term than those who focus solely on winning.

Stage 4—Training to Compete
Age: Males 16-18/Females 15-17 years
Objectives: Optimize fitness preparation and sport,

individual and position-specific skills as well as performance. The training-to-competition ratio now changes to 50:50 ... High-intensity individual event- and position-specific training is provided to athletes year-round ... This emphasis on individual preparation addresses each athlete's individual strengths and weaknesses.

Stage 5—Training to Win
Age: Males 18 years and older/Females 17 years and older
Objectives: This is the final phase of athletic preparation. All of the athlete's physical, technical, tactical, mental, personal, and lifestyle capacities are now fully established and the focus of training has shifted to the maximization of performance. Athletes are trained to peak for major competitions. Training is characterized by high intensity and relatively high volume. Frequent "prophylactic" breaks help to prevent physical and mental burnouts. Training-to-competition ratio is 25:75.

Stage 6—Retirement/Retention
Objectives: Retain athletes for coaching, administration, officials, etc.

For Americans who grew up during the Cold War, trusting a sports scientist who first learned his craft behind the Iron Curtain may be a challenge. The Soviets and their comrades were the bad guys, supposedly (certainly, in some instances) focusing children exclusively on sports performance for the sake of national glory. But the emphasis on producing champions at the Olympic level lifted some of the pressure to win at the youth levels—to have a child "peak by Friday," as Balyi puts it. Their scientists were encouraged to think critically about the value of competition as a developmental tool, which if overemphasized at an early age, he writes, "will always cause shortcomings in athletic abilities" later in life that cannot be corrected. Note that Balyi doesn't recommend even entering the sports system until age 6.

His message: Kids must be allowed to play before they can be expected to play hard.

"What we have in the U.S. are parents trying to get their kids into game environments as soon as possible," says Randy Huntington, former technical coordinator of sports science for USA Track and Field, the sport's governing body, and a consultant to elite athletes who play football, hockey, baseball, and other sports. "We're slotting kids in the Train-to-Compete phase and largely bypassing the FUNdamentals and Train-to-Train stages. Soccer is the worst offender."

It's often the first sport that kids get signed up to play. Parents figure, What's it take? Running? Kicking? Any little kid can do that. They're urged on by the American Youth Soccer Organization, which knocked down its starting age from 5 years old to 4 in 2004, for no reason other than to build the customer base and keep kids from committing to other sports. Problem is, rarely do volunteer coaches at the lower levels have enough knowledge to create a practice session that hits on both fun and fundamentals, so kids get placed in lines and perform drills. And often, formal games are scheduled, which inevitably promotes the assigning of positions, tactical play—and parents on both sidelines screaming instructions that kids often cannot appreciate.

Scholars who have studied child development have found that most children only *begin* around age 8 to develop the cognitive and social abilities necessary to understand the complex relationships in competitive, action-oriented team sports. Sports sociologist Jay Coakley notes that parents and volunteer coaches often plead loudly with children to "Stay in position!" or "Get back where you belong!" without realizing kids' brains just aren't formed that way yet. Understanding the concept of positional play asks that a participant do three things simultaneously: Mentally visualize where his teammates and opponents are on the field at a given moment, assess their relationships to one another and the ball, and decide where he or she needs to be. Most children do not fully develop these skills until 12. Adults "mistakenly think that children are not concentrating or trying hard," Coakley says. "This frustrates children who *are* doing the best they can at their level of psychosocial development." Many of the frustrated kids quit the game.

Those who stay often lose out, too.

"A coach of a team of 8- or 10-year-olds might have great intentions, but what's the first thing they feel they need to do? Organize and manage," says Bob Jenkins, director of coaching education and youth development at U.S. Soccer. "That's not what kids need at that age. These well-meaning adults feel like they have to manage things so the other team doesn't score on them. They plant a defender 18 yards from their goal and have him kick the ball downfield. Well, that may work when kids are young, and his team may get a trophy at the end of season. But the player doesn't learn how to move forward. After a few years, he might be fast and physical, but there's a lack of comfort with the ball.

"Go watch a high school game and count how many times the ball turns over. These kids have been playing for 10 years, but what have they learned? They can't control the thing bouncing around in front of them. And everyone all the way up the line ends up being affected. The better everyone is with the ball, the tougher it is to stop a team, so the defenders get better, and the game evolves in terms of the sophistication. Everything gets ratcheted up.

"The World Cup wasn't a revelation to me. It's the same problem we've been dealing with for years. We don't have enough special players in our talent pool, players who have suppleness with the ball. Yes, you need mental toughness in soccer, and you need to be a smart thinker. But you also have to have good feet. If you look at Zidane and Henry, the magic is in what they do with the ball."

U.S. Soccer is starting to recognize that its grass can only grow so high if the roots are overwatered with adult-style competition. In 2006, a few months before the World Cup, the organization published a paradigm-shifting, 70-page document compiled by Jenkins that essentially begs coaches to turn the game over to the fertile minds of children. Called "Best Practices for Coaching Soccer in the United States," it attempts to find a place for loosely structured play within the society's need for adult oversight. "Coaches can often be more helpful to a young player's development by organizing less, saying less, and allowing the players to do more," the document advises. "Set up a game and let the kids play. Keep most of your comments for before and after practice and during water breaks. Comments should be kept short and simple. Be comfortable organizing a session that looks like pickup soccer."

Detailed recommendations are offered for each age group, beginning with kindergartners. No organized games through second grade, just three-on-three scenarios in practice. No lines, no laps, and no discussions about "commitment." Just one game a weekend through fourth grade, with no tournaments and rosters small enough to allow for close to 100 percent playing time for everyone. No assigning of players into specific positions until the teenage years.

If much of this sounds familiar, it should. In 2000, Aimé Jacquet, manager of the French team that won the '98 World Cup, was flown to Philadelphia by Adidas to speak to the U.S. Youth Soccer Association. There, and at the national conference in Las Vegas the next year, the esteemed coach laid out the philosophy and architecture of the French system. Jacquet, who worked with Mérelle and considered coaching education to be his most important responsibility within the federation, helped give shape and support to notions that had been percolating in small pockets within the U.S. coaching community for decades. Those ideas would continue to languish, though, as U.S. Soccer's focus during the Bruce Arena era was on the national teams, the elite of our (modest) elite.

Arena resigned after the '06 World Cup and was replaced by Bob Bradley. The new coach has taken a more direct role in youth development, leading the selection process for a U.S. Soccer initiative, started in fall 2007, that aspires to work with 80 premier clubs around the country. Those clubs must agree to shift the emphasis away from game play and toward effective training—a response to the nation's top high school freshmen telling shocked U.S. Soccer coaches that they're already tired of the sport. The program, called the U.S. Soccer Development Academy, starts at the under-16 level, though Jenkins and others hope its philosophy trickles down to those working with younger kids.

"We have a tendency to overcoach kids in this country, and part of it is the culture," says Ivan Gazidis, deputy commissioner of Major League Soccer. "The idea that the game is improvised from moment to moment is alien to most people who grew up on football and baseball, sports that are less chaotic and less player-driven. Maybe the easiest way to win at an early age is to punt the ball downfield, have some big kid cross it, and another big kid head it in. But that doesn't develop a player. When I coach my kids' teams, people look at me like I'm crazy, because they know I'm involved in pro soccer and yet I'm not trying to impose structure on them. I don't insist on positional play. I want them to work it out."

"Making the quarterfinals of the 2002 World Cup was an anomaly," says Gary Allen, who holds the same position as Jenkins with Virginia's state soccer association. "Bruce did a great job of getting the team ready to play that year but just about every major star in the world was injured or coming off injury except Ronaldo of Brazil. And we had speed, which does make a difference when people are injured. Then 2006 comes along, and we say, 'What happened?' Nothing happened. I was at a training session right before Bruce named the final team. He had 40 cookie-cutter players to choose from; there was nothing to distinguish one player from another. Most of them were huge, but there was no creativity, no ability to adjust and solve problems. And that's because since they were young they've been told that speed trumps all."

There are a few American prospects who don't fit that mold, among them Benny Feilhaber—who was born in Brazil. The young midfielder supplied what was hailed as the best goal in U.S. Soccer history when he picked a volley out of the air on a corner kick and sent the ball screaming through a pack of players and into the Mexican goal for the winner in the 2007 Gold Cup final. He moved to California when he was 6, but he regards those first few years in the land of samba soccer as critical in forming his concept of the game. (The few girls who play the game in that country benefit from the same seasoning. With fewer than 5,000 registered female players to draw upon, Brazil's national team was runner-up in the 2007 women's World Cup, frustrating the U.S. 4-0 in the semis with an inventiveness that the Americans lacked.)

There's also Freddy Adu. When Allen first scouted Adu, the 10-year-old was lighting up the fields of the Washington, D.C., area with his footwork. By 13, he was enrolled at the federation's under-17 residency program in Florida (which was created after the U.S. finished last at the '98 World Cup). On April 3, 2004, when Adu was drafted by the D.C. United of Major League Soccer, the 14-year-old midfielder became the youngest athlete to play in an American professional team sport since Fred Chapman played baseball for Philadelphia of the American Association in 1887. As Adu's 17th birthday approached, he was not yet polished enough to make Arena's World Cup roster—no one that young ever has locked down a spot. But his technical mastery of the ball remains superior. And for that, he gives credit to the system in which he was groomed during his first eight years.

Which was no system at all.

Before Adu immigrated in fourth grade with his family to the U.S., he lived in a town called Tema, in Ghana—the same nation whose team would send the U.S. packing at the '06 World Cup. No one formally introduced Adu to soccer. No one taught him any moves. Instead, he kicked balls made of socks around the neighborhood lot, an unruly patch of sand, rocks, and broken glass that the locals called Stone Park. "You had to keep the ball in control at all times," Adu tells me. "The field was so bad and uneven you had to keep it close to you." He played barefoot, perfecting the double step-over he had seen Ronaldo do on TV. *Fake left ... fake right ... juke your man. Ha!*

He never played organized ball, as there were no leagues for kids under the age of 14. Just impromptu games of five-on-five, sometimes overseen by teenagers on the block who had, you might say, a different sort of rooting interest than American soccer moms and dads do. "In all honesty, the older guys probably were gambling when they were picking the teams," Adu laughs. "I was the first pick every time." The teenagers complimented him constantly—which made him only want to play more.

Travel ball? Once, when he was 7. Realizing they had a ringer in Adu, the teens arranged a match between the best little kids in Tema and their peers in a neighboring town. They played, as always, using small goals with no keepers. With less overall talent, Adu's team fell behind 2-0. But he scored three goals to rally his crew, nailing the winner in the final minute when he beat three guys off the dribble and curled a shot around a defender. When it was over, the older guys rushed the field and put him on their shoulders.

"That was the moment when I decided I wanted to be a pro player," he says.

There's a saying in soccer: Let the game be your teacher. "We'd be right up with the rest of the world if we did that," says Adu, who now plays with one of the top European clubs, Benefica in Portugal. "It's too structured in the U.S. If you're telling kids to do one, two touches, and pass—when they get older, they can't learn the game. You don't create superstars that way. Plus it's just boring. That's why I think kids get to a certain age and say, 'I don't want to play soccer anymore.' They're just not able to have fun. You shouldn't get yelled at if you express yourself and lose the ball."

• • •

Youth soccer registrations have more than doubled over the past two decades as programs have been created for kids of increasingly younger ages. The U.S. now has more boys running around in uniforms, 2.3 million, than any nation in the world—and three times as many as World Cup opponents Italy, Ghana, and the Czech Republic combined. When girls are added to that total, we have three times as many registered youth players, 3.9 million, as either France or Brazil. All the gear they wear makes the U.S. the largest soccer market in the world for retailers. But research by the SGMA shows that participation levels peak at age 9, just as kids in Brazil are *starting* to play organized soccer.

American kids drop out of soccer sooner than they do from any other team sport. And most kids quit the game in all forms as they get into their teenage years. Those who do keep playing into adulthood are often immigrants who were first introduced to the sport in other countries. The one-team, one-school bottleneck drives this weeding out of participants. But soccer is doubly cursed by the native impulse to control the play of children. For many boys and girls, it's not a spontaneous, kid-directed game. It's their parents' idea; something to eventually grow out of, like braces.

I want to know more about how this came to be, so on a winter day I drive over to a new, 130,000-square-foot indoor soccer facility in Farmington. "It's pressure through fear," says the mother of one 9-year-old girl. "If you don't get your kid in, and you don't get them played, and if they're not getting any better, they're behind. Nobody wants to wait, so people go with it early, at 4 and 5 years old. And we're looking for all the different places they can go."

I am told this tan, taut woman with an Audrey Hepburn haircut has been a nuisance at games, screaming belligerently. She doesn't disagree that she's out of control. "I'm sick," she concedes with a halting laugh. "I mean, I'm ill. I need treatment for this. It's so intense. There's just so much going on, so many teams, and so much competition at this age."

But giving the game back to the children isn't going to come easily. Because, as I would discover, kids never truly owned this or any other game. In the U.S., organized youth sport was, from the first, the brainstorm of adults.

AGE 5

BLING, BOMBS, AND THE BIBLE

New York, New York

In 1981, a sparkplug of man with a short neck, bony cheeks, and deep-set, blue eyes stood before a cadre of Wall Street analysts at New York's Pierre Hotel and laid out his vision as the new chairman and CEO of General Electric. In his distinctively working-class Boston accent, Jack Welch told the assembled crowd that his mission was to make GE "the most competitive enterprise on earth." At the time, it was the 10th largest company in the nation, with 411,000 employees in an array of businesses, most of them in the manufacturing sector. It was a lumbering, bureaucratic behemoth that he was determined to remake into a nimble, entrepreneurial powerhouse. That meant trimming inventories, selling off lackluster units, and shutting down factories.

Within four years, GE was down to 299,000 workers, earning Welch the nickname "Neutron Jack" because he left entire company buildings empty. He was despised by many, especially at first, but in time he became the most admired corporate chieftain in the nation. He added new businesses, made them efficient, shifted the company's focus to service industries, entered the media business with the purchase of NBC, attacked global markets, and embraced the Internet as a means of modernizing operations. When he retired in 2001, GE was the most valuable company in the world, with $400 billion in wealth created during his tenure. Along the way, he inspired the reinvention of the American corporation, which over the past two decades has fueled a rapid expansion of the economy.

In suburban communities like mine, with its fair share of professional managers, Welch is more of a hero than any athlete—and better paid, too, one year having made $94 million. He's a role model for can-do executives, whom he encourages to think big and get results. I have friends who buy his books, line up to get them signed, and read them cover-to-cover. They outline passages in ink and highlighter, with stars for triple emphasis. I have other friends who work for companies run by former Welch lieutenants, firms in which versions of Jack's Rules are part of the corporate culture. Those friends work like hell, logging hundreds of thousands of airplane miles, acquiring new business units, and moving factories from places like New Britain to China.

They are good at what they do. They are rewarded with big homes and big cars, which are used to ferry their kids on weekends to an endless string of travel soccer and baseball games. My family is rewarded for their efforts when the value of our stock portfolio grows. These people perhaps will help send our kids to college.

Welch's most significant—and controversial—innovation was in how to motivate talent. Each year, GE would give A, B, or C grades to all of its employees depending on which category they fell into: Top 20 percent, middle 70, or bottom 10. The first tier would get treated like stars, with bonuses, stock options, training, public praise, and new opportunities; to Welch, these people were the drivers of company growth and he wanted everyone to know who they were. The middle 70 was made to feel like they belonged, although more energy went into identifying people who just might be able to step up their performance into the upper echelon with some seasoning, as opposed to trying to prevent people from falling. The bottom 10 percent of managers and workers was simply and openly targeted to be fired. Each year—even if the company was thriving, even if the very worst employee was productive—the imposed bell curve dictated that the designated laggards got pink slips. Critics around the world assailed the 20-70-10 model as cruel, inhumane, and perhaps foolish, given that at some point so much fat has been removed from the operation that only meat is left to cut. But Welch defended it until the end and beyond, into retirement, arguing that shleps need to know they are shleps so they can find a better fit—anywhere but here.

And where did Welch get his model of "differentiation," as he calls it? He lays out the origins in his 2005 book, *Winning*, written with second wife Suzy Welch:

> I learned it on the playground when I was a kid. When we were making a baseball team, the best players always got picked first, the fair players were put in the easy positions, usually second base or rightfield, and the least athletic ones had to watch from the sidelines. Everyone knew where he stood. The top kids wanted desperately to stay there, and got the reward of respect and the thrill of winning. The kids in the middle worked their tails off to get better, and sometimes they did, bringing up the quality of play for everyone. And the kids who couldn't make the cut usually found other pursuits, sports and otherwise, that they enjoyed and excelled at.

Intrigued, I rung up Welch's office in Boston, not far from the Salem, Mass., ball fields of his youth. At first he declined my request for an interview, relaying through his assistant that he didn't feel qualified to talk about kids and sports; he's not a child psychologist, his assistant said. I persisted, reminding him via e-mail of the esteem he is held in by many executives in suburban communities where youth sports are arguably most intense. He agreed to carve out 15 minutes from a daily schedule that is only marginally less hectic now than when he was power-lunching in Manhattan for GE. He has an adjunct professorship at the MIT business school, weekly speaking engagements for which he is rewarded at $150,000 a pop, paid consulting arrangements, and a regular gig on a regional television show offering fans' perspectives on their beloved Red Sox.

When I get Welch on the line, he gives me a half hour. The topic seems to matter to him. "I was never the biggest kid by any means, but I was competitive," he says to me. I ask him where on the 20-70-10 scale he fell as a baseball player. He says that he started in the bottom 10. "When I was young, I was barely in rightfield," he says. "But as I got older, I got to pitch." He had a big, roundhouse curve that would earn him innings on the mound. "I didn't want to be in rightfield because you never got any action out there," he says. "So I just got better. I don't want to overstate this part of it, but there was a competitive fire put in you by a very ruthless selection process."

He loved it. "It was total meritocracy," he says. "Pure." He hits that last word hard, which in Boston-speak comes out as *PYUUU-uh.*

The quest for victory that took shape on the Salem ball fields would inform the entire culture at GE. Welch considered himself a jock, so he surrounded himself with former jocks. (He also liked ex-military officers.) In the manner of the late Green Bay Packers coach Vince Lombardi, he insisted for years that each business unit be No. 1 in its category, No. 2 at worst—otherwise it would be sold. He had been obsessed with golf since doing some caddying at age 10, and now he had the money to play the finest courses in the world, so deals got done on the links. The brightly lit, multitiered lecture hall at GE's management training center in Croton-on-Hudson, N.Y., got named The Pit, in honor of the dusty lot in Salem where neighborhood games of Welch's youth came together. When his overt ranking of workers was accused of pitting people against one another and undermining teamwork, he'd swallow his Red Sox pride and figuratively wrap himself in pinstripes, asking if differentiation kept the New York Yankees from winning championships. In that clubhouse, journeymen making $300,000 and young bucks pulling $18 mil a year worked together just fine, he'd say.

In many ways, Jack Welch was precisely the kind of American that the founders of youth sports wanted to breed.

• • •

Youth sport is, like organized sports itself, a modern invention brought on largely by the rise of industrial capitalism. Well into the 1800s, religion was the dominant influence in children's lives, and honest labor was promoted as the moral way to serve God. The Puritans who first settled Welch's hometown saw any form of play as frivolous and therefore wicked, so extreme restrictions were placed on the pursuit of games. Even among the less devout, the notion of sports as a tool to develop useful social skills had not yet been dreamed up. The culture began to change only with the Second Industrial Revolution and the emergence of massive steel, oil, rubber, and other manufacturing corporations, which built factories that drew large groups of workers to urban centers. By the end of the 19th century, the U.S. was taking its place as a global economic power.

When Theodore "Teddy" Roosevelt looked around, he didn't like what he saw happening with teenage boys. He had grown up an asthmatic, the sickly son of a wealthy New York investor who implored his second child to "make your own body" by embracing a life of vigorous exercise. Teddy took up boxing, wrestling, gymnastics, and weightlifting, and as his chest grew so did his health and confidence. He continued to box even after ascending to the presidency in 1901 and was disappointed to see that more boys did not share his commitment to exercise, adventure, and conquest. He developed a discernable hatred for sissies, a term coined at the time that reflected the growing fear that the comforts of urban life had rendered middle- and upper-class boys soft and effeminate. He lamented the "mere animal sloth and ease" and "gradual failure of vitality" among native-born boys, many of whom were being raised by their mothers. They hardly seemed fit to take over the industries that their more manly fathers were hard at work creating. "Only aggressive sports can create the brawn, the spirit, the self-confidence, and quickness of men essential for the existence of a strong nation," Roosevelt said. Aided by Roosevelt's public example, sports became widely seen as a tool that could infuse masculine qualities into the next generation of leaders.

At the same time, the nation needed pliable laborers and warriors to pave the expansion into new markets. As assistant secretary of the Navy in 1898, Roosevelt had advocated for military actions that pushed the Spanish out of Cuba, Puerto Rico, and the Philippines—successes that encouraged the building of enough warships to make the U.S. a naval power for the first time in its history. As president, Roosevelt used his new and intimidating Big Stick (while diplomatically speaking softly) to reduce European influence in the Western hemisphere. Then he had the audacity to chase the Colombians out of Panama, which he declared an independent nation so that the U.S. could build a canal that would open up the West Coast and Asia to East Coast companies. Roosevelt was setting the stage for what historians came to call the American Century, fortified in the coming generations by a military and a labor force that were stocked largely with young immigrants.

Team sports were promoted as a way to teach boys from the working class how to work together productively. In industrial centers such as New York City, where family structures often were frayed, many boys roamed the streets, wreaking havoc and destroying property. They operated in gangs, regularly clashing with police. Team sports were seen as a way to channel those youthful energies in a manageable format—with the coach standing in for the boss, it was a form of initiation into industrial and military roles the kids would enter later in their lives. It was also believed that sports would breed patriotism and divert the revolutionary energies that were percolating at home and internationally in places like Russia. Children of laborers grew up in cramped tenements, listening to their parents and neighbors complain about the exploitative work conditions imposed on them by greedy monopolists and their bought-off politicians. Some boys and girls knew the misery of this life firsthand; a federal child labor law wouldn't be passed until 1938, when Franklin Delano Roosevelt, Teddy's distant cousin, pushed it through.

Protestantism still was a major cultural influence at the beginning of the 20th century, but it had been reshaped by the "Muscular Christianity" movement that first came to life in upper-class England. The goal of Muscular Christians was to recruit more males into church life by counteracting the creeping notion that religion was primarily a feminine pursuit. Sport was their angle. At local chapters of the Young Men's Christian Association, boys were told that the Lord's only son was not some passive, bookish figure but a dynamic, sinewy force ready to take on the world. Jesus was now a stud (in a *morally* reproductive way, that is). Play was no longer the work of the devil, it was a way of praising God. Young Teddy was an early subscriber to Muscular Christianity.

So was Luther Halsey Gulick, a towering, if largely forgotten, figure from the pages of sports history. His actions shaped the landscape of sports in America, and especially youth sports, into what it is today. A top official at the YMCA Training School in Springfield, Mass., Gulick was responsible for changing the curriculum of YMCAs from gymnastics and calisthenics to team sports. Most notably, he was the man who in 1891 assigned James Naismith, one of his students, the task of coming up with a game that could be played indoors in the winter and would integrate the YMCA's holistic principles of mind, body, and spirit. "Basket ball" was an instant hit whose gospel Gulick then spread around the world through various prominent roles he played at the YMCA, the Amateur Athletic Union, and the American Olympic Committee, among other groups. For that, he would be inducted into the Basketball Hall of Fame. He also played a part in the invention of volleyball, which like basketball is now one of the world's most popular sports.

Gulick was a man of his time, which is to say that he embodied the essential contradictions of his era. He was pious, yet innovative. He was obsessed with rules, yet basketball—his favorite offspring—was the most spontaneous of games. He was preoccupied with adolescent boys taking control of their sexual impulses (Muscular Christians were determined to discourage masturbation), yet he was rational in his response to such sin—thanks in part to having been trained as a medical doctor in Victorian-era New York, where everything was easy to come by on the streets, including $1-a-date hookers. The son of Congregationalist missionaries, he was an altruist who later fought for the humane treatment of the mentally retarded, yet he also was an early advocate of eugenics, a social philosophy that sought to improve the human gene pool. Gulick's beliefs in this vein may have been relatively benign, with a focus on not marrying into the family of "degenerates," but eugenic thought paved the way for such atrocities as forced sterilization and, under the Nazis, extermination.

Like other Muscular Christians, Gulick reconciled his moral principles with those of Social Darwinism, a philosophy that stood in contrast to the more humane tenets of traditional religious thought. Promoted by some in the wealthy class as moral justification for the colonialism and exploitation that it had benefited from since the start of the Industrial Revolution, Social Darwinism used Charles Darwin's findings in the natural sciences to justify the idea that struggle, survival of the fittest, and elimination of the weak were essential to progress in human societies. Winning—a favorite word of Social Darwinists—became seen as the just reward of the superior individual; losing was taken as the consequence of inferiority. "The fundamental qualities to be cultivated in the boy are those of muscular strength, the despising of pain, driving straight to the mark, and the smashing down of obstacles," Gulick wrote in his book, *A Philosophy of Play*. "The world needs power and the barbaric virtues of manhood, together with the type of group loyalty which is based upon these savage virtues."

Gulick was not technically a Social Darwinist, as his goals were more egalitarian. He hoped to improve the health and citizenship of the masses. He professionalized the training of P.E. teachers, and the Playground Association of America he founded helped the number of playgrounds around the country multiply from less than 100 in 1905 to nearly 4,000 a dozen years later. But he was worried that "evil rather than good" could come from unsupervised play, so he worked to direct kids' energies. ("The playground is a device by which a single leader can effectively control the play of a large number of children," he wrote.) And he had sufficient respect for the motivating qualities of high-stakes competition that he stitched a winner-take-all thread into the fabric of kids' games.

In 1903, as the first-ever director of physical training for New York City schools, Gulick introduced interscholastic sports to the nation's largest school system. The Public Schools Athletic League was the most ambitious effort ever undertaken to get urban boys interested in organized sports, and it included citywide school, class, and individual competitions in baseball, basketball, soccer, and other sports—all the way down to the elementary-school level. By their very definition, competitive games are a zero-sum exercise in that each match creates as many losers as winners. Tournaments are negative-sum propositions, since among multiple entrants, there is just one winner. But imagine the glory of standing atop a pyramid that includes 600,000 students at 630 schools! The newspapers loved the idea; the city's industrialists loved it even more. The PSAL was bankrolled exclusively in its early years by John D. Rockefeller, Andrew Carnegie, J. Pierpont Morgan, William K. Vanderbilt, and other members of the elite merchant class.

The first PSAL tournament was held December 26, 1903, at Madison Square Garden just a month after the PSAL was formed, with the high school basketball champion laying claim to a perpetual $300 trophy—that's 7,000 in today's dollars—donated by a copper mining heir who previously had underwritten Gulick as a board member at the Springfield Y. There also was a track meet on site that pushed the total number of athletes, most of them of elementary-school age, past 1,000—a participation figure that surpassed that of the first three modern Olympics. Not until the 1908 games in London, at which 1,971 athletes from 22 countries participated, did the Olympic numbers surpass those of the inaugural PSAL tournament. Gulick grandiosely declared the one-day event the greatest spectacle in the history of modern sports. "Not since the days when gladiators entered Roman arenas in thousands have so many contestants decided the question of superiority with the same time limit we have brought," he said. President Roosevelt would soon issue a hearty endorsement of the PSAL and sign on as honorary vice president; he even wrote an annual personal letter to the city's top marksman, er, marksboy, in the riflery competition.

Gulick was not so much an inventor as an adept blender of powerful forces that were already in play. That certainly was the case with the PSAL, which merged the interests not only of Muscular Christians and wealthy industrialists but also of child welfare advocates, who were pushing to make school mandatory for all kids, and of military recruiters, who wanted ready soldiers. Once Gulick brought the cocktail together in New York City, organized sports for boys would explode around the country. By 1910, 17 other cities had formed athletic leagues patterned on the PSAL, which, beyond elite interschool tournaments, also included fitness competitions designed to encourage the least talented children to participate in athletics.

The school-based model worked, for some. It supplied talent, folk heroes, and a fan base for emerging professional sports leagues. It helped occupy the rising tide of children who filled orphanages, those leaky safety nets for the victims of unchecked industrialism. But within a decade of Gulick's death in 1918, teachers began to complain that his ideal of "sports for all" was being lost. The focus had shifted from a physical education curriculum to the teaching of sport-specific skills that could help school teams win games. "Schools were hiring a coach first and then asking him, 'What do you want to teach?'," says Jack Berryman, a University of Washington medical professor who has studied the early history of organized youth sports. In a harbinger of a dilemma that would reappear later in the century, the participation opportunities had coalesced around the best athletes, which Gulick knew was no recipe for public health. And there were concerns about the demands placed upon prepubescent children who were being asked to compete for elite championships. Eventually, in 1938, a committee of the American Association for Health, Physical Education, and Recreation—an influential body for which Gulick had once served as secretary—issued a statement that read, in part:

> Inasmuch as pupils below tenth grade are in the midst of a period of rapid growth, with the consequent bodily weaknesses and maladjustments, partial ossification of bones, mental and emotional stresses, physiological adjustments, and the like, be it therefore resolved that the leaders in the field of physical and health education should do all in their power to discourage interscholastic competition at this age level because of its strenuous nature.

Other key groups came to similar conclusions and school sports for children under 12 were eliminated in most communities. But just because educators stepped out of their coaching roles didn't mean that kids stopped throwing balls around. After all, they still had those playgrounds that Gulick and his peers had helped carve out. They still had fathers and uncles who had been indoctrinated into the team games that now permeated everyday culture. They had the World Series on the radio. And they had World War II as a backdrop.

This was the American childhood that awaited Jack Welch.

• • •

MYTH NO. 5
Children want to win.

THE TRUTH
They do, but it means far more to adults.

Later in the century, sociologists studied the way children play sports when not organized by adults. They watched thousands of kids interact in parks, vacant lots, school grounds, and backyards. They found that the way children compete is distinctly shaped by the availability of participation opportunities. When they are allowed to create their own games—and everyone gets to play—their priorities are:

1) Action, especially action leading to scoring
2) Personal involvement in the action
3) Challenging and exciting experiences
4) Reaffirming friendships with peers

Kids prefer close scores, not blowouts. So they divvy up the talent more or less equally, and sometimes place handicaps on the better players. Less skilled players are granted "do-overs" and "interference" calls to compensate for deficiencies or mistakes, minimizing the embarrassment that could cause them to walk off—and leave the game short on players. Abuse of such special exemptions is regulated by teasing. Rules go ignored provided that it doesn't interrupt the flow of the action. In baseball, called strikes are verboten so that everyone gets a chance to hit (and there are more balls to field). In football, every kid is eligible to receive a pass on any play.

The ethic changes when access to the playing arena is limited. When there isn't room for every kid to participate, performance becomes critical. Winning emerges as a priority. Rules get enforced with rigor. Roles get more specialized. And the weak perish. At The Pit in Salem, behavior followed this pattern. "If you weren't good enough, you were brutalized," Welch says. "You were sent home."

The Pit on North Street was created out of, and named after, an old gravel pit. It was a neglected space, so inelegant that the city didn't bother to give it a name a few years before, when a small baseball field had been carved out of the rocks. There was no outfield fence and the park was surrounded by cliffs. But it was all that the boys of Welch's neighborhood in north Salem had in the early and mid-1940s. These were not the children of Brahmins, the descendents of original Puritan families who had long since traded their piety for establishment privilege. They were kids of first-generation immigrants from Eastern Europe, African-Americans, orphans of vague origin, and Irish Catholics like Welch, poor enough that they couldn't afford admission to the Y. Up to two dozen of them would show up every day at The Pit, lunch bags in tow, hoping to play from sunup to sundown. Those breaking balls Welch threw were also broken balls—their covers worn bare and made playable with a new skin of tape.

Sometimes there weren't enough kids to field two full teams, in which case they would play with two outfielders. In those neighborhood games, "There wasn't a lot of cruelty," says Samuel Zoll, a childhood friend of Welch's who was also a regular at The Pit. "Even if you were a medium athlete, you could play at the park." The brutality, as Welch refers to it, became a factor only on the occasions when a game would be arranged against a team comprised of the best kids from another inner-city park and some boys were deemed not good enough to make the top nine. Those crosstown rivalry games meant a lot to kids who had very little, and Welch's instinctive competitiveness would redline. Zoll recalls that Welch never ridiculed anyone but often was very direct in his comments—*Hey, you gotta make that catch!* Playing first base, the taller, less athletic Zoll once booted a couple of balls in a row, infuriating his pitcher. Next thing he knew, he and Jack were rolling around on the ground. "Let's just say he wanted to perfect my performance as well," Zoll says with a chuckle.

Basketball games were always fierce, even the in-neighborhood variety. Again, it was a numbers game, a supply-demand equation that promotes aggressive behavior in any realm where opportunity becomes scarce. For years the kids could only play three-on-three, as the dirt court had just one basket, which the boys had erected themselves. Even when a second hoop was added and games grew to five-on-five, court time was hard to come by. World War II had just let out and young veterans had returned to north Salem, further populating The Pit. Two teams of five could be waiting to challenge the winners, who by custom kept the court until they lost. The notion of taking turns was folded into a structure—now codified in the architecture of pickup hoops—based on rewarding achievement.

In time, Welch took this core, *PYUU-uh* principle to heart. "Our turn, losers out!" he once barked at a group of older teenagers who didn't want to cede the court after getting beat. He was in junior high school, much smaller than the high school boys, but his sense of justice was being violated. It was a cold, early-winter day and his pals had shoveled the snow to clear the court alongside the high schoolers.

To his teammates' surprise, his antagonists backed down.

And Welch went back to work, with no intention of losing the court. "Zoll, you cover this guy ... " he ordered.

Welch and his buddies couldn't have known it at the time, but they were growing up in an era when moral notions about victory and defeat were being culturally fortified and elevated. In 1943, when Welch turned 8 and first joined the action at The Pit, the Nazis were in control of much of Europe. They had occupied Warsaw for four years, Paris for three, and Athens for two. In the Pacific Theater, the war had begun to turn against Japan. But the forces of fascism had already left tens of millions dead around the world, and the outcome was still far from certain. The boys at The Pit got used to eating rations and listening for the air raid siren. They wondered if Ted Williams, who won the Triple Crown in 1942 and then joined the Marines as a fighter pilot, would ever return to the Red Sox.

On June 6, 1944, Allied forces stormed the beaches of Normandy. Within a year, Paris was liberated, Hitler was dead, and Winston Churchill was standing on a balcony with a cigar in his mouth and V sign formed from his right index and middle fingers—a victory that was made possible by the U.S. athlete-warriors that Roosevelt and Gulick had cultivated through youth sports. Contrary to popular assumptions, wars don't always produce obvious winners and losers. (A reminder of that would be served up within a decade in the Korean War, where the loss of

33,000 American lives produced a ceasefire that saved the south for democracy but abandoned the north to nut-job totalitarians.) But World War II was as clear and symbolic as triumphs get, even with the rise of Communism and the Soviet Union. Evil had been put down by superior firepower, and by industry. Might made right, just as the Muscular Christians had preached, and America reaped the material rewards. Within a decade, the U.S. produced most of the world's steel, refined most of its oil, and was flush with cash.

Winning isn't everything; it's the only thing. Lombardi, the Pro Football Hall of Fame coach used versions of that phrase in the postwar years to motivate his teams, insisting later that what he meant to say was, "Winning is not everything—but making the effort to win is." He had endured a rash of criticism from the subsection of American society whose notions about the nature of competition were more comfortably reflected by the spiritual, and perhaps pleading, words of sportswriter Grantland Rice, who in the 1930 poem "Alumnus Football" wrote:

For when the One Great Scorer comes
To write against your name,
He marks—not that you won or lost—
But how you played the Game.

Despite Lombardi's partial recanting, his ethos won the culture war. It even pushed aside the creed of Baron de Coubertin, who had founded the modern Olympics at the height of the Industrial Revolution and famously declared, "The most important thing ... is not winning, but taking part." While discomfort with the notion of unbridled competition remains in the culture at-large today, the psychic landscape has shifted to such a degree that touting sportsmanship as an ideal is now seen as a sign of weakness in sports circles, a chink in the armor that could open the door to defeat.

One of the leading youth sports organizations today is the Positive Coaching Alliance, a nonprofit based in Palo Alto, Calif. The group has trained roughly 200,000 coaches and administrators since 1998 on how to work effectively with kids. One of the keys to its growth has been its careful use of the word "sportsmanship," which tends to make the eyes of youth coaches glaze over. Instead, its trainers talk about becoming what the PCA calls "a Double-Goal Coach": that is, one who "strives to win and, even more importantly, uses sports to teach life lessons through Positive Coaching." One of its catch phrases is "Honoring the Game," which the PCA describes as "a deeper, more focused evolution of sportsmanship." It means showing respect for the rules, officials, and your opponents, without whom there would be no game, no tableau for personal challenge. In other words, the ghosts of Rice and de Coubertin are featured guests at the PCA party, but they have to show up dressed as Lombardi.

The son of Italian immigrants, Lombardi was another one of those boys Gulick wanted to mold into a great, moral American. Born in 1913, he attended Brooklyn public schools until eighth grade before joining the seminary in the hope of becoming a Catholic priest. He left after two years so he could play high school and then college football, where his offensive line coach at Fordham was Frank Leahy, future head coach at Notre Dame, where Muscular Christianity was, unlike the seminary, embraced and even elevated to art. (Hello, Touchdown Jesus.) But as a coach, Lombardi didn't do much of note until after age 35, when he joined the staff of West Point coach Earl "Colonel Red" Blaik, a legendary taskmaster whose mantra was, "Good fellows are a dime a dozen, but aggressive leaders are priceless." Blaik wasn't really a colonel, and football is a pale substitute for real combat, but Lombardi was deeply shaped by his five years at West Point in the decade after World War II. He, like the nation itself, was transformed. That academic fraud was rampant among cadets on those teams is a mere footnote to history.

When Jack Welch got around to penning his book *Winning*, Lombardi earned mention as one of the people Welch admires most. Right up there with Mahatma Ghandi.

• • •

The line between winning and winning at all costs is hardly drawn in bright ink. It's a bit like the line between art and pornography, which one Supreme Court justice famously argued was something you just know when you see it. Welch tells me he loves the Little League World Series because it strikes just the right balance between all-out competition and civil behavior. "That's a great experience," he says. "You see kids lose well, win well. You gotta learn to lose, too. Life is not all winning." But what he sees, sitting in front of the television reminiscing about his youth, is a filtered truth. The parents of players who make it to Williamsport are given talks on appropriate behavior. Coaches know they're going to be miked during the game. Little League officials use the media spotlight to model behavior they hope will be replicated back home.

When network cameras aren't rolling, adults are less restrained. On the day I reach Welch, the morning shows are playing a home video clip from a Pop Warner football game in Stockton, Calif. In it, the quarterback gets knocked down by another boy after the whistle. He is crumpled on the ground when his 36-year-old father, an assistant coach, enters the screen from the left in full sprint. The enraged dad levels the offending boy with a forearm to the back of the head. On NBC's *Today Show*, Welch's former employees gasp with horror.

"It's a *game*, people," Matt Lauer says.

"I don't understand what makes people so upset," Ann Curry concurs, bewildered.

Events such as these aren't limited to Lombardi's game. I've seen parents fly out of the stands and attack AAU refs. A Pennsylvania grandfather was killed in 2007 over a local Little League eligibility dispute. A few years earlier, a Boston-area truck driver was sent to prison for killing the ref at his son's hockey scrimmage after an argument over rough play on the ice. These are extreme incidents, but lesser expressions of the same behavior can be found in every town in America where the games of children are organized by adults.

Welch has seen as much at his grandkids' youth hockey and football games, and concedes that he's thrown by the level of passion on display. "The parents are fiercely involved," he says. "Not necessarily the parents of my grandkids, but the other ones. There's an enormous involvement here. It's almost as if the parents are reliving their youth through their kids. It's a whole different game, you know?" One that effectively has been hijacked, however benevolently or self-servingly, by moms and dads.

That was never part of the original plan. When Gulick adapted the games of children to the purposes of nation-building, he placed kids under the care of trained professionals. His YMCA instructors were educated in physical activitites and the PSAL coaches he recruited were teachers with expertise in child development. When grammar school sports got shut down, volunteer-based organizations fill the void. That shift inserted parents into the action, by both necessity and design. Indeed, they were invited onto the playing field, as reflected in a 1958 article in *The Sporting News* on Little League Baseball, which was founded in 1939 and added thousands of leagues in the decade after World War II:

> To the countless thousands of adults who voluntarily give their time, services, and often money to help maintain Little League baseball, the program affords an opportunity to fashion lasting benefits to the community and the youth of the nation. It gives them a chance to participate, rather than to "spectate," in a great sport. In so doing, they may relive their youth. To the parent, LLB is a means of being with his son at a time in the youngster's life when he needs the parent most ... during the formative years of 8 to 12.

The hazard with recruiting untrained adults into children's playing arenas is that adults have different needs. And in the course of reliving their youth, they're not all that good at remembering it. Parents often presume that kids are most interested in winning, when in fact that's not the case. A 1989 survey by Michigan State researchers found that the No. 1 reason children give for participating in sports is, "To have fun." That was the case with boys and girls, in school sports and nonschool sports. Children want the excitement and challenge of competition, but "To win" only cracks the top 10 reasons given for playing sports by boys on school teams. (They rank it No. 8. For the full lists, see Appendix A.) With most kids success at the expense of an opponent isn't a high priority. While winning is preferable to losing—and many children will try hard to win, even crying when they come up short—they don't linger on the result. Ten minutes after the final whistle, they've moved on. It's coaches and parents who keep talking about the game at dinner. Adults exist in an adult world that dispenses rewards based on the bottom line, where the destination matters more than the journey. They often work for companies that move quarter-to-quarter, with earnings and not effort juicing the stock price, often until Mom or Dad are out of a job because they were judged in the bottom 10 percent of producers. Even if the company delivered record profits that year.

Gulick certainly was convinced that boys are bent on conquest. (He viewed the psychology of girls differently—for more on that see Age 7.) "If the masculine individual is turned loose where there is anything to kill, he wants to kill it," he wrote, his conclusion informed by his own days as a child roaming through the forest in search of small animals to shoot. "Not only boys, but men, good men, educated men, do that and enjoy it. When such men as President Roosevelt want to rest they go out into the woods and hunt, satisfying their consciences by collecting, or other excuses." He built a system to reward such instincts.

But Gulick knew enough about child development to recognize that promoting competition in the very young was counterproductive. He felt that premature exposure led to "unfair play" when they got older. And that adults shouldn't even try to direct the play of children below the age of 6, an ironic observation from a man who played such an important role in the growth of an organization, the YMCA, that now sponsors 30-minute games in his sport, basketball, for tots half that age. Parent-run town sport associations rarely show greater restraint.

Cole, our first child, entered organized sports at age 5. We signed him up for "micro-soccer," as they call it in my town. I have warm memories of his first practice, watching him chase the prize across a marked field that seemed open to nothing if not possibility. I remember laying on the sideline grass, stretched out beneath a cloudless sky so wide it appeared to reach down to meet the elevated field, thinking, This is pretty close to heaven. Not because I harbored a dream of Cole someday taking penalty kicks for the U.S. of A., but because I'm as idealistic about sports as Welch or anyone else is whose character was shaped by the childhood presence of a ball and a field and a team. That Cole was being introduced to structured play, with parents framing the action on both sidelines, three years before I had been—well, it seemed odd but not necessarily alarming. Just a modern update to an American tradition.

But it's fair to wonder if any of this will serve him better than if he were just left alone with friends in the backyard.

Gulick greatly underestimated the benefits of gangs being left to their own devices. A salient feature of Welch's childhood was that he was never coached. In fact, none of his sporting activity was supervised by adults until high school. Little League didn't come to Salem until the 1950s, after he had moved on. He played hockey on frozen "ponds" with buddies who had uncapped fire hydrants. He grew up in that sliver of 20th century history after educators had largely ducked out of kids' games and before parents took over. He is a veteran not so much of youth sports as of sports in which children had to supply the equipment, organization, and energy. When invested that deeply in a game, maybe it's easier to care what happens.

One of the reasons Welch enjoys the Little League World Series is that the players' passion is visible and abundant, at least when magnified by television. It reminds him of his days at The Pit. At his grandkids' games, he says, "I don't see the same competitive feel." There, it's often the parents who bring the heat. Which begs an interesting question: Is it possible that in our quest to teach kids to compete we have achieved just the opposite by flooding the zone with grownups? With most kids, says Hall of Famer and youth baseball organizer Cal Ripken Jr., making winning a priority should be held off until, at the earliest, the late elementary-school years. "If competitive strategies are introduced too early, kids will not have the confidence they need to be truly competitive," he has advised parents.

Differentiation, the 20-70-10 tool Welch introduced to GE, is the most-promoted concept drawn from his days at The Pit. But talking with his childhood pals, I get the sense that an appreciation for ruthless efficiency may have been the least of the lessons learned. Perhaps much of the actual value of the experience was that Welch, and not some adult coach, had to prepare for those crosstown challenge games. He had to have the candid conversation when he got good enough to lead (and it's worth noting that even when he was, by his own admission, in the bottom 10 percent at The Pit, he never got cut for good). He had to work through the playground politics. He had to get himself across town for games, motivate his teammates, and solve on-field problems. He picked up transferable skills that one day would help GE see more than 100 consecutive quarters of growth in net income and make Welch, in the opinion of *Fortune* magazine, Manager of the Century. "It was a very maturing process," Zoll says.

Welch wasn't the only denizen of The Pit from that era who rose to prominence. Zoll became mayor of Salem and chief justice of the district court system in Massachusetts. Another boy became a major general in charge of the Army's special forces. One became a Navy pilot and captain of a commercial airline fleet. Another served for 35 years as, fittingly, superintendent of Salem's parks and recreation facilities. Teachers, businessmen, and a Carmelite priest emerged from The Pit's gravel. Few of them had the means to go to college, but nearly all did well in life. These were hard-luck kids who, in the absence of adult coaches, used team sports to help them become not just productive workers—i.e., solid role players—but leaders capable of giving directions. Maybe the robotic children in the Tom Emanski coaches' training DVDs will someday find similar success as citizens. But it sure looks like they're honing little more than their baseball skills.

Not that Welch cares to get sentimental. It's just not his style, and it's not his legacy as the man who remade the American corporation, for better or worse. Like Roosevelt and Gulick a century ago, he's all about moving forward. "That's a day gone by," he says. "It doesn't matter anymore. That's the old guy talking about the good ol' days when they weren't that good. Now, the kids have much better facilities."

And a lot more for which their parents can compete.

AGE 6

FOLLOW THE MONEY

Concord, Massachusetts

Carl Gray warned me.

"Ya have to dress wahm," he said, in his clipped Boston accent. "Ya get cold in ya bones."

Of course, I thought. It's winter in New England. But I couldn't appreciate the wisdom of the founder of the Assabet Valley girls' hockey program until I arrived at Valley Sports Arena, a corrugated metal barn painted utilitarian beige, and pushed through its swinging front doors. It was chillier inside than out—the kind of still, dense cold you might find in a walk-in restaurant refrigerator. The cold starts low, at rink level, and moves up; you feel it first in your toes, and eventually it numbs the ears, nose, chin, and finger tips—not a good thing when you grew up 10 blocks from the beach in South Florida, as I did, and you're trying to take notes. Henry David Thoreau, the 19th-century philosopher who once did his writing in a cabin on nearby Walden Pond, never would have penned anything if he had had to work out of this place. Valley Sports Arena isn't one of the modern rinks Jack Welch was talking about when lauding the facilities kids get to play in these days. It's an icebox from the Bobby Orr era, its tenure clocked by thousands of puck marks in the Styrofoam-lined ceiling.

But youth sport isn't about facilities, it's about opportunities. And opportunity is in the air here. You can actually smell it. It's the scent of near-frozen sweat and hot, if thinly disguised, ambition. It suffuses the main rink and wafts through the tunnel leading to the rear rink where the trophies from dozens of national club championships are stacked on rows of shelves. The scent billows from the cramped locker room, where moms and dads are getting girls dressed for a practice session that begins in 10 minutes sharp. Once the Zamboni finishes its sweep, the Neutrons are on the ice, and it's theirs for the next 55 minutes—ice time is precious, so there's no room for screwing around. The hands of parents move with the efficiency of assembly-line workers. Shoulder to shoulder at the knees of their giggling if compliant daughters, they slide pads over shoulders, helmets over heads, and skates over elfin feet, making the girls seem more imposing—they now look like pint-size gladiators. The Ninja Turtles of the Frozen North. In one corner of the dimly lit room, the youngest member of the team, 6-year-old Karly Aguirre, is getting her shin pads cinched up with tape. Then—*whoosh!* The girls are through the swinging metal door and within two strides out on the glassy ice, where in a rapid-fire succession of drills they will be taught puck skills, how to play one-on-one, and, by the dragging of deflated car tire tubes that forces blades to dig into the ice, proper skating form. But first, they arrange themselves in lines for warm-up sprints.

"To right, to left— Go!" their coach calls out to the first of four lines.

"Go!

"Go!

"Go!"

Go get your Division I scholarships.

• • •

For Karly, for now, the rewards of being on the ice are all intrinsic. She loves chasing that puck. It's all she's ever wanted to do since going to see her first hockey game at age 1. She would press her tiny nose up against the glass at her teenage aunt's town games, mesmerized by the power and grace of the helmeted players. The sight of a ponytail was like a green light. *Girls, Mommy, girls!* she'd say, and by age 3 she was on skates too, determined to get all the way around the rink without holding anyone's hand. So her mother, Karla, signed her up for the town team, and when a taste of hockey made Karly only want more, Karla found the website for the top all-girls club program in Greater Boston. She typed out an e-mail:

> Dear Assabet Girls Hockey,
> I was just checking to see if the minimum age for your U8 team was 5 or 6 by Dec 31, 2005. My daughter, Karly, is 5 on 5/10/05 and really loves hockey, and she learned to skate last summer and started to play this 2004-05 season in Waltham. She is signed up for hockey camps with Pro Ambitions this summer and Bay State Hockey in the spring and summer. Please let me know what the minimum age is for your organization.
> Thank you,
>
> Karla Aguirre

Three days later, there was a response in her inbox:

> Karla Aguirre ,
> You can show up and check in with me on Sat 1:40 p.m. I should be there this weekend for all Assabet Girls activities.
>
> Carl Gray

At the tryout, Gray liked Karly's spunk so he extended her an invite, the first he's given to a 4-year-old. She's been with the team a year and a half now. She's scored three goals. Whenever she nets one, she lifts her stick above her head in spontaneous celebration. She's the only girl on the team who does that. She gets so excited about that moment and about what she just proved to herself and to Rico the Penguin, the well-worn stuffed animal she sleeps with every night and that she brings to every game because she is sure he wants to see her play. "Funny story," says her affable head coach, Chip Labonte. "She had pneumonia three weeks ago and was going back and forth to the doctor. He was talking about when she can go back to school. She was like, 'I don't care about that, when can I play hockey again?' "

Karla doesn't talk to Karly about athletic scholarships. She reminds herself that Karly is still a little girl who wants kisses on her boo-boos. But everyone else talks to them about scholarships. Sometimes it's fellow parents, who often half joke among themselves about the carrot dangling before each of them. *Better work on her edges, we need scholarships,* they'll say with a wink; or, *Gotta listen to the coach, scholarship money's on the line.* Sometimes it's the coach himself projecting a dozen years out. One day at practice Chip says to Karly, "See you in D1 hockey." On the ride home, Karly blushed at the seeming absurdity of the notion. "Coach is talking about college," she told her mom. "I'm not old yet!" She's just started first grade. Still, Karla concedes that she would be lying if she said the idea hasn't penetrated her consciousness. "It's nervewracking because I don't want to say something to her that might take the fun out of it, like I'm pushing her," Karla says. "But I think about it. She could potentially get scholarship money for doing something that makes her happy."

If any of this sounds slightly premature and a lot like a feeding frenzy, it's also an inevitable development. In recent years, the NCAA has thrown a lot more chum into the choppy waters of youth sports. During the 1992-93 school year, NCAA member colleges and universities handed out $377 million in athletically related financial aid, across all sports and divisions. By the turn of the century, the pot had passed $1 billion. In 2006, in response to an inquiry asking the NCAA to explain why athletic programs shouldn't pay federal taxes given the extremely commercial nature of their most prominent sports, association president Myles Brand told Congress that athlete scholarship payouts had reached $1.5 billion. So, in just a decade and a half—about the same amount of time that it will have taken for Bill Clinton to settle in at the White House and his successor George W. Bush to check out—the amount of money awaiting young athletes at the end of high school has quadrupled.

But chum does not a meal make. An athletic scholarship carries with it many conditions that favor the NCAA member institution, notably: 1) Four-year deals that guarantee the student-athlete access to an education were prohibited in 1973 after coaches complained that they didn't have enough control over players given multiyear commitments. Athletic scholarships today are more like one-year performance contracts, renewable entirely at the discretion of the university—and more specifically the coach—which can terminate aid if the player isn't performing well. 2) Most of these deals are partial scholarships that cover no more than half or a quarter of an athlete's college costs. And 3) even when so-called "full rides"—a package that includes tuition, room, board, and required books—are awarded, they don't pay the full cost of attendance, an official figure that accounts for such incidental expenses as transportation, clothing, and laundry, which typically add up to about $2,500 to $3,000 beyond the scholarship.

But chum *does* come cheap. The NCAA is, in effect, a cartel whose members long ago agreed not to get into monetary bidding wars over recruits, so athletes are in fact the only students on a college campus who are restricted in terms of the amount of school-based aid they can receive. At public universities, the maximum value of a typical scholarship is less than $14,000 a year for in-state and $24,000 for out-of-state students; even an athletic gold mine such as former Ohio State quarterback Troy Smith could not bargain for more than the annual $18,860 grant he was given. But the expense to the university is even lower than that, as economist Andrew Schwarz has pointed out. Tuition is not a payment made in cash to an athlete—unlike the salary paid to Smith's coach, Jim Tressel, who made $2.4 million during the quarterback's senior year. Awarding a scholarship is effectively an internal bookkeeping maneuver with no real overhead—the promise of a chair in a classroom to a student who agrees to play sports for the university. For a school that does not have a hard cap on its enrollment, as most do not, the cost is negligible because athletes need not displace students who do pay.

And there are wholesale discounts involved that Brand made no mention of in his letter to Congress. Books might be charged at retail to the athletic department—but in such an arrangement, the school's campus bookstore makes a profit. Room and board are the rare expenses for which schools must actually cut a check to an athlete, but only if he or she lives off campus.

The net cost of an athletic scholarship to a typical university: $5,000 to $10,000. In return, the college gets an athlete who typically devotes north of 30 hours a week to their sport. For football players it's 45 hours a week.

Deal or No Deal, Dr. Brand?

Deal!

Unlike pro sports, most of the money flowing into college sports does not flow back out to athletes. Total annual operating revenues for all NCAA divisions has skyrocketed to $7.8 billion a year, so scholarships (even disregarding all those phantom costs) usually soak up fewer than one of every five dollars that are collected. Division I universities hand out the vast majority of athletically based aid—the remainder gets distributed to Division II athletes—but even the most ambitious programs do not spend the majority of their winnings on athletes. Take Ohio State, again. It has one of the largest programs in college sports, with nearly 923 athletes on 14 men's and 15 women's teams. Yet the cost of all scholarships gobbles up only $12 million of the $109 million in revenues that come to the athletic department. Across Division I and II, four in 10 athletes won't receive *any* aid; they play for free.

Still, for up-and-coming child athletes and their parents across the country, $1.5 billion is a real, and magical, number. Because that's how much cash will be saved by the 25,000 high school seniors each year who convince a coach that they can help his or her team win some games. College costs have risen drastically in recent years. A full athletic scholarship at an elite private school such as Duke or Stanford is worth about $45,000 a year. That's a figure comparable to the net salary of the typical pro athlete, believe it or not. According to U.S. Department of Labor statistics, the median annual gross earnings of the 17,000 pro athletes who drew paychecks in 2004—from the lowliest minor league baseball players to the highest-paid NBA stars—was $48,310.

The NCAA, as a registered nonprofit, characterizes itself as engaged in the exercise of amateur sports. The association works hard to draw a distinction in the public mind between its school-based model and that of the clubs in Europe and elsewhere that sign promising teenagers to professional contracts. But even in the most popular international sport, soccer, and in the country that produced the reigning World Cup champion, Italy, there are only 3,541 pros ... of all ages. In the U.S., where soccer isn't a marquee game even at the collegiate level, about 3,700 freshmen each year will receive formal commitments totaling $32 million annually from NCAA soccer programs. And far more get deals in other sports.

In practical terms, no sports organization in the world offers greater financial incentives to focus children's lives on athletic achievement than does the NCAA. And no sport offers better odds at cashing in than girls' ice hockey.

• • •

"C'mere, I want you to see this," Carl Gray says after practice, summoning me from the locker room where the Ninja Turtles of the North are getting de-taped and de-padded. "This is four years later," he says.

Gray is not a man you comfortably say no to. He is tall and commanding and sure of his place as the king-, er, queenmaker of Assabet Valley hockey. He decides who's in, who's out, and who gets the rink when. He runs Valley Sports Arena with the no-nonsense precision of a Space Shuttle engineer, a job he held before "retirement." Back out on the ice, he walks more gingerly than I do, as his knees have gone bad; at 68, he's not spry enough to coach on skates anymore. But he still can blow a mean whistle, and he's eager to show me what might lie ahead for Karly and the other Neutrons if they continue on and play with the 12 Reds, the club's top 12-and-under team.

"You ready?" he barks from the terra firma of the players' box.

"Ready!" the girls yell back, slapping their sticks on the ground in programmed eagerness. They are spread out on the ice, evenly spaced, and set to begin a grueling skating drill that forces them to change direction each time he blows that ornery whistle of his.

"Ladies, the goal is I want you to WORK," he says, and commences: *Tweet, tweet, tweet, tweet, tweet!*—all those crisp blades moving in tandem sound like a jumbo jet lifting off in the distance—*tweet, tweet, tweet, tweet, tweet!*—the girls are tired after 30 seconds but all are determined not to show exhaustion as Gray approaches the final, fading whistle that allows them to relax ... *twEEEeeeeeet*!

The girls come to a rest, sticks now held above their heads to open up their lungs. I'm impressed with the effort displayed. I ask him: How many of these 16 girls will play coll—

"All of them," he says, anticipating the rest of my question. He pauses for a beat. "And the financial numbers are big."

Gray figures that around $1.4 million in future financial aid is on the ice at the moment, given that many of the girls will attend private colleges where the game is most popular. And that estimate does not include the scholarship money that some receive to play at elite New England prep schools, where students are charged as much as $35,000 a year. The prep school payoff can begin when the girls reach high school age, and sometimes it comes even earlier. "Like this girl in white, a seventh grader," Gray says as one of them flashes by the boards. "She's already getting almost a full scholarship—30 some odd thousand a year. She only pays $2,000. Seventh grade. Right there."

I do the math in my head. That's potentially $200,000 in aid between now and the end of high school, then another $200,000 in college (costs will surely rise by the time she gets there). Which begins to explain why some of the parents of these girls spend 3 ½ hours a day driving them to Assabet Valley practices and games four days a week between Labor Day and Memorial Day. You can be sure that they've done the math in their heads, too. Later, when I enter the trophy room from which the parents watch practice, and I ask how many of them expect their 11- and 12-year-olds to play college hockey, virtually every hand goes up. "Pretty much all of us do," says one mother, acknowledging the obvious with a shrug.

"It's always on their minds," says Gray, who likes his customers best when they're ensconced in that trophy room. "I stay away from parents, okay? I don't even like to sit up in the stands near the parents. It's a whole 'nother world. There are expectations. 'Why isn't my daughter on a particular line?' 'She's playing lefty, and she ought to be playing righty.' So I just stay away from them."

MYTH NO. 6
Athletic scholarships support amateurism.

THE TRUTH
The lure of a payoff turns peewees into mini-pros.

Gray can afford to tout the financial bonanza and be dismissive of those who see the same because he delivers top product. He's lost track of all the Assabet Valley players who have gone on to play college hockey over the years, from Harvard and Yale to the public universities. He can call up a college coach and tell her to offer a scholarship, sight unseen, to a given player; that's what he did with Providence, where Cammi Granato, who became a star of the 1998 U.S. team that won the Olympic gold medal, enrolled. There were six Assabet Valley alums on the '06 national team. That year, his newest crop of girls won the national championships at the U12, U14, and U16 levels, bringing the club tally to 32 such titles since Gray founded the program in 1974. He says this year's U12s—whom he spends 80% of his time with because this is the age when USA Hockey first crowns a national champion—might be his best team ever. Right now the team is 26–0–0, with 178 goals for and 19 against.

But girls' hockey, in general, is a relatively good bet if playing in college is your goal.

The NCAA's method of estimating the chances of a kid making it to the collegiate level is to divide the number of high school seniors participating in the sport by the number of freshmen on college teams. By that formula, American football offers long odds—just 1 in 42 boys will go on to suit up in Division I (and 1 in 77 in the Football Bowl Subdivision, formerly known as Division I-A). Boys' basketball is even more of a sucker's play—1 in 111; the sport of March Madness is tied with volleyball for the lowest odds. (For a sport-by-sport list of the odds of playing in college, see page 361.)

The casino game called Scholarships offers better odds for females, though not by much in some of the most popular sports. In basketball,

1 in 100 will go on to play in D1. Soccer and outdoor track each come in at 1 in 42, softball 1 in 72, and volleyball 1 in 91. Girls' hockey blows them away: 1 in 11. Plus, scholarship dough is abundant, an average of $348,000 per team, tops among women's sports.

Credit for those handsome numbers goes to three factors: 1) Title IX of the Education Amendments to the Civil Rights Act, the 1972 law that mandated equitable opportunities for students, regardless of gender, at institutions that receive federal funds. 2) The gluttony of Division I-A football, in which the NCAA allows colleges to pass out 85 scholarships and, counting walk-ons, teams often carry twice as many players as NFL clubs; the abundance of football players compels universities to create women's teams just to balance the numbers. And 3) physical infrastructure—which is to say that colleges already had rinks on campus for the men's team, so why not simply add a women's team?

You could also note that Carl Gray deserves some props. He was one of the first men to get behind girls' sports in a big way. He started his program soon after the arrival of Title IX. Like most males of his stripe, he was a sports-loving dad, righteous about egalitarian America giving his two daughters the same access to organized sports as his two sons. It all started when he was coaching Little League and local officials refused to allow his best player—a girl—to take the field. At the time, Little League Baseball honchos at headquarters in Williamsport, Pa., were fighting lawsuits around the country in response to its boys-only policy. They claimed that the game was too dangerous for girls. Among the more dubious pieces of medical evidence to support its position: That boys are born with more muscle fibers, and that by age 10 the fiber ratio was 3:2 in favor of males. (That girls often reach puberty sooner and are sometimes larger muddies the argument hopelessly. A New Jersey judge ultimately laughed Little League out of court and ruled that discrimination is illegal on public grounds, which in turn forced the organization to back down.)

Says Gray, "I got so pissed. I said, 'I'll find a sport where they can't tell us that girls can't play.'" He took an ownership stake in the arena and, in the town where the second battle of the American Revolutionary War was held, his all-girls hockey club was born. Most of his first group of players showed up wearing figure skates.

Enforcement of Title IX lagged during the Reagan era, so at the start of the '90s, Assabet Valley was still an anomaly. In 1990, only 5,068 females under age 20 were registered with USA Hockey, the sports' national governing body. There weren't many opportunities for girls to play on the club level, which the federation regulated, and school-based hockey was largely limited to the prep schools. But two years later, the Supreme Court put a hammer into the hands of gender-equity advocates, ruling that a person could be awarded monetary damages if she (or he) proved that a school had intentionally violated Title IX. With a penalty attached to ignoring the law, educational institutions began rapidly to add teams for females, and not just in ice hockey. By 2000, two out of five high school girls played sports, up from 1 in 27 when Title IX was signed into law by President Nixon—who probably had no idea that the amendment would be used to grow women's sports so forcefully. He was more football fan than feminist, and the bill at the time was neither controversial nor discussed much in terms of its impact on sports.

After the Supreme Court victory, girls' club hockey boomed. By the 2004-05 season, there were 40,301 youth players, nearly half of them below the age of 10. There are still far more boys playing the game than girls, but Assabet Valley has ample competition now at most age levels. Tournaments such as a Christmastime event run by a rival club in Connecticut draw more than 220 teams down through the U10 level—it's one-stop shopping for college and prep school recruiters. NCAA institutions have kept pace with that growth. The number of college teams had more than tripled in the decade leading up to 2004-05 to 74, and another seven were added a year after that. On the D1 level, there are now about 700 athletes on 34 teams.

It's not just schollys that are up for grabs.

The Ivy League doesn't do athletic scholarships. That would be too mercenary. But those genteel northeastern schools do like hockey, and they do have institutional egos, ancient rivalries, and scads of cash. Harvard has a $29 b-b-billion endowment that, among other benefits, helps defray the cost of tuition for students. Resources abound. There's a saying about financial aid for Ivy League athletic recruits: *It's all on a need basis. If they need you, they'll get you.* Harvard women's hockey coach Katey Stone conceded as much when I called. "We haven't lost a kid for a financial reason since I've been here," she said. "Often, the package from an Ivy League school is better than a full athletic scholarship elsewhere."

No less significantly, Stone also can be the key to unlocking admission to the nation's most prestigious university—even if you have academic credentials that otherwise might not impress state colleges. Each year, Harvard gets about 3,000 applicants with perfect SAT scores, or nearly twice as many slots as are available for the entire freshman class. "We wouldn't have a hockey program if we only admitted perfect SAT scores," Stone says. "I have not seen one hockey player yet with perfect SAT scores." Like other coaches, she gets to submit to the university each year a list of prospects she wants to see considered for admission. She sends a list of five to eight athletes and, usually, they all get in. Of course, Harvard isn't the only elite school where strings get pulled: Recruited athletes are four times as likely to gain admission to Ivy League colleges as other applicants with similar academic credentials, according to William G. Bowen and Sarah A. Levin's 2003 book, *Reclaiming the Game: College Sports and Educational Values.* The authors found that the admissions advantage was even greater than that given to legacies or minorities. Call it Affirmative Action for athletes.

Stone declines to share the average SAT scores for the players on her team, so I ask what sort of SAT score it would take for a girl like, say, Karly to play hockey for the Crimson someday. (The question is complicated by the fact that the SAT added a written section in 2005, on top of the math and verbal tests, and a perfect score changed from 1600 to 2400, so I ask her to give me a number that corresponds to the old test which people are more familiar with). "I would say that getting over 1200 is a good thing," she says. "Not to say that we haven't admitted people under 1200." Karly must also have at least a B average, Stone says. With strong recommendations. And a good interview with the admissions people, who want to know if athletes are going to be discontented if they blow out a knee and can't play anymore. It's a rich irony: The ultimate liberal arts college wants the specialized athlete—as long as she can prove that she's not specialized. "She would need to present herself as much more than a hockey player," Stone says.

Otherwise Karly might have to settle for, *egads!* Yale. Or Ohio State.

"The sky's the limit, particularly if she continues to be a good student and good athlete," says Stone, who has two Assabet Valley players on her current team with two more on the way next year. "Tremendous opportunities will come her way."

Better than most would imagine. In October 2005, the coaches of a boys' hockey team in central Michigan were suspended for three games for overseeing a practice drill in which the teenagers paired up, dropped their gloves, and began slugging one another in the face. A retired police officer who witnessed the exercise described it as "orchestrated brutality." Community outrage ensued. But there was plenty of support for the coaches, too, by those who viewed their actions as a way to build the toughness needed to play the game at the next level. In a letter to the local newspaper, the father of one player on the team wrote, "If my son is to move on to college, or higher, he will not get there wearing a dress."

Not true. Just 1 in 22 boys go on to play D1 hockey. He'd have twice as good a chance if he were a girl.

And even better odds if his parents were wealthy.

AGE 7

FOLLOW THE MONEY, TOO

Concord, Massachusetts

When Karly gets a couple of years older, she'll get to take the Carl Gray Aggression Test. It's his personal tool for figuring out who has what it takes to excel at the next level. He'll hold two quarters in one of his steely fists and tell the girl she can do whatever she wants to try and pry it loose—scratch, punch, spit, bite, kick him in the groin—no act is too uncivil so long as she does not break eye contact. If the girl doesn't retrieve the coins, she gets a rating on a scale of 1 to 10. "I want to find out how they are going to be in a competitive situation," he says. "A few of them have taken a piece of meat out." None have gotten the quarters, though. Or a score higher than an 8.

Karly is Gray's kind of prospect. She's a sweetheart at elementary school, everyone's playmate because she's so inclusive. Her teacher can't believe this little girl who stuffs Rico the Penguin into her backpack every day plays the sport associated with missing teeth. But get Karly on the ice, and those soft, brown eyes harden, especially when the disc is anywhere near the end of her stick. Gray swears she skates faster with the puck than without it. In a one-on-one practice drill near the front of the net, her shot gets trapped in the crease by the square-faced girl tending the net today, Amanda Reilly. Karly whacks away at her teammate's oversize glove anyway, determined to pry the black pearl loose from its closed-up oyster shell.

"Okay, enough Karly," an assistant coach says. He shakes his head, looks at me, and chuckles. "Karly's a madwoman," he says.

An athlete gets nowhere without a passion for the game. It's an asset of Karly's. But she's handicapped, too. At bedtime, she and her three preteen siblings lay their heads down in the happy, modest home of her grandmother, a Salvadoran immigrant who helps 33-year-old Karla make ends meet. An office assistant in the financial aid division of nearby Bentley College, Karla is the only single mother among the Assabet Valley team parents—Karly has no contact with her father—and meeting commitments is a stretch, both financially and logistically. Just with transportation, Karla needs ample help from her mother, who often makes the 30-minute drive to Valley Arena two or three days a week, as well as to the games 50-minutes away at a different arena.

Youth hockey has become an expensive sport. Gray's registration fee of $1,000 a season is less than that of comparable clubs. But there's the expense of gas, tolls, and hotel rooms for the occasional out-of-state tournament. This year, the team is signed up for one weekend event in Vermont, which the Aguirres plan to make their big vacation for the year, "since we don't go to Disney" and other faraway theme parks, Karla says. To avoid breaking the family budget, she starts saving for Karly's hockey six months before the start of the next season. New blades make old skates last longer, and as Karly gets older, she'll wear hand-me-down boots from siblings. Still, the cost of select-level hockey will grow measurably in the coming years. Some parents on the 12 Reds will easily drop $10,000 on one child's hockey involvement during the year, between nationals in California, their town team, and other commitments.

These costs won't be an issue for Amanda Reilly, the girl in goal, and her fraternal twin, Shannon, who also plays on the Assabet Valley team. They live in an exclusive neighborhood of million-dollar homes several suburban towns over from Karly's working-class enclave. Dad's a Harvard-educated chemical engineer who's taking time off to "play the market" with his investments, and mom is a whip-smart civil prosecutor in the state attorney general's office. The Tudor home in which they will lay their heads down tonight doesn't qualify as a mansion, but it's large enough to comfortably accommodate five children, one sheep dog, and a backyard ice rink (which, in the present clement weather, is just a large puddle).

In short, it's a home with everything except a maid.

"This is our locker room," Kristen, the mother, jokes, nodding at a family room that is more stylistically frat house than Martha Stewart. Scattered everywhere are socks, jerseys, helmets, sticks, pads, bags, and skates—she says the family has 58 pairs. A tennis-racket-stringing machine sits in the corner. In an adjacent room (ostensibly the library), a pyramid of children's books rises from the carpet in the shape of a campus bonfire. Academics are important in this home, but so too are sports, and with all the kids' scheduled activities, something's got to give. It's tidiness.

Kristen's organizational efforts go into the making of the daily youth sports schedule, printed out from a Microsoft Word document and distributed the night before. She hands me a copy of today's grid, which, she insists, is relatively light for a Saturday:

5:55 a.m.	Leave for twins' Mite A 6:50 a.m. game at Hockeytown.
6:40	Leave to get Karen to her 7:40 a.m. Squirt game at Fessenden.
7:30	Leave for Barry (8 to 10).
10:00	Leave to get twins to their 11:00 a.m. Mite A game at Wilmington rink.
10:15	Leave with Karen for her 11 to 1 Igor skate.
1:35 p.m.	Karen has U10 White game at Northboro (miss).
1:45	Leave with Jimmy for his singles match at home at Win. Bld. No. 1 ag. Woburn Red.
2:30	Leave with twins for their 3:00 Assabet dryland and 4:00 Assabet practice. Leave there by 4:45 at the latest due to 5:40 Top Gun game.
3:15	Leave with Josh for his doubles match at home at Win. Bld No. 2 ag. Woburn Red w/Ross.

5:40 Twins have Top Gun game at New England Sports Center ag. Eagles (big game!).

So, to translate and recap: The 7-year-old twins played two games today with their town team and one more with their (otherwise) all-boys select team based in New Hampshire, in between two hours of practice with Assabet Valley, at four separate rinks. Eldest daughter Karen, 9, played one game with her town team and also got two hours of group instruction with Igor, the $4,000-a-season former Soviet Red Army skater whom the twins also see on Saturdays when not booked solid with commitments to their three teams. The eldest boy, 13-year-old Josh, a nationally ranked tennis player, and little brother, Jimmy, 11, whose main sports are hockey and football, got a lesson and played some club tennis, but that's all—they were done in time to go see the new Bond movie, *Casino Royale*, with their dad/chauffeur, Mark. "I was home for two hours today," Mark says with a wry smile, scarfing down a Whopper he picked up on the way home from the cineplex. (The family usually eats its fast food in transit.) "It was great."

The Reillys already spend more than $10,000 a year per twin on hockey, if you include the $2,500 in figure skating lessons they use to sharpen their edges. Amanda and Shannon also have twice-weekly lessons at the Harvard courts in tennis, a sport in which both are ranked in the New England region. But Josh's private tennis instruction, for eight hours with a couple of different pros, is the big ticket there. He and Joey also see a $60-an-hour personal trainer, who works with them on speed, strength, and balance. ("The best investment, because it's injury prevention," Kristen says.) Kasey, who has yet to specialize in a sport, takes private lessons in tennis and figure skating in between games for her two soccer and two hockey teams. Throw in fees and miscellaneous costs for gymnastics, golf, baseball, lacrosse, skiing, cross country, and Pop Warner football, and it wouldn't surprise me if the Reillys are dropping a hundred grand a year on their five kids' athletic endeavors.

And none of them are even in high school.

So over the 10 years leading to college, that's conceivably a bill of ... $1 million on youth sports? "Hey," Mark says, "it's not like we go out to a lot of fancy dinners."

He and Kristen are coy with the actual figures. They understand how ridiculous this all sounds. But they also understand that they are in an arms race of sorts. They hear the stories: Of the girl who gets $900 in tennis lessons *a day*; of the fifth grader whose father moved into a rented trailer in Florida with her so that she could train at a top sports academy; of the parents of a New York club hockey team who reward its blue-chip coach with a $2,000 gift each Christmas. (This isn't out of line with other people's efforts in other parts of the country: Some families drop $70,000 a year, soup to nuts, to get *one* kid professionally groomed in golf or tennis at the famed IMG Academies in Bradenton, Fla.) In the land of plenty, it's pay or perish in some sports.

Since she has the resources, Kristen sees it as her duty to seek out the best sport training for her children. "Parents believe they're supporting their kids by showing up for games," she says, "but I think it's cruel to ask a kid to entertain you and not prepare him or her to do well. It's like you're going to the game to *watch* them? When you've done little to support them? And they might not be on team next year because they're no longer good enough? I don't know. I guess they're showing emotional support."

Sometimes the prosecutor gets put on the defense for this stance. A few years ago one of her boys had a hockey game that made them late to a friend's birthday party. When they arrived, she apologized and explained the circumstances. It was like walking into a bear trap. One of the parents in attendance happened to be Bob Bigelow, a former NBA player who co-wrote the 2001 book, *Just Let the Kids Play: How to Stop Other Adults From Ruining Your Child's Fun and Success in Youth Sports*, which argues for, among other things, the elimination of travel teams before grade seven. Bigelow, who happens to live across town from the Reillys, has railed for a decade about the intensification of kids' games, firing away from lecterns and television talk shows. And now the 6-foot-7 hometown hero was about to breathe fire on the red-haired, red-faced Kristen, 16 inches shorter and surrounded by kids.

"You're apologizing for being late because you missed half of this party for a hockey game? In September?"

He asked for the team schedule. She handed it to him.

"Why are you playing a team 30 miles away from here?"

"It's the schedule I got," she responded meekly, not wanting to create a scene.

The counselor has done a lot of thinking about Bigelow and his sermon since that night. And here's what she's decided: Nice guy, good intentions, outdated message. Like Bigelow, she enjoyed the more casual youth sports environment of the 1960s and '70s. She won two Virginia state championships playing high school soccer, a sport she didn't even pick up until sixth grade. She went on to participate as a gymnast on the club team at the University of Virginia. But she believes modern reality is that without focused training when her children are young, they might not have the chance to play even high school sports. "Let kids be kids? Is that possible anymore?" she says. "Can you develop an athlete that way these days? I don't care about winning. It's just the price of being on a team.

"I'm way past Bob Bigelow."

When I call Bigelow later and remind him of the party and relay Kristen's thoughts, he at first remains on the offensive. "What does she know about child development?" he says. "She only knows more, more, more—the code of the West. She's swallowed the Kool-Aid and swallowed it early." He grudgingly concedes, though, that she's "probably right" in surmising that a kid can no longer wait until his teenage years to take up hockey and hope to play in high school. "But that's only because of the clueless idiots who are ruining the system by insisting on getting their kids on the right team early," he adds.

Bigelow or no Bigelow, hockey season keeps the Reilly family from getting to Mass as much as they would like—not that the twins complain about that. More hockey + less church = win/win. They *do* miss the play dates that are sacrificed. We're sitting at the kitchen table now, and Amanda smiles shyly when her mother, who is stroking her shoulder-length brown locks, mentions the absence of down time with town friends.

"Yeah, that's all we think about," Amanda says, glass half empty.

"Sometimes they come to our house," Shannon says, glass half full.

"They know so many kids from New Hampshire, from their Top Gun team," Kristen says, reconciling. "Those are their play dates."

Kristen says their goal in hockey is ambitious: To make the Assabet Valley U12 Reds. Once that happens, everything else falls in place.

I ask the twins what their goal is, just 'cause I want to hear it from them. There's silence for a moment. Amanda fiddles with a painted toy soldier among the Christmas decorations on the table. Shannon looks at her mom for guidance. "I know what *her* goal is," Kristen says, filling in the blank. "It's to take the puck. And the harder you work in practice"—she's now talking directly to Shannon—"the easier it is to take the puck. So if you don't have it, you go get it. You steal it. Even if someone is taller than you." The twins listen intently.

The truth, of course, is that most 7-year-olds don't have long-term goals. They're still in the moment. Kristen, in no small measure, is inserting her ambition for theirs. But again, you could call it an act of love, as every kid wants to be good at what she or he does, and no 7-year-old could find the pathway to the U12 Reds without ample amounts of planning, sacrifice, and financial investment by parents such as Mark and Kristen. At practice, I had asked the U12 Reds as a group when each of them first played hockey. Six of the girls were on skates at age 2. All but two were on teams by age 5. The player who started at the latest age, 7, raised her hand meekly, in embarrassment. They are Massachusetts girls. In most states where hockey is popular, girls usually join teams somewhere between the ages of 9 and 14. On a chart, youth-participation levels through high school are shaped like the classic bell curve, with a bulge in the middle school middle. But in Massachusetts, home to some of America's leading prep schools and universities, where the scent of educational advantage is omnipresent, the largest chunk of girls registered with USA Hockey is in the youngest category—6 and under. The participation rate tapers off gradually from there, as girls quit their town teams. "The stakes are higher, sooner here in Massachusetts," says Ben Smith, who coached the 1998 U.S. women's team to the Olympic gold medal.

Hockey is a game that could take the twins far—if they make the commitment. The greatest barrier to entry is ice time, which is scarce and thus expensive. Pond hockey, the pick-up form of the game that launched the career of many NHL old-timers, is all but dead, the casualty of residential development, global warming, and jittery parents. Opportunity now runs almost exclusively through rinks like Valley Arena, which opens at 4:30 a.m. and keeps the lights on through midnight to accommodate demand. Inevitably, it's a not a game accessible to much of society. Only one percent of Americans pick up a stick even once a year, and among females, just one percent of those come from a household with less than $25,000 in annual income. Fully 85 percent come from families that take in more than $50,000. The demographics are more blue collar on the boys' side, but not by much. Nearly a quarter of all frequent players, of both genders, are drawn from households with incomes of at least $100,000.

These are the kids who will have first dibs on college hockey. Up-by-the-bootstrap success stories like those of Jack Welch, who started with no family wealth and went on to play for the University of Massachusetts, are now rare. In fact, college athletics in general are more the province of the privileged than the poor.

The images that dominate media coverage of college sports are of basketball and football, with more than a few of the players coming from distressed families. In his 2006 letter to Congress justifying the NCAA's tax-exempt status, Myles Brand went out of his way to mention that the $1.5 billion in athletic scholarships that gets doled out annually helps "many low-income students who would otherwise have to forgo the college experience." But a decade earlier, a survey by the U.S. Department of Education debunked the notion of college sports as a tool of broad social uplift. Tracking students from eighth grade through college, it found that children with a high socioeconomic status (those in the top 25 percent on a measure that considers their parents' occupations, education, and income) were 10 times as likely to play Division I sports as those with low socioeconomic status (those in the bottom 25 percent). Even among elite high school athletes—defined as those who were MVPs or captains on their team—only four percent of kids from disadvantaged backgrounds went on to play at the D1 level.

Look at the list of sports that offer the best odds of playing on the collegiate level (page 361). Most of those at the top—rowing, equestrian events, fencing, gymnastics, lacrosse, swimming, water polo, golf—draw athletes from or are popular in suburbs that are wealthy or at least middle class. Not surprisingly, two-thirds of all D1 athletes are Caucasian.

Down in the Norman Rockwell zone of Division III, by far the largest NCAA grouping, with 443 schools, there are no athletic scholarships. Of course, the affluent have less need for athletic scholarships. Admission to a small, prestigious college such as Amherst or Williams can be a bigger prize, and a coach's nod may be reward enough for a sizable investment in youth sports. (Schools in the New England Small College Athletic Conference accepted just under two-thirds of the athletes they recruited as compared with only 31 percent of other applicants.) All told Division III appears to pull from poor or minority homes even less frequently than D1. "We certainly don't have those stories here at Ithaca, and really at many of the private schools," says Ellen Staurowsky, a sports management professor and the former director of athletics at Division III Ithaca College (N.Y.). "College athletics caters to the upper economic strata. There's a big mythology out there that these opportunities are going to inner-city kids. But that's not our clientele." Even in men's hoops, only one in five D3 players is black, some of whom of course are from middle-class, suburban areas.

So, beneath the thin layer of sports entertainment that makes its way onto television are the bulk of college athletes: Well off and white. That's not to say these athletes and their families don't have their own struggles; but they are, frankly, more Shannon and Amanda Reilly than Karly Aguirre.

• • •

We all know the storyline of the celebrated, revenue-sport college jock.

I'll keep it to one sentence. If you're gifted, really gifted, and lucky (right team, right coaches, right scheme, no wrecked knees) and play by the unwritten but uncompromising rules of the NCAA establishment—devote 260 days a year to your team and don't make a habit of questioning the fairness of a system that uses your ability to perform in order to make hundreds of millions of dollars while you are on campus—then you *might* end up like Ohio State quarterback Troy Smith, with a hunk of wood and metal in your left hand and a stirring national feature story (set to soft jazz) that memorializes your childhood descent into a Cleveland foster home and emergence as a student-athlete-celebrity, and how that Heisman Trophy you just won is going to motivate other kids to rise up from the ghetto in a similar manner, thereby helping to recycle the myth—critical to existing public policy—that big-time, commercialized college sports like D1 football and basketball are a viable route to a better life, when in fact there's no real evidence to suggest that collectively the poor have been lifted by all that sport-centric dreaming and, besides, the Heisman isn't what kids in the ghetto dream about anyway because chunks of metal and wood don't put dinner on the family table and sometimes don't even guarantee an NFL career, even if you so far have beaten the odds.

MYTH NO. 7

The poor benefit the most from college sports.

THE TRUTH

Rich kids are far likelier to get roster spots.

For a handsome young man like Smith—just the kind of poster boy that colleges can use effectively to keep the IRS from taxing their take—life is good. For now. Which makes the rest of us feel good. For now. We can safely continue to cheer the spectacle of desperate young men chasing deliverance under hot lights, which, let's be honest here, makes for *damn good entertainment.*

The Ninja Turtles of the North aren't nearly as entertaining. But there are moments of hope and inspiration, just the same.

"Shannon, are you fired up?" Bonnie half yells, tapping her teammate's face mask.

Shannon nods, turns, and chirps, "Karly, are you fired up?"

Karly responds in kind and says, "Amanda, are you fired up?"

So the chant moves around the locker room, the pregame ritual connecting every player orally, viscerally, and spiritually. We're at an arena in

Westborough, Mass., the morning after my visit to the twins' home, and in this space it's easy to appreciate the influence of Title IX. These girls are not cheering for boys but for themselves, bonding so they can *beat* boys—in today's case, the Tri-Valley Indians from nearby Franklin. In such a crucible, with their helmets on, all ethnic and class distinctions fade. The girls are just athletes.

One of the original advocates of youth sports in America was Catherine Beecher, who wrote influential books in the mid-1800s on the need for girls and boys to exercise. She was among the first Muscular Christians, a predecessor to Luther Gulick and Teddy Roosevelt. The invention of the bicycle got many girls moving, as did a Harvard essay in 1876 that found that exercise during school hours reduced menstrual pain. But Victorian notions about ladylike behavior and fears that exercise might inhibit the girls' ability to have babies discouraged participation at a time when youth sports was being institutionalized in boys' lives. Gulick supported exercise for girls. But he also believed that girls lacked the natural killer instinct of boys, and that they neither could nor should engage in rough activities. When the Girls' Branch of the New York Public Schools Athletic League was launched in 1905, cooperation and access were the cornerstones of its five precepts:

- Sports for sport's sake—no gate money.
- Athletics for all girls.
- Athletics within the school and no interschool competition.
- Athletic events in which teams (not individual girls) compete.
- Athletics chosen and practiced with regard to their suitability for girls and not merely in imitation of boys' athletics.

Folk dance, walking, and "other games" were promoted among girls of elementary school age. We can safely assume that ice hockey against boys was not among the approved games. Then again, Gulick and his disciples probably never got to see a girl do what Shannon does to the ruddy-cheeked boys of Tri-Valley—which is to forever deny them credibility should they ever use the words "play like a girl" in an insulting manner. Under Armour headband peeking out from beneath her gold helmet, stick at the ready, she commandeers the puck on the rear wall and heads up the left wing, whisking easily around one ... two ... three boys, before a defender swoops in and stops the run. If the rules allowed Shannon to lay a shoulder into that kid, I'm sure she would: She wishes she could body check like the older boys. (She finds it especially "stupid" that there's no checking at the Harvard women's games she and her Assabet Valley teammates attend.)

No matter. Her team's up 4-1. Another easy win is pretty much in the bag, and plenty of time remains. All that's really left is to see if the parents on the other team—Assabet Valley is the only all-girls team in this particular league—are going to get ugly. It's happened before; although by now most of them realize that girls of this age have no problem competing with boys.

"The good thing is, they're not pioneers," says Kristen, who volunteers as an assistant coach on the team. In recent years, Americans have gotten used to watching girls do battle in team sports, and not just on the Olympic and collegiate level, but in their own communities. The number of girls between the ages of 6 and 11 who engage in strenuous sports activities two or more times a week rose 86 percent in the decade after Title IX began to be enforced in schools and public facilities. And for the most part, Americans like what they see. Athletes such as Granato, soccer's Mia Hamm and basketball's Sue Bird have become the iconic faces of women's sports—buoyant, self-possessed, and still feminine. They embody the traits many of us, me included, want to see in our daughters. Studies show that girls who play sports have more confidence in their physical and social selves than those who are sedentary. They are less likely to get pregnant, smoke, or use illicit drugs as teens. They get better grades. They grow up to become leaders—four out of five executive businesswomen in a 2002 national survey played sports, and a vast majority said that lessons learned on the playing field contributed to their success. Count Kristen among that group.

But many of those studies were conducted before the world of girls' youth sports had become organized to such a degree around the lure of athletic scholarships. Select teams and the tournaments they play in primarily serve the needs of NCAA colleges because they aggregate talent in a limited number of places, thus minimizing: 1) recruiting costs and 2) recruiting mistakes. The potential to win scholarships and gain access to good colleges encourages the formation of elite club teams that aspire to identify top young prospects or at least those whose families can foot the bill. It pushes the process of weeding out less-promising child athletes down to the lowest levels that the market (meaning parents' pocketbooks) will bear. It places a premium on making a select team, such as Assabet Valley, at the first age offered, since coaches tend to hang onto the players they are most familiar with. The process encourages unprecedented amounts of time and financial commitment just to stay on those teams. There's no reason to think that the current generation of girl athletes won't receive many of the same health benefits as their predecessors, but their bodies are also under greater stress. Girls' knees, in particular, are more susceptible to injury than those of boys. Karly is already on the ice seven days a week. Minds could become weary, too. Karly and the Reilly twins may never know a youth team on which the mere potential of a financial aid jackpot does not loom large, competing with love of game as the club's raison d'être.

One family spending a hundred grand a year on kids' sports might sound nuts, but it could be viewed as a rational number—should all five Reilly children continue to play at a high level and get full rides to private schools. Athletic scholarships aren't necessarily the goal of Kristen and Mark, who don't need the assistance. But that's how much incentive colleges and the NCAA have given parents to invest in a kid's sports training. As another shift of Assabet girls rises from the bench and heads onto the ice, Kristen turns to me and says, "To say the problems in sports are all the parents' fault, I don't know about that. The NCAA is a huge factor in all of this." For the record, she says, her goal is merely to provide her children with fitness habits for life—"which I suppose makes all of this even more absurd," she laughs—and perhaps some bonus points in the college admission process. She isn't sure she'd even want her child on an athletic scholarship, given that it's a contract for sport services rendered. She wasn't on one at Virginia and was fine with that because she didn't feel beholden to the coach and could prioritize her studies. She not only got her degree but also went on to graduate from Georgetown's law school. "It's great to excel in sports, but where do you draw that line?" she says. "I guess it's your tolerance level for school being irrelevant."

As for Karla Aguirre, it might be madness to be thinking of college scouts at a time when Karly mostly wants to impress Rico the Penguin. But Karla is only responding to the opportunities presented. At her administrative job at Bentley College, she hears about the hockey coaches working the angles for the prospects they want. On the ice, hockey is all about finding 2-on-1 scenarios that create scoring opportunities. A numbers advantage works in the financial aid game, too.

As Kristen and I talk, Assabet Valley goes up 5-1 on a breakaway.

She doesn't see the goal, distracted by our conversation. Like the rest of us with children in youth sports, she's trying to sort it all out in her mind, how we got to this place where so much seems to ride on the outcome of a child's game. She also brings a legal mind to the discussion, musing about the larger concepts in play when an industry gets built up around the pursuit—not just in girls' hockey—of an economic payoff.

"At what point do you call it child labor?" she asks. "At what point do you call it a job?" She's thinking of the 16-year-old boys who skip high school hockey altogether to play in the United States Hockey League, a junior hockey league based in the Midwest that's every bit as commercial as those in Canada—except that the NCAA lets players remain eligible for college hockey because their host families get only expense money and season tickets. She's thinking of the parents who home-school their kids so that they can train harder. She's thinking of NCAA coaches increasingly signing foreign tennis players who came up through pro circuits overseas. How do *they* qualify as amateurs? "The NCAA does this wink-wink, nod-nod," she says. "You don't even know who you're competing against now—it's some kid in Europe you've never heard of."

The truth is, there's no legal definition of amateurism. If the NCAA wanted to declare Carmelo Anthony an amateur so he could play again for Syracuse, it could. If it wanted to let Florida quarterback Tim Tebow sign a $1 million contract with Nike, it could do that, too. The NCAA won't because member schools favor the existing business model—Brand calls it the "collegiate model"—that keeps available revenues flowing straight into the university's pocket, not the athlete's. Plus, any moves like those could invite IRS scrutiny of the NCAA, since the distinction between D1 and that of overtly professional leagues is already pretty much cosmetic. But the NCAA *will* let athletes take Major League Baseball paychecks and retain their football eligibility. It *will* certify the eligibility of soccer and basketball players who were groomed at professional clubs in Europe. And it certainly *won't* stand in the way of the women's hockey team at the University of Minnesota at Duluth filling two-thirds of its roster with Canadians and Euros—including the Swede who scored the winning goal to shock the U.S. at the 2006 Turin Olympics.

That might not have been the intent of Title IX, to provide foreigners with taxpayer-funded educational opportunities (and athletic training that can directly deny the U.S. a gold medal), but it's the contemporary reality in sports. In Division I, there are now more than 8,000 male and female athletes from foreign countries. They are being added to college rosters at a faster rate than any ethnic category of U.S. athlete. The trend is especially pronounced in hockey, in which one of every four D1 players now is from another nation. In contrast, there are so few U.S. minorities on those rosters that if everyone were brought together there would be just enough to form one men's and one women's team. No more than a half dozen or so of the females are, like Karly, Latino; and none is on Harvard's squad, which gets most of its talent from prep schools and Canada.

"Athletics is about winning," Brand said in his 2004 NCAA Convention speech. In other words, it's not about giving Karly a chance to play—unless she earns it, that is, in what has become a global marketplace for talent.

She's paying her dues right now. "Karly just got decked," Kristen says, halting our conversation. The littlest Neutron is crouched on the far end, gloves off, holding a wrist in pain. Play stops. She comes off the ice, weeping. Chip Labonte, the head coach, puts an arm on her shoulder, whispers something comforting in her ear. Her teammates on the bench bang their sticks on the floor, a support ritual, as she takes a seat. Kristen leans over her shoulder and says, "You gotta be tough when you have the puck because they're gonna come after you."

Within a minute, the tears are dry. Karly's sitting up again, inching toward the gate, trying to get back in the game. A few seconds later, the buzzer sounds, and all the girls pour onto the ice, piling on to one another in a heap, because, well, it's fun to celebrate and be silly when you're 6 or 7 or 8 years old.

After handshakes with the vanquished, the kids pour into the locker room. Coach Chip wants to say a few words. It's the usual postgame palaver. Good game, hard game, made some mistakes, but congrats. He's holding in his right hand a clear plastic cup with the printed inscription: TODAY IS A GREAT DAY FOR HOCKEY! It's a saying from his childhood that he treasures, capturing a once-revered ethic he wants to encourage, even as the scent of tomorrow's rewards cannot be ignored. He gives out the mementos for special performances.

"Amanda, what a game!" he says, handing her one. "Terrific in goal!" She smiles broadly, her cup running over. For now, for her, this will more than suffice.

• • •

In 2006 and without much fanfare, the NCAA marked the 50th anniversary of the athletic scholarship. Even the fact that we call it a *scholarship* is something of a rhetorical coup for the NCAA, which since the inception of the "grant-in-aid"—the official term—has waged a public relations campaign to link such compensation with the educational mission of universities. The NCAA had been formed half a century earlier at the urging of Teddy Roosevelt, whose notions about the nobility of amateur sport were enshrined by the organization in its basic principle that "no student shall represent a college in any intercollegiate game ... who has at any time received, either directly or indirectly, money, or any other consideration." That edict didn't stop ambitious programs from finding ways to entice talented football players, though. So to compete with the richer Northern colleges, the Southern schools pushed for the creation of the grant-in-aid, which soon drew judicial scrutiny as to whether or not such compensation constituted the formation of an employee-employer relationship. The NCAA responded by crafting the term "student-athlete," and embedded it into all rules and interpretations as a substitute for such words as "players" and "athletes." "We told college publicists to speak of 'college teams,' not football or basketball 'clubs,' a word common to the pros," Walter Byers, NCAA executive director from 1951 to '87, wrote in his 1995 book, *Unsportsmanlike Conduct: Exploiting College Athletes*. "I suppose none of us wanted to accept what was really happening." That college sports had embraced pay-for-play.

Byers, now retired and living in seclusion on a ranch in Kansas, advocates the abolition of the athletic grant-in-aid. He argues that assistance should be based strictly on financial need and academic merit. That the NCAA no longer set the terms of a scholarship, and that financial aid offices control the renewal of funds. In short, that an athlete be treated like any other student. Because aid would be need based, athletes from poor families would still get help paying for college. It would be children from affluent backgrounds who wouldn't receive a subsidy.

Remarkably, given Byers' stature, his proposal was summarily ignored. But looked at in a different way, the response is understandable. The year was 1995, and women's sports were finally blooming, thanks to belated enforcement of Title IX.

The core value of Title IX is participation, not commerce. Spiritually, it is about intrinsic, not extrinsic, rewards. But technically the law is about ensuring that girls have access to the same opportunities as boys, who, for better or worse, have been chasing athletic scholarships for decades. Scholarships can be counted and quantified, so they became a key measuring stick to determine which schools were complying with Title IX and which weren't.

Women's sports advocates weren't interested in giving up that hammer. And the NCAA, after years of fighting implementation of Title IX, had come to appreciate the public relations value of promoting gender equity. What better way to justify the growing revenues of big-time football and basketball programs than to plow (some of) the profits into the creation of women's teams? What more effective way of demonstrating that amateurism was still an ideal at the NCAA level than to fund athletes for whom professional leagues are rarely an option? Title IX would help save NCAA's image as an agent of not-for-profit service.

In truth, the football team at Ohio State owes as much to the women's hockey team as vice versa. The former makes the money; the latter keeps those athletic department winnings from being taxed. The need to fund women's sports also blunts arguments for an open marketplace for cash cows such as Troy Smith, whose compensation package was limited by NCAA rules. (The same sort of protective relationship exists between Division I and Division III, which lends its amateur patina to the NCAA enterprise as a whole in exchange for an annual subsidy of $17.9 million, which flows mostly from the March Madness contract. Ithaca's Staurowsky argues that Division III, whose allocation amounts to just three percent of the NCAA budget, has been "bought off too cheap.")

It's a fine arrangement, certainly for the chief beneficiaries: The football and basketball coaches making as much as $3 million a year, the conference commissioners and athletics directors with salaries in the hundreds of thousands, and the massive NCAA bureaucracy required to oversee Division I's ever-expanding, Byzantine rule book. The size and scope of college sports have never been grander, with more teams and more competitors than ever before. And there will always be instances in which some of those athletes—just like some nonathletes—succeed fabulously after their college years.

Less clear is whether the athletic scholarship serves the needs of public health. Since 1990, the amount of aid made available to NCAA athletes—not just women but to men as well—has risen considerably. So has the number of Americans who are between the ages 5 to 19, from 53 to 62 million. Yet, somewhat paradoxically, the number of team-sports participants between 6 and 17 has actually declined; girls' ice hockey is among the few sports that have bucked this trend (in part because it essentially started from scratch and the opportunities to continue playing into college are not yet remote). Far from encouraging broad participation, competition for athletic scholarships in most games appears to be driving kids away. For every child who gets slotted early as a potential college prospect, one or two or three kids must be eliminated. These are often the ones who quit exercising altogether.

Basketball pays the bills at the NCAA's central office, which derives the vast majority of its revenue from its $6 billion contract to televise the men's Division I tournament. Those who say the game is healthier than ever are usually attached in some way to that spectacle—whether they be bookmakers, game analysts, coaches of elite AAU teams, or marketing agents. Down in the grassroots of what is the easiest, cheapest team sport to play, down in the driveways and musty gyms of America, Luther Gulick's game is fading in popularity. Since 1990 the number of children who play basketball at least once a year has fallen by more than three million. Even with an increase in organized play on the high school and AAU levels in the decade leading up to 2000, there are fewer women of all ages playing basketball now than in 1987, before Title IX was enforced. The decline in recent years has been even steeper among males.

Casual players: Down

Frequent players: Down.

Loyalty to the game: Down.

First-year players: Way down.

Even so, there's a team of 8-year-olds in Memphis that can call itself national champions.

AGE 8

MANIFEST DESTINY

Memphis, Tennessee

In the Dominican Republic, where some of the world's best baseball players are cultivated, young boys train daily on grassless fields, in rock-strewn vacant lots, even on the sides of tree-lined hills—just about anywhere that open space can be found. They use old gloves, balls, and bats often provided by a *buscón,* or "finder"—an adult who works kids out by the dozen in the hope that maybe a couple will, when they turn 16, draw enough interest from a Major League Baseball team to get signed. These boys spend their after-school hours developing the hitting, fielding, and pitching skills that stand out in cattle-call tryouts run by major league scouts. The only sounds you hear at the *buscón*'s training sites are the crack-crack-crack of batting practice and some leisurely chatter among boys shagging balls. There are few games played and, thus, no spectators. I've reported on this scene for ESPN, documenting the abuses of *buscones* who change the identities or ages of players then take up to half of their signing bonuses, sometimes with the complicity of major league teams.

When I was in Santo Domingo in 2004, my translator was an easy-going former minor league pitcher named Henry, who at night entered his prize roosters in cockfighting events at the neighborhood *gallera.* He asked if I wanted to join him there one time, just to watch. I said sure, out of morbid curiosity. After paying a small fee at the front we entered the mini-thunderdome, with its 15 rows of seats encircling a combat zone the size of a huge sandbox and lined with artificial turf. Two young roosters in sacks were carried into the ring by their owners. Blindfolds were removed, a referee took his place, and a bell was rung. At first, neither bird seemed all that interested in ripping the heart out of the other. But they were given the tools to do so—steel talons attached to their heels and a limited amount of space in which to engage their territorial instincts. So after walking around aimlessly for a couple of minutes, and hopping out of the ring only to be escorted back in, the cocks found themselves in a corner, beak to beak. Fearfully, one of them jumped into the face of the other; its rival responded in kind. The battle was on, delighting the customers. They feverishly yelled *"Vamos, azul!"* and *"Vamos, blanco!"* until a winner was declared. He celebrated with a cock-a-doodle-doo.

In the U.S., we do sports the other way around, at least when Michael Vick isn't at the helm: The animals get left alone while the children get placed in the ring.

• • •

"Can I have a sub?" Ethan Pangelinian says to his coach during a timeout in the fourth quarter of a pool-play game at the Amateur Athletic Union's 8-and-Under/2nd Grade Boys Basketball National Championships in Memphis. His team, the Basketball Town Pharaohs of Sacramento, Calif., had sprinted to a big halftime lead over the Maryland Heat with a full-court press that caused turnover after turnover. But the Heat are no less relentless on defense, and they have numbers. They brought 15 players to the tournament—only seven Pharaohs made the trip—plus a 75-person support unit that roots with more conviction and attachment than you will find in your average *gallera* or just about any sports setting anywhere. These are mothers, fathers, grandparents, siblings, and cousins who are invested not only financially, as benefactors of the trip, but emotionally, as the boys on the floor are their babies. And babies deserve to be protected and rewarded. So every borderline call from the $22-a-game refs elicits full-throated howls of protest that fill the Hickory Middle School gym. The lead ref, an older man with thick glasses, gets annoyed at first and clenches his fists with each insult absorbed. But the AAU doesn't offer any real guidance on how tightly to officiate games with kids this young—incidental contact is common—so after a while he gets weary of the abuse and begins calling everything on the Pharaohs. One by one the starters foul out. Ethan is exhausted, as he's been on the court most of the second half, and his spotty handle makes him a target. Each time he receives the ball, the Heat players jump in his face, clawing at the prize, as they've been instructed to do by their gyrating, cursing coach. The lead is now down to five points, with a minute to go.

Ethan, with pleading eyes, wants a breather to collect himself, as nothing in his young life has prepared him for such a cauldron. He's not going to get one.

"Nobody left," says his coach, Rod Greene, waving at his three fouled-out players slumped on the chairs behind him. Only four Pharaohs remain and they're all on the court. So Ethan, his dark blond hair matted with sweat, heads back out for what has been reduced to a desperate game of four-on-five. He's still panting.

The Heat, smelling blood, move in for the kill. And well they should. National championship tournaments demand that much.

As recently as 1995, 8 was the average age that boys *began* playing organized sports (it was 10 for girls). Now, 8 is the age at which more than a few of them begin to compete for national titles. The shiny new hardware is dispensed by a growing array of youth sports organizations—one count found 21 such groups in the sport of baseball alone—but few if any entities have been more aggressive in the push downward in age than the Orlando-based AAU, one of the largest actors in youth sports with nearly one million dues-paying child athletes, coaches, and administrators. In '95, the organization put out for bid to local organizers about 100 national championship events, few of them involving children below age 12. Now it sanctions more than 250 such events in which a total of 1,900 age-group champions are crowned, starting around age 6. More often, these tournaments begin at age 8.

It's hard to call many of these events true national championships. Any team could have signed up for the Memphis boys basketball tournament, for instance, as long as it forked over the $625 in registration fees, agreed not to stay in certain unofficial, non-participating hotels, and indemnified the AAU for any harm that might come to its players during the week. The branding of the event as a "national championship" is effectively a marketing gimmick allowing the AAU to charge a robust tournament fee and sell all manner of merchandise to memorialize participation in the event. Teams don't have to qualify through state and district tournaments until the third grade, next year to Ethan and his teammates, when the national championship tournament moves to the Wide World of Sports complex at Disney World. Here in Memphis, scores of 31-3 and 43-0 are not unheard of.

It's also hard to say that anything like the nation's best young basketball talent can be found on the 30 teams that made the trip to Memphis. Some players, such as Coach Greene's son, Devin, show early promise—he can yo-yo the rock and score from as far away as 18 feet. But with most kids, little hands on big balls make it hard to call traveling violations with any precision. Refs feel they must let some of it go

Development of Fundamental Motor Skills

Ages at which 60 percent of children were able to perform at specific skill levels for several motor functions related to athletics.

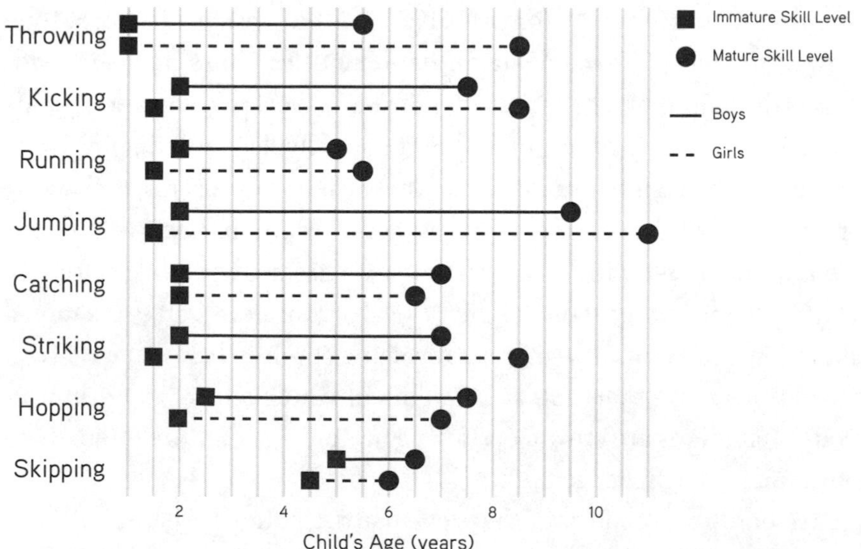

Source: From "Patterns, Phases, or Stages," by V. Seefeldt and J. Haubenstricker, from The Development of Movement Control and Coordination, *J.A.S. Kelso and J.E. Clark, eds., John Wiley, 1982.*

(enter screaming parents) to keep games from going on forever. Shooting on regulation 10-foot baskets by children less than half that height also produces absurdity. Even Devin must heave the ball from his chest, using a technique that will have to be broken as he gets older and grows into his body. The Heat make just 5 of 25 free throws. And rebounds? Kids of this age are pretty much ground-bound. Most cannot begin to jump in what is considered a "mature" biomechanical form until age 9, according to a motor skills study by researchers at Michigan State University (see chart, previous page); and 40 percent of all boys don't reach that benchmark until later. Jumping ability for all boys continues to improve through age 19 (age 16 for girls). So predicting the future for any of these athletes before the end of puberty is a fool's game, especially in basketball with its bias for height.

Finally, it's hard to take seriously an event the magnitude of which its participants can barely comprehend. A day earlier, back at the team hotel, I sat in the sun-splashed lobby with three of the players. One of them was snaggle-toothed Ethan, who says his dream is to be the streetballer Hot Sauce because he saw an And1 video clip and liked that the refs didn't call traveling. The second boy was Devin, the current star of the team, who wants to both play in the NBA and hunt for dinosaur fossils when he grows up. The third was Jay Hope, whose round face, easy smile, and tranquil manner would seem to make him a fine candidate to be the next Dalai Lama; he's the wise point guard, of course, and the son of assistant coach Mickey. The coaches sat nearby, on the lobby's polyester sofas. When I asked the boys if they knew what a national championship was, I got blank stares. So I broke it down, asking if they knew what the word "national" meant.

Ethan shrugged.

Devin said in a barely audible, high-pitched voice, "I forgot."

Jay looked up at me with his Zen-filled mug and offered, "Like, the whole country? The whole world?"

Ding-ding, I said, we have a winner, sort of. Dalai Lama's certainly sharper than I was at his age. In second grade, my world pretty much ended at the edge of town.

Devin was excited to be here, though. "I've never gotten to swim in Tennessee before," he said, and we adults all smiled at how adventurous he finds that to be. In fact, all of the boys were eager to splash around in the hotel pool.

"You win, you get to swim," his father-coach said, knowing full well that a victory in the Heat game also ensures a top 10 finish and automatic bye into next year's national championship at Disney World.

"Yeaaah!" Devin said.

Little kids are easily bribed. But it's hard to get them to care as much about winning this event as the adults who underwrite the affair do. There's just something about those two words—national championship—that engages the competitive impulse and induces fever in the otherwise stable, mature mind. The Assabet Valley parents had great ambitions for their daughters, but USA Hockey holds off on sponsoring national championships until the 12-and-under level, so until then one game or one goal can only mean so much. The prospect of being declared the best 8-year-old basketball team in the land brings those subterranean hopes and fears to the surface, mandating their immediate parental expression. Nowhere in my travels through the youth sports landscape have I seen crowds as intensely engaged as those at this tournament. Early in the Pharaohs-Heat game, one of the Sacramento moms objected to belligerent language used by the Heat moms, turning around in her seat to remind them that these are just 7- and 8-year-olds on the court. "Don't you talk to me," the Heat ringleader shot back defiantly. Her group didn't much appreciate the cute-yet-provocative banners ("Brrr—it's cold in here" ... "The Heat's in California") made by the Pharaoh supporters. The women had to be separated to avoid a fight.

Like the Assabet Valley parents, these parents too can begin to whiff the aroma of college scholarships. One of the leading scouting services, Hoop Scoop, has ranked players as young as those in fourth grade, and the AAU national championships are where those sorts of judgments are first made. Get on the list early, the belief in AAU circles is, and it's hard to fall off. By eighth grade, the NCAA begins mentoring and grooming select players that AAU officials help identify as the best in their class. By ninth or tenth grade, colleges are accepting oral commitments from prospects. No scouting services make an appearance here in Memphis, but get to Disney next year and you're almost into the pipeline. Success here also can raise your profile high enough to pique the interest of sports-apparel companies laying bets on future stars. In Baltimore, just up the highway from where the Maryland Heat's Washington D.C.-area players live, there's an Adidas rep who is about to drop $20,000 in free sneakers and travel money on the team of one especially desirable 9-year-old. Also, kids with reputations have marketing value, so college coaches may recruit them to their lucrative summer camps to encourage sign-ups from other, less-known players. The manic behavior on display in Memphis, while excessive, is effectively encouraged by a system that rewards early talent.

Coach Greene, a vacuum cleaner salesman by day, is a cool character, like the comedian to whom he bears a faint resemblance, Martin Lawrence. But Greene concedes that he, too, has been somewhat obsessed with the "Road to Memphis" since learning 10 months before that the AAU sponsored the tourney. There wasn't even a Pharaohs club team in the age category at the time; the allure of the national championship encouraged him and Mickey Hope to create one. They recruited kids from all over the greater Sacramento area, held tryouts, and picked 15 of them. A couple of weeks before the tournament, though, only six remained. Some had dropped out because of cost; most peeled off because of playing time. "Parents get pissed off if their kids aren't getting minutes," Greene says.

"Some of the kids just weren't good enough," Hope adds.

"Yeah, we got parents who are watching the AAU tournament website right now, checking for scores, and hoping we don't do well," Greene says with a self-conscious chortle. He realizes he's made some adversaries in town by prioritizing the needs of the travel team at the expense of kids interested in less serious forms of basketball. "Our national team was taking so much time, our rec teams got neglected," says Greene, who like Hope runs his own non-profit recreational league in the Sacramento area, the Youth Basketball Alliance in El Dorado Hills. "The parents actually had a meeting and said, 'This isn't what we signed up for.' "

The trip to Memphis became precarious. If they hadn't found Ethan through a friend at the last minute, Greene says, the Pharaohs probably wouldn't have made it. His presence gave them a bench of two, just enough hairless bodies to pull the trigger on a trip that collectively would cost the families of team members about $18,000 between airfare, hotels, meals, transportation, fees, and other items. Ethan, who just lost his baby teeth, became the enabler of others' dreams in exchange for the promise of playing time.

But Hot Sauce Jr. is getting more than he bargained for against the Heat. He's played nearly the whole game. With 41 seconds left on the clock, he fouls out and heads to the bench.

Now there are just three on the court for the Pharaohs. The Maryland boys swarm, smothering Jay, the lone remaining ball handler. One of those flailing arms whacks him across the nose and eyes; he wants to cry. But there's no time for that. The Heat steal an inbounds pass and cut the lead to five.

The clock reads :08. The noise is deafening. The parents are courtside. There's another panicked inbounds pass by the Pharoahs. No player touches it. But the clock starts running anyway. As the ball rolls across the court, the Heat parents scream at the ref to stop the clock. The seconds keep ticking off.

:07

:06

:05

:04

:03

The Heat score at the buzzer, but it's over: 32-29, Pharaohs.

Jay collapses like a punctured balloon at mid-court, buries his face in his hands, and finally allows himself to cry. They are not tears of joy, but of stress from being pushed as far as little kids can or perhaps should be. Later, the Heat coach will crow with pride about how his team broke down the little point guard—evidence, as he sees it, of his team's effective press. He won't be able to claim the W.

"WHOAAAH!" Rod Greene says, sprinting into the locker room ahead of his proud, exhilarated, relieved miniature crew from Sacramento.

In rooster-speak, that's cock-a-doodle-doo.

• • •

The Pharaohs celebrate at Burger King. Kids at one table, adults at another. Then we all caravan across town in rental cars to the massive public high school that serves as headquarters for the 8-and-under and 13-and-under tournaments, the latter of which the AAU had also granted to Memphis and which was simultaneously underway. The AAU has its banners up in the hallways, empty since school let out. "Don't Just Settle for Doing Good," one reads. "Good is no longer good enough," another proposes. Here, good is bad, best as I can tell. Only greatness will do.

The boys take their place in the front row of a cavernous auditorium for the one-hour "Complete Athlete Seminar" that the AAU requires each participating team to attend once during the week. A middle-aged white man in pink shorts walks on stage and, looking at the several dozen kids slumped in their seats, earnestly lists the four characteristics of the AAU's notion of the complete athlete: 1) Sports-mindedness; 2) Seriousness in school; 3) Staying alcohol/drug-free; and 4) Good citizenship. The subject matter appears to bore the teens; the little kids seem more mystified than anything else.

But the man onstage, Steve, is dispensing cash so no one falls asleep. "Name one of the components of the Complete Athlete," Steve asks Devin.

"Good citizenship?" Devin responds.

With that, a five-dollar note is peeled from a stack of fresh bills and handed over, easy as that. Devin smiles down at Abe Lincoln, then up at his dad.

After that, I wander out to the merchandise tables in the hallway where everything from official AAU national championship rubber bands ($3) to programs ($12) to briefcases ($25) to fleeces ($33) to balls ($47) to "NBA style" jersey-and-shorts sets ($60) are sold. One of the reasons so-called national championships have pushed down to increasingly lower ages is that promoters have come to realize that the younger the children are, the greater the money that gets spent. Teenagers often travel to tournaments by themselves, with their teams. But with the little kids, whole families come along for the ride, paying for lots of hotel rooms (for which the tournament's host often gets a referral fee), tickets ($35 for adults, $25 for children for a tourney pass here), concessions (no outside food allowed in gyms), and miscellaneous merchandise. So far, the Greenes alone have purchased $270 worth of T-shirts to bring home, plus a $100 CD of photos from the Heat game.

One T-shirt on the hallway display struck me as ironic, given the behavior at the game. The back read:

I PASSED THE BASKETBALL MOM TEST
☑ WASHED HIS UNIFORM
☑ PAID FOR HIS CAMP
☑ CHEERED FOR HIS TEAM
☑ YELLED AT THE REF

Soon as I begin taking notes, I hear an agitated, deep Southern voice over my right shoulder.

"You a reporter?"

I turn around. There's a big-cheeked man with disheveled hair and a slight paunch that makes his untucked T-shirt drape at the waist. It's Bobby Dodd, president of the AAU and nobody's fool.

"Yes," I respond.

"I'd like you to leave the premises," he says, pointing to the side entrance. "*Now.*"

I figured that this might be how a member of the media would be greeted, which is why I didn't call to let the AAU know that I was coming to Memphis. Dodd has never liked scrutiny of his operation. A few years earlier, for an *Outside the Lines* piece on the lengths to which some travel coaches will go to recruit young talent, I went to Orlando for the 17-and-under AAU national championships. Looking at rosters, I decided to focus on the best local club, the Nike-sponsored Team Florida, whose new center, Amare Stoudemire, was starting get some buzz on the summer circuit but was still an unknown quantity nationally. "You don't want to look at that team," I was told by one of Dodd's lieutenants. Which, of course, made me all the more interested in looking at them.

And the AAU had good reason to worry: Stoudemire had recently moved into the sparkling, new suburban home occupied by his coach, Travis King. That home was, it turned out, owned by Bobby Dodd. He had bought it for the family of King, whom Dodd considered a surrogate son. After working at the AAU national office outside Orlando, King's ambitions shifted to grooming Stoudemire. The high school junior had a miserable academic record and had played almost no organized ball, but he was also extremely quick for a big man. King was among the first to feel *amore* for Amare. In the King family living room, a puffy-haired Stoudemire explained that he had every intention of financially rewarding King once he hit the big time—as he would a few years later in 2002, when he signed a $73 million contract with the Phoenix Suns. If Stoudemire weren't a young athlete, the arrangement might not have raised an eyebrow; his father was dead, his mother was in jail, and he needed a safe place to live. King, and Dodd by extension, can easily be seen as good guys helping an at-risk kid. But amateurism remains an ideal in American sports culture, largely because of the tracks laid down a century ago by the very organization that Dodd now runs, so the subsidizing of a future straight-to-the-NBA man-child just didn't look good.

At the time, Dodd was rather upset by my report, though when I encounter him in Memphis I can't tell if he remembers me.

One thing I remember about him, though: Bobbidodd—as people in Memphis say his name—likes to be understood. So, standing in front of the merchandise counter, I explain to him that I want to understand how young is too young when sponsoring national championships for children, and how low might the AAU go? Might we some day see teams of kindergartners fighting for national bragging rights?

"We're a democracy," Dodd says a few minutes later, after we get talking. "I can't tell ya what a democracy will do. I couldn't tell ya that George Bush would go attack Saddam Hussein, but he did." He's trying to say the massive AAU, which has committees for each sport and 600 board members, will decide. But I want to know what *he* thinks, since Dodd has held great sway over the direction of the organization since rising to its presidency in 1992 and, a few years after that, solidifying his power with the removal of term limits and assumption of the title of CEO as well. Dodd may enjoy a good debate but he remains a czarist figure with a micromanager's touch. "Well, you're talkin' to a man who ran a sports program for 3-year-olds, so that oughta speak for itself," he says. "I ran programs for 3-year-olds as a professional YMCA director. In every sport: basketball, T-ball, soccer. Kids would run over, sit in mama's lap, go pick clover on the soccer field, just have a grand ol' time. I ran those programs for 35 years. I'm living off that retirement now. It's great, you know. And we started around 3." Did you keep score? "Oh, yeah," he says with an obvious sense of pride.

Dodd grew up right here in Memphis. The town formed his values. Situated at the corner of three states—Mississippi, Arkansas, and Tennessee—the River City has always been a magnet for those who prize opportunity. Elvis found his way here, as did Tennessee Williams, B.B. King, and Hulk Hogan. It's a free-spirited, eclectic outpost that values art over science and independence over conformity, then slathers the cultural vibe in a barbeque sauce that the common man can appreciate but will remain a house secret. You see characters in Memphis you just don't see anywhere else. Driving here on this 90-degree day, for example, I cross paths with a middle-aged woman in tight boots, an even tighter camouflage-pattern tank top, and a feathered black cowboy hat who was *sloooowly* pushing an enclosed baby stroller across the street at a suburban intersection. A hot pink thong was wildly exposed, and she wagged her caboose for the idling cars. Hooker with innovative prop? Soccer mom with an outsize sexuality? Who knows?

Dodd encountered much crazier things as an adolescent in Memphis, not all of them so benign. As a 10th grader in 1965, the year his school system was integrated (and three years before Martin Luther King Jr. was shot at a Memphis motel), he noticed a large group of white students beating up a black kid under a tree where smokers normally hung out. "It was just brutal," he says, "so I jumped in to help him. Didn't know him from Adam. Just didn't like the odds. Just didn't think it was fair." The blacks were shocked, the whites even more so. Bobbidodd had been raised in the traditional Southern manner, which meant that he played football, went to church, and honored the prevailing social order. But he says he also took to heart what his Baptist minister preached: Respect everyone. That's what he told mother and daddy when he was asked what the hell he had been thinking.

The brawl left Dodd with scar on one arm and a new perspective on what it means to be a true American. He made black friends, campaigned for black Congressman Harold Ford Sr., and dated a black woman whom he says he would have married if their families would have been more accepting. Dodd even created a word—"ecra"—that didn't stand for anything except his hopes that someday white and black people would have children together and that racial categories would fade. "I coined it and I think I really believed it," he says. "Now I realize the world is bigger than the ecra picture." A trip to China with the U.S. Olympic Committee, of which the AAU is a member, got him thinking about the magnitude of the Asian population. The war in Iraq got him thinking about Arabs and their issues related to cultural understanding and integration. The more he learns, the less he knows. One thing is for sure: The world's a complicated place.

For many years, he also coached basketball teams made up largely of African-American kids from the tough side of town. Longtime NBA guard Anfernee "Penny" Hardaway, who joined Dodd's AAU team as a 10th grader in the late 1980s, told me Dodd opened up his home and wallet to the kids on his teams. "He'd feed you if you were hungry," he said. "You gotta understand, a lot of these kids didn't have clothes to wear. You might have one pair of pants to your name. Whether it was at the Salvation Army or wherever, he'd get you taken care of."

And generally speaking, Dodd wasn't in a financial position to help anyone. During the '80s, he had made what he calls "some bad investments," spent "a lot of money on a lot of things," and built up a mountain of debt. In August of the year he was elected AAU president, in fact, he filed for personal bankruptcy. Court records show that he owed $95,475 on 26 credit cards, another $6,065 in phone bills, and $25,000 on a home loan. He had 12 Visa cards, 11 Mastercards, and no means to pay off any of them. He listed himself as unemployed without an income stream, and told the court he hadn't made a penny in the previous two years. He claimed to have no savings, no stocks, no pension, no annuities. He had $50 in cash, an old Chevy pickup truck, and a couple hundred dollars' worth of clothes. Total assets: $1,450, plus $5,000 in home equity. He was living on $100 a month in food, and $10 in transportation expenses. He had no health or life insurance.

Dodd's track record with money perhaps made him an odd choice to run a major sports organization. But he never told the AAU board of directors that would elect him about his financial distress. Even his closest allies in the organization insist they had no idea Dodd was a debt-strapped pauper—until I asked them if it had been a concern for the AAU, whose history of leaders included such dignitaries as Avery Brundage (who later presided over the International Olympic Committee). "This is the first time anyone has told me Bobby went through personal bankruptcy," said Ron Crawford, longtime AAU treasurer. "I am shocked. I didn't know that." The next morning, Crawford called his good friend to confirm as much, which Dodd did. Then Dodd called me to explain why he hadn't shared that situation with the AAU board.

"I thought it was a personal issue," he said, adding unprompted, that he was not giving money at the time to Hardaway. Just in case anyone was wondering about NCAA rule violations.

His inner circle isn't holding the bankruptcy or the lack of disclosure against him. "I'd still vote for Bobby Dodd," Crawford said. "I've known him since 1980. His heart is as big as a barn." Adds Jeff Hammer, chair of the AAU finance and investment committee: "You know what the scourge of credit cards is. It's hard to have the discipline not to spend."

Besides, the AAU has grown dramatically under Dodd, who brought a big idea to the ancient organization: When a child plays ball, someone's going to make money. "Youth sports is a business," Dodd says. "Across America, it's a business."

Dodd's genius was in figuring that out before anyone else. It was a revelation borne of desperation. For the first 90 years of its existence, the

AAU concerned itself primarily with athletes at the other end of the pipeline. One of its chief functions was choosing the teams that would represent the U.S. in Olympic competition. As the NCAA rose in prominence under Walter Byers in the 1960s, colleges grew less willing to free up their athletes—whose services they effectively had bought and paid for—to represent the U.S. in international events. Some of the nation's top jocks got caught in a nasty jurisdictional battle, finding themselves disqualified from one event or another as the AAU and NCAA fought for control of amateur sports in the United States. At one point, President Kennedy even brought in a retired Gen. Douglas MacArthur to mediate the intractable dispute; history will record that MacArthur was far more effective at resolving World War II. The American public finally lost patience with the situation during the 1972 Olympics in Munich when, at the height of the Cold War, the U.S. surrendered its place atop the medal count to the more organized sports machine of the Soviet Union; the hammer and sickle even beat the U.S. in men's basketball. In 1978 with the passage of the Amateur Sports Act, control of athlete selection was handed to the previously unimportant U.S. Olympic Committee, which until then handled little more than teams' travel plans to the Games. AAU officials were shocked, and for a while many insiders thought the organization might go out of business. Dodd was a low-level zone representative at the time, and he remembers the AAU leadership, a haughty bunch, moaning at their national convention about lost privilege like aristocrats whose trust funds just got pilfered. "When you're selling Chevrolets and Chevrolet takes your franchise away but you still got an auto lot, you gotta figure out what the hell to do," he says. "In essence, Congress took away our license to sell Olympic athletes."

Dodd's idea was to sell little kids instead. Go where Little League had famously gone in baseball a generation earlier, but with more entrepreneurial vigor. As chair of the boys' basketball committee in the 1980s, he helped make that sport the powerhouse of the revitalized AAU by creating more elite tournaments in more age groups. After he rose to the top of the organization, the number of local, district, and national tournaments for kids continued to proliferate across all sports. There are now

48,000 of these events, about 30 of which are held at the 240-acre sports complex that Disney built outside Orlando in 1998 as a tool to help drive up theme-park attendance. The availability of such showcases, in turn, encouraged the creation of more travel teams, whose players and coaches buy annual AAU individual and team memberships in order to be able to play in tournaments. The number of boys playing AAU basketball has doubled to 125,000 since the early 1990s, and there are just as many girls in the fold.

Dodd also has turned the AAU Junior Olympics into a franchise. Like all AAU events, it gets scant media coverage because most child athletes are not yet stars except in their own homes. But a Junior Olympics can bring more than 14,000 children (plus their relatives) to town—that's a lot of heads in beds—so cities compete fiercely to host the annual summer event, sometimes bidding as much as $225,000 for the honor. Then the games begin, and medals are handed out to children in about two dozen sports, and, again, age is not much of a limiting factor. I attended the Junior Olympics in New Orleans a month before Hurricane Katrina hit. I saw a skinny 7-year-old girl dressed in a pink leotard perform clean-and-jerks in a power-lifting event and a 4-year-old from Chicago accept a gold medal in tumbling.

Every expert on child or athlete development who I've spoken to isn't big on dispensing national titles to kids of elementary school age or younger. Colleen Hacker, a Pacific Lutheran University psychology professor who works with the U.S. women's national soccer team, summarizes their concerns best. "It's not that national championships per se are evil," she says. "It's the question of what we lose by focusing on winning when young. Parents and kids think that in order to win, maybe you need to practice longer and year-round. Then kids get asked, 'Are you sure you want to play these other sports and activities?' It's the coattails that come with a focus on excellence that begin to concern many of us who deal with youth athletes. Gradually their world begins to shrink so that all of their achievement, all of their self-worth, all of their confidence at a very young age is from one place. That's where the danger occurs.

"For many parents and coaches, we sort of play with words a little bit when we enter kids into these events. We call it encouragement or support or facilitating their interest. Kids call it pressure, and I think that's the most accurate take on it. Again, it's not that pressure is negative. But it can't be pressure all the time. Everything is not do or die. And the problem as we move through national championships is everything becomes do or die. You win, you advance; you lose, you go home. It's very immediate. And the problem with that is kids begin to get tense. They begin to fear failure, yet failure is part of the process of achievement. We problem-solve, we learn, we grow through our mistakes. In national championships, we can't afford mistakes. And when a mistake does occur, you feel as though the entire team outcome is resting on what you did wrong. We want sports to be a fun experience. The focus needs to be on mastery and developing skills, rather than a focus on beating the other guy. Unfortunately, with many elite programs it's a case of focused excellence at the expense of individual development. And it's focused excellence at the expense of broad-based participation."

MYTH NO. 8

Grade-school travel teams identify future stars.

THE TRUTH

They reward early bloomers, leaving the rest behind.

The American Academy of Pediatrics, too, recommends a "focus on enjoyment rather than competition" in organized sports through age 9. Dodd wonders who made the experts the experts. He didn't consult them or their research about what's age appropriate in youth sports when adding all these tournaments, and he isn't going to start now.

"I don't know how much all this really impacts an 8-year-old," he says. "Prolly the only thing an 8-year-old remembers 'bout bein' here was he mighta got a five dollah souvenir from Steve. And I'm not sure he'd remember that."

• • •

One state without a team in this tournament is Minnesota.

For a decade and a half, Dan Klinkhammer was Dodd's man in the Land of 10,000 Lakes. As co-founder of the Minnesota Youth Athletic

Services (MYAS), a non-profit dedicated to creating athletic participation opportunities for children, he became the AAU's service agent for all sports in the same year that Dodd was named president. The contract gave him the responsibility of organizing AAU teams and events in the state—and incentive to bust tail for his cut of the fees collected. A former high school football captain, Vietnam vet, and parks-and-rec director, Klinkhammer was so dogged in his promotion of the AAU that he twice won the annual President's Leadership Award. Crisscrossing the state in a four-wheel drive pickup that finally quit after logging 192,000 miles, he signed up enough new members to make the state the fourth-largest AAU district. Basketball is the crown jewel of the AAU, and for three years running Minnesota, once a backwater, had the largest boys and girls' hoops programs in the nation.

Before long, though, coaches and the families of players became upset with the expense involved with playing what is a simple game. Between the mandatory annual AAU membership fees for players ($12 minimum today), coaches ($14), and participating clubs ($30 minimum), a team can spend more than $200 before it ever takes the court for an area invitational tournament, which typically costs it another $150 to $400. The fees were half as much in the 1990s, yet teams back then still could drop a grand for a weekend tournament, including the hotel costs. For clubs from less wealthy areas, it seemed more like an exercise in profiteering than participation. "You guys are nothing but thieves and crooks," one small town coach told Klinkhammer after getting bounced from a tournament after two games.

Klinkhammer found it hard to justify the fees. The overwhelming majority of annual club and individual dues went to the national office in Orlando. What exactly were Minnesotans getting in return for that investment? It wasn't clear. They couldn't see the value in funding AAU national conventions in exotic locales such as Maui and Puerto Rico, where its massive board of directors—a cast of hundreds—tweaked rules, shared ideas, and acquired tans. And few local teams had interest in competing for national championship tournaments, which usually were held in some Southern state. Many teams just wanted to play in two or three weekend tourneys in the spring, before the snow disappeared and kids' interests turned to baseball and softball. The big selling point for AAU annual membership was that it paid for secondary medical insurance in case kids got injured. But only $2 of each player's dues fee goes toward insurance and, Klinkhammer says, 93 percent of the Minnesota kids were already covered by their family's insurance. "Very few people here got anything from the AAU's insurance," he says. One year, he says, fewer than five Minnesotans filed claims and only one received a payout. (The AAU's insurance broker says that about 750 members nationwide—roughly one of every 800—receives some payout annually, in amounts ranging from $1 to the policy max of $50,000.)

The AAU's individual sport committees also wring significant revenue from event operators. The committees control the rights to tournaments, which in the case of a national basketball championship can sell for upwards of $25,000; they also get a large chunk of each team's entry fee. The AAU charges lower fees for local or district tournaments but, remember, there are tens of thousands of these events. The dollars flowing to these national committees drive up the fees that end up getting passed on to local organizers and local teams, inevitably limiting the pool of children who can afford to compete. The cost structure begs for total commitment to the sport, or none at all.

Frustrated, Klinkhammer began affiliating some of the events he was running with other organizations, such as the Minnesota Golf Association and the U.S. Sports Specialty Association. Upfront fees to teams got cut by 90 percent in many cases, he says. Sign-ups rose dramatically. And Klinkhammer made it clear to all those organizations that no outside affiliation would be needed for MYAS events in which qualifying for national championships was not a goal, so don't lean on him to get his customers to pay pre-tournament dues. "We were never designed to be the slave to any national organization," he says. "We were designed to serve the citizens of Minnesota."

The AAU terminated his contract in 2005. It hardly hurt his group. Even without a national affiliation, MYAS has been able to create one of the largest basketball tournaments in the country. Each March, 1,100 boys' and girls' teams from fifth through ninth grade compete in the Grade State Championship. The key to its success is spreading the wealth. There are no bid fees for host sites, just a sharing of revenues with MYAS. More local money stays local, defraying the costs of running community-based teams. "We're not just catering to the elite athletes," Klinkhammer said. "We are literally getting everyone to play."

He doesn't miss the AAU. By the time they parted ways, Klinkhammer already had a strained relationship with Dodd. He had fought Dodd over his insistence on requiring tournament teams to stay in hotels that agreed to give rebates to the AAU event organizer. There's plenty of money to be made via such a policy: Youth and high school sports now account for about 35 percent of all overnight stays that Americans make related to travel for organized sports events. Klinkhammer felt that if a family could save money by staying at grandma's place or at a campground or cheaper hotel, so be it. When hosting the 12-and-under AAU national baseball championship, he placed no restrictions on team accommodations.

Klinkhammer also objected to the cozy relationship Dodd held with one AAU executive who would later admit to a felony. Mike Sweeney, former member of its executive committee and head of its New England district, pleaded guilty in 2002 to bank fraud for bilking New Hampshire financial institutions of $257,000. He had juggled deposits and checks in accounts tied to a bingo operation that the AAU district had been allowed to set up, based on its status as a non-profit. Sweeney ran one bingo operation under the business ID of the New England AAU, the other under that of the national AAU. Together, the two charitable gaming initiatives reportedly brought in an average of $4.97 million from 1997 to '99.

Sweeney was hardly a stranger to Dodd during that time. He had helped Dodd gain access to discount cars for himself, four staff members, and two of his unadopted "kids." Also disclosed by the *Orlando Sentinel* was that for at least two years Sweeney had sent $1,500 a month to Dodd's AAU club that hosts the national championship tournaments, the Youth of Memphis Competitors Association (YOMCA). Dodd would later tell me his club received money over a longer period: $15,000 a year between 1995 and 1999, for a total of $75,000.

Given the unusual nature of a district leader providing cash to a club in another part of the country, Dodd was asked to explain himself at a meeting of top AAU leaders at national headquarters in February 2002. Microphone in hand, he responded that his executive committee had given him the OK to take the money, "that they would take any sponsorships on any events that they could get, however they could get them." Privately, Dodd had his own questions about the propriety of the YOMCA payments. "What I did do after that," he told me later, "because it did make me wonder, I took one more check and then I told New England, 'I'm not going to do that because it could be perceived as something wrong.' " But at the time, he defended his judgment. Klinkhammer, who was in the room, sat in stunned silence, questions running through his head. *Were they laundering money? Was this a kickback to Dodd for keeping Sweeney as chair of the AAU insurance committee? Was this hush money so Dodd wouldn't tell anybody that New England was using the AAU's tax ID number for gaming?* Klinkhammer realized this was all just speculation, and Dodd quickly moved on to the next agenda item. But Klinkhammer later shared his dismay with the man who until then had treated him as AAU Golden Boy, or at least its Golden Goose.

"I am still amazed that Bobby survived that situation," Klinkhammer says now. "He made a special trip to Minnesota back in 2004 just to try to smooth things over with me. When I asked him again about his acceptance of money from Sweeney's gambling operation, he told me he had 'made an error in judgment.' I told him, 'Where I come from, we don't call that bad judgment. We call that bad character.' "

One thing that Dodd cannot be accused of is lacking loyalty to his longtime associates. On the morning that Sweeney entered his guilty plea in a federal courthouse in Concord, N.H., Dodd testified to the quality of his character. Just a few months before, the AAU's executive committee had created new guidelines to keep felons out of the organization. "My take is you had a well-meaning person and something happened," Dodd says. "I would have owed [testifying] to any volunteer." Sweeney appeared before the judge wearing a tan golf shirt with a red, white, and blue AAU logo sewn on its chest. He would be sentenced to a year and a day in prison.

The AAU is run by volunteers, but questions about its leaders profiting from their positions within the organization are not uncommon. Some conflicts of interest have been readily disclosed. In its 2004 federal tax filing, the AAU notes that the organization's investments are managed by the same New York firm that at the time employed Jeff Hammer, chair of both the AAU's finance and investment committees. Hammer, who would retire as a Morgan Stanley vice president in 2006 while continuing on in his AAU capacity, said he did not personally manage or profit from the account, which controlled all of the organization's securities ($5.1 million in '04).

Other potential conflicts are not discussed in the tax document. One of the AAU's sponsors is Nike, which Dodd says pays a "very minimal" fee to the national office—he implied that it was between $25,000 and $100,000 a year, but wouldn't commit to a number. Meanwhile, the apparel company has separate financial arrangements with individual AAU clubs run by Dodd in Memphis and Marcellus "Boo" Williams in Virginia. The influential chairman of the AAU's Boys Basketball Committee, Williams runs a summer league which for many years has received cash and products from Nike ($115,000 worth in 2004). "We're consultants," says Williams, who also sits on a Nike advisory board on grassroots basketball. Given that Nike money is highly coveted on the travel basketball scene—Williams says the company funds only 45 clubs—the fact that two of those clubs are run by high-ranking AAU officials naturally begs the question, How do those relationships affect Nike's ability to cut a favorable sponsorship deal with the AAU's national office? Could the larger body of child athletes get shortchanged for the sake of those on two well-positioned clubs? Nonsense, says Dodd, who claims his Memphis club is getting less than $25,000 a year from Nike. "The AAU is lucky to have Nike as a sponsor," he says. "If anything, we've been able to hold on to them because of Boo's involvement."

Ron Crawford, the AAU treasurer, also runs a Nike-sponsored club in Arkansas, but that's not the conflict that drew criticism when he was running for re-election several years ago. Klinkhammer, who ran against him, objected to Crawford's ownership interest in a company that in the 1990s manufactured the AAU's official clothing sold at events, a marriage Crawford had arranged. "As I think about it in hindsight, I can see where someone would be uncomfortable about that," Crawford says. "I won't do business with the AAU again for any price. Quite frankly, even though I saved the Union money, I don't want the perceived conflict of interest." Crawford says he is unsure how much business the company, Gameday Apparel, did with the AAU before it was closed earlier this decade but that the amount was "insignificant."

Dodd, like each of the top five AAU officials, for many years has been listed on tax forms as receiving no salary. It's been a selling point during his re-election campaigns. But he's received the use of an Orlando-area house owned by the AAU, a car allowance, and all his food for free. The organization lets Dodd live in the house because, according to the AAU's tax filing, he is a Tennessee resident who "travels to Florida for work with the organization. The house is provided for him in lieu of providing a hotel room." Dodd, though, told me he spends only two weeks a year in Memphis, much of it running the two national championship tourneys.

AAU insiders moan about the propriety of the organization granting those tournaments to Dodd's personal AAU club, the one to which Sweeney contributed. Officially Dodd is listed only as a director of the Youth of Memphis Competitors Association, but he holds the club's financial books, signs its tax forms, and claims to donate more time—10 hours a week on top of the 40 he logs at the AAU national office—than any other officer. During tournament games, the Pharaohs drank out of water coolers that were marked, simply, "Bobby Dodd." That year, 2005, the YOMCA reported revenues of $298,841 from tournaments and leagues, against expenses of $203,538; most of the surplus went to team travel. Here, as with the AAU national office, Dodd listed himself as taking no salary.

All of which has made Dodd one of the most philanthropic people in youth sports, or one of its cleverest. Since filing for bankruptcy in '92 and taking his unpaid position with the AAU, he has managed to find the resources to buy the house for King's family that Amare Stoudemire lived in—funds he says came from inheritance from his father's death in 1998—and financially assist several other children he came to know through his Memphis basketball program. He's paid for flutes, cars, and college tuitions. "Like they are your own kids," he says. Photos of these children line the walls of his cluttered office on the Disney property, where the AAU has been based since Dodd moved the national office from Indianapolis in 1996.

Though it's not publicly disclosed, Dodd has derived some income from the AAU. Remember that Complete Athlete presentation at which Devin earned a five-dollar souvenir? On a tax filing signed and provided to me by Dodd, the AAU claimed to have spent $712,000 that year on these presentations, which are held at national basketball championships and reach approximately 5,000 athletes. That works out to an average of $142 spent on each kid. It's hard to fathom where all of that expense might be going. As far as I could tell, the seminar consisted of Steve—the site coordinator—talking on stage about making good choices and then handing out small amounts of cash to several boys. In closing, he invited all of them on their way out to grab a "Smart Athlete Strategizer"—a spiral-bound homework organizer that costs the AAU $5 a unit.

Dodd, when pressed, allows that he received a consultant's fee from the basketball committee for presenting the Complete Athlete program where he sometimes speaks. But he says the figure was modest—he got just $16,500. So how did the AAU end up claiming $712,000 in expenses for the program? "I think there might be an extra zero on the end," he suggests at first. Later, in a subsequent e-mail, Dodd offers up a different reason: The AAU accidentally gave incorrect information to the IRS. When his finance director researched it, he wrote, she "discovered that the $700,000 represented all training, education, and expenses associated with AAU such as training, workshops, conventions, sports meetings, etc. and included the Complete Athlete. The auditors had simply picked up the first topic of the list which was the Complete Athlete."

Dodd declined to make available a copy of the AAU's annual audit, which would provide more detailed financial information than the tax filing. The only audit from any year to which I had access is from 2002, forwarded to me by an AAU delegate to the national convention who has since left the organization. The report, by the consulting firm KPMG, says a total of $123,400 that year was "paid to sports chairpersons and Board and Executive Committee members for services provided to the Organization during the year;" no names of the recipients, or the services provided, are listed.

None of which means that anyone is getting rich on the sly. Just that volunteer service isn't always volunteer service. And that it's not clear who exactly is benefiting from the reconstructed, kid-funded AAU—starting with Dodd himself, who once suggested in an executive committee meeting that the "loosey-goosiness of this association is the real question." He made that comment during the Sweeney scandal, but the sentiment holds today amid the AAU's many pockets of robust, mysterious cash flows. Not that his trusty executive committee is concerned.

"I can assure you there is no hidden chateau or Maserati," Jeff Hammer says. "Bobby doesn't drink wine, and he's not a fancy food guy. And God knows he doesn't spend money on clothes. He doesn't even have nice sneakers."

His allies on the executive committee are so sure he's doing a good job they want to give him a big raise. In 2006, they would approve a formal CEO's salary of $200,000 to $250,000, according to Dodd. Now that he's approaching his 60th birthday, Dodd says he's leaning toward taking it, even if some of his perks go away. He's already starting to phase out his Complete Athlete speaking gigs. "I'm getting too old and can't relate to kids today," he says. (Crawford, the treasurer, confirmed in December 2007 that Dodd has begun to take a salary of an undisclosed amount.)

In Minnesota, the AAU's one-time missionary is moving on as well, to a more open church. "The AAU leadership is extremely unethical, and I don't want to be associated with that," Klinkhammer says.

He doesn't need to be, anymore. Without the AAU's front-end fees, MYAS now serves 110,000 children in eight sports. That's more than one-sixth as many child and adult members as the AAU has nationwide. "The AAU's motto is 'Sports for All, Forever,' but that's not the motto they live by," he says. "They're more concerned with elite teams and championships." Crawford denies this allegation, while allowing he does have concerns about the impact of these tournaments on the quality and quantity of players coming up through the system. In 2006, he cancelled all teams under the age of 14 in his Arkansas Wings AAU club. "I just don't want to fight the battles with parents anymore," he says. "You want your 8-year-old ranked? Gimme a break."

When Bobbidodd was 8 years old, he was, in his own words, "a fat Johnny" who sat on the end of the bench of his church-league basketball team because his coach didn't want to play him. That much he does remember about age 8. After his freshman year of high school, he was done with organized sports. So he's not unsympathetic to the need to keep as many kids as possible active and engaged. Every year, he says, he lobbies to add an "everyone plays" rule to AAU basketball in the youngest age groups. Every year, the committee for that sport shoots him down. "I do worry about the message we're sending in terms of competitive travel teams," he says after we've been talking for a while. "How do we get parents to realize that the prize is that you get to travel and not that your kid's going to be the next LeBron? Twenty years from now, I think all of us who are responsible—youth sports organizations, the media, the NCAA, and the professional leagues—are going to look back and say we should have done things differently."

Not that he feels empowered to change course now. He has a business to run, and its model revolves around national sponsors, clubs panning for elusive scholarships, and obligations to partners such as Disney, which contracts with many organizations to bring 180 youth sport events a year to its $150 million complex.

"The horse," he says, "is out of the barn." And chewing on the grassroots.

AGE 9

MOSCOW ON THE MIND

Washington, D.C.

Travel teams are no longer an add-on to the youth sports landscape, like the postseason all-star teams of previous generations. In many communities, after the age of 9 or 10, they effectively *are* youth sports. That's the case with soccer in my Connecticut town of 10,000. Once the travel squads are formed, the in-town rec league begins to feel second-class and shrivels in size. By fifth grade, if you don't choose to go out for travel or don't make the team, your only option might be to cobble together a team from several age grades and play in a rec league run by a larger neighboring town. And the fifth graders who make travel are usually the fourth graders who made travel, who are the third graders who made travel. These are the kids who survive tryouts because they have some experience, understand the system, and the coach knows them. They will go on to populate the lone middle school team, the lone high school jayvee team, and, unless they burn out, the lone high school varsity team. It would be nice to think that my son Cole could wait a few more years before taking up the game, but it just doesn't seem realistic. He'd have to be a gifted athlete—and have a coach who was willing to interrupt practice to teach him remedial tactics. So, for us, letting Cole try out for the town travel team starting in third grade was, oddly enough, a conservative move, the preserving of an option. I suspect that's the rationale of many parents.

Cole and 13 others made the team. On the whole, it's been a positive experience. He's with a great group of kids who support each other and play with remarkable discipline and selflessness. Our sideline can get intense at times, but most of the parents try to adhere to the pledges signed before the season not to bark instructions (I'm no saint; I've done it on occasion) or not to work the refs (I've managed to restrain myself there). It's gotten easier to do with each passing year, as the realization sets in that all this emotion is expended not for the boys' benefit, but for our own. Cole enjoys his coaches, who have been fair with playing time and understand when a Little League game in the spring conflicts with a travel soccer event. From his regular position at left fullback, Cole plays with tremendous pride, and rarely gives up a goal. Learning other positions would help his development, but all in all, he's happy. He keeps asking to be signed up—as long as room is left in the schedule for friends, skateboarding, and other sports. For him and most teammates, early travel ball has been a good thing.

I'm less sure that it's been good for other kids, the community, or even the sport.

Most of the boys who didn't make the team the first year didn't try out the next year. Did they lose interest? No confidence? Hard to know. They weren't around to be asked. But those who work with children will tell you that the earlier kids are told that they're not good enough at an activity, the less likely they are to set out to prove the community wrong. They get the hint; they move on. In Year 2 of Cole's travel team, there also weren't many *new* kids who mustered the courage to try out. In the third year, as the boys entered fifth grade, a second "B" travel team was created—but only because just enough energy had been drawn out of the town rec league that the rec league no longer had enough bodies to remain viable. Travel was the only fifth-grade option for the remaining boys, most of whom were less game-ready than the "A" teamers who were closer to (if still far from) the 10,000-hour mark that some contend is required for expertise in any activity. One new kid was added to the "A" team and one was subtracted to make room for the newcomer. If that sounds like a simple mathematical equation, you probably weren't the parent who had to tell the lone 10-year-old boy he was no longer deemed good enough to play with his friends.

Around age 12, the pyramid will narrow further. If history serves as any precedent, about half a dozen of the better players could be recruited away to what in New England are called "premier" teams, which are expensive, private programs that draw talent from anywhere, not just within the town's boundaries. The loss of those bodies will soon bring an end to the travel teams, as fielding even one team gets more difficult once play moves from eight-on-eight to 11-on-11 on the larger pitch.

Premier programs are led by paid coaches with impressive credentials who work with the players year-round. They justify their fees by pursuing state and national championships and providing access to the tournaments where college scouts congregate. They also use their connections to help their players gain roster spots on the state's Olympic Development Program (ODP) teams, an initiative for which the stated goal is to "identify players of the highest caliber on a continuing and consistent basis which will lead to increased success for the U.S. National Teams in the international arena." These kids, in theory, are the best of the best, and inclusion on the team offers exposure to top regional and national team coaches.

The result of all this early aggregating and winnowing of presumed talent?

"I started it," says the godfather of Connecticut soccer, Al Bell, "and it's been a massive failure." As former president of the state Junior Soccer Association, Bell opened the door to the creation of premier teams in 1989 by lifting the residency rule requiring kids to play strictly for town-based teams. Forget the national team, he says: "We've hardly had anyone even play in Major League Soccer who has come out of a premier club. We've had no success stories."

Larger states can claim better outcomes, but success is relative. The problem is the same everywhere: Soccer isn't focusing its development resources on the best prospects. The pipeline narrows at too early an age for scouts to know where to place their bets. The child who stands out in elementary school is typically the one with a physical advantage. "By selecting out players at 12, 13, even 14, we miss a lot of players," says Gary Allen, director of coaching education in Virginia. "I wouldn't start travel teams until 14. Otherwise we favor the bigger, stronger, faster players." And the financially secure kids, whose families can afford the thousands of dollars it costs to play on premier and ODP teams. The economic structure of elite soccer is one big reason why the sport in the U.S., unlike everywhere else in the world, is largely a game of the suburban middle class.

There is talent in urban, lower-income areas—lots of it. In some immigrant communities, especially those such as Hartford where many Latinos live, parks are busy on weekends with pickup and league games. What the best of these kids sometimes lack in tactical knowledge and physical stature they make up for with creativity and technical skill. But my son's travel team rarely plays any of these teams, as few of them are registered with the state soccer association. These players rarely come out for ODP tryouts, and scouts aren't driving into these communities to find them. These prospects exist outside the mainstream, never fully honing talent that could be electric if plugged into a good system.

In basketball, promising talent is harder to miss. Eventually, the kid whose head bobs above those of his peers when walking down the street is bound to be asked if he wants to play the game. The dysfunction in the development process occurs once the genetic outlier can demonstrate that he is coordinated enough to put the ball in the hoop a bit, too. He becomes a commodity to be endlessly recruited by travel-team coaches whose access to sneaker money and goods depends on acquiring and retaining players with potential NBA futures. Unable to sign players to contracts without sacrificing their future college eligibility, these coaches are in no position to force their rainmakers to learn the less glamorous parts of the game lest they lose them to a rival, which happens all the time.

The U.S. national team that took bronze at the 2006 World Championships was merely the latest to emerge from the youth hoops' star-centric paradigm. Their athleticism was breathtaking. Their enthusiasm was admirable. LeBron James, Carmelo Anthony, and pals listened to their coach and earnestly tried to play like a team. But many of them did not know how to move without the ball, so the offense stagnated. And they struggled to defend plays as simple as the pick-and-roll. The U.S. fell to unheralded if fundamentally adept Greece in the semis, denying the team a shot at redemption after placing third at the '04 Olympics and sixth at the '02 Worlds. "It was an AAU game all over again," says Brian McCormick, a Sacramento-based youth basketball trainer, author, and analyst who has coached and given clinics on four continents. "Everyone was standing around, waiting for their one-on-one. Our guys didn't know how to make their teammates better."

I suggest that perhaps the addition of Kobe Bryant and other new players at the Beijing Olympics might bring gold. Perhaps, McCormick says, but that will only mask the system's underlying flaws. "We need to change the culture, not just the names on the back of the Team USA jerseys," he says.

In the U.S., the developmental challenges that soccer faces differ from those of basketball, which differ than those of baseball, and so on. Each sport has its unique issues to confront in serving kids and athletes well in the new century.

But most of them share a common partner.

Right now, that partner is largely silent.

• • •

The Amateur Sports Act of 1978 not only put the U.S. Olympic Committee in charge of directing international competition, it also made the organization the coordinating body for grassroots sports—and by extension youth sports—across the nation. This was thought to be a fine idea at the time, for the key to beating back the Soviets and East Germans, it was argued on Capitol Hill, was to crush them with sheer numbers. While our ideological rivals were selecting out 9-year-olds for elite year-round training, we would counter with mass participation under the assumption that the very best talent would naturally and inevitably emerge. The heartless sport chieftains of the Eastern Bloc were welcome to throw eggs against the wall to see which of them did not break; we would give our chicks time to hatch before introducing the best of them to a rigorous training regimen. We would do it the American Way, and democracy would rule. Cue the fife and drum.

"This legislation is not a bill merely to assist Olympic and 'elite' athletes. Far from it," declared a young Republican from Alaska, Ted Stevens, on the Senate floor during the debate leading up to the vote. "I am hopeful that with the new goals and directives for both the Olympic Committee and the national governing bodies, it will be easier for all Americans to find programs and facilities through which they can further their athletic interests."

A few minutes later, the bill's cosponsor, Richard Stone, a Democrat from Florida, made his plea. "This country's lack of success in amateur sports is not due to any shortage of talent or lack of resources," he said. "Our problem stems from a failure to encourage physical fitness and better athletic programs." The nation was beginning to see the first signs of both the obesity epidemic and the trend toward lavishing training resources on select preadolescent athletes. "If our people have greater opportunities to compete in athletics at the grassroots level," Stone said, "America's performance at the international level will be second to none."

The Senators' intentions were reflected in the original draft of the bill, in its statement of purpose. Above all, the goal of the law was to "encourage participation in amateur athletic activities by citizens of the United States." Its vehicle, the USOC, would be required to establish national goals for amateur athletic activities, protect the opportunity of any athlete who wanted access to competition, expand access to sports by women and racial minorities, promote physical fitness, and "assist organizations and persons concerned with sports in the development of amateur athletic programs for amateur athletes."

How would the USOC achieve this vision? The blueprint had been laid out by the President's Commission on Olympic Sports, a panel of coaches, athletes, and legislators assembled under President Gerald Ford. Its members included NFL quarterback Jack Kemp and 1936 Berlin Olympics sprint medalist Ralph Metcalfe—both congressmen at the time—and its urgent report, which prompted the hearings, called for the funding of amateur sports to "reach across the whole system rather than remain confined to a few niches of affluence." For new research in sports science and medicine that would get pushed down the pipeline. For the creation of "high, clear standards" of certification for coaches. For the strengthening of club systems "to mesh with school sports programs." For the building of facilities in the "most needy" amateur sports. The commission estimated that all of this would cost the public the relatively modest sum of $83 million a year.

By the time the bill left the House of Representatives, however, the last of the proposed subsidies had been stripped out of the law. The USOC would have to make do with whatever cash flowed from its designated monopoly on the Olympic marks, such as sponsor and broadcast revenues. With a stroke of President Jimmy Carter's pen, the USOC had a mandate—an unfunded one, but a mandate nonetheless.

At the time the USOC was little more than a travel agency. The committee consisted of a handful of desk jockeys in Manhattan waiting on the AAU and other controlling bodies to submit the lists of athletes who needed transportation to the Olympics. Among its biggest decisions was the choice of blazers, ties, and hats worn by the delegation as they shipped off to overseas Games. Now the private, not-for-profit corporation was being moved to an abandoned Air Force site in Colorado Springs, Colo., where it would oversee a training facility and coordinate the hodgepodge of organizations that serve young athletes in the country—everything from the sport federations to the YMCA to the now-disgruntled AAU. This would be no easy task. Not only was the USOC one of the only Olympic committees in the world without taxpayer funding, its governance structure wasn't even made all that clear by the law.

Despite the obstacles, some progress was made. One of the first initiatives was the annual U.S. Olympic Festival, which brought together as many as 3,000 up-and-coming athletes in 38 sports. Many of them were teenagers who were among the best prospects in their region. It wasn't a true grassroots solution—the number of participants was too small to qualify as such—but the festivals did spark the construction of velodromes, swimming halls, and other facilities built by host cities such as San Antonio, St. Louis, Oklahoma City, Raleigh-Durham, and

Indianapolis. Those venues would become training sites for athletes from newbie to elite levels. The festivals didn't offer the marquee names necessary to make the event a television spectacle, but as many as 1,400 journalists were credentialed to cover their hometown heroes. These festivals bred the Olympic beat writer, a species that few newspapers had employed previously. The event recruited medical personnel and sports administrators into the Olympic movement, creating opportunities to throw knowledge into the pipeline. It brought fans, athletes, and funding to obscure sports. Eventual stars picked up valuable experience: Most medalists who won summer Olympic medals in subsequent Games passed through the festivals, from boxer Mark Breland to gymnast Mary Lou Retton to sprinter Carl Lewis. "Never has there been an event associated with the USOC that has generated more goodwill around the country," says Bob Condron, longtime USOC director of media services. "The festivals probably helped the grassroots as much as anything else."

Then came the 1988 Winter Olympics in Calgary, where the U.S. won just two gold and six total medals. It was the nation's poorest showing in 52 years, good for ninth on the international medal count. Watching in horror from his Manhattan living room, The Boss was livid. Ordinarily, George Steinbrenner losing his cool is only of consequence to his highly paid chattel in the locker room of the New York Yankees, the baseball club he owns and, to that point, had had mixed success with. But the boat builder from Cleveland had the ear of USOC president Robert Helmick and strong opinions on how to right America's ship. He was named chair of an outside review committee, the USOC Overview Commission, a.k.a. the Steinbrenner Commission, whose charge was to audit the direction of the USOC. "We're going to tell it like it is, and that may not please some people," Steinbrenner huffed, patriotism coursing through his veins.

The performance in Calgary wasn't all that shocking, actually. America has never been a powerhouse in the Winter Olympics, dominated as those Games are by Scandinavian and Eastern Bloc nations farther north of the equator. Most of the medals being handed out were in events that require the wearing of long, thin boards on the bottom of one's feet. The rank of a nation could rise and fall dramatically based on the showing of a couple stalwarts. Four years earlier, with alpine skiing twins Phil and Steve Mahre leading the way in Sarajevo, the U.S. had the third-most gold medals—with just four (and eight total medals).

The Steinbrenner Commission called for greater government support of the USOC. But that wasn't the take-away message of its report, released the following February. It was this: Priorities needed to shift further to supporting those athletes who had the best chance of standing on the podium at upcoming Games. "With the limited resources available, the USOC must focus on activities that are central to its mission, and not weaken its effort by trying to be all things to all people," the report concluded. It construed the USOC's mission as delivering immediate performance results. It was a move straight out of the operations manual for the Yankees, who have traditionally been willing to trade away farm system talent for stars who might help the big club win now.

Monetary awards for medal performances were created—and support for organizations that develop nonelite athletes withered. In 1995, research by the *Atlanta Journal-Constitution* found that since the release of Steinbrenner's report direct grants to community sports groups totaled slightly more than $1 million—an amount equal to less than one-fifth of one percent of all revenues the organization collected during that time. A Senate hearing was called. Donna de Varona, a former Olympic swimming champion and USOC board member who helped draw up the Amateur Sports Act, testified that the USOC hadn't lived up to the mandate of the law. Tom McMillen, then co-chair of the President's Council on Physical Fitness and Sports and a former Olympic basketball player, objected to the drift toward an elitist model, pleading, "When will America wake up? When we pay $100 million for a superstar's salary and have nothing left for our children: no physical education, no bats, no balls, no grassroots sports at all?"

McMillen was exaggerating for effect. But he knew the soul of the organization, and by extension amateur sports in the U.S., was up for grabs. And, for a moment, it appeared that he and his allies were gaining traction. Just as the Atlanta Olympics arrived, a Carnegie Commission report found that "sports in America represent a highly exclusionary process, with only the elite performers accorded a share of the spotlight." Separately, a watershed report by the Surgeon General (see Age 3) was released noting that 60 percent of Americans were not regularly active and that physical activity declined dramatically during adolescence. It called for a "massive national commitment" by public and private leaders to turn around the ominous trends. And the USOC had fresh resources to do its part, thanks to a 10 percent cut of the stunning $2.3 billion contract NBC had inked with the International Olympic Committee to broadcast the Games through 2008. McMillen suggested that at least 25 percent of the USOC's annual budget be directed to the needs of youth sports.

But here's the thing about having to pay your bills largely with sponsorship dough: You gotta listen to your sponsors. And the broadcast and corporate partners were telling the USOC leadership that they, like The Boss, wanted winners *now*. They had Fortune 500 businesses to run and to them the Olympic movement was the Olympic Games. (Jack Welch, who ran GE during the years that NBC bid up the Games' television contract, told me he didn't even realize that the USOC was charged with coordinating grassroots sports, too). The Atlanta Games became the most commercialized Olympics in history. It was Times Square in the middle of Baron de Coubertin's herb garden, with a billboard on every exploitable space. That the chief advertisers included corporations shilling beer, fast food, and soda—not exactly foodstuffs consistent with the Amateur Sports Act's mandate to promote fitness—was not up for debate. The USOC made no apologies about its embrace of the consumerist ethic, with its bias toward marketable athletes who can move product. "If you have stars on the top," one former official rationalized, "you will get people involved on the bottom."

The festivals died, never to return. The shift in resources to elite athletes continued unabated. With Atlanta barely in the rearview mirror, the USOC created Podium 2002, an $18 million program whose sole aim was "increasing the number of U.S. medalists" at the 2002 Winter Olympics in Salt Lake City. Funding was now restricted to the top eight athletes in selected sports and events. The cash could be used to acquire an extra coach, a physical therapist, or access to an off-season ski camp; a handful of figure skaters got $580,000 to buy better choreographers and more ice time. "We didn't give money to the guy who would place 35th and have the best finish of his life," says Condron, a member of the committee that distributed the support. "We funded the guys we thought might make a difference. There was nothing democratic about it."

Nowhere in the Amateur Sports Act has there ever been language about medal counts, only a general instruction that the USOC assemble the best teams possible. But the USOC was now explicitly moving in that direction anyway, like a publicly traded company managing quarter-to-quarter earnings in order to meet Wall Street expectations. Leadership made ambitious predictions for total medals in upcoming Games, tied 50 percent of staffers' bonuses to hitting that number, and doubled the reward for any athlete who reached the podium (gold brought $25,000). Within the USOC family, everyone was incentivized to stay laser-focused on the needs of those at the very top of the pyramid, the tip of the iceberg that sat above the surface of the water—the part everyone could see.

Research grants for topics important to the lower levels of sport began to dry up. Support for local partners around the country managing Community Olympic Development Centers, which were used to introduce children to lesser-known sports, was weaned from the budget. The USOC was now allocating less than one percent of its resources on creating clear athletic development pathways for children and the training of coaches at all levels. Fittingly, given the win-at-all-costs sports culture that had been allowed to emerge, the USOC was spending three times as much just on doping control for its elite competitors.

By 2003, the mission of guiding the development of younger athletes had become such a nuisance that USOC leaders no longer wanted even to pretend that they had such a responsibility. They asked that the Amateur Sports Act be rewritten so the purpose of the organization would be focused narrowly on fielding and promoting the national teams. Gone would be its historic obligations to tend to the pipeline, everything from setting national goals for amateur sports in the U.S. to encouraging physical fitness. "It's a very long way from the couch to the podium," a member of the USOC Executive Committee, Jim McCarthy, complained at the time. "If we need to do all of these things, we probably won't do any of them well."

Yet, the 10-member USOC Governance & Ethics Task Force that came up with the recommendation acknowledged the obvious in its report: "It is clear that the USOC has never really attempted to fulfill directly several of the USOC purposes specified in the Act."

The Senate approved the restructuring, but the House never signed off. The original language remains.

No matter. The USOC has moved on. On the front page of the "About Us" section of its website, the organization describes its mission as:

> To support United States Olympic and Paralympic athletes in achieving sustained competitive excellence and preserve the Olympic ideals, and thereby inspire all Americans.

Personally, I'm more inspired by the lawn at the entrance to the U.S. Olympic Committee complex in Colorado Springs. Thick and green, lush as a feather bed, it's the product of seed and fertilizer applied to rich soil, encouraging a million blades to stand tall. It represents a fine commitment to the grassroots.

• • •

The irony is that just as the USOC was dismantling the final vestiges of any direct investment into the athletic pipeline, it was discovering with startling clarity the importance of quality youth sports programs. Literally the same month that the task force issued its recommendations on a streamlined mission, a report was produced by the USOC's Coaching and Sports Science division confirming what federal legislators had suspected was likely a quarter century earlier: "The successful development of a U.S. Olympian is the result of a long-term process, which requires high levels of training and support."

The 47-page analysis, "Reflections on Success," was drawn from an extensive survey that had been filled out by 760 athletes from a wide variety of sports who had competed between 1984 and 1998. The same rich data set had been used two years earlier to produce a related, 84-page report, "The Path to Excellence," the first-ever comprehensive study of the training patterns of U.S. Olympians since early childhood. Together, they offered a roadmap for anyone or any organization interested in making champs out of children.

MYTH NO. 9

No national body coordinates grassroots sports.

THE TRUTH

The U.S. Olympic Committee is supposed to.

The survey delivered several important findings, some of which are highlighted elsewhere in this book: That Olympians were most often introduced to their sport through unstructured activities. That once enrolled in organized sports, quality coaching was important in the acquisition of technique. That clubs and community-based programs, not school teams, were primarily responsible for the training of these athletes—but that school physical education classes played a key role by developing fitness and, surprisingly, skills. That it took the average Olympian three years to find competitive success at the local level as a child and that the gap was more like five years in sports such as soccer and hockey in which players start young. That it took 12 to 13 years after introduction to a sport before they made their first Olympic team. And that many played multiple sports as teenagers, dispelling the myth of early specialization.

In short, growing great athletes took patience and an application of kids' need to explore. Yes, Olympians needed the USOC support that began flowing to the elite after Steinbrenner shook his fist at his TV screen in '88. But their path to glory ran much, much deeper than that. The authors of the first report implored the USOC to "take a leadership role in promoting relationships" between the community groups, clubs, schools and national governing bodies "to ensure a seamless system of athlete development in Olympic sports." (See chart on the next page.)

Few people heard about this survey. No press releases were issued. No news stories were written. The reports got linked on an obscure corner of the USOC website, and went without mention in the annual report that went out to the public. Politically, it wasn't the time to make the case for the grassroots—not with the task force trying to shrink the size of its dysfunctional board by eliminating representatives from community-based organizations.

Quietly, one square-jawed, former Olympic wrestler named Jim Scherr appreciated the findings. The fact that he soon would be given the reigns of the USOC as its CEO offers at least a glimmer of hope that those insights will be acted upon.

"The development system in the United States is pretty chaotic," Scherr tells me. "We have a very cobbled-together system made up of independent volunteer groups and community-based organizations that are trying to drive more people through their turnstiles and reach their missions. They do a good job at that but they are really baby-sitter services for athletes who walk through their doors. So what we really need to do is develop across that system more comprehensive pipelines in each

The Progression of the Olympic Dream

The average age at which athletes who competed for the U.S. at Olympic Games from 1984 to 1998 reached milestones in their events.

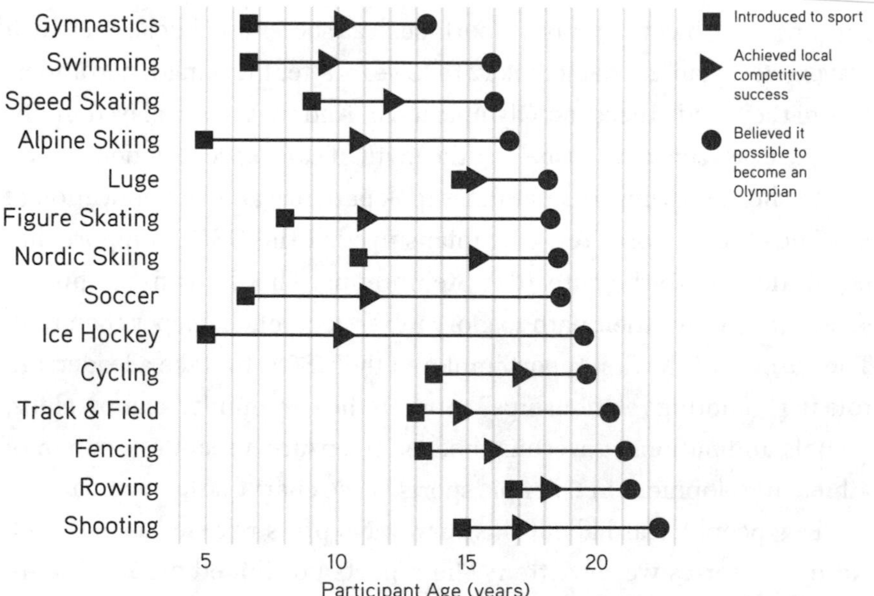

Source: "The Path to Excellence," T. Gibbons, R. Hill et al., U.S. Olympic Committee

sport that make more sense." And widen those pipelines. "Our biggest concern is that we get a broader and broader cross section of society participating in amateur sports," he says. "It's a matter of building the base by getting people participating in a sport and giving them an experience that's meaningful and positive, then, for those few who are able and interested, providing an opportunity to go to the Olympics."

Still, change comes slowly. The USOC continues to devote the mother lode of its attention and resources to the 1,200 or so most immediate medal contenders. Meanwhile, the hazards of neglecting the base are becoming more apparent.

The U.S. won nine gold medals at the 2006 Turin Olympics, most in a Winter Games except for the 10 in Salt Lake City in 2002. Even so, much more was expected. The number of events and thus available medals has grown significantly since Calgary, and many of the most high-profile Americans failed to live up to their hype. While the women's hockey team settled for bronze, the men beat only Kazakhstan in the preliminary round and washed out in the quarterfinals. Alpine skier Bode Miller folded under the pressure of expectations he had never courted. Perennial runner-up Sasha Cohen came up short again in figure skating. The skeleton team went from three medals in Salt Lake, to none. To boot, TV ratings were low, especially among the young. *American Idol* trumped American idols.

The U.S. delegation was saved by two distinct forces.

One was diversity, both geographic and racial. Speed skaters won three golds (plus three silvers and three bronzes). Joey Cheek and Chad Hedrick are Southerners who come from the world of in-line roller-skating. Shani Davis, the third gold medalist, is from the South side of Chicago, where, in a stroke of dumb luck, his mother once worked for a lawyer who happened to be a speed skating official. That man hooked up the kid with a club in the suburbs. With victory at 1,000 meters in Turin, Davis became the first black athlete to win an individual gold medal at a Winter Olympics.

The other force in play was, in a word, fun. Americans won three golds (plus three silvers and one bronze) snowboarding, a teen-driven sport that stands in contrast to the mainstream, adult-organized sports culture. On her gold-medal ride in the halfpipe, Vermont flower child Hannah Teter dialed up on her iPod a song by her boyfriend's band. When asked about the rules of her sport, she said, "Rules? Snowboarding is free. You make up your own rules." That doesn't mean she didn't train with purpose. She had a coach and, really, scores of informal coaches, as the open-source culture of alternative sports is to share what you've learned with your peers. But these are sports that do not heap excessive amounts of pressure on children at an early age.

"I don't think athletes should specialize in one sport until at least age 14," Scherr says. "Obviously there are exceptions with gymnastics or figure skating, but a broader sports experience is better. Our way of attacking that is through coaching education."

As the designated coordinating body for amateur sports, the USOC has the best Rolodex in all of jockdom. While the corporation has never had the money to pay for more than a few bats and balls at the community level, it has always been uniquely positioned to push knowledge and education down the pipeline to coaches, the most influential figures in youth sports. A 1992 study found that when coaches received training in effective skill instruction and positive motivational techniques, only five percent of children chose not to play the sport again. With untrained coaches, the attrition rate was 26 percent.

The USOC has two tools to encourage productive behavior from its affiliates, the 39 national governing bodies (NGBs) for Olympic sports that in turn work with an array of smaller groups that sponsor youth sports. There's a carrot: The USOC allots each NGB's share of $35 million in annual direct funding. And there's a stick: The USOC can remove any of those groups as the official NGB of their sport. Lose that designation, and some other group gets the money, the prestige, and right to select the teams that represent the U.S. in international competitions.

So far, the USOC has been reluctant to exercise that power. "I'm not sure that coaching education would ever apply itself as an issue of decertification for an NGB, but it's clearly a priority that we're asking each of them to do," Scherr says. "For the most part, coaching in the United

States is an afterthought. Athletes and parents become coaches, and they're not trained to be coaches. In Europe and other societies, coaching is held up at a much higher level as a professional standard. They have to have significant education in sports science, kinesiology, sports psychology, coaching principles. We don't do that in this country."

Very few of the nation's 2 to 4 million youth coaches—perhaps as little as 20 percent—have received any form of training, even if it's just a three-day course on skills and drills. And even fewer have been taught how to coach for character. So most of them wing it, using disciplinary techniques that experts say aren't developmentally appropriate for elementary and middle-school kids: extra exercise (64 percent), verbal scolding (42 percent), public embarrassment (18 percent), suspension (8 percent) and striking or hitting (2 percent), according to survey results presented to the American College of Sports Medicine in 2006.

In recent years, a growing number of state sports associations have begun to mandate training. And some NGBs have been proactive in this area as well. USA Swimming is the gold standard. Every club coach, no matter the age group they're working with, must receive training in first aid, cardiopulmonary resuscitation, and basic water safety. By the start of their second year, they must pass an additional "Foundations of Coaching" test that covers everything from rules and regulations to strokes to age-appropriate workout sessions. Coaches can only miss 20 of the 180 questions on the online, open-book test, so they are strongly advised to read three specific textbooks. If they want to dig deeper, the website is packed with helpful information: There are sections on Biomechanics/Technique, Physiology/Biochemistry, Sports Medicine, Race Analysis, Dietary Supplements, and Growth & Development. Coaches are offered strategies on how to keep the late-maturing kid engaged early—and how to prevent the early-maturing kid from getting down on himself when the other kids catch up. Articles point out that only 25 percent of the kids who are outstanding in elementary school are still outstanding in later years. That female swimmers release higher levels of the stress hormone cortisol than boys, especially when coached by men (so gentlemen, don't train everyone the same). That it's best to have kids between the ages of 9 and

12 practice at longer distances because that's the key window of opportunity in which to lock in aerobic capacity and stroke mechanics. Need to find an orthopedist, asthma specialist, or nutritionist for one of your athletes? Use the drop-down menu, searchable by state, which links to a database of certified experts. With such a comprehensive, grassroots-to-elite program in place, little wonder USA Swimming is the nation's most consistent summer Olympic medal producer.

Oh, and the federation now does criminal checks on all 11,000 of its coaches.

Then there's USA Basketball, which is closer to the norm. There's nothing on its website that speaks to coaches' education or athlete development. The front page is dominated by a series of press releases that highlight the feats of adults who happen to wear USA jerseys during their off-seasons ... *Kobe Collects NBA All-Star Game MVP Honor ... Marquette Retires Dwyane Wade's Jersey ... Carmelo Anthony Honored as USA Basketball's 2006 Male Athlete of the Year*. The site has a strong NBA and NCAA promotional flavor because, although the federation is based in Colorado Springs, it is effectively run by the powers that be in pro and college hoops. In the president's seat at the moment is a former WNBA president, Val Ackerman. Behind her are a 25-member board of directors and a 10-member executive committee whose primary responsibility consists of little more than approving the coaches and players recommended for the national teams by various committees.

The federation's most significant investment in its pipeline is the USA Basketball Youth Development Festival, which every other June brings together 48 of the top high school juniors and seniors for several days of teaching and games led by AAU and high school coaches. In all, the federation invests less than $150,000 annually in youth development—or about three to five percent of its budget in any given year. In 2004 it spent more just on insurance premiums for the NBA stars participating in the Athens Olympics, where the men's team lost to Puerto Rico, Lithuania, and, in the semis, Argentina. The USOC gave USA Basketball $1.5 million that year, the fourth-largest check written to an NGB (USA Swimming received $2.3 million).

Want some guidance from USA Basketball on how to coach kids? Don't bother. A couple years ago, Brian McCormick, the private trainer from Sacramento, wrote USA Basketball to ask if he could get certified as a coach. He already had completed such programs with USA Track and Field and USA Weightlifting, and, while he knew the principles of coaching kids better than most, he figured parents might want some help figuring out who's qualified to work with their child. "The federation responded by telling me they don't do certification," McCormick said. Sadly, it's true—there is no such program.

Which brings us back to the AAU, the de facto youth arm of USA Basketball. The AAU holds a seat on the federation's board and promotes that fact as evidence of its credibility on the anything-goes summer scene, yet has resisted calls to perform background screens on all member coaches. In 2003, *The Seattle Times* and the AAU checked the rosters of 4,236 coaches and volunteers in Washington and Idaho and found 38 felons. Some had a history of incest, theft, and delivering drugs. One convicted murderer said he missed reading the part of the AAU membership form requiring him to disclose his crime; others hid theirs in order to avoid review by the national office. AAU president Bobby Dodd told the *Times* that he considered a one percent felon rate to be low—but promised to examine ways to perform background checks nationwide.

By the time I met up with Dodd three years later, he had talked himself out of mandatory checks. He said an insurance adviser suggested that random checks would be sufficient to protect the organization legally. Besides, Dodd said, he wasn't sure which screening company to trust. They reminded him of the chemical salesmen who tried to sell him hard-to-understand products back when he was managing a pool in Memphis. "I've talked to many people and can somebody tell me where 1-800-background checks is—one place that has all the information? There's no such thing," he said. "You can hire the Internet companies and pay anywhere from two to 20 dollars to pull up the data. But you know it will only be as good as the folks that have put it in. And our belief in that process is: Who knows better if a person committed a felony than the person himself?"

Dodd is right that there's no perfect product. Even FBI databases are incomplete. But his logic that felons can be expected to rat themselves out is either hopelessly naïve or dangerously cheap. Either way, his stance places him at odds with that of the National Council of Youth Sports, a trade group whose members include the AAU and 179 other organizations. The Florida-based nonprofit recommends that all coaches be screened through the National Center for Safety Initiatives, a company specifically created for background checks on coaches. For $25, a name gets run through two national criminal databases.

Little League does it for even less money. Using its scale to negotiate down the price, it offers its affiliates a more basic criminal and sexual offender check at $1.50 per coach. "There's no excuse for not requiring background checks," Little League president Steven Keener tells me. "I don't understand what [Dodd] is talking about."

Dodd is also skeptical of requiring training for coaches. Sure, there are some AAU coaches who just roll out the ball. But Dodd himself won four AAU national championships with his Memphis club, and he's no Yoda of the hardwood. His success was based on recruiting the city's top players away from other programs, then lighting a fire under them with go-get-'em rhetoric. (Penny Hardaway says of Dodd, "He was just a guy who motivated the crap out of us. We got speeches every day.") Dodd adds dismissively, "'Coaches' education' are nice words to use, kind of like 'background check.' God Almighty they sound good, like motherhood and apple pie. But what do they really mean?"

McCormick has a few ideas, many of which are drawn from models in Europe where he has coached: Games with less than five players per side until age 10 to create the floor space and access to the ball that builds technical skills; emphasis on general athletic movement abilities through puberty as bones tend to grow faster than muscles do; a focus on tactical imagination and moving without the ball in the early teenage years ... He could go on and on. And he does in his 2006 book, *Cross Over: The New Model of Youth Basketball Development*, which is built upon Istvan Balyi's five-stage framework for "Long Term Athlete Development" (see Age 4) and was written as a response to USA Basketball's lack of initiative in coaching education.

"The reason guys like me have a job is because thousands of parents see their kids aren't getting better," McCormick says. "Many of the existing programs are based on the goal of how we can win the next game or the next championship. It's that 'Peak by Friday' mentality. They basically try to put together an all-star team by finding the quickest kids and cutting the rest. Then they have them use the press to create turnovers. Or, with the younger kids, they try to teach really organized offenses that take away their decision-making, which ultimately stunts their development.

"Twenty five years ago, Americans had the highest basketball IQ in the world. Now, it's just the opposite. It was unheard of in the past that a non-U.S. player would be a point guard in the NBA or even at the D1 level. Now the guys with creative flair are Steve Nash, Tony Parker, and Manu Ginobili. There certainly are Americans who know how to play the game, like Jason Kidd, but the foreign players come here with a much better understanding of it at a young age. In that respect, basketball and soccer share the same problem in our country. Basketball just gets the better athletes, so it covers better."

• • •

Need an AAU coach? My dog is now available.

Out of curiosity, I went to aausports.org, punched in the name, kennel, and birth date of my Nova Scotia Duck Tolling Retriever, clicked "No" when asked "Have you ever been convicted of a sex offense or felony?," and supplied my credit card information ($33.95 for a two-year membership, with free T-shirt). Just like that, her printable AAU Membership Card showed up in my e-mail inbox.

Nutmeg of Wausakeeg
Membership ID: PQSED998Y6978NK
Birthdate: 9/26/1998
Tom.Farrey@espn3.com
BA—Boys Basketball
District: CT

The T-shirt arrived a few days later. No one called to ask any questions.

To pin all the shortcomings of American basketball on the AAU, or USA Basketball, wouldn't be fair, though. Structurally, the sports clubs of Europe more readily lend themselves to teaching and to long-term athletic development. Though each country does things differently, the local clubs that players come up through often own their own facilities and receive some government subsidy. They're staffed by paid coaches who are often certified and overseen by their sport federations. They offer teams in a range of ages, from 6-and-under through, in many cases, the professional level. The goal with the children is to develop talent that someday could play for the top team or, after they can enter into contracts around age 16, be transferred to another team for a profit. The incentive, then, is to produce sound athletes who ripen in their early twenties, not on winning national titles at age 9. That's how Italy delivered the first player taken in the 2006 NBA draft, Andrea Bargnani. The foundation for Kobe Bryant's highly skilled game was laid in that country, where fundamentals were drilled into him between the ages of 6 and 13 when father Joe played pro ball with top clubs.

The U.S. sports system, on the other hand, relies on altruism—the generosity of volunteers. When it works, it's a lovely thing. My son Cole has had several coaches who were excellent. These people not only knew the games they were coaching, but had some notion of how to teach it to children of varying ages and, more important, understood that most kids play sports for fun, friendship, and skill development. I can tell you that when Cole has one of these coaches, he comes home from practice and often asks to play more in our backyard or driveway. To me, that is the clearest sign that a youth coach has done well—when they have sparked a love for, and then let kids take ownership of, the game. These coaches are community treasures.

Sometimes a coach can get by on little more than good spirit. When my daugthter Anna was 7, she played on a rec-league soccer team run by a local lawyer, a sharp woman who knew almost nothing about the sport but took a genuine interest in each girl. Anna was as fit and coordinated as any pigtailed second grader, but hadn't really grown into her body yet. As a result she enjoyed the practices more than the games, in which the bigger girls dominated play, urged on by amped-up parents. There were times when I would look at Anna, who mostly ran around on the outside of the beehive, and knew that she was asking herself if soccer was really for her.

We encouraged her to try soccer again the next year anyway, and she found more success. Her more assertive instincts were starting to kick in. She attacked more often and wasn't so afraid to get trampled by the pack. Her confidence soared when she brought home a "Co-Most Improved Player of the Week" card that her coach, the same one as the previous year, had printed out at home. That card went on our refrigerator—as did the next week's "Co-Most Valuable Player of the Week" card. You could see this child, and maybe an athlete, blossoming. Her coach was improving her own game, too; coach now carried around a spiral-bound guide that recently had been created by the U.S. Soccer Federation and included suggested drills for kids of Anna's age.

Then we got word that her coach was effectively retiring. The coach's daughter, one of the team's better players, was going out for travel the next season and so were a couple others. The travel team already had its coach and several assistants, and it wasn't an environment Anna felt she was ready for, with its nearly year-round commitment, star system, and emphasis on winning.

"Are any of my friends still going to play rec?" Anna asked, looking up at me with her big dark chocolate eyes.

And that was it for Anna and soccer.

I suspect the national team will do just fine in her absence. I'm not worried about Anna, either; she's a happy, resilient kid who has options. As parents, we'll do everything we can to help her join the one-third of students at our town's middle school who pass the annual fitness test. But surely in the land of opportunity there is one girl, or one hundred, or maybe one thousand, who might have gone on to become a special athlete if she hadn't been weeded out prematurely by a system geared toward aggregating the early bloomers. The USOC's own survey of Olympians shows the average soccer player of a generation ago, before travel teams dominated the landscape, didn't find success at the local level until age 11.

At the very least, a lot of potential fans of the sport have been lost along the way. And not because their dream was taken away. They just never got the chance to dream.

It was around that time that I asked Kathy Zolad—president of the Connecticut Junior Soccer Association, which governs the sport in our state—why the organization doesn't ban travel and premier soccer until age 14 given the hazards of unnecessary attrition and faulty talent identification. The coaching directors of the U.S. Youth Soccer association (USYS) formally recommend as much. Zolad appreciated the question but pointed right back up the ladder, to USYS, which runs the Olympic Development Program and begins forming state teams at the under-12 level. "When they decide they're not going to have a U14 national camp, we'll go along with it," Zolad told me, rejecting the prospect of unilateral disarmament by her state. "They need to make a decision about what's best for kids and take a leadership role." So then I called USYS coaching coordinator Sam Snow, who acknowledged, "Yeah, we're kind of shooting ourselves in the foot there. But U.S. Soccer expects us to have an ODP pool at U14."

Snow isn't just passing the buck. USYS gets its clout from the U.S. Soccer Federation.

Which gets its sanction from the USOC.

Which got its monopoly from Congress.

Which just after midnight on Oct. 13, 1978, wasn't quite sure what it was creating with adoption of the Amateur Sports Act. On the House floor, one Ohio Democrat predicted the birth of a "nice bureaucratic boondoggle." A weary colleague from Hawaii said, "I do not think at 12:30 this morning we are qualified to spend $30 million of anybody's money for what I have heard so far. I would hope that we would take a noble position and put it to work in another session of this Congress to do it as though it makes sense, and that we will be proud of what we have done." But there were communists to catch, so minutes later, in a classic case of Capitol Hill sausage-making, the chamber stripped out the last of the requested funds and signed off on the landmark bill. The vote was 54 to 42. The House has 435 members, but most were gone by that hour.

"It's a disaster," the youth sports scientist Robert Malina says now of the act's offspring, the empowered-yet-impotent USOC. "A political disaster."

Forced to pay for itself, the USOC continues to make moves that stand in conflict with what its leaders know is in the best interest of future Olympians and ordinary child athletes. Scherr might not believe that kids should specialize too early in one sport, but in 2007 the USOC threw its support behind the creation of the Youth Olympic Games, an International Olympic Committee event for the adolescent elite. The USOC sees the event, which is slated to begin in 2010 and inevitably will encourage premature specialization, as programming for an Olympic Channel it is trying to develop. The dangling of gold medals also could promote drug use among the young. In 2007, a Florida father was sent to federal prison for six years after providing steroids to his son starting at age 13. Corey Gahan was a youth champion in in-line skating, an emerging sport that many in the community believed soon would be added to the Olympic slate.

Cheering for a kid on sideline of a community rink or field, it's hard to fathom the web of institutions and events that shape the behavior of the moment. A youth sports contest is at its core a local affair. But everything rolls downhill, including chaos, so if elements of the youth sports culture now resemble a wild, town-by-town, libertarian response to the sports factories of the old Eastern Bloc, perhaps no one should be surprised.

The best that can be said about the Amateur Sports Act is that Americans got exactly what they paid for.

AGE 10

THE AUSSIE RULES

Canberra, Australia

Ten is the age at which the average future U.S. Olympian in some sports achieves local competitive success, according to the USOC's survey. A talent begins to reveal itself, and often within a year or so, a child starts fantasizing of representing his country one day. It's still going to be another few years before they actually commit to their dream, and not until their late teens will they come to believe that it's indeed possible for them to make an Olympic team.

Now, what if every kid knew what his natural talent was?

And what if that talent revealed itself earlier, at say ... birth?

These are big questions worth flying around the world to explore.

It's noontime in small-town Connecticut when my youngest son, Kellen, just shy of his first birthday at the time, awakens from his noontime nap. The shades are drawn, the room dark, the air purifier on a low hum as I slowly push open the door. He's sitting up in his crib, one hand holding his favorite blue blanket, the other rubbing blue eyes that blink back the hall light. Next to him is the music-box pillow that had sung him to sleep to the ting-ting-ting of "Here Comes Peter Cottontail."

"Hi, kicker boy," I say, using his nickname du jour, so given because of his diaper-time obsession with whacking his heels on the changing table as rapidly as possible, like a Benihana chef with new knives. Kellen, of course, does not get my reference, as he does not yet talk, or walk.

But he does drool. And it's a sample of that saliva that I'm looking to harvest right now—because his wipe-away spit, nearly as clear as a crystal ball, offers some genetic insight into his athletic future. As Kellen (that's him on the cover of this book) squints back up at me, I slide the end of a Q-tip into the side of his mouth, rub it around the gum area for 20 seconds and drop it into a "Sample Transportation Bag"with his name scrawled in pen on the outside.

In two hours, my plane leaves for Australia.

"All right, kicker boy," I say, sealing the baggie. "Let's go find your destiny."

The man I am headed to see is Deon Venter, a top medical executive at Genetic Technologies, a midsize Melbourne firm offering what it calls the world's first DNA test for sports performance. The test was launched a few weeks earlier, in December 2004, and is being sold over the Internet to Australians for the equivalent of $100. (The test isn't being made available to Americans generally.) You mail in a cheek swab, and a couple of weeks later, the company sends back your results. But I want to see the process for myself, to glimpse the future of athlete development—and perhaps that of my baby boy, too. Venter hasn't screened many young children, much less an infant, but sure, he says with a chuckle, come on down.

The test is based upon the findings of an academic study that *Discover* magazine hailed as one of the Top 100 scientific advances of 2003. Working with the Australian Institute of Sport (AIS), researchers at Children's Hospital in Sydney screened the genotypes of 429 of Australia's top athletes in 14 sports. From their previous work on muscular dystrophy, they had a hunch that one gene, ACTN3, might play a key role in the creation of muscle used by athletes.

Muscle matters in sports. But it's not all the same. Fast-twitch fiber provides explosion, the bursts of speed that helped our forebears escape from lions. Slow-twitch fiber has survived because it aids endurance, the picking of berries for hours under the sun. As suspected, tests showed that the Australian athletes in sprint and power events were more likely than other athletes to have an ACTN3 structure that produces the protein that fires fast-twitch muscle.

Every human gets two copies of each gene—one from mom, one from dad. So for ACTN3, the genetic lottery determines whether a child gets two, one, or zero copies of the form linked to fast-twitch fiber. In effect, half of the Australian sprint and power athletes got a double shot of fast-twitch espresso, and all but five percent got at least one shot. By contrast, the endurance athletes more often got the ACTN3 equivalent of double-shot decaf, leading the authors to conclude that these genetic differences might be able to predict talent in sports.

Within a year, Genetic Technologies had turned the findings into a commercial test and posted a marketing pitch on its website: *For the first time anywhere in the world, we are able to offer a genetic test to determine whether you are naturally geared toward sprint/power events or toward endurance sporting ability ... So whether you're an athlete, or young athlete-to-be, the ACTN3 Sports Gene Test will help direct you toward achieving your maximum natural potential.*

One day and 7,000 air miles later, I meet Venter in the quiet laboratory at the company's urban headquarters. He hardly fits the image of a mad scientist. A former British Ironman champion, he is thin but taut. His gray-specked hair, cropped short and combed neat, sits atop a thin face and a pair of eyes that twinkle through rimless glasses. Behind Venter on the counter is a machine that robotically extracts samples of DNA, including those of Kellen, and drops them into tubes for processing.

"There's always a knee-jerk response to anything having to do with genetics," says Venter, who, in addition to his role at Genetic Technologies, serves as chief pathologist for seven Australian hospitals. His previous work has included the development of cancer-related gene tests. "People think it might involve the creation of superhumans or something like that. None of that has really happened with the disease gene tests. In terms of ACTN3, there's very little to fear, with potentially enormous amounts to gain in terms of helping people enjoy sport more, and making them healthier."

Researchers around the world have already associated 165 genes with physical activity, up from 29 when the first "Human Gene Map for Performance and Health-Related Fitness Phenotypes" was published in 2000 by the American College of Sports Medicine. But the focus of most studies has been on fitness characteristics, not athletic performance. And most involved the general population. That is what made the ACTN3 study a watershed—it looked at international-caliber athletes, including 50 Olympians.

"Sports performance is a jigsaw puzzle, and this is just piece No. 1," Venter tells me. But as we stare at a monitor that gradually displays Kellen's results, which are being decoded in a gene machine about the size of a microwave oven, I am filled with anticipation and queasiness. How bizarre would it be to know that he's cut out for sprinting while he still can only crawl? As a parent, even one whose instinct is to expose my kids to as many sports as they might want to try and let them find their own way, can I be trusted with such information?

A lab tech copies the results onto a CD, converts them to a graphically pleasing format and hands the disc to Venter, who pulls up a series of bar charts on his laptop. "Well, Tom, here are the results," he says in a gentle voice. The vertical bars on Kellen's graph are absent. In ACTN3 terms, he's a zero.

"This is more likely to fit with an endurance athlete," Venter confirms.

"So we'll skip the 100-meter dash," I say.

"He can do it if he wants to do it," the good doctor replies, "but statistically speaking, based on what we know now, he's less likely to do well because he will not apparently make sufficient power."

Venter is a geneticist, not a physiologist, so I'll save the question of which sports might best fit Kellen for tomorrow. That's when I meet with the world-renowned experts at the AIS, a three-hour drive hour north of here, in the capital city of Canberra.

Before I leave, though, I feel compelled to ask Venter a question: As an accomplished endurance athlete who happens to have the same ACTN3 architecture as Kellen, does he think my boy has the stuff of an Ironman?

"He might, if he can stand the pain," he says, with a wink. "That's something we don't know how to measure yet."

• • •

I'm not sure how to feel about this knowledge. But it should come as little surprise that Australia would deliver a DNA test for athletic traits. No nation on the planet is better at identifying and developing athletes, with success in realms well beyond its traditional sports of rugby, cricket, netball, surfing, tennis, and that indigenous brand of football known for its comically robotic refs.

Where to begin? In 2007, Australia was home to reigning world champions in cycling, swimming, women's basketball and lacrosse, squash, rowing, sailing, running, walking, mountain biking, motorcycle racing, and other sports—30 individual teams or athletes in all. The Socceroos, as the national team in that sport is called, made the round of 16 at the 2006 World Cup. That year, the U.S.-based PGA Tour featured a whopping 22 Aussie golfers, including headliners Stuart Appelby and Adam Scott. In basketball, the land mass farthest from where the game was invented produced the first pick in the '05 NBA draft, Andrew Bogut, leader of Australia's junior team that won the world championship a couple of years earlier. On and on, the national résumé goes. In recent years, the sun-splashed nation has even claimed world titlists in snowboarding and moguls skiing. Back at the '02 Winter Olympics, gold in aerials freestyle skiing went to converted gymnast Alisa Camplin, who practiced by jumping into a pond near Melbourne.

Australia is so adept at making champions that in preparation for the '08 Beijing Olympics, China asked to send 300 officials to Australia to study its methods. AIS leaders politely explained that they couldn't accommodate that large a contingent, and a lesser partnership was struck. But it was a smart request by the world's most populous nation. At the '04 Athens Olympics, Australia was fourth in total medals behind the U.S., China, and Russia. But the former penal colony for the British empire got there with just 20 million citizens from which to select its talent—about the same population base as Sri Lanka (or the state of New York). The U.S. has 290 million citizens, China 1.3 billion, and Russia 142 million.

On a per capita basis—comparing medals won to the number of people living in each country—Australia was virtually without peer in Athens, as the chart on the next page shows.

China isn't the only country that could learn a thing or two from the Aussies. Australia was seven times more efficient at delivering medalists

2004 Olympic Medals per Million Citizens

RANK	COUNTRY	GOLD	SILVER	BRONZE	TOTAL MEDALS PER MILLION
1	The Bahamas	1	0	1	6.309
2	**Australia**	**17**	**16**	**16**	**2.461**
3	Cuba	9	7	11	2.383
4	Estonia	0	1	2	2.294
5	Slovenia	0	1	3	2.018
6	Jamaica	2	1	2	1.868
7	Latvia	0	4	0	1.750
8	Hungary	8	6	3	1.729
9	Bulgaria	2	1	9	1.533
10	Belarus	2	6	7	1.523
11	Denmark	2	0	6	1.488
12	Greece	6	6	4	1.458
13	The Netherlands	4	9	9	1.356
14	Norway	5	0	1	1.318
15	New Zealand	3	2	0	1.281
16	Croatia	1	2	2	1.132
17	Slovakia	2	2	2	1.110
18	Lithuania	1	2	0	0.877
19	Austria	2	4	1	0.862
20	Romania	8	5	6	0.853
21	Georgia	2	2	0	0.7883
22	Sweden	4	2	1	0.7878
23	Czech Republic	1	3	4	0.782
24	Trinidad and Tobago	0	0	1	0.765
25	Switzerland	1	1	3	0.698
26	Russia	27	27	38	0.646
27	South Korea	9	12	9	0.626
28	Germany	13	16	20	0.594
29	Azerbaijan	1	0	4	0.592
30	Italy	10	11	11	0.558
31	France	11	9	13	0.546
32	Kazakhstan	1	4	3	0.519
33	Great Britain	9	9	12	0.505
34	Ukraine	9	5	9	0.478
35	Spain	3	11	5	0.462
37	Finland	0	2	0	0.384
36	Mongolia	0	0	1	0.380
38	Canada	3	6	3	0.378
39	**United States**	**36**	**39**	**27**	**0.343**
40	United Arab Emirates	1	0	0	0.328

Sources: International Olympic Committe, United Nations Population Division

than the U.S., which has the raw materials to dominate with its wealth and ethnic diversity. "If we did what the Australians do, it would be downright scary," David Martin says, his chipper, Stateside brand of English still fully intact after a decade Down Under. "It could be that no other country in the world would win a medal if the U.S. got serious about a lot of the Olympic sports."

A senior sports physiologist originally educated in Michigan, Martin began his career at the U.S. Olympic Training Center. But funding for sports science there was scant, and guys like him were stretched thin trying to serve the needs of dozens of teams. Now he works here at the AIS, the Aussie equivalent of the Olympic Training Center, which feels like some grand project that Microsoft and Nike got together to dream up. It's the training headquarters for 700 scholarship athletes in 26 sports, each of which has its own team of nutritionists, physiologists, bio-mechanists, psychologists, and therapists, all of whom work side by side with some of the world's best coaches.

The geeks and their toys are everywhere on this tree-lined, 160-acre campus. I meet Martin under the "biomechanics dome," where, next to us at a table on a red rubber track, a bearded technician taps furiously on a laptop, calibrating a device analyzing the stride of a female runner. Down the hallway is the Hematology and Biochemistry Lab where vials of bodily fluids are being evaluated. In another building, a boxer slips into a bodysuit with affixed sensors that allow lasers to create a computer rendering of his movement patterns. Basketball players hoping to be the next Bogut or Lauren Jackson (the 2003 WNBA MVP) wear 3D goggles and throw balls against a wall, sharpening their decisionmaking process with the aid of video that simulates game situations. In the cafeteria, the next generation of elite Aussie athletes dines on carefully selected entrées that come with "nutrition cards" that reinforce lessons on proper eating for athletic performance.

The AIS was created by the Australian government after the 1976 Montreal Olympics, where the Aussies fared poorly against the Eastern Bloc powers. Australia won only five medals, none of them gold. (Thirty-one countries fared better, including Jamaica, Denmark, and, horror of horrors, New Zealand.) Unlike their political counterparts in Washington, D.C., however, Aussie leaders chose to invest in the nation's revitalization effort. The Australian Sports Commission, the government agency that distributes funds and provides strategic guidance for sports activity, now receives $205 million in federal money, one fifth of which goes to the AIS. That's on top of occasional cash infusions for infrastructure upgrades, such as the cutting-edge $14 million lap pool with underwater windows on each lane, force pads on the walls that measure turn speed, and two dozen cameras that feed data into a custom software program. The AIS also recently opened a winter sports training center in Italy. All in all, the operation is more sophisticated than anything the Soviets and East Germans concocted in their ideological war with the West.

But that's where the similarities with those old, notorious sports factories end.

Far from pushing little blue pills on teenage prospects, the AIS is a world leader in the fight against the use of performance-enhancing drugs. Drug scandals involving its athletes are rare, largely because: 1) direct government funding brings direct government accountability, and 2) shortcuts don't seem as attractive when legal options for improvement are more readily available. In the U.S., by contrast, the public face of sports science is Balco labs founder Victor Conte, a former rock musician who was the go-to guy for scores of Olympic, NFL, and baseball jocks until the Feds cracked down on his cowboy chemistry outfit in the Bay Area.

To the Aussies, sports science is something to be embraced, regulated, and disseminated. They conduct lots of original research, freely sharing much of it with the rest of the world. Domestically, the government insists that coaches and administrators involved in youth sports educate themselves on how to structure training and competition for kid athletes. "It is important," declares the website for the Australian Sports Commission, "that decisions made about junior sport are based on the most current research available." The guiding ethic is reason, not faith or simply old habits.

Australia has a detailed national policy on sports based on the philosophy of "Sport for All," not just the elites as was the case in the Eastern

Bloc. It has a law that specifically forbids the abuse of child athletes and a top-down mandate, the Junior Sport Framework, that integrates the goals of grassroots and elite sports. Australia, like all industrialized countries, wrestles with an obesity problem. The crisis is less pronounced than in the U.S., but the government is attacking it with a new $116 million program that pays for two hours of after-school sports. That's on top of the $2.1 billion that federal, state, and local governments have spent annually on sports and recreation activities ($110 per citizen). AIS officials support the after-school measure—it helps keep the pipeline of potential Olympians as wide as possible by promoting basic motor skills in children.

One of the key features of the Australian system is the National Talent Identification and Development program, which is run by the same people who co-authored the ACTN3 study. Its coordinators are always on the lookout for genetic aristocrats, reaching out to AIS athletes about the interests of brothers and sisters. But the heart of the program is a testing regimen given to thousands of children each year. In some years, the AIS has screened as many as 100,000 school children, measuring them, starting around age 13, in seven ways: by height, body mass, arm span, seated basketball throw, vertical jump, 40-meter sprint, and shuttle run. At the moment, the AIS is moving toward more of a targeted approach, spending larger sums on the initiative while testing a couple of thousand teens a year who have some experience in sports. About one in 10 earn invitations to join elite programs, either at the AIS or in an affiliated state academy closer to home. When a hundred Aboriginal boys were screened, for instance, the AIS found six boxing prospects.

The idea behind Talent ID, as the program is known, is that Australia has a relatively small pool of potential elite athletes—about 280,000 people between the ages of 10 and 19. The program uses analytic tools and broad historical data to identify the best prospects, then the AIS blankets them with top coaches and state-of-the-art training tools, with the hope that ultimately a few of them will shine on the world stage.

"If Australia behaves like the U.S., they'll always lose," Martin says. "In the American system, you have hundreds of thousands of kids who want to get involved in a limited number of main sports—football, basketball, baseball, hockey, golf, and so forth. There's pee-wee league competitions and if you're no good, everyone makes fun of you and you quit. And if you are good, you just keep going and going and going until a few become millionaires. So it's just a Darwinian concept of the strongest surviving through these progression pathways of youth programs into the elite professional programs. In Australia, that happens a bit in the major sports, Australian Rules football and rugby. But in Olympic sports, they actually go out and recruit young talent and match them up with sports. They ask kids, 'Is this something you want to do?'"

Michelle Steele got that question when she was 17. A former gymnast who had maxed out her potential in the sport, she had moved on to surf lifesaving (a form of competition that springs from Australia's beach culture) when she received an e-mail from her coach. He had heard that the AIS was canvassing the nation for females to create a skeleton team. She had no idea such a sport existed. She had seen snow just once, on a school field trip.

Her coach explained: *It's a sliding event, like luge or bobsled.*

"He didn't tell me it was headfirst," Steele says with a wry smile.

Five months later, in November 2004, she would find herself at a world-class track in Calgary, Canada, training with nine other Aussies whose only time on a sled had been on dry land at an AIS evaluation session. One candidate from the Outback had tried to prepare for the tryout by lying on a detached car hood and having her boyfriend drag her in his truck. But every last one of them was a greener-than-green rookie. And now Steele was in wintry Alberta, getting her tongue stuck to a frozen pole because she just had to know if what she'd been told was true.

Being fearless like that helps in skeleton. It's a sport in which a racer whips down the course at speeds reaching 80 miles an hour, their chin just inches above the ice. The AIS criteria that singled them out as candidates to represent the nation, though, were focused on physical traits. Martin's team studied the times of the world's top skeleton racers and determined that 50 percent of the "shared variance" in performance—geek-speak for half the credit—was attributable to the running start. Each of the AIS recruits selected proved to be fast and explosive in a series of tests that included the 30-meter sprint, the distance a skeleton athlete often runs before flopping onto the thin, heavy sled.

The AIS did *not* test for neck strength. "The first time down the track, I was facedown the whole time," Steele says. "I couldn't see. My head was slammed to the ice because of the G's, and the harder I tried to lift it the more it got pushed down." Recalling that day, she flashes a weary grin. "It was a bit terrifying, actually."

She eventually built up her neck muscles. Once able to actually see the course, she began to excel, quickly picking up the nuances of driving, which require subtle shoulder and leg manipulations on the sled. Her long torso and short legs that the coach, American Terry Holland, noticed in tryouts served her well in that respect, as did the fine motor skills honed during her years as a gymnast. A year later, Steele placed sixth in her first World Cup race. She qualified for the Olympics in Torino, Italy, where, on the most technically difficult track in the world, she finished 13th, a letdown to her but still a startling achievement. The best racers on the planet usually take the better part of a decade to reach that level. "It was like a little leaguer going up to the majors and hitting a double or triple in his first at-bat," says Holland, who previously coached the U.S. men and women to gold medals at the 2002 Salt Lake City Olympics. "It sent shock waves through the skeleton community."

Steele's success was no anomaly. Another AIS skeleton recruit had won the Junior World Championship a month earlier. A third recruit delivered top-15 finishes on the World Cup circuit. Soon after that, the international skeleton federation—seemingly offended by the Aussies' overnight success—changed its rules so that only riders with at least two years experience could enter World Cup races. "I think it shows that if you put the right people in the right sport, you can really get something out of them in a short time," Steele says.

The leader of the Talent ID division is Jason Gulbin, a former cyclist and runner whose program's methods are now being adopted by leading nations around the world. Just about everywhere, that is, except the U.S., where sports science is distrusted and children almost always are guided into a given sport by: 1) parents, who typically sign them up for their own favorite games; or 2) serendipity, i.e., the chance conversation with, say, the rowing coach who lives across town.

A few weeks before my Australia trip, Gulbin roamed a mountainside in Park City, Utah, where the skeleton team was training. Holding a video camera at the top of a track, he stood with Holland, who clapped wildly when the split time for Steele, halfway down the hill, popped up on the electronic race board. Tan and sturdy with short, curly hair, Gulbin was the picture of cool in his wraparound shades. The sun, like the future of Talent ID, was—and is—quite bright.

MYTH NO. 10

Children inevitably find their best sport.

THE TRUTH

Most are never exposed to sports they might excel at.

"I guess what we're doing is making sure the right athlete bumps into the right coach," Gulbin says. He sees his methods as merely helping nature take its course. "I think there's nothing more unethical than battling away at a sport that ultimately you're not suited to. The window of opportunity is so darned small to become an elite athlete and specialize in a particular sport that you need maximum information to make the right choice."

But could there be such a thing as too much information?

• • •

When Kellen was an infant and had trouble sleeping, Christine and I would sometimes bring him into our bed. When he awoke in the morning, he would smile, and I would smile back, which only made him smile more. And since it really would be wrong to end this silent joyride, we would keep grinning at each other until my jaw hurt or it was obvious from the commotion downstairs that Christine needed my help getting Cole and Anna out the door for school. I'd scoop Kellen up in my arms, struck by the truth that in our obsessive, what's-next society, the littlest kids might be the only human beings who truly live in the moment. The rest of us have bills to pay, ladders to climb, plans to make.

Gene tests for athletic traits, the logical extension of Talent ID, are all about the now in one respect—DNA is fixed for life. But they make it hard not to think of what may lie ahead.

Under the biomechanics dome, Martin lets out a chipper laugh when I ask if parents can be trusted with test results for sports genes. "Parents can be crazy," he says. "They live through their children, and sometimes they want things for their kids that are bordering on insanity. So I don't think parents can be trusted."

The AIS officially shares his skepticism. The Talent ID section of its website actually ridicules an unidentified mother who wrote the AIS seeking advice on how to maximize her child's presumed gifts for elite swimming after she had noticed her 3-month-old baby splashing a lot at bath time. More than other sports bodies, the AIS preaches against premature specialization. For every Tiger Woods, there are many more Roger Federers, who played a variety of sports into their early teenage years and seemed to benefit from the experience.

Still, gene tests have arrived in the commercial sphere. It seems only a matter of time before they can be purchased at Target, which recently began selling a "Baby DNA Kit" that identifies one's ancestral history, with the results printed on a wallet-size Profile Card that a doctor can look at in prescribing custom medicines. So Martin plays along in my whimsical hunt to identify the optimal sport for Kellen, perhaps the world's first baby to get checked for athletic traits.

I share what I now know of his evolutionary stew: that his skeletal muscle gets no ACTN3 protein, as is the case with 18 percent of European descendents (the only racial group studied). I also know his maternal grandmother, who played college tennis, marvels at his coordination, how well he whacks a rolling ball with either hand. Starts low. Finishes high. Topspin deep into the corners?

"With tennis," Martin says, "you want to have fast-twitch fibers to move dynamically."

Huh. "What about basketball?" I ask.

"Same thing."

"Baseball?"

"I'd be going for fast twitch."

"Football?" Kellen has the first name of a Hall of Famer and his current NFL player son (the Winslows). But I'm guessing that doesn't help his odds.

"The most explosive guys on the planet."

Martin is now chuckling sympathetically. "Good hand-eye coordination and endurance," he says, mulling the options for Kellen. "How about biathlon? They ski for long distances and shoot a rifle."

And so it shall be. Meet the next Ole Einar Bjørndalen.

All kidding aside, I have something of a dilemma now, right? In the U.S., most kids get funneled into the same four or five mainstream games, all of which favor explosive muscle action. Cole and Anna got signed up in several of those sports not because their bodies and minds are necessarily tailored for success but because that's what my wife and I once played. It's that way with most kids—and many kids quit sports by age 13, usually because either they can no longer make the team or they're not having fun. Now, two thirds of Couch Potato Nation is overweight or obese. Maybe biathlon isn't the answer for Kellen, but a more thoughtful approach to sports selection is beginning to have its appeal.

Some genes hold the potential to identify sports a kid should avoid altogether. Among them is APOE, a gene associated with increased risk of brain damage from head injuries in contact sports. In studies of professional boxers and football players, people with one form of the gene, APOE-4, were shown to be more likely to develop problems than those with other forms. For boxers, Chronic Traumatic Brain Injury (CTBI) is pegged as the most serious public health concern. It's characterized by cognitive impairment, clumsiness in balance and speech, and Parkinsonism—a neurological disorder marked by a masklike face and slow gait. CTBI is why some retired boxers seem punch-drunk. The results are slightly more equivocal with football players. In a study of 53 active pros during the 2000 season, only the most veteran players with the dubious APOE-4 form of the gene exhibited problems. The younger guys appeared to be fine, suggesting that such brain damage only occurs—or at least reveals itself—after a decade of knocking skulls.

There's still much we don't know about head injuries and the associated genes. But out of curiosity, in the course of my research I got Kellen tested for APOE through a Belgian company, Gendia. He turned up negative, which, yes, offers some comfort to dad should Kellen someday find the urge to strap on a helmet.

Back in Melbourne, Venter insists his goal is to help adults and children find lifelong avenues for exercise, not contribute to the manic development of kids as athletes. "We don't see how a genetic test is going to put any more pressure on children than has already been applied by parents for generations," he says. "In fact, it might help stop a father from pushing his child in a sport he wishes he had done well in but for which the child is not genetically suited."

Venter advises me not to act on what little we know about Kellen's genes until after he has had time to climb trees, experiment with a few sports, and define his interests on his own. I agree. It's his life, not mine. Besides, his ACTN3 results say only so much about his supposed strengths and weaknesses. The AIS study looked exclusively at the elites, the physical freaks at the far end of the bell curve, not the ordinary athlete. Closer to the middle, the association between genotype and performance is surely much weaker. The Olympics might be out of question, but high school basketball, say, seems plausible—if that's what Kellen really wants.

"The bottom line of which sport you go into," Gulbin told me up on the mount, "is how much you love the sport. You may theoretically on paper have the right profile for a sport, but you need the passion, the enthusiasm, the day-to-day training to deal with the knocks that these skeleton girls put up with."

Sports performance is a complex interplay between genetics, coaching, psychology, diet, and other factors, as Genetic Technologies acknowledges in its marketing literature. Venter assigns 80 percent of athletic aptitude to genetic factors, but he's just speculating. And even a trait as seemingly straightforward as muscle power might, like hand-eye coordination, involve a cluster of genes—most of which have not been studied. "ACTN3 could be just one of 10 genes that relate to muscle power performance, and it might not even be the most important one," says Stephen Roth, a University of Maryland kinesiology professor whose own ACTN3 study of nonathletes supports the AIS finding.

Sports gene testing has the potential to be the killer app of athlete recruiting. As more elite athletes get tested and more genes get identified, the database will grow, revealing patterns and allowing for predictions with greater accuracy, based on statistics. Ultimately, it's possible that when a boy like Kellen is born, the vial of blood taken to screen for diseases could also be used to spot athletic traits. Plug the results into the All-Jock Database, and before leaving the hospital, the baby's parents could get a report on which stars best match his DNA—quite the head start if they hope to raise the next Justine Henin or Lance Armstrong.

But that day is a long way off. For now, the AIS doesn't even bother to screen for ACTN3 in its Talent ID protocols. It's just not all that clear how useful the knowledge is at this point. Physical tests and skilled observation already offer a pretty good idea of whether a teenager is suited for a power or endurance sport.

Beyond that, the Australian government wants the AIS to proceed cautiously with genetic research, given the potential for abuse. It's data, not Dolly the Sheep, but the knowledge gleaned from identifying sporty DNA could be used by rogues around the world for the purposes of gene doping, a next-generation form of cheating.

"The Minister doesn't want cameras knocking on his door at 6 a.m.," says Gulbin, whose group has agreed to a moratorium on such testing while the ethical issues get sorted out. He's getting anxious to move forward with such research, since staying ahead of the competition has gotten harder as rival nations raid AIS staff to replicate Aussie-style programs. With China rising, Australia is expected to win fewer medals in Beijing than in the previous two Summer Games. But genetic research can wait, for now.

There's still room to maneuver—as long as the sleeping giant on the other side of the Pacific doesn't wake up to the Aussies' more proven methods.

• • •

The closest thing to a national Talent ID that Americans have known is the Presidential Physical Fitness Award, a program started back when

Lyndon Johnson was in the White House. Maybe you remember the annual drill from your days in PE. Shuttle run. Pull-ups. Sit-ups. Push-ups. Endurance run. Some got the patch; some didn't. Some got publicly embarrassed; some got pegged as future stars. Inevitably, word of the most impressive 10-year-old performers might reach the local coach, who might invite those kids to join his team or league, if they weren't signed up already.

The awards program is still around, sanctioned by the Department of Health and Human Services. But it's not much of a change agent. It gets no government funds, so school districts must pay for the patches. Only a quarter of them choose to do so. The program technically is run by the AAU—Bobby Dodd's AAU—which holds the government contract. But for years the work has been handled by a full-time staff of three affiliated with Indiana University. The AAU pays their expenses, keeping a small fee for itself.

So, how 'bout that: Bobby Dodd as the nation's de facto Talent ID chief. Another big hat for the AAU big man.

Steve Spinner has another idea. It's called Sports Potential, and it just might be a more comprehensive, grassroots-to-elite solution than anything put forth by the Aussies. One that holds the promise of both keeping marginal kids involved in sports and identifying top prospects for the USOC's smaller NGBs, whose sports are clamoring for more participants and richer pipelines.

Shortly after returning from Australia, I meet Spinner at the company offices in Menlo Park, Calif. It's an aluminum barn that the Bay Area start-up has rented, a sparsely decorated building with more than enough room for half a dozen desks, some exercise and testing equipment, and a shingle. The products he's building out don't take up much space anyway. They live on a computer, software and databases that help recommend sports to children and adults.

The Harvard M.B.A. first pitched his idea to Bill Bradley, the former New York Knick and three-term U.S. senator. He saw Bradley, who had just run for the presidency in 2000, on a random flight. He approached him in first class, explained that he was a longtime admirer, and told him his own story: Growing up on New York's Long Island, Spinner had discovered his best sport by chance. He was playing middle school soccer when the high school track coach stopped by and noticed that Spinner, after three hours of running, was barely winded. The coach challenged him to try cross country. He did and went on to run in college. "Luck should play a role in life—but it shouldn't play that big a role," he told Bradley. "There has to be a better way for me to have discovered this latent talent."

Bradley got it, and signed on as chair of the company's advisory board.

"Really what the product is designed to do is unlock the athlete that lives in all of us by matching that person with five or six sports they are most likely to succeed in," Bradley told me. "I don't think kids have a lot of fun if they're on a team and they're failing." At the same time, Bradley wasn't interested in a service that ramped up the pressure on kids to train like future pros. "I think that any organized sport with kids younger than 10 is counterproductive," he says. "Football teams for 8-year-olds? Kids ought to be able to play for a while and follow their own interests." He's downright old school in that respect.

Spinner would build out separate tools for two age groups.

Preteens (boys and girls ages 8 to 12) would get the Sports Matching and Readiness Tool, which is designed to identify which sports they are developmentally ready to play, physically and cognitively, based on their individual characteristics. The custom evaluation would draw heavily on science that speaks to activities that are age appropriate for children during a time of rapid growth. "Kids under the age of 12 should not take a Talent ID test. The science doesn't support it, and it's ethically and morally wrong," Spinner says. "But we can help a parent identify whether or not they should put a child in a sport at a given age and at what level. Does the child have the minimum requirements needed to have a positive experience? There are plenty of stories of kids who had tried baseball, basketball, all these sports, and had a miserable experience. And so the kid thinks sports are not for him, and he quits all sports. But he really is deficient only in hand-eye coordination—he's fine in every other area. The parent just mistakenly put him in there a little too early. We're not going to tell a kid to avoid certain sports, but we'll make them aware of which 25 of the 38 sports, say, he or she is prepared to play."

I brought Cole with me to Sports Potential when Spinner and his staff were first developing this assessment. They had him kick a ball against a wall, throw at a target, jump high, and jump long. They tested him for flexibility, strength, balance, agility, and reaction time. I laughed when the endurance shuttle began, as the recorded voice that marked each passing minute was Aussie—the same voice I heard at the AIS while watching women's basketball players get put through their paces. Spinner borrowed from the best.

Cole had fun, did well, and eagerly awaited the results. Then he bugged me about letting him try archery, one of the activities he's developmentally ready for—it sounded cool to him. I just wish I would have brought Anna here, too, as she's the child in our family more in need of finding a new sport, now that her confidence is shaken from playing soccer before she really had the tools to compete.

The second Sports Potential tool is a full Talent ID workup, for teenagers on up. For this, people submit to an even more extensive evaluation—a battery of 30 tests that makes the NFL combine treatment seem basic. Spinner and his staff calculate the circumference of calves and biceps, the breadth of hips, the length of legs, the span of arms, the size of hands and feet, the resting heart rate, body-fat percentage, and height and weight. They check concentration with a visual memory quiz, grip strength with a hydraulic gadget, and fine motor reflexes with a test involving the catching of a yardstick dropped between thumb and index finger. (Bradley's idea.)

Collecting all of this data is not a contemporary idea. The desire to analyze and quantify such traits goes back more than a century. Basketball founder James Naismith was so fascinated with the mortal machinery of athletes that he measured every entering freshman male at the University of Kansas in 19 ways, from height to weight, breadth of shoulders to girth of chest. What's original with Sports Potential's tool is that the data gets fed into software that compares his or her characteristics with those of their age peers around the country—as well as elite athletes from 50 sports and

100 positions. The base information was collected during the previous three years from pro, college, and national teams that agreed to work with Spinner's staff. So now Sports Potential knows, for instance, that baseball infielders have a 50 percent faster reaction time than the average male. That long jumpers concentrate and focus 70 percent better. That wide receivers leap 60 percent higher.

One of the first people to go through the exercise was Tehuna Mahoni, a 13-year-old eighth grader from nearby East Palo Alto. Growing up just across the 101 Freeway, in a rough section of town where the sound of police choppers fills the night sky, she had never played sports on a regular basis. Her Tongan-American immigrant parents worked long hours trying to make a life for their four children and found no room in their schedules for the games and ever-increasing commitments of youth sports. Then, when Tehuna got to middle school, so scant was her classmates' interest in sports—other than chasing boys, that is—there was no demand for teams for girls.

But now her parents want their big-boned daughter to get involved in sports, in part to keep her out of trouble. They have some idea where to start. The top five recommendations are right there on her Sports Potential custom evaluation, accessible with a password on the web:

1) Track and field - Discus
2) Softball - Catcher
3) Softball - First base
4) Track and field - Javelin
5) Rowing - Open

Her workup has reams of bar charts with detailed breakdowns and a list of local clubs and facilities that sponsor each sport.

"I'm going to give discus a try," she says, "even though I haven't heard of it."

With calf, hip, and hand sizes in the top 10 percentile for girls her age, she has an ideal physique for softball according to her Sports Potential profile. Indeed, twice in middle school, competing on a lark, she won first place in softball-throwing contests. "But I don't like the game," she says.

More to the point: She doesn't like objects being thrown at her, a fear she noted in her Sports Potential questionnaire. So in addition to softball, the ice hockey and lacrosse recommendations in her chart are highlighted in red, suggesting sports she might excel in—if she confronts her dread of hard, flying objects.

And if she gets good coaching, of course. One of Spinner's goals is to get schools to adopt the Sports Potential tests and screen all students. Another one is persuading the respective NGBs of sports to help subsidize the training of athletes who get identified as potential stars of the future. Like his colleagues at the AIS, Spinner isn't worried if his grand plan bears the faint echo of the former government-run, Eastern Bloc sports factories. "Those systems were all about taking choices away from people and pushing them to do something whether they had an interest in it or not," says Spinner, who's initially launching the products, at $125 and $200 a pop, in health clubs with the plan of bringing the price down if he can get schools and USOC support. "We're an American company trying to do it the American way. It's an opt-in service that someone can choose to pay to take. It's information, not decisionmaking."

Tehuna, after all, might just want to pursue tennis in high school. It's farther down on her recommended list, but she's dabbled in it, and she thinks she might like that sport, too. Mostly, the big girl with the soft black eyes just wants to find a way to transcend the self-conscious tattoo on her right arm, the one that reads "Shyness," her nickname at school. "I just want to be really good at one sport," she says. "And to be outgoing."

• • •

A few months later I'm back in the nation's capital. A couple of blocks from the White House where America's unfunded mandate, the Amateur Sports Act, was signed into law 27 years earlier, a stocky man in a suit and reading glasses steps up to a podium—nothing Olympic—in a room at the National Press Club. It's Dan Gould, a former college wrestler and now one of the leading researchers on the athletic lives of children. He's been brought to Washington, D.C., to deliver what is being touted as the first-ever "national report card" on youth sports.

He looks out at the crowd of a couple of dozen attendees, some of them journalists, some of them teenagers associated with the sponsoring group, and wonders how much the information he is about to deliver will sink in. He prefers to use well-known athletes to get out the message about important topics, because people listen to celebrities. He's just a Michigan State professor sitting on a panel of experts assembled by a nonprofit group called the Citizenship Through Sports Alliance (CTSA), a coalition of pro and amateur sports leagues whose stated aim is to promote character in youth sports.

Gould doesn't have a familiar face. But he has a recognizable problem.

"We are losing our child-centered focus," he says. "It's real easy to forget that sports are about producing better kids—physically, socially, developmentally."

Gould makes no mention of the USOC, which was once a member of the CTSA but had recently stopped paying the $25,000 in annual dues. He had worked with the USOC for years as a consultant and has no interest in bashing an organization whose structural limitations he can appreciate. Still, the CTSA report card he unveils may as well be the medal count of youth sports under the guidance of the organizations the USOC oversees:

Child-centered philosophy	D
Coaching	C-
Health and safety	C+
Officiating	B-
Parental behavior/involvement	D

I grab a copy of the grade sheet and drive up the highway to Baltimore, where merely having a team to grade counts as an achievement. As Gould reminds me as I am heading out the door, youth sports in America are now largely a suburban exercise.

AGE 11

THE GREATEST CITY IN AMERICA

Baltimore, Maryland

Oriole Park at Camden Yards is, in my estimation, the best modern-era ballpark in the land. Others will disagree. Since the Baltimore Orioles took occupancy in 1992, there have been larger and far swankier facilities built around the country—full-service entertainment zones with every amenity from children's playscapes to on-site breweries to retractable roofs that weigh 22 million pounds and quite effectively separate fans from moisture and heat. That's why Camden Yards is a gem. It does not aspire to perfection; instead it strives for connection. Connection to the city from which it springs and to the history of a sport that is nothing without its history. The architects who drew up the lines not only gave ticket-buyers a JumboTron, escalators to the upper deck, and seats with ample leg room—the basic needs of the modern fan—they also gave them a glimpse of life beyond the confines of the venue and the moment. In a nod to the ballparks of the early 1900s, steel columns, beams, and trusses are used to support the structure instead of concrete. Just beyond the right field seats is Eutaw Street, a pedestrian-only promenade where fans can buy ribs and look at plaques of Orioles Hall of Famers, and just beyond that is an old, eight-story brick warehouse that was refurbished and made into team office space.

When I first visited Camden Yards a couple of years after it opened, the Orioles were regularly playing before sellout crowds, with nearly a third of all fans coming from the D.C. area. Some took the train that pulls right up to the ballpark; others drove on I-95 and parked in the many lots just off the highway. Camden Yards was a place to fall in love with, and an inspiration for more than a few pro sports owners who at the time were stuck with alien, multisport flying saucers that had touched down in the '70s and never left. Among those were the owners of the Seattle Mariners, who desperately wanted a replacement for the gray, soulless Kingdome. They saw the same thing I did in Camden Yards, a place that could be enjoyed even when the team didn't win. There was value in merely sitting there, following the arc of a well-struck ball. Here's what I wrote about that for *The Seattle Times*:

> It floats up, past the redbrick B&O Warehouse, into the infinite Baltimore evening sky, white leather on black canvas. Then, on its way down, it draws a path that uses the city as a backdrop, like the set of a play that runs 81 times a year (and sometimes longer). The ball passes in front of the modern skyscrapers several blocks in the distance, then the antique Bromo-Seltzer tower with its Big Ben-like clock, finally setting down in a cushion of bluegrass in short center field, mere feet from where Babe Ruth's father ran a saloon early in the century.
>
> Baltimore wins!
>
> Baltimore—not just the Oriole ballclub—wins!

I wasn't oblivious to the even bigger picture; I noted that the bonds used to build the ballpark were being paid off through proceeds from a state sports-themed lottery, a regressive form of financing that relies disproportionately on the poor. Baltimore had plenty of poor people, with high murder and AIDS rates, and a failing school system.

Still, in retrospect, I wish I had gotten into my rental car and also driven a few blocks past the ballpark, beyond the Inner Harbor and into the inner city, into the neighborhoods that aren't on the tourist maps handed out at the better hotels. I should have crossed over to Martin Luther King Boulevard, made a left on historic Pennsylvania Ave., and pursued the no less important story that was unfolding, entirely overlooked: Just as public funding for stadiums was exploding, sports and recreation resources for city children were imploding.

If I had made that trip, I might have stumbled across a boy named Carmelo Anthony, his basketball gear paid for by drug dealers.

• • •

Anthony saw his first street death around age 11, three years after he and his mother had moved from New York City into a two-story row house in a section of West Baltimore that once was the proud heart of the city's African-American civic life but had fallen into disrepair. Globalization had exported the steel-industry jobs that previously had floated Baltimore for better than half a century and crack had joined heroin as a favorite street drug in the 1980s, so now the marble steps in front of the row homes were populated with more than one city's fair share of users and dealers, pimps and prostitutes. One day, a guy on a motorcycle came barreling around the corner chased by the cops. The bike tipped over and he slid under a car. "Got killed like that," Anthony says. "Dude wasn't even from my neighborhood."

A couple of years later, he saw a man stabbed to death. That one was worse to witness, because it took longer for the man to expire. On the other hand, all blood is the same color and dead men have the same cold look in their eyes. Anthony, now a NBA All-Star, says he never got used to the experience. "It's like your body just goes numb," he says. "You don't realize that the person's done, like he's dead completely, until you sit down and think about it." And when Anthony thought about it, the premature finality made him want a better end for himself.

But where to aim, and how to get there? He had few tools to help him carve a path out of the ghetto. His Puerto Rican father died of cancer when Anthony was 2, depriving him of a bond that as a boy he wanted more than anything else. His two brothers and one sister were much older so they stayed back in New York. His mother, Mary, is a strong woman with deep religious beliefs, but as a $9.85-per-hour housekeeper at the University of Baltimore she lacked the resources to expose her youngest son to much beyond the grimy sidewalks of Myrtle Avenue. Anthony did have some aptitudes: He's always had an ability to memorize words, so he was a good speller in elementary school. And basic math came easily to him. But showing up on the honor roll can be an invitation to pariah-hood, placing a target on one's back in a city where getting respect is a daily struggle. It was easier for him to play the role of class clown ... and to assume the position of statistic-in-waiting. "I was looking for a role model when I was growing up," he says. "But, you know, our role models wasn't any corporations, any owners of Fortune 500 companies. My role model was the guy up the street who was making $500 a day without a job, doing whatever he was doing out there." The Robert C. Marshall rec center, on Pennsylvania Ave., kept him from following the same path.

Each weekday, Anthony spent the late afternoon hours playing ball at the facility two blocks from his home. Like other parents around Baltimore, Mary Anthony used the rec center to keep an eye on her kid until she got off work. There were rooms inside the windowless box of a building where kids like her son could do their homework, and play spaces inside and out in which to burn off excess energy. The rec center didn't transform Anthony into a solid student—he screwed around until his senior year when he barely acquired the minimum ACT score to accept an athletic scholarship to Syracuse—but it did offer an alternative to the action in the streets. He played all the main sports for the local teams, pitching in baseball and playing tight end in football. And of course there was basketball, in which he flashed talent from the moment he arrived in town. In one 36-35 loss, he scored 33 of his team's points. Not bad for a kid who would be asthmatic until age 13.

Soon, though, the cops took control of Marshall and a couple dozen other rec centers in the city. They were renamed Police Athletic League (PAL) sites. The familiar rec staffers were let go, replaced by uniformed officers who laid down a new rule: No one above the age of 18 could enter the rec center. It was an attempt to flush out the adult drug dealers who sometimes played ball there. But the move backfired, as law enforcement effectively was asking kids in the neighborhood to pick sides. For children in a suburban environment where crime isn't an everyday reality, such a decision might be a no-brainer. But in places where dealers can be found on every corner, and some cops have learned to assume guilt and ask questions later, standing with the men and women in blue has its perils. "After that, drug raids went sky high in Baltimore because people wouldn't go to the PAL centers," Anthony says. "The police would be sitting in the front office of our rec center with they hats, they badges, they suits on. Like, we had rallies over there. *Rallies*."

Yet, the cops only had assumed responsibility for the centers because city budgets for recreation were continually being slashed. The first big cuts came in 1993, just months after the Orioles moved into the $200 million Camden Yards with a sweetheart lease. Club profits that year hit $25 million, allowing team owner Eli Jacobs to sell the once-struggling franchise to a local attorney, Peter Angelos, for $173 million—at the time a record price for a sports franchise, and $100 million more than Jacobs and his partners had paid for the club four years earlier. (The franchise is now estimated to be worth more than twice what Angelos paid for it.) Meanwhile, a fiscal crunch at the state level reduced the amount of annual taxpayer support flowing back to cities. Faced with deep and immediate needs related to police, schools, and emergency services, it seemed far easier to whack away at funding for recreation and parks.

By the end of the decade, two-thirds of the city's 143 neighborhood rec centers had been shut down or, in the case of a few, taken over by the police. The cops were only able to step in because of grants flowing from President Clinton's community-policing initiative, which was successful elsewhere in reducing crime. (Not however in Baltimore, where, in key sections of the city, drug lords *were* the community leaders.) No longer comfortable using his neighborhood facility, Anthony began playing ball at the still city-controlled Mount Royal Recreation Center, about 13 blocks north of his home. It was just far enough away to discourage many kids from making the daily trek, which could be dangerous given the intra-neighborhood rivalries. "That area where Melo grew up was so vital," says Darrell Corbett, the rec leader at Mount Royal and Anthony's youth basketball coach. "Kids used that field at Marshall all the time. Melo was there every day. It was his safe haven."

The cuts thinned out staff at the existing rec centers, making mere supervision a challenge. Activity fees rose, which always disproportionately affects those most in need of such services, the indigent. The citywide youth football league shrank in size, and baseball all but disappeared from the urban landscape. Part of the problem was that funds were lacking to maintain the fields properly. And with each demoralizing cut, the city recreation and parks department slipped further into bureaucratic dysfunction. At one point, the mayor shifted the responsibility of field maintenance to the public works department, which already was overwhelmed with the tasks of delivering clean water and picking up trash. It couldn't prioritize the repair of rusty and splintered equipment at the city's 300 play lots, 80 percent of which were deemed unsafe for children. So the next mayor handed that job back to recreation and parks—albeit without a full lawn-mowing and metal-welding staff. The department would have to make due with one maintenance worker for every 101 acres.

Oriole Park, by contrast, has a 26-person grounds crew to tend to every need of one field that gets used sparingly by grown men who have every expectation that the bluegrass will be trimmed before each game, and that the infield dirt will be raked and reraked until the chances of a bad hop are near zero.

"Funding pro sports was supposed to help the local economy, and that was supposed to get more money into the rec centers," Corbett says, learning forward in his office chair at Mount Royal, where he still works. "Well, I guess things change. I think they ought to charge a $1 tax on every ticket sold to those games, with the money going straight to parks and rec. I thought that was a great idea." He's referring to a proposal made by the city council back in 1999, after the Baltimore Ravens had moved into another publicly financed stadium next to Camden Yards. The state enticed the owner of the Cleveland Browns to relocate his franchise with a 30-year lease that became the envy of the NFL: No rent, just the reimbursement of annual maintenance costs and the levying of a 10 percent ticket surcharge. The proposal to add an additional dollar to all tickets fizzled after the Ravens and O's balked at a direct subsidy to recreation.

All around the young Carmelo Anthony, then, there was decay. The outdoor court in his hood that he and his friends balled at got shut down due to neglect and complaints about noise that once was largely confined to the rec center. Midnight basketball, a national initiative that had been ridiculed by conservative Republicans after Clinton proposed federal funding for it as an anticrime tool, disappeared as a late-night option for teens. A popular inner-city, neighborhood-based basketball league also lost many teams as cheap, rec center courts became scarce; school gyms were still available but expensive (it costs $100 an hour to open a school gym because staff needs to be brought in to secure and heat the facility at overtime rates). As for middle-school-based teams, there was nothing.

Fortunately for Anthony, he had flashed enough talent on the court to find opportunities. He wasn't much interested in playing defense, but he was smooth with the ball. He could score, which is how players in grassroots hoops get noticed. AAU clubs from across town wanted his services, as the hunt for national championships for little kids was taking hold in the mid-1990s. The neighborhood businessmen also figured he might have a future—one different than their own—so they stepped up as benefactors, filling a void that might never have existed with a better-subsidized recreational operation.

"I probably wouldn't have had to help if that was the case," says Corey Jones, one of the drug dealers who lived on the block.

I find Jones in front of Melo's former home on Myrtle Ave., which has lost a lot of life even since both of them moved out of the neighborhood. Several homes are abandoned, boarded up. There's no sign of commerce within blocks, other than the usual illicit varieties. Jones, a stocky man in his mid-30s whose street name is "Fred," tells me he's just driving through the old hood, that he hasn't dealt drugs for the better part of a decade, that he's moved on to renovating old homes. But back then, he says, he was among a group of dealers who would give Anthony rides to practice, cash for out-of-town AAU tournaments, whatever assistance he needed to focus on basketball. "He didn't need to be in the street too much because older guys like us kept him out of it," he says.

Anthony's mother did her part, too, buying his shoes and putting food on the table. Corbett bought a $2,700 used van to truck his players around in. But, Anthony allows, "Drug dealers funded our programs. I was like 10 when they started buying my uniforms, and it went on until I was 13 or 14." He says they never asked him for any favors in return, such as delivering product. "They just want to see you do good," he says. "They want to come support you, show you love. Then after they come show you love, they go do what they gotta do. You can't fault them for what they do. They grown men. That's a decision they made."

If there was any form of repayment that Anthony has made to his former sponsors, it lies in the fact that a national celebrity, and thus inevitable role model, has refused to condemn them for their trade.

• • •

This posture creates a dilemma for anyone who wants people to stop killing people in Baltimore. Anthony's take emerged in the aftermath of his appearing in a local underground DVD, *Stop Snitchin'*, which discourages cooperation with the police, specifically by drug dealers who might try to avoid mandatory prison sentences by fingering other dealers. Anthony appears in a few scenes, mostly in the background. He says little, and never advocates drug dealing, much less violence. In fact, Anthony would later argue, "stop snitchin' " is the ghetto way of saying, "stop the violence." Still, thanks to his cameo the DVD went national, and since then he has rejected a request by Baltimore police to film a clip encouraging witnesses to come forward. His street cred has never been higher.

Dr. Edward Cornwell is trying to see that as an opportunity.

"Athletes and rappers, it's what it is in our society," he says. "Let me use their celebrity to get our message across."

As chief of trauma at Johns Hopkins Hospital on the east side, Cornwell is tasked with stitching up the victims of Baltimore's ongoing drug war. Those who don't come through his emergency room doors DOA, that is. He's a busy man and doesn't have time to do anything other than fix momentary problems. Surgeons in ERs are taught to stabilize the patient, move on to the next crisis, and leave it at that. Compartmentalization is a survival tool that keeps a surgeon mentally fresh. But over the past decade he's seen enough shot up and stabbed young men, usually between the ages of 15 to 24, to step out of his comfort zone and try to confront the problem of youth violence before it reaches him professionally.

For now, that means showing groups of school kids and teachers what he's seen, in a graphic multimedia presentation called "Hype vs. Reality." He'll roll a video clip showing a gunshot chest wound of a lucky-to-be-alive gang member, dropping the jaws of little boys in cornrows. "The problem didn't start on that night when they were shot," Cornwell tells audiences. "The problem started when they were 8, 9, 10, 11, 12. That's when we form our attitudes, right? That's when we develop or accept the messages from our culture."

He wants to turn his presentation into a public-service announcement and take it national. He's been looking for an athlete who can help him do that. Eager to counter the *Stop Snitchin'* publicity, Anthony and his handlers have agreed to make the spot. The doctor is moving ahead with the effort, despite his reservations about the spokesman, because he figures he needs Melo's cache with kids. "What do I have?" he says. "White coat, black face, bloody hands. That's all I'm bringing."

A little historical perspective would serve us well here. Just over a century ago, the scourge of rampant juvenile delinquency in American cities was attacked not through the media, but, as much as anything else, through organized sports. The professionals leading the charge—the Cornwells of their day—were called "child savers."

The Progressive-era movement, in fact, saved George Herman Ruth. Though The Babe, as Ruth would later become known, now seems like a mythical figure, he was a real person who had a real boyhood—one that bears relevance to the historic role of recreational sports in both addressing urban ills and developing pro athletes.

In his early years, Ruth was a street kid. He lived with his parents near the Baltimore waterfront, above their saloon, where the action was rough and rowdy (his dad would later be killed breaking up a bar fight). He skipped school, resisted any form of discipline, and, as he would later say, didn't know right from wrong. He came to hate the cops. Labeled "incorrigible," his parents finally handed him over to the Xaverian Brothers who ran St. Mary's Industrial School for Boys, where, after a couple of brief stints, he was enrolled full-time at age 10. He was one of 800 boys at the city- and state-funded institution, among the many created around the country during that era to manage the growing number of orphans and wayward boys who threatened to disrupt the social order.

Effectively, St. Mary's was a prison, as no boy could leave campus without permission from the Brothers (akin to male Catholic nuns). But the school had its upside, too: Daily doses of recreational sports. Each afternoon for an hour or two, even in the cold of winter, the boys would head out to "the yard," a basic if perfectly functional patch of dirt and grass where several types of games were played. Baseball was the favorite sport, and every boy, no matter their skill level, was placed on a team and given instruction. It's where Ruth, who until then had had no interest in the national pastime, learned to play and love the game. There were no hovering parents, no contests against outside teams until high school age—just him and his fellow incorrigibles challenging each other and fielding the mighty fungo blasts of Brother Matthias, a 6-foot-6, 250-pound baseball aficionado whom Ruth came to call "the greatest man I've ever known." Today, the notion of developing an elite athlete largely through intramural sports seems ludicrous, but by 1914 when Ruth was signed to a minor league contract and released from St. Mary's one week after his 20th birthday, he was a finished product. For that, he credited Brother Matthias, the mentor who had taught him how to field and had insisted that he learn to play every position.

Ruth was soon the best lefthanded pitcher in baseball. Naturally strong, he applied his physical gifts and refined technique at the plate, becoming the game's first great slugger. His charisma, legendary home runs, and larger-than-life persona elevated Americans' affection for pro sports and the otherwise regular guys in uniform. Ruth was The Bambino, the Sultan of Swat, the Maharaja of Mash, Homeric Herman, the Wali of Wallop, the Colossus of Clout—sportswriters couldn't come up with enough nicknames to capture their affection for the player who would retire in 1935 with 714 dingers. In 1936, the Baseball Hall of Fame itself was created and Ruth among the first five players inducted, marking the start of an era in which great athletes were to be recognized as immortals.

When Ruth was a boy, athletes weren't particularly revered members of society. The most outstanding of them—such as baseball's Christy Mathewson and Honus Wagner—were admired for their on-field abilities, but the true cultural heroes were more likely to come from the ranks of the military or politics, like Teddy Roosevelt. Likewise, the athletic infrastructure wasn't set up in a way that was effectively designed to identify and develop emerging talent for the pro sports leagues, as football and basketball hadn't yet taken off at that level yet and salaries in baseball were still quite modest. Instead, the emphasis was on providing broad-based recreation, as the child savers of the era strongly believed in the value of physical activity as a tool to channel potentially destructive male energies. Beyond the thousands of playgrounds Luther Gulick and his peers got built during the first two decades of the 20th century, large urban parks offered opportunities for kids to run, jump, and play catch.

Without ever intending to do so, these play spaces served as the launching pad for professional sports as a mass-entertainment phenomenon. They were so popular, Gulick wrote in 1920, that in some "it was impossible to see through the group for ten yards in any direction" because several games were going on in one space. A ball hit was a ball lost in the masses of boys.

One of the great mysteries among baseball writers is why offensive numbers in baseball jumped so dramatically in the 1920s. Steve Hirdt, a statistician with the Elias Sports Bureau, has observed that the increase was even more robust than the period beginning in 1994, which is roughly when baseball's steroid era began and home run records began to fall. Comparing the 12 years before 1920, Ruth's first year with the Yankees, to the 12 years after that, the batting average across the majors improved from .253 to .285. The increase in runs per game was 27 percent; the increase in homers per game was 173 percent. This period has become known as the "live-ball era," but that's a misnomer. Tests done at the time found no difference between the ball used in the majors in the late 1910s and the one used subsequently. Hirdt suggests several alternate theories to account for the spike: new rules limiting trick pitches, more frequent use of clean balls, and batters imitating the Babe's uppercut swing. I'll offer one more: The players of Ruth's era were the descendants and first beneficiaries of broad-based recreational sports for youth.

Child saved. Athlete made.

Fan made, too.

The enthusiasm for pro sports that was born during that era was so great that cities eventually began competing to attract franchises in top-tier leagues. At the front of the pack was Baltimore, whose political leaders shortly after World War II laid plans to bring major league baseball and football teams to town. The lure was a recently built, city-financed venue: Memorial Stadium, located five miles north of downtown in a neighborhood of row houses and mom-and-pop stores. In 1953, an NFL team from Dallas and a baseball team from St. Louis relocated to Baltimore and became the Colts and Orioles, respectively. Spectator sports and citizen recreation were still connected at the hip, as reflected in the fact that the city's recreation and parks department ran Memorial Stadium. But the era of the publicly built stadium had arrived, giving club owners the power to extract subsidies for their for-profit companies. Everywhere, taxpayers would become partners in jacking up franchise values and player salaries across pro sports.

Live by the sword, die by the sword. In the spring of 1984, the Colts franchise snuck out of town in the middle of a snowy night, a line of Mayflower moving vans rumbling toward Indianapolis where a greener, artificial pasture awaited. Baltimoreans were heartbroken at the loss of the Colts, whose bond with fans was forged through legendary games (the club's televised victory over the New York Giants in the 1958 NFL Championship came to be known as the greatest in league history) and blue-collar heroes (Johnny Unitas, John Mackey). Still, most citizens weren't so desperate that they wanted to keep playing the stadium blackmail game. The city had been losing jobs and was already straining to provide basic services. When the Maryland legislature proposed to build state-of-the-art facilities that could keep the O's in town and eventually recruit another NFL club, there were signs that it would fail if it went to a public vote. But an effort to force a referendum was quashed in court, on the grounds that the funding was technically an appropriation—i.e., something the state needs to keep running—not an item subject to the will of the people.

When Oriole Park opened for business, free luxury boxes were set aside for the governor and the mayor.

The next year, there were a record 353 murders in Baltimore.

• • •

So now B'More exports two forms of national entertainment: Pro sports on TV. And gritty dramas about a city compromised by the drug trade, most recently HBO's *The Wire*. The Game and The Game.

It's hard to blame the subject matter of the latter on that of the former. But publicly financed stadiums are supposed to deliver a real financial dividend for cities—money that can be spent to improve quality of life for its citizens. In 1996, when the O's were playing before sellout crowds each night, an economics professor at Johns Hopkins produced a 47-page analysis concluding that Camden Yards is "most definitely not a success as a vehicle for job creation and economic development." The report estimated that all those fans coming from out of state created 460 local jobs and lifted Baltimore home values a grand total of $6.50. (The Ravens, who play far fewer games, hadn't yet moved into their new stadium so the impact wasn't fully analyzed).

A decade later, Orioles' home attendance had fallen to 20th out of 30 MLB teams, due largely to nine consecutive losing seasons. Still, the Maryland Stadium Authority released a report insisting that Camden Yards supported nearly 2,500 jobs and $72 million in regional wage income and that all those fans coming from out of state spun off $7.6 million in local sales taxes. But mysterious "multiplier effects" were used in the calculations, and the study didn't account for lost investment opportunities related to the public subsidies. Generally, experts discount the conclusions drawn in these types of stadium analyses. Either way, it's clear that not much of the alleged winnings have trickled down to the infrastructure that services youth sports.

MYTH NO. 11
Money is pouring into youth sports.

THE TRUTH
It is, but not in the communities that need it most.

The most famous basketball court in the city is called The Dome, located not far from Johns Hopkins Hospital. It's a covered, well-lit outdoor space where every great Baltimore baller has played, from Muggsy Bogues to Reggie Williams to Sam Cassell. The city, which is allowing Nike to reference the court on the side of one of its basketball shoes as part of an urban marketing effort, restarted Midnight Basketball there a couple of years ago. Just don't try and play there any season other than the summer. After the longtime director of the attached rec center retired a few years back, games at The Dome during other seasons became scarce. When I drove by on a warm spring day, it was locked up and caged off. The funeral parlor on the corner was open for business, though.

The most extensively used recreational space in the city is Patterson Park, across town from where Anthony grew up. It's one of those thoughtfully laid out urban parks from the 19th century that has an ice rink, pool, running trails, rec center, and half a dozen or so athletic fields. But the soccer goals are without nets and some of the baseball fields are covered with weeds. There's a distressed quality to the place that matches the chipped, fading benches which bear signs reading, perversely, "Baltimore ... The Greatest City in America" (the rah-rah slogan of the previous mayor). You can tell the recreation and parks staff is trying to shine the old jewel, maintaining the nets on the tennis courts and clearing debris. But there's only so much they can do with 365 full-time workers. In 1990, there were 1,400 employees in the department.

"If you don't fund amateur athletics, what do you expect?" Corbett says. "It's not free, and it's not cheap." Corbett is a thickly built man with a no-nonsense demeanor who commands ample respect from the kids he oversees. But he could use help. As I pulled up to his rec center, a boy a couple of years older than my son Cole was getting his brains beaten in by another kid being egged on by a dozen peers who just wanted to see someone get hurt. The bigger kid had the smaller kid pushed backward over a chain rope above a small patch of grass in front of the rec center, and the smaller kid was just taking it—punch after punch to his gently lined, terrified face. It appeared to be a petty dispute, an early alpha-dog exercise, but the result left an impression on the pummeled boy. As word traveled down the alley that Mr. Corbett was coming and the beat-down came to an end, there was a look of deep humiliation in the kid's eyes.

If Corbett had an extra body to watch the front door, or, better yet, could organize a game to occupy those boys, all that emerging testosterone might not have been channeled into a violent episode that will surely beg retaliation.

Funding for recreation has crept up under new mayor Sheila Dixon, the aunt of Juan Dixon, a NBA player and rec center alum who lost both parents to AIDS-related diseases before he was 17. But, Corbett says, "We need more, much more." The department gets no dedicated cut of the local sales tax, as do rec departments in some other cities. And no further run has been made at an Orioles or Ravens ticket surcharge—just an inquiry by a city councilman, quickly dismissed, asking the stadium authority to forgive the city's annual $1 million payment to the authority.

Here and there, the city's pro teams have chipped in.

A few years after Anthony left the Robert C. Marshall rec center, the Oriole organization helped bring in dirt to improve the surface of the adjacent baseball field (the renamed "Orioles/Saturn Field" has fallen into disrepair again). The club also offers a free skills clinic each spring and sponsors a baseball program for fourth and fifth graders. Its most significant commitment is as local administrator for Major League Baseball's Reviving Baseball in the Inner City initiative, providing uniforms and equipment for 20 teams of teenagers. An Oriole spokeswoman says the club's total contribution to city sports comes to about $87,000 annually. She said another channel for charity is the Baltimore Orioles Foundation. But a check of that entity's tax filings from the most recent three-year period shows that little of $443,000 in donations collected by the foundation was disbursed to organizations with ties to youth recreation. Half of the donations received, in fact, weren't disbursed to any community group; they stayed with the foundation. (More than anything, the franchise has contributed dubious role models to the community in recent years. Nineteen current and former Orioles were linked by the Mitchell Report to steroids or other banned drugs.)

The Ravens are more engaged. Four or five players have relationships with high school teams, and they provide varying degrees of support. The club itself spent $500,000 refurbishing the best high school stadium in Baltimore it could find, replacing the rocky dirt with artificial turf and installing lights to allow night games; the NFL chipped in another $300,000 as part of a national initiative to restore urban fields. In 2005, the Ravens outfitted city teams with $250,000 worth of uniforms and equipment. That year, one in which the club established itself as an NFL leader in community service, the Ravens provided $1 million in charity to local organizations related to grassroots sports or otherwise.

Still, such gifts are table scraps in the all-you-can-eat feast that is pro sports.

Consider: The Ravens dropped $12 million in 2006 on just one player, quarterback Steve McNair. That's as much as the city of Baltimore spent on the recreational and athletic needs of the 20,000 children it could afford to service, in all sports.

"If we're to the point where the value of one player exceeds that of the general population, then we're in trouble as a society," says Portia Harris, who runs all recreation programs for the city. "People want to see star players on their teams, so that increases their market value. I can appreciate that. But what's not increasing is the investment in kids that helps them achieve in the first place." Harris, an African-American woman in her forties, speaks from personal experience. She was a rec center kid in the 1970s who learned to play tennis at a city camp and went on to earn an athletic scholarship at the University of Maryland. "In my mind, either you pay the price now or you pay the price later," she says. "There are certain things you learn though recreation—socialization, interpersonal skills, commitment, discipline. If those things aren't taught now, when youth are impressionable, the question becomes: How do you deal with that when they become misguided adults? We've seen what happens. The penal system is exploding. They don't have enough space to keep people behind bars. A lot of that is because we didn't pay when they were younger. When I was a kid, these social programs made a difference in my life. My family was important, too, but for many, these programs are the only thing they have. If we don't give kids the opportunity to see outside of their current situation, it'll come back to hurt us."

Camden Yards sparked the largest construction boom in the history of American spectator sports. The great majority of MLB, NFL, NBA, and NHL teams have moved into new or significantly renovated homes since, or gained the approval to do so, at a cost of more than $20 billion. Most of that tab has been picked up by the public—and it's not just cities and states that are paying. Federal taxpayers contribute as well. The Camden Yards project, for instance, used $48 million in federal transportation funds that allowed out-of-town fans to get in and out of the stadium area more efficiently. Beyond direct grants, dozens of facilities also have been financed with the use of tax-exempt bonds, a federally supported method of borrowing money at a lower interest rate. More commonly used to build schools and other public projects, such bonds devoted to sports stadiums cost the U.S. Treasury more than $100 million annually. "In our view, this is a very expensive public housing program for millionaires," a spokesman for Sen. Byron L. Dorgan (D-N.D.) told *The Washington Post* in 2003. Yet, efforts over the past decade to ban the practice have been rebuffed.

Meanwhile, at the other end of the athletic pipeline, federal support for the recreational sports infrastructure has dried up. The primary vehicle for encouraging the creation of playing fields is the Land and Water Conservation Fund, a legacy from the Kennedy Administration that offers matching grants to states and cities to carve out and maintain these spaces. Many of the 40,000 athletic fields created through this program were introduced long ago. Funding was whacked to a tenth of its previous level when Ronald Reagan took office, disappeared entirely in the late 1990s, restored to some degree when runner-biker George W. Bush took office, then virtually eliminated again as the Iraq war and other priorities took their toll on the budget. A month after the November 2006 elections that gave Democrats control of Congress, advocates of the program finally won a dedicated funding source—a small cut of royalty revenues from future offshore drilling in the Gulf of Mexico by oil companies. Thus, the nation is now wildcatting for youth sports, with the potential, a decade down the road, of a windfall. (Go Exxon!)

Baltimore has received nothing from the fund since 1980. It has benefited more from a much smaller program, the Urban Park and Recreation Recovery Act, which is designed specifically to help economically distressed cities rehabilitate their deteriorating parks and recreation facilities. Created in 1978, the same year, ironically, as the Amateur Sports Act, the initiative has provided Baltimore with $4.6 million in matching grants, one of the last of which was used to help Anthony's rec center, before it was taken over by the police. As with the LWCF, the Urban Park and Recreation Recovery Act has received less than half of its originally authorized funding. The last check written to any city under the act was in 2003, despite the recommendation by the Centers for Disease Control and Prevention that more parks and playgrounds get built as tools to fight growing obesity rates. The epidemic is especially pronounced among African-American youths, who on average sit in front of the TV seven hours a week more than white kids do.

Baltimore gets some state assistance for its parks and recreation facilities. It would be hard to imagine a municipality in America that needs it more. (Except perhaps Detroit, the only large American city that is more violent than Baltimore—and a city where recreation services, notably, have been slashed over the years.) Only one in nine Baltimore children now are involved in city-run athletic programs, not a good omen in a town where beating the odds can mean just getting a high school degree. Studies have shown that kids who play sports are more likely to stay in school and less likely to commit crime as juveniles.

Much of the concern about physical inactivity has centered on minority girls. In a random, unscientific, drive-around survey of a dozen or so parks and rec centers in Baltimore, I saw no more than a handful of girls outside playing any sports in any capacity. Almost by default—weeds can't grow in gyms—Baltimore has become known as a basketball town, so surely there were some bouncing balls inside gyms that I missed. But after a while their absence was so glaring that I began looking specifically for girls with softball bats, tennis rackets ... anything.

Then it occurred to me: I'm not seeing that many boys playing ball, either. Sam Cassell, the longtime NBA guard, tells me this isn't a mirage.

"It's unbelievable," he says. "When I was growing up, every court was filled with kids playing basketball or doin' whatever. Now, on a lot of the courts, they're just not out there. I think that's why the younger generation is suffering athletic-wise."

Across the nation, no group has suffered from the obesity crisis more than black kids. You'd never know that by the looks of pro basketball and football, which have come to be dominated by African-Americans over the past three decades. Popular images of black celebrities enjoying the very, very good life might suggest a new athletic class has emerged. But pull the U.S. Department of Education statistics, as I did, and a different story emerges. In 1980, most black teenagers played sports. Back then no ethnic group had a higher participation rate. Not anymore. In fact, no other ethnic group has lost more sports participants.

In other words, enjoy the game at your favorite pro venue. Just know that the full truth cannot be glimpsed from even the best seat in the house.

• • •

"It's like playing the Lotto, with a one in a million chance of making it out," Corey the former drug dealer says of his old friend Melo. "He's the lucky winner."

That much is obvious on a bright afternoon in December 2006, as an extra-large SUV with tinted windows pulls up in front of a handsome brick building a few blocks south of the Johns Hopkins Hospital. An elderly black man in a coat and tie, the chauffeur, opens the right rear passenger door and out pops Carmelo Anthony, all 6-foot-8 of him. Draped in a cool blue Brand Jordan warmup suit and a matching baseball cap turned backward and pulled low over his eyebrows, he thrusts a right arm triumphantly into the chilly air, eliciting shrieks from the elementary school kids who have gathered for the grand opening of the Carmelo Anthony Youth Development Center. Two Baltimore cops part the crowd, and the Denver Nuggets star steps into a ring of cameras from the assembled media.

"This is a dream come true for you," a local TV reporter says, as if reading from script.

"This *is* a dream come true," Anthony confirms, looking out over the microphones and into the distance. "I'm doing it for Baltimore. Tryin' to bring some life back to Baltimore. We kind of lost it for a minute but, you know, ultimately this is a shot at a new beginning."

Call it a win-win. Anthony still has a little P.R. problem to solve, the lingering resentment from *Stop Snitchin'*, plus a marijuana bust and a bar fight from a couple of years before that chased off big-time corporate sponsors. News of him helping to reopen the private rec center—abandoned by the Boys and Girls Club—should improve his image and standing on Madison Avenue. Plus, he has his own Brand Jordan shoe to sell, the latest in a line that has celebrated and exploited his ties to the dead-end streets of B'More. He shot a commercial last year on the unkempt outdoor court at, of all places, the neighborhood PAL center he once abandoned. In the spot he's presented as a black man being harassed by police, whose helicopters hover above, trailing him with a spotlight as he walks through the hood and nods at a series of little kids and hard-faced characters. His $125 kicks became No. 1 among shoes endorsed by active (i.e. not Michael Jordan) players, out-selling that of corporate darling LeBron James.

One could argue that if Anthony was truly the inner-city angel he's trying to show himself to be, he'd endorse a cheaper shoe. That's what Stephon Marbury of the New York Knicks did earlier in the year, lending his street-credible name to a $15 model that began to make it okay for a kid to step outside in shoes he could afford to buy without help. From whomever. It could also be argued that Anthony's commitment to donating $300,000 annually over the next five years to the nonprofit organization that runs the renamed Carmelo Anthony Youth Development Center is little more than pocket change to the player, who just months earlier re-upped with the Nuggets for $80 million and, with his Brand Jordan and other deals, should make well north of $100 million over the next five years. The money has gotten so crazy in pro sports, it's sometimes hard to fully comprehend how rich some of these guys are.

But to expect more from Anthony might not be fair. Babe Ruth codified the social contract between athletes and their public nearly a century ago. He bought a car in gratitude for Brother Matthias, and raised money for St. Mary's when a fire burned down part of the school. But the first jock to pull a bigger salary than the President of the United States—Ruth made $80,000 in 1930—left Baltimore and hardly looked back. He lived large, indulging in the best cars, clothes, clubs, and cigars that his era had to offer. He smiled a lot for the photographers, as does Anthony, and dabbled in movies, as does Anthony. Melo's first effort was a documentary, *Prison Ball*, about inmates in Louisiana playing hoops and reflecting on the circumstances that led to their incarceration. Anthony saw an early version of the doc, paid six figures to make himself executive producer, and inserted himself as the narrator and main character. He revisits the old neighborhood court in Baltimore, noting that he's from the ghetto, too. It's a touch self-aggrandizing, but the viewer does get the sense that Anthony laments the lack of safe places for kids to play.

So, thank you brother, for the much-needed love. Having laid down a couple sound bites, Anthony makes his way to the front entrance of the Carmelo Anthony Youth Development Center, where he is greeted by Elijah Cummings, who offers a conciliatory handshake. Time to mend fences. Cummings, the longtime Congressman and resident of inner-city Baltimore, had chastised Anthony for not sticking up for the police more forcefully after the *Stop Snitchin'* video hit the streets. He'd met with him in his office and implored him to set a better example, starting with an appearance in Dr. Cornwell's anti-violence PSA. "I realized that Carmelo, while he never will admit this, still has a lot to learn," he told me at the time. "He's still a very young man. He's trying to keep one foot in the neighborhood where many young men who have not had the good fortune he has had spend large parts of their day chasing or selling death, and then you have the other foot of Carmelo in the NBA making millions of dollars. He's stretched by both worlds." In other words, he's not ready to lead. Yet people have lost such faith in institutions that Cummings, like Cornwell, respects the influence of celebrity athletes. "As one of the top five basketball players, he automatically has a much louder voice than Elijah Cummings," he conceded.

A politician knows nothing if not how to read power. So after a quick hello, the two of them move together through swinging doors, the lawmaker whose efforts to save funding for youth sports programs had gone ignored and the ballplayer who has become Baltimore's chief beneficiary of America's investment in spectator sports. They pass a pair of floor-to-ceiling wallpaper posters of Melo in repose, one of them showing him holding a many-diamonded Jumpman necklace—the kind of jewelry one could acquire only with scads of loose cash. They enter the gym, where a couple hundred kids in blue T-shirts with Melo's mug on the front wait. Kids are sitting all over the refinished court, but not on the Melo logo in the tip-off circle. The walls are papered with artistic shots of neighborhood children, interspersed with ... six more larger-than-life shots of a laughing or smiling Melo. This is what happens when a city tells a kid he's Nobody, and he turns himself into Somebody who constantly gets reminded of his new status.

The bald, jowly Cummings steps up to the microphone stand (in front of another Melo painting propped up on the floor) and composes himself. In a moment he'll present the featured guest, and he must choose his words carefully. While the success of pro athletes can be inspiring, it also can reinforce the American belief, based in Social Darwinism, that the poor deserve to be poor. That hard work, and hard work alone, is the great separator of winners and losers in sports as in society—when, truth be told, Anthony probably isn't here today if he didn't happen to grow five inches the summer before his junior year of high school. In the past, Cummings has winced at the sight of young ballers swooning over Anthony, thinking that level of success might be theirs one day. Cummings has nothing against dreaming big, but not everyone can grow big. He wishes kids would approach the game as a means, not an end.

So Cummings, considering his options, issues a measured plea. His message is directed as much at Anthony as it is to the crowd before them. "What I hope happens here today," he says, "is our children will look at this brother here and say, 'This is a brother who grew up in our neighborhoods, and he grew up to be a great man, and he's not a great man just because he can put a basketball through a hoop. That he was great because he never forgot and he came back and gave so much of what he had so that we all could be better.' And for that, on behalf of *all* of us, and even for generations yet unborn, we thank you brother.

"Ladies and gentlemen, the No. 1 scorer in the N-B-A ... Carmelo Anthony!"

Everyone gives it up for Anthony, who takes the mike and smiles sweetly. Two days later, much of America would be calling him a thug again after he sucker punches a New York Knick, eliciting a 15-game suspension from an NBA commissioner who has grown tired of players, and particularly Anthony, acting out the code of the street. Cornwell, too, dismisses the idea of ever using Anthony as an antiviolence spokesman. But right now, at Anthony's new rec center, it's all good.

"I got my family here today. I got the whole Baltimore city," he says, waving his arms. "I probably had more doubts than anybody in the whole wide world in opening up this rec center. People said I wasn't giving back, I wasn't coming home. But how could I forget a city like this where I grew up at?"

Starting today, his local Team Melo AAU club will have a regular, and free, place to practice. Starting today, kids will get help with their homework in a well-lit reading room. Starting today, kids will fill the building with the sounds of African drums they're learning to play. Starting today, 250 kids a day will be serviced.

Now if the city could just find a way to take care of the other 160,000 in need.

• • •

The farther you get away from central Baltimore, the better the athletic fields. On the outskirts of town is Cardinal Gibbons High School, where a team of boys—all but one of them white—can be found taking batting practice in cherry red T-shirts that read "The House that Built Ruth." It's the same space where the boys of St. Mary's Industrial School once played, before the private Catholic high school moved in and took over the place in 1963. But the field is by no means a green cathedral. The outfield tilts because of the old tunnels dating back to St. Mary's that run between the buildings, and the infield grass is spotty, inducing bad hops.

The coach has tried to raise money for improvements. He's found that folks are more likely to subtract than add to the diamond. Every now and then, he'll find some stranger on his knees in the batter's box, scooping dirt into a jar.

"You'd think a lot of people might want to pour money into Babe Ruth Field," says Lee Schwarzenberg, the coach. "Nah. But a lot of people come here."

Fame is a powerful thing.

Forty-five minutes up the highway in Aberdeen are the nicest youth fields in the state. Carved out of the red dirt of rural Maryland are a series of miniature major league ballparks, including a replica of Oriole Park, that were built in 2005. The facility is the home of the annual Cal Ripken World Series, where, in association with the Babe Ruth League, the retired Orioles shortstop runs one of the top international youth events. He also hosts a series of well-regarded tournaments and camps, teaching baseball "The Ripken Way"—which emphasizes simple instruction so kids can grasp the coaching, and fun so they stay engaged. Sometimes Ripken hosts teams from inner-city Baltimore, as his foundation works to bring baseball to underprivileged youth. But the Ripken complex is a business that depends on paying customers. So he's built a park that you just gotta see, with events you just gotta be a part of. It's a place where a kid can ... well, I'll let the website make the case:

> Become a big leaguer at age 10: Hit a home run over the Green Monster at Fenway Park, slide into second on the

> Polo Grounds, or even swing for the Warehouse at Oriole Park at Camden Yards. Get your heart racing as you hear over the PA system: "At bat, Number 8 ... "
>
> Coaches can make calls from big league dugouts and glance over at the professional scoreboards. Fans and spectators can grab a seat in the shade and cheer on the games in-between trips to the concession stands.
>
> From the professional major-league quality fields, to the covered dugouts ... From the incredible practice facilities, to the lighted fields ... From the ponds, fountains, and trees throughout the complex, to the on-site photography, merchandise, and concessions ... You haven't experienced youth baseball at its finest until you've been to a Ripken Tournament.

The Hall of Famer has serious competition in the youth baseball marketplace. That was never more evident than in August 2005 when a team of 12-year-olds from the Hawaiian island of O'ahu won the Cal Ripken World Series. People back home were excited. But it didn't compare to the delirium that greeted another O'ahu championship team whose returning flight from the mainland a week later was met at the Honolulu airport by a six-firetruck escort, 700 delirious fans, candy leis, stretch limos, and "We are the Champions" as strummed by the Royal Hawaiian Band.

After all, no event dishes preadolescent fame quite like the Little League World Series.

AGE 12

A SPECTACLE OF INNOCENCE

South Williamsport, Pennsylvania

Much of the 60-person television crew had previously been working the PGA Championship in New Jersey, where, two weeks earlier, Phil Mickelson had birdied the final hole for a thrilling, one-shot victory before a national audience. Others drove from Connecticut and New York, specialists in the craft of live sports entertainment. They set up shop on the third-base side of Howard J. Lamade Stadium, in a cordoned-off enclave of production trucks, simple trailers, and makeshift cafeteria tables. More than $20 million in state-of-the-art equipment was now on-site, plus nine hard cameras (one more than can be found at most Major League Baseball game telecasts), two jib cameras (for beauty shots), a dozen microphones stationed around the field (to capture such natural sounds as the ping of metal bat on ball), Brent Musberger and Harold Reynolds in the booth (for star power), and two reporters on the field (one with each team). All of which and all of whom are linked together with the aid of wireless devices and 60,000 feet of snaking cable—a mass of metal sheathed in green, yellow, blue, gray, black, and red that gathers at and plugs into the sides of four 53-foot-long production vehicles. Inside the dark of the main truck, 85 mini-television monitors come alive, offering the director a mind-boggling array of angles and graphical presentations from which to create each

Television Moment. It's akin to ordering from a Chinese menu, written entirely in Mandarin. Except this director knows Mandarin, as well as the menu, and he doesn't appear the least bit flustered by the daunting task of selecting just the right dish for the several million Americans tuning in to the ABC broadcast, expecting nothing less than total satisfaction. He's a seasoned pro at grabbing and holding viewers.

Some days it's the NFL playoffs or an MLB game. Today it's the 2005 title game of the Little League World Series between defending champion Curaçao and the U.S. challenger from Ewa Beach, Hawaii. Nothing the guys in the booth can't handle.

"This room," the jut-jawed director says cheerfully, making eye contact with his assistants manning the truck's audio and video boards, "let's kick some butt." The producers, mostly men and women in their 20s or 30s, nod in return.

"Team!" he says, issuing the universal "work together" command.

With that, they proceed to cover the game.

A children's game that's already been transformed and made adult—by TV cameras merely being here.

• • •

Set in the green, rolling hills of central Pennsylvania, Williamsport is a place that exists in the deepest recesses of the American imagination. It's a quaint landscape of Victorian-era homes and small downtown shops, where life moves at the steady, if unhurried, pace of the nearby Susquehanna River. Once the Lumber Capital of the World, with more millionaires per capita than any other city of its size in the world—that was before overcutting and floods gutted the industry—the town of 30,000 now primarily exports nostalgia, via the broadcast of the Little League World Series each August. In culture and imagery, Williamsport is a long way from Ewa Beach, a bedroom community outside Honolulu precisely 4,813 miles to the southwest. Too far for any crow to fly. But even in the middle of the Pacific Ocean, five time zones behind the East Coast, Layton Aliviado felt the tug of Williamsport.

It was 2003, and the volunteer coach from the western side of the island of O'ahu already had the foundation of his team. The core consisted of his son, Layson, who usually goes by his Hawaiian name, Keao; nephews Myron Enos and Shane Baniaga, respectively known as Kini and Bubbles (for his ample rear end); and a powerful slugger, Vonn Fe'ao. The boys were playing in the Pony League of an adjacent town, Waipahu, and made the all-star team that won the state tournament. But Aliviado, the field manager, and Kini were suspended for the tourney when it was discovered that Kini was not living within the league's geographic boundaries; his listed address was that of his uncle, not his parents. Seething because he felt like officials should have stepped in earlier in the season if there was a problem, Aliviado considered his options: stay with Pony League, or find some other organization in which to groom his young ballplayers.

"Just seeing the World Series on TV, that's what drove us to Little League," Aliviado told me. "A lot of people said to us, 'Why are you going to Little League? You're going backward.' " Some people consider Pony League to be more competitive, since managers aren't forced to give innings and at-bats to every player. The basepaths are longer in Pony League (70 feet instead of 60), and base runners can take leads, forcing pitchers to keep runners honest. In some ways, Pony ball is more conducive to developing individual talent. "Little League is more like mini-baseball," Aliviado concedes. But Little League had the best media deal in youth sports: an agreement with the Walt Disney Company to carry dozens of games on its networks. This year, ESPN is carrying 36 games and ABC another three (the semis and today's final). The *Baseball Tonight* crew is also now on-site, analyzing the day's MLB and Little League action. Nifty catches and hits get highlighted on *SportsCenter*.

Television has long been used as a marketing tool by Little League Baseball, which is headquartered in Williamsport. In fact, ABC's broadcast of the Little League championship game, which began in 1963, represents the oldest continuous relationship between a network and a major sports organization. The event was carried live for the first time in 1985, and with the growth of cable and ESPN, more and more early-round games in Williamsport were added to the schedule in the ensuing years. In 1997, U.S. regional championship games—the winner of each goes on to Williamsport—were televised for the first time. Four years later, the Williamsport tournament doubled in size to 16 teams, producing yet more television as well as Internet, radio, and newspaper content. In 2005, 527 media credentials were issued, just under half of which went to ABC and ESPN personnel.

All that extra publicity has not stoked participation levels. In fact, the number of kids signing up for Little League baseball at all levels, from T-ball through the divisions for teenagers, has dropped from 2.6 to 2.3 million over the past decade. When MLB commissioner Bud Selig states, as he has, that "by almost any criteria you choose, the sport has never been more popular," he's talking about revenues and attendance at the highest level of the game. He's *not* referring to kids' passion to play in Little League, with which MLB has been a partner since 1997. (MLB produces a magazine mailed to all kids in local leagues that serves as a marketing tool for its teams and products as well as the Little League World Series.) In the division in which kids compete to play in Williamsport, typically for 11- and 12-year-olds, there are just over 450,000 kids, down from a high of 575,000 in 1997.

So TV (and MLB) got on board in a big way. And kids quit in droves.

Coincidence?

Steve Keener says yes. He's the clean-cut president of Little League, and his leadership has been marked, paradoxically, both by a promotion of a broad-based participation ethic and by a hearty embrace of the emerging multimedia opportunities. He says coverage of the Little League World Series allows the organization to promote its core values through ESPN and ABC announcers and producers who are encouraged, though not required, to present the games in a certain manner. Reynolds, for instance, offers basic playing tips to kids watching at home. "I don't think TV has ever hurt participation, and for many years it helped," Keener says. "The thing that's hurt participation is travel baseball." He's referring to the push to create select teams at increasingly younger ages to play in tournaments sanctioned by bodies that are less scrutinized than Little League, the only entity in all of sports with a federal charter. "Television keeps us honest," he says. "We're certainly under a microscope like no other youth sports organization for 10 days in August."

But some say the high-definition display is more of a spotlight than a microscope. "When you put the media on any type of activity, you highlight and elevate the game. It makes winning more important," says Dr. Linn Goldberg, a professor of medicine in Oregon and one of the nation's leading experts on youth steroid abuse. "When the game gets placed on a pedestal, it tells everyone that this is important, that it's not just a kid's sport. There's a lot of pressure on these kids." Goldberg speaks from personal experience: His son quit Little League at age 11 after the coach on his all-star team pressed him to play despite a broken knuckle.

The evidence would suggest that use of the mainstream media, at the very least, is overrated as a tool for getting kids excited to pick up a ball. The most historically popular team sports—those that receive the lion's share of coverage at the youth, high school, college, and pro levels—have seen participation drops at the community level over the past decade, according to annual surveys that look at both the organized and the unorganized play of adults and children. The lone exception has been tackle football, which has held steady. The sports with rising participation rates all come from the second tier of media attention: lacrosse (up 78 percent), karate, paintball, snowboarding, surfing, and skateboarding. Even tennis, which in the 1990s fell out of the national conversation among general sports fans, has rebuilt its base, thanks in part to the industry's offering free or low-cost lessons to attract new members.

I'm thinking back to my childhood: I suspect that my enthusiasm for Nolan Ryan, whose California Angels baseball card still sits on my desk, helped make me a baseball fan. But I can't say that watching him on TV is the reason I kept signing up to play, or ultimately why I left the game. I got into it as a little kid because I thought the game would be fun, which it was, and departed when I couldn't make my high school team as an undersized, weak-hitting second baseman. My participation was a function of homegrown opportunity, not distant inspiration.

Perhaps the rise of female athletes over the past two decades is instructive. The estimable advocates of women's sports clamor for more media coverage of their pro and college events, yet the most prodigious wave of new athletes—and the most positive development in the nation's physical fitness in half a century—rolled over society while all those chauvinist sports editors were looking the other way. Take another bow, Title IX.

Kids play, then they become fans. Not the other way around.

But a national television event can be intensely motivating to an adult. In Ewa Beach, Aliviado was the first to dream of making the Little League World Series. The planning started two years beforehand, shortly after he left Pony League and when the boys were 11. The fact that there were only two teams in the West O'ahu Little League—it had been formed in 2002 as a result of rapid population growth in the area—played to Aliviado's advantage, allowing him to control the training environment. All 24 of the boys who signed up were subjected to intense workouts, with the top dozen being selected at the end of the regular season for the all-star team which would represent the league in the postseason. They practiced five days a week, often three hours at a time. "I was preparing them for the 12s," he says. "All I wanted to do that year was make them stronger." The all-stars advanced to the state tournament, where they lost a pair of one-run games, an impressive result given that the other teams were largely composed of 12-year-olds.

Aliviado, a quietly intense man with a thick pile of straight black hair, was an unlikely candidate to mount such a charge toward Williamsport. He had played Little League as a boy three decades ago but found baseball boring and gravitated to basketball instead. In high school, his interests turned to surfing. He looks like he's still in decent enough shape to ride the waves of the North Shore, with a solid, fairly muscled middle and a youthful bounce to his step. His job certainly is not ideal for coaching any team that begins practice at 4 p.m. He starts work at 1 a.m., driving a truck for the U.S. Postal Service. He would come home midmorning, sleep a few hours, and begin loading up his pickup truck with the pipes, nets, backstops, and batting machine that he and his assistant coaches would assemble each day at Mahiko Park, a barebones community field that once was a tract of sugarcane on a sprawling plantation. Ewa Beach is not Waikiki. It's a working-class town of small homes with large rents and mortgages—living anywhere in Hawaii these days is expensive—so don't assume that anyone associated with the team spends their afternoons sipping mai tais like some tourist. Still, it *is* Hawaii—paradise, where the trade winds and gorgeous sunsets have a way of calming the restless soul. What could rural Pennsylvania offer that couldn't be found here? Aliviado had some idea.

Three months before the start of the 2005 regular season, he let everyone in his group know what it would take to go back east: total dedication. He printed up T-shirts that on the front read, "One Team, One Dream," and on the back, "Work Hard, Play Hard." He gathered the parents around a picnic table before practice and gave each of them one T-shirt if they promised to get their child to daily practice on time, pitch in with potlucks, help out where needed—and accept his decisions without complaint. If their kid played no more than the minimum Little League requirement of one inning a game, with one at-bat, so be it. Then after getting the parents' buy-in, he asked each boy, "Do you commit to this team?" An affirmative answer was rewarded with three shirts, to be worn at all workouts. No exceptions.

"I knew the mainland teams would be tough to beat," he explains to me. Some international teams were even stronger, having won five of the past six Little League World Series. He knew all this because he had reviewed video of the past two years of the Series, studied every nuance of the finalists. He set the batting machine to 70 miles per hour because that seemed to be the typical speed of pitches in Williamsport. The boys ran until they vomited, because Aliviado wanted them to have the endurance to make it through the long postseason, which includes the district, state, and regional tournaments that lead up to Williamsport. They ran through cones and ladders and swung at softly tossed whiffle balls for form and hanging tires for power. Practices often ran past sunset, followed by half-hour coaches' talks in the dark. Parents sometimes had to shine their car lights on the field so the batting cages could be disassembled.

Like the other parents, Mack Memea spent a lot of time at Mahiko Park, waiting under the yellow sidewalk lights for his son Mike to finish up so he could get home for dinner and homework. As devout Mormons, the Memeas actually had left Pony League before the team's other families, as the local Little League doesn't schedule games on Sundays during the regular season. Sports was important to the Memea family, but it didn't trump all priorities. "I thought Layton's practices were too much," says Mack, a retired Navy mechanic. "But then I thought, He knows what he's doing, because the kids are listening to him. He kept them focused on the World Series." So Dad stayed on task too.

Keeping Mike in the fold would prove to be, like the boy himself, huge.

• • •

The championship game broadcast begins with Musberger's familiar voice reading an essay on the innocence of Little League baseball. His words are set to the tinkle of soft piano music and layered with shots of little boys hopping over outfield fences and casually tossing balls to each other in alleyways. "There was a time in all our lives when the world was small enough that only the important things mattered. Back then, the good guys wore white. The sweetest sounds came from an ice cream truck. And baseball games would fill an entire summer ... "

The tease does its job quite ably, hooking channel-surfing viewers by locating the emotional appeal of the event from the outside in. For adults old enough to don rose-colored glasses, there's something sentimental about the idea of the Little League World Series, "where," as Musberger proposes, "for one brief moment, memories are allowed to live. And breathe. And play a game called baseball."

When glory is up for grabs, though, the truth can get a bit grittier.

"Hi, Mom!" Vonn Fe'ao enthuses into the camera, in a preshot montage of Americana moments at the top of the broadcast. He's one of the stars of the Hawaii team and, due to the wall-to-wall coverage of the tourney this year, its most famous player. The Tongan-American boy has curly, shoulder-length hair dyed golden blond, and a fierce, slugger's swing that can send a ball 100 feet beyond the 205-foot fence if he really gets ahold of it. Coming into the game, he is leading all tournament players with three home runs, one ahead of Mike, Bubbles, and one other teammate. He also has a backstory for the ages, one not ready for mass consumption. Vonn, in that television shot, is waving to a mom who gave up legal custody of her son so that he could play on this team.

That's right. Vonn's mother and father relinquished control of their 12-year-old boy for the sake of Little League baseball.

Here's what happened: A Little League rule requires that all players representing a district "reside within" its specified boundaries, usually a geographic area no larger than 20,000 people. When a local official discovered, the previous year, that the Fe'ao family had moved to Nanakuli—a half-hour drive from Ewa Beach—Vonn was prevented from joining his team at the state tournament. With Vonn relegated to the stands, the West O'ahu Little League all-stars, as 11-year-olds, failed to advance to the regionals in California. "It was hard to watch," Vonn says. "We had won every game, and then we just lost."

So the next year his parents, Heather and Sese, went to family court to transfer custody of Vonn to an aunt who lived in Ewa Beach. I would be told this later by three sources: the local Little League administrator who reviewed the paperwork, Aliviado's wife, Debbie, who handled it on the team's side, and Vonn himself.

Did Vonn actually live with his legal guardian, Pativaine Scanlan? "Oh, no," Vonn tells me, a guileless admission that forces me to pursue the angle, much as I like this kid. He says his mother would wait for him at practice and drive him home at night to Nanakuli, that "she made the sacrifice," he says.

When I relate this conversation to Debbie Aliviado, she sighs, as none of this is information that has come out publicly. A high-cheeked woman who like all the Hawaiian mothers in Williamsport wore a lei around her neck and a flower behind one ear on game day, Aliviado says nothing improper was done. "Vonn's family is confusing," she explains. The Fe'aos move around almost annually, sometimes based on the needs of extended family. They had relocated to Nanakuli "on a whim" to take care of Vonn's ailing grandmother, Aliviado says. Other times they have simply moved to towns where Sese, a car mechanic, could find work. Further complicating Vonn's everyday life is the fact that his mother takes off for California for weeks at a time to stay with relatives. Aliviado insists Vonn did live with his aunt at times, though she allows it was "just when the mother was on the mainland."

The area Little League administrator who vetted this arrangement is Mike Victorino, who happens to be a private investigator on the island (and the uncle of Philadelphia Phillies outfielder Shane Victorino). The previous year, he had checked on the eligibility of team members after rival coaches suspected Ewa Beach of using out-of-district players. He had knocked on doors at addresses provided by the team as proof of residency, ultimately disqualifying only Vonn. With the submission of the legal guardian papers for Vonn in '05, though, he had no choice but to drop the Magnum, P.I. routine. The loophole was right there in the Little League rules:

> A player will be deemed to reside within the league boundaries if:
>
> A. His/her parents are living together and are residing within such league boundaries, OR;
>
> B. Either of the player's parents (or his/her court-appointed legal guardian) resides within such boundaries.

Technically, there's nothing requiring a kid to spend even one minute at his guardian's home. Only *the guardian* has to reside there.

"I sat there with my staff for 20 minutes after receiving his document, and we just stared at each other," Victorino says. "We said, 'My god, these people are intense.' " In his 11 years as an administrator, he's seen parents do a lot of desperate things—like create fake residency papers—but never anything like this. "They followed the letter of the law, not the spirit," he says. "But I couldn't turn the boy down, or I'd have a lawsuit on my back."

Ultimately, Williamsport gave it the green light too. "Somebody had convinced a judge as to why this [legal guardianship] was necessary," says Little League president Keener, who confirmed for me basic facts on the controlling document. "That's all we can base our ruling on. We can't start asking how many nights he slept there."

MYTH NO. 12
Media coverage drives up participation.

THE TRUTH
Kids play a game—then they become fans.

Keener says he'd be surprised if a judge would allow such a transfer for baseball reasons. But Vonn says that's why it was done: "My mom got my auntie and uncle to get the legal rights to me so I could play that year."

Keener knows situations such as these can become contentious, even deadly. The latter would happen right in the national headquarters' backyard a couple years later. In Gilberton, Pa., just 90 minutes southeast of Williamsport, the father of one boy killed a neighbor who had threatened to call Little League headquarters and report his son for playing in the wrong territory. According to prosecutors, the 40-year-old assailant shoved the 60-year-old man, struck him in the head, and a fight ensued. The man died of chest and abdominal injuries.

Understandably, any of the teams beaten by the Ewa Beach All-Stars on their 18–0 march to the championship could feel cheated by Vonn's inclusion. The foundation of the Little League system is community-based teams, a feature that sets the organization apart from select or travel teams which can draw talent from areas with few or no boundaries. As far back as 1959, Williamsport has penalized local leagues for using players who lived out of district. A team from Zamboanga City in the Philippines won the 1992 series but was stripped of its title after it was revealed that eight players were from far outside the established boundaries.

Vonn, in his defense, doesn't qualify as a classic ringer. Aliviado had been his coach since age 8, first on the Pony League team and then in Little League. Vonn was the rare player on the team who actually went to school in Ewa Beach, at Ilima Intermediate; in 2005, half the team's players were enrolled in private schools or had transferred to better public schools on the island. Vonn's situation appears to be similar to that of two boys on the Harlem Little League team that advanced to the 2002 World Series; Williamsport declared the pair eligible to compete because they had played in the league for four years before they moved out of the area.

Debbie Aliviado says any objections to the use of Vonn are rooted in jealousy. "People want to see these kids go down," she says. "They cannot stand to see kids doing well."

For Ewa Beach, the toughest competition on the road to Williamsport, ironically, was on the island. Once at the regionals in San Bernardino, Calif., the team rolled, outscoring opponents 87-19 in six games. Defense, pitching, hitting, total team play—Layton Aliviado's all-stars were showing that they had it all. The sense that they could actually go all the way and win the Series, which would be a first for a Hawaiian team, seemed real. No longer were they in awe of the mainland teams, which they had assumed played the best brand of baseball.

Confidence wasn't the only thing soaring. Literally, a couple of the key players have been growing at a hellacious rate, as well.

Mike, already the team's best line-drive hitter—the only kid who had ever sent a ball into the parking lot beyond leftfield at Mahiko—has sprouted two inches during the summer, to 5-foot-6. Vonn, meanwhile, has added *four* inches in the four weeks before the World Series, pushing him to 5-7. His bones are expanding so rapidly that he often sleeps late and eats three helpings at mealtime. His father had bought him new cleats, as usual, larger than they needed to be, but by late August, they could barely contain his suddenly size 13 feet. To add strength to his new length, he's been doing 100 push-ups a day in his room.

It's common for kids going through growth spurts at this age to temporarily lose some of their coordination. Mike has been struggling with that, having trouble putting bat on ball. Not Vonn. At a postgame barbecue, after hitting a walk-off grand slam against Oregon in the regional, the boys on the other team gently teased him, saying that he must be taking steroids.

Danny Almonte.

That's what some of the players called Vonn, a reference to the infamous case of the 14-year-old pitcher who lied about his age in 2001—a fraud that led to the forfeiture of games by his Bronx Little League team in its celebrated run to Williamsport. Vonn just smiled, taking it as a compliment. At school, only a couple months earlier, he had to defend himself constantly, as the new kid in the hallway with neither the size nor the friends to fend off the bullies who suggested his hair looked funny. He was in fights since his first day at Ilima. Now boys—hotshot athletes from the mainland—seemed to genuflect his way. Atop his buffed-up body, his shockingly blond hair—originally his mother's idea—became an extension of the Vonn Fe'ao swagger, one of those earned luxuries of stardom, like Ali's rap. "I felt like I could put the ball over the fence anytime I wanted to," he says. "I would get this certain feeling, like I was about to hit one."

Spiritual. That's what it was. And Vonn never fails to thank his up-above guardian, the late uncle he was named after. The man was murdered in Oakland shortly before Vonn was born, but Vonn felt like he knew him, and he supposedly had seen his apparition as a little kid. "That's what my mom said," he says. "I couldn't remember it, but she said I saw him out a window. I just know he's been around for me. When I play ball, I ask him to help me." With each new and mighty jack, Vonn crosses his chest and points to the heavens.

The supersizing came just in time. Every serious Little League World Series contender needs an XL man-child or two. In 1982, Taiwan's five-year monopoly on the series was dismantled by a 5-7, 175-pound pitcher from Kirkland, Wash., Cody Webster, who threw 75 miles an hour. Seven years later, also against Taiwan, chubby-cheeked Chris Drury provided the winning edge for Trumbull, Conn. In 1993, it was Sean Burroughs leading Long Beach, Calif., to its second consecutive title with two no-hitters and a batting average of .600. In 2002, Aaron Alvey threw 44 strikeouts in 21 shutout innings and hit a 250-foot rope to beat Japan 1-0 in the title game. Then there's the 1971 giant, Lloyd McClendon, all 5-foot-8 of him; in 10 plate appearances for Gary, Ind., he was intentionally walked five times. The five times he was pitched to, he homered.

McClendon and Burroughs went on to play in the majors. They are the exceptions. Of the more than 7,000 children who have played in the series over six decades, only 31 have gone on to spend even one day in the bigs. Thus predicting future success based on achievements at the Series is a dubious exercise.

Late-maturing boys, who are in rare supply in Williamsport, often end up taller than the kids who sprout early, according to growth and maturation researcher Robert Malina. That irony begins to explain why so few kids who have passed through Williamsport end up in the majors. It also begs questions of fairness with the Little League World Series, given the stated ideal of a level playing field (which is why an Almonte gets scrutinized). Indeed, 12 might be the worst age at which to hold a meaningful championship, due to the vagaries of puberty. A child might have the body of a 10-year-old or that of a well-muscled, testosterone-fueled 15-year-old. One boy on the team from Saudi Arabia this year is 6-foot-6 and growing by the day.

These disparities have led to occasional calls, never heeded, for the application of size limits, as is the case in Pop Warner football. "When the next hulk-child comes along, a Little League official needs to stand up, on a chair, if necessary, look him in the eye, and tell him to go play somewhere else," *Slate*'s Josh Levin wrote in 2003. "By knuckling under to a few dominant players, Little League implants a lasting lesson in the heads of the millions of youngsters that play in its leagues worldwide: The big kids always get their way."

Watching the Little League World Series on TV for the first time, my son Cole's reaction was different. Maybe it's because he's an early bloomer too, taller than most of his classmates. "Whoa," he said, marveling at the majestic blimp shots, fancy graphics, and Kellogg's Frosted Flakes-sponsored player intros. "Are the players paid, Daddy?"

• • •

Returning from a commercial break, Musberger sends it down to on-field reporter Sam Ryan, who is going to give viewers a flavor for the team from Willemstad, Curaçao. Above the din of the upbeat ballpark music, she notes that its boys are heroes on the quaint Caribbean island nation of 135,000 just north of Venezuela. The players who won last year were showered with gifts. A graphic appears on screen with a partial list of items:

Computers
Printers
Scanners
Digital cameras
KFC for a year
52 six-packs of Pepsi
Savings account with $600 balance

"So how's that for some incentive?" Ryan begs.

A couple of innings later, Musberger weighs in. "I hope the NCAA wasn't looking at that," he says, trying to keep it light. "That spells professional."

"Got that right," says Reynolds, the color analyst and former major league second baseman.

We can scarcely imagine how Little League founder Carl Stotz might have taken the Curaçao team's material rewards. He died in 1992, so I call his daughter, Karen Stotz Myers, the de facto family historian and the local county treasurer. "I'm sure he wouldn't have approved of those boys getting all that stuff," she says. But then, Stotz had grown uncomfortable with many aspects of the Series by the time of his passing.

A 29-year-old clerk at a Williamsport-area lumber yard who had never run anything in his life, Stotz created Little League in 1939 with the modest goal of giving his nephews and their neighborhood friends a format in which to play baseball under the guidance of adults. It was a vision based on local needs and local controls. He drew up field dimensions two-thirds that of the major leagues', based on what seemed appropriate for boys between the ages of 8 and 12—or at least the Williamsport kids, who helped him figure out the scale by racing around an open field with experimental bases made of newspaper. As a coach, he kept the largest boys off the mound so the smaller ones might have a chance at the plate. Rosters were limited to 12 kids, to promote playing time. For years, he resisted advice to register Little League as a corporate entity. "I think he was simple and good in his orientation," Keener says. "All he was really interested in was giving kids the opportunity to play ball."

Stotz argued that commercialism and professionalism were fine for business but not for youth sports. Like Luther Gulick at the start of the century, he became evangelical about making his little idea work on a broad scale, traveling from town to town, selling the gospel of community-based, volunteer-driven organized ball for the preteen set. In 1947, he created the "Little League National Tournament"—a grandiose notion given that all but one team hailed from within 20 miles of Williamsport. But sure enough word got out, and within a few years, there were national sponsors, a write-up in the influential *Saturday Evening Post*, and newsreel footage in movie theaters across the country.

At first, Stotz embraced the attention as a means to encourage other towns to start chapters; it was an era when American fathers, many of them back from World War II, were looking for new ways to get involved in their sons' lives. But rapid growth also brought a board of directors comprised of New York businessmen who didn't necessarily share Stotz's small-town sensibility. A devout Lutheran, he clashed with the board over the playing of games on Sundays. He fought the addition of international teams—like Curaçao—to the renamed Little League World Series, reluctant to raise the ante for leagues that already were starting to take extreme measures to win the year-end event. He disagreed with the board's use of celebrities to promote the Series, an event he feared was becoming the focus of, rather than an add-on to, the Little League experience. Little League had started as a summer league, with a June opening day. But the regular season had been pushed back into the spring, to make room for the World Series qualifying tournaments.

Stotz came to resent "the corporation," as he called it, that Little League Inc. had become. He and the board parted ways, bitterly, in 1956. He never would attend another Series game, nor would he set foot in Lamade Stadium after it was built, three years later, even though he lived just a few miles away. Near the end of his life, he suggested that the tournament he created be abolished. He was quoted as saying that a county or state championship would be sufficient to end the season—"a tournament close to home and inexpensive, financed the same way the leagues are financed, by local sponsors." His daughter tells me he felt the World Series had outgrown its purpose and that the competition had gotten elitist. "He thought more kids should be allowed to feel special," she says. "The Series was a tool for him to get people interested in Little League. But that tool had become obsolete. People already were interested. They were playing the game all over the world."

Evidently, Stotz had underestimated the consumer appetite for miniatures.

Adults have long been fascinated with little people doing big things. In medieval France, nobles living in countryside châteaus liked to be entertained by dwarves. The circus promoter P.T. Barnum used a midget he called Tom Thumb to build his show in pre-Civil War America. One of the most popular Hollywood actors of the 1930s was the singing, tap-dancing Shirley Temple, who set the stage for many child stars to come, from Danny Bonaduce to Gary Coleman to Drew Barrymore. *The Wizard of Oz,* released the same year Little League was created, was set in an alternative universe populated by really small, friendly folk. Without intending to do so, Stotz had created an entertainment platform for Little League by simply dressing the boys up in spiffy uniforms and rigorously organizing their play. All that structural concordance with the major leagues remains irresistible to many adults, allowing for predictions and comparisons that otherwise would be hard to make. In fact, here comes one right now ... from Reynolds, as Hawaii's Kini Enos rushes in from his shortstop position to lift the ball off the perfectly manicured lawn and whip it over to first for a tough out: "You see Derek Jeter make this play all the time for the Yankees."

It's now the top of the seventh, the first extra-inning game since McClendon's team won its title in 1971. Game tied at 6, with Vonn on the mound in relief. He's scowling, talking trash to a Curaçaoan batter he thinks gave him a smug look.

Musberger says, "Vonn's favorite athlete is Ray Lewis. And he showed us a little Ray Lewis there."

Not wanting to play it up too much, Reynolds says, "This is not the sportsmanship you like seeing. But he is competing."

And mowing 'em down. The righthander strikes out the next batter on three pitches, throwing so hard, his shirt comes untucked. The fastball that retires the side is clocked at 77 miles per hour, which, since the mound is only 46 feet away, offers the batter less reaction time than is afforded most major leaguers when they face the hardest throwers in the game. An on-screen graphic compares Little League pitch speeds to their Major League equivalents. "If you want to change that over to the big leagues, it's *a hundred!*" Reynolds enthuses. "Oh, it's getting hot in here."

"Mercy," Musberger adds.

These kids are good. But that's not why we're drawn in. Once they become teens, we don't care to watch them play baseball again until, if any make it, the College World Series. The appeal here lies in their youth—at least their chronological youth. We're amazed at how cute *and* competent these children are.

Karen Stotz Myers, ironically, loves the spectacle of innocence. And she welcomes the extended television coverage that allows story lines and characters to develop over the month of August. "I watch the games," she says. "Not everyone can come to Williamsport, and tuning in to a ball game during the World Series is more fun if you know something about the players ahead of time. If you're in Kalamazoo, Michigan, and you don't have team in there, you get to establish favorites. I think it all makes for very interesting, healthy entertainment."

Others are hostile to the event. "Let the kids play in anonymous safety, free from the enormous pressure that television brings," Sean Horgan of *The Sun News* (Myrtle Beach, S.C.) has written. "Let them learn to play the game somewhere other than on 'The World Wide Leader.' Let Orel Hershiser critique somebody his own size and relative age. Let our little people go."

It's not an uncommon sentiment. A week after the Hawaii-Curaçao game, ESPN.com users were asked, "At what age should the media begin televising and reporting on youth games?" This was an unscientific online poll, so the results must be judged accordingly. Still, the numbers were interesting, given that the website's users are sports fans, the segment of society with the greatest appetite for spectator sports. Of the 20,530 votes received, 82 percent said the media should wait until child athletes are at least in high school.

Of course, the media makes programming decisions based on business, not democratic, principles. It's not a matter of how many Americans choose to tune out, but how many choose to tune in. In a fragmented, 500-channel universe, getting just one percent of households to watch a cable show is a rousing success. Get six percent, as CBS pulls in for the NCAA men's basketball tournament, and you have March Madness. This phenomenon is how *Gardening by the Yard* and *The Jerry Springer Show* stay on TV for more than a decade when neither you nor anyone you know watches these shows; it's just that enough of your non-friends do. The 2005 Little League World Series games on ESPN and ESPN2 have average viewership of a little less than one percent of households, comparable to *SportsCenter*.

The era of network broadcasting, in which much of the citizenry sat around the tube and listened to what Howard Cosell or Walter Cronkite had to say, is long gone. The reason that rights fees paid to sports leagues have grown exponentially over the past two decades is not because ratings are better than ever—they aren't—but because an event such as the Super Bowl offers a rare opportunity for advertisers to reach, in one place, a sizable chunk of the viewing public.

Most of the time, however, television must cater to niche audiences. Those niches are organized by affinities and natural feelings of identification. Relatively speaking, lots of people can identify with Little League, still the largest organization in youth sports. Its jewel event also benefits from regional affinities, as cities swoon over their fresh-faced ambassadors in Williamsport. When these kids are from major markets, look out: The 2001 U.S. championship on ABC, featuring Almonte's Bronx team against a squad from the Orlando suburb of Apopka, outdrew everything—NFL, MLB, or otherwise—on ESPN that August. And Almonte didn't even pitch. The international title game the next day produced an even better rating, despite Apopka losing to Japan. In the Orlando market, nearly half of all people watching TV saw the game.

With hits like that, the well of programming possibilities runs deep. Keener says he's hesitant to offer up to television any games below the regional final level, for now. But he could see those early-round games shown on broadband. "Maybe you want to have the game for your digital scrapbook," he says. The Internet changes the whole paradigm. In an affluent district of Houston, one Little League chapter just added webcasts of games. That way Dad and Mom can watch games on their computer when they're stuck late at work. If they get in an electronic queue and wait their turn, they also can control the zoom and directional features on any of the three cameras (at first base, third base, and the scoreboard) for 45 seconds at a time. "In the future, I think you'll see a lot more of that," Keener says. League websites are now common, so the online venues are in place. San Diego-based eteamz.com, the official online community of Little League Baseball, now serves more than two million teams in 120 countries. The co-founder? Gary Weinhouse, the same guy who now sells college athlete sperm at California Cryobank (see Age 1). He and a friend started eteamz.com in 1998 as UCLA students and sold it off two years later to Active.com.

Small community newspapers have gotten hip to the opportunities. The free weekly that shows up in my mailbox has pages of sports coverage that consists entirely of youth team photos and headlines such as "Simsbury American 9-10 Baseball Boys Stay in Early Section II Contention." Major metropolitan papers have been slower to embrace youth sports, but they're getting there. "Local, local, local," says Curtis Murayama, the sports editor of the *Honolulu Advertiser*. He's citing the mantra of publishers across the country as they try to stem circulation losses. With the national news organizations pushing out reports electronically on a 24/7 basis, the major metros have had to find new ways to become relevant to readers, especially to young people. For Murayama, that means increasing high school coverage at the expense of college and pro sports. "Instead of the focus going up and out, we're going down and in," he says. "Now we're starting to cover youth sports." Most of the 99 print reporters issued media credentials in Williamsport are from local papers. Two are filing articles for Murayama.

If the Ewa Beach All-Stars win today's game, the *Advertiser* is prepared to blow out the front page to trumpet the achievement. No other news story will appear on the cover of the A section. Since it is Aug. 28, 2005, the morning before Hurricane Katrina is set to barrel into the Gulf Coast, that is saying something.

Hawaiians are just so damn proud of their boys. "We're very, very provincial," Murayama explains later.

In truth, we all are, right down to the family room. And therein lays the dilemma.

All parents wants their kids to shine. With the Little League World Series, sometimes the trick is knowing when to pull them off the biggest stage of all.

One reason Ewa Beach is in the championship game is because other teams ran out of quality pitchers. In the U.S. final, the formidable squad from Rancho Buena Vista, Calif., was unable to use its star, Kalen Pimental, because the 5-8 fireballer with hair on his chin had gone six innings the previous game in a defeat of Maitland, Fla. So Vista went with its No. 2 pitcher, Nate Lewis. Problem was, Lewis had injured his arm at the Western Regional and was still throwing the ball underhand just a few days before. He lasted three innings in the 6-1 loss to the Hawaiians. When the team returned home after the long postseason, the third-best pitcher for Vista also would find out that he had fractured his elbow.

Coaches on other teams rode their top pitchers hard too. The previous year, USA Baseball recommended that kids of this age throw no more than 75 pitches a game, but some here have gone well over 100. ESPN analyst Larry Bowa watched one game in which a boy threw more than 130 pitches. In receiving the William A. Shea Distinguished Little League Graduate Award before the Hawaii-Curaçao final, Bowa shared his concern about this practice. "You've got to look at the long-range goals, look at the future," he told reporters. "For a kid to throw 130 pitches in a game is ludicrous, really." The former major leaguer also chafed at the prevalence of breaking balls, the frequency of which had risen from 23 percent of pitches in 1991 to 37 percent a decade later. Experts who have studied injuries to young pitchers say curveballs should not be thrown until at least age 14 or until puberty is reached, because of the stress that is created when arm joints are twisted while bones are still developing. (Little League would restrict players to 85 pitches per game starting in 2007 while advising against, but not banning, breaking balls.)

Medical professionals also warn against playing baseball year-round. One study showed that kids who pitched at least eight months a year were 500 percent more likely to injure their elbows. When this guidance goes ignored, Little League can scarcely be faulted; the vast majority of its games are held in the spring and summer. Other national organizations aren't so restrictive, and independent event promoters have flooded the baseball scene in recent years—so select teams can find tournaments during pretty much any season. Ten of the 12 Rancho Buena Vista boys play on a year-round travel team coached by Pimental's father, Joe. Keener argues that Little League for years brought a measure of control to the scene by prohibiting kids from playing with other organizations during its season. But Little League got challenged on the rule in 1992 and quietly backed down two years later on the advice of lawyers. "That was the first crack in the dam," Keener tells me. "The trigger point for the whole evolution of travel baseball was when we had to revise our rule against dual participation."

Anecdotal reports suggest that the incidence of most serious arm injuries has risen dramatically. One of the best-respected orthopedic surgeons in the nation is James Andrews, an Alabama doctor who performed Tommy John surgery, a reconstructive procedure on the elbow, on 21 high school baseball players between 1995 and 1999. That number jumped to 124 over the next five years. Andrews would later suggest to Charles Euchner, the author of the 2006 book *Little League, Big Dreams*, that all those injuries were depriving the major leagues of talent. "The best pitchers in the country never make it to the majors because they're the ones in the youth leagues and high school who are overused," he said. There's no way to prove as much, but it's an intriguing theory. On one hand, the majors right now are seeing some very good pitching prospects emerge. On the other, there might be more if not for injuries. It's notable that one of the best southpaws in the game, two-time Cy Young Award winner Johan Santana, didn't pitch until his midteens. He didn't even throw with his left arm until age 11, because, as a child in rural Venezuela, he used his father's righty glove.

Aliviado did not limit Ewa Beach to Little League games on the team's road to Williamsport. He had the boys play a partial schedule in their area's Cal Ripken winter league and signed them up for a couple tournaments on the island. But all told, they suited up for fewer than 50 games in the year leading up to the championship; some travel teams log more than twice as many. One reason Ewa Beach didn't play more games is because there simply is no local league for youth baseball in the fall. "That's the time for football," Aliviado says. "The community knows to expect that."

Aliviado's pitchers aren't worn out, and it shows. Curaçao finally gets to starter Quentin Guevara, who until now has been solid in the Series. But behind him are three more pitchers with Series ERAs under 1.00, including Vonn.

His ERA is 0.00. Untouchable.

• • •

At 6:17 p.m. Eastern Daylight Time, the game moves to ESPN2 in most parts of the country so that ABC News can get on with its Katrina coverage. The producers had hoped the championship would be wrapped up by six o'clock, and when it wasn't and Hawaii made its stunning comeback, the decision was made to send the game to cable if it went into extra innings. No one in the booth or the main truck complains, as the hurricane reached top speed earlier in the day, and it is apparent from the in-game news bulletins that a major disaster is looming. I step outside to call my mother, who lives just outside New Orleans and is driving north, anywhere north, in her Toyota Corolla, with a few personal belongings in the trunk. She is, and will remain, fine. A little scared, but fine.

I go back inside, where Michael Memea's half-boy, half-man mug fills a couple of the many blinking screens. It's about 6:30 now, and he is the leadoff batter in the bottom of the seventh. He looks a little spooked, and the on-screen graphic explains why: He's 0-for-3 with two strikeouts. It's the third straight game in which he's struggled at the plate, after having gone homerless in San Bernardino, where his father sarcastically told him that he hit like a girl, a comment that only made the boy cry. (Dad later apologized.) The centerfield camera shows a big strike zone, made larger by his growth in recent weeks, which has thrown off his dexterity and self-confidence.

"That face, Vonn Fe'ao, will be the second hitter," Musberger says. "Unless Memea ends it right here with one mighty swing." The leftfield camera shows Vonn in the dugout, pacing back and forth, head down, helmet on, pointing to heaven again, working himself into a focused, faith-based fury. Musberger: "He's like a caged lion."

Mike whiffs at two medium-fast pitches, and the count goes full. It looks like Vonn's going to have to supply the fireworks. Which is fine with Vonn, because all along he's been thinking, he would say later, that playing on national TV is his chance to "show the scouts what I have." Then ...

Ping!

A fastball on the high outside corner rebounds off the end of Mike's blue aluminum bat. It's less a swing than a stab, a desperate lunge. But for a mustachioed slugger with a teenager's frame, it doesn't take much to send a ball over the 205-foot fence. It scoots out of the upper left corner of the screen, the camera angle switches from centerfield to behind home plate—and no more than two seconds later, the drive is landing on the hill beyond right centerfield. "Gone!" Musberger enthuses. "Hawaii wins it!"

After Mike rounds first, he pushes up his right arm and index finger, almost as if he needs convincing that he, little-big Michael Memea, could induce the delirium that has erupted outside his team's dugout, in the stands where his thickly built father is tearing up, and, presumably, thousands of miles away in a state whose adult sports teams have never won anything this ... huge. By the time he rounds third, though, the quality of his achievement, of having met fire with ice, has set in. The controlled smile on his wide face after he stomps on home plate suggests that he may have grown up, right now, in this very moment. Peeling off his black batting gloves, he already looks like a been-there, done-that major leaguer.

Then the postgame interview sets us straight.

Musberger: "Let's go down to Penn Holderness with the hero. Penn?"

Holderness: "I am here with the new Mr. August, Michael Memea. Awesome home run. What's going through your mind right now?"

The ABC Sports microphone inches from his chin, Mike looks up, looks down, looks back up, now sideways at Holderness. He's speechless, smiling, trying not to embarrass himself in his national TV moment.

Holderness leans in, rephrases: "What's on your mind right now?"

Memea: "The home run?"

Holderness: "Yeah."

Memea pushes out five words: "Excited for the home run."

Interviewer and interviewee are doing the best they can. This is how 12-year-olds talk, especially to journalists. Like they have inner worlds to protect.

Since it's taped, they redo the Q&A. It gets better. A little. With a mention at the end about Coach maybe taking the team to Disneyland. Mike smiles again.

• • •

To cover the Little League World Series from every dimension, you have to check in with the players at least a couple years later. Because the event changes lives. Keener knows this, so his staff sits down with the final four teams to prepare them for what to expect after Williamsport. "We try to explain to these kids that they should go home and celebrate their accomplishment," he says. "Do the parade. Then put it in a scrapbook and look at it 20 years from now."

He knows that's easier said than done.

Two years after shutting down Taiwan in the '82 championship game, Cody Webster was still good, but not dominant. Strangers would yell, "I thought you were the World Series hero. You suck." He could never get away from the expectations, made more difficult by the fact that: 1) The field dimensions would grow considerably after Little League; and 2) he himself would not (adding just four more inches). Webster's high school team went on to win the state title, but he was done with the sport after one year at Eastern Washington University. "It was hard for me," Webster told *The Seattle Times* in 2001. "I mean, I had a lot of pressure throughout my baseball career to produce. It just got to the point when I was 17, 18, 19, I just wasn't as good anymore." Fewer than half of the members of the Spring, Texas, team that lost to Taiwan in '95 went on to play high school baseball. One of those who did was shortstop Kyle Foster, whom the Houston Astros were considering drafting out of high school. But the night before the draft, he told the Astros to take his name off the board. He was burned out. "The exposure is nuts," Don Turley, manager of the Spring team, would say to a reporter on the eve of the Hawaii-Curaçao final. "Ten years later, I still have guys telling me it was the highlight of their life so far. I don't know if that's such a good thing, you know? The question becomes: Where in life will I be able to experience the same attention and elation and adrenaline as I did then? The answer is, you probably never will." Chris Drury is the rare Series star who can say otherwise—he went on to win NCAA hockey and Stanley Cup titles—but his discomfort with his childhood celebrity was immediate. He was horror-struck when *Sports Illustrated* photographed his bedroom, and by the time he joined the Boston University hockey team, he was so eager to leave the past in the past that he didn't mention Little League when filling out a questionnaire for the sports information department.

Vonn Fe'ao's mother had a sense of what was to come. A couple hours after winning the championship, he got on the phone with her. She was back in Hawaii, engulfed as it was in communal ecstasy. "Be ready," she warned, "because when you come back here, you're going to be a different person."

Vonn recounts this conversation from the front room of his family's latest home, a sparsely decorated apartment in the mountainside town of Mililani. He's 14 now, a high school freshman. "Sure enough," he says, "everything changed." Most of it's been good. The team never made it to Disneyland—that was just wishful thinking—but it got to ride a roller coaster nonetheless. At the Honolulu airport, the boys were met by the mayor, the governor, and a throng of fans. So many leis got stacked on their necks that it looked as if their heads were peeking out of the tops of technicolor volcanoes. The boys filed away the *Advertiser*'s front page—which indeed was all about the championship, with Katrina relegated to a Page 1 tease and a story inside the front section. They accepted kisses from pretty girls whom they'd never met. They did the parade before 20,000 fans in Waikiki, then another one in Ewa Beach. They gave speeches at assemblies at their schools. They signed autographs on commemorative T-shirts. They met the Los Angeles Lakers. They were honored at a University of Hawaii football game, where some fans held up a sign saying "Put in Fe'ao." They took questions from IBM executives at a company convention. Exhausted, the team stopped accepting appearance requests after a year, at which time the invitations were still coming in weekly.

Along the way, companies gave the players DVDs, clothes, sports equipment, and a year's worth of McDonald's—hey, everyone knew what the Curaçao kids had received a year earlier. Parents scored too: After Reynolds mentioned on air that Kini Enos' father had quit his job as a cement-truck driver to attend the Series, six new job offers came his way. Layton Aliviado took a part-time position as jayvee baseball coach at St. Louis School, a Catholic school in Honolulu. He brought with him his son, two nephews, and Vonn. Each of them receives some tuition help, as do Mike and one other player who attend private school. "Just from the recognition that ESPN gave them on TV, schools wanted them," Aliviado says. Vonn got a full ride, courtesy of a couple of philanthropic-minded teachers. One reason the Fe'aos moved to Mililani was to be closer to the school. Still, Vonn must leave his house at 4:30 a.m. and take two hours' worth of bus rides to get to school in time for tutoring before first bell. He makes the effort because St. Louis offers a far superior education to what he was receiving in public school.

Parents giving away the legal rights to their son for the sake of Little League baseball surely qualifies as a sign o' the times in modern youth sports. But it paid off handsomely for Vonn Fe'ao.

The boy did have to lose his famous locks, though, as St. Louis requires all students to have short hair. Vonn had mixed emotions about it. The golden curls had become part of his identity and part of his story. Now that his brown skin meets a short crop of brown hair like that of so many other Hawaiian teens, he's more anonymous. Only the eyes offer a clue that he's the same hyperkinetic kid who thrived in the World Series cauldron—and it's not a solid clue, as the energy flowing from them is far gentler than it used to be. It's almost as if Vonn is starting over. And maybe there's an upside to that. He hates when people say to him, *Hey Little Leaguer*. He answers that he's changed a lot. He just hasn't grown much height-wise, only two inches. Still, he says, "That's the past. I'm trying to move forward."

Like Vonn and his other '05 teammates, Mike Memea almost never watches a replay of that championship game. It's too frustrating seeing himself strike out in the early innings—that's what he focuses on, not the walk-off home run. His dad watches, though. "Almost every day," Mack says. "It still brings goose bumps." The following year, a Mormon team from Utah would forfeit a game in their Little League World Series regional rather than play on Sunday. But the Memeas made an exception in Williamsport. Mike played, and they never looked back.

Father and son have a tight bond. They muse about whether Little League was prompted to back up the fences to 225 feet the following year because of the "Hawaiian Punch" of '05. (Really, how could it not be related?) Mack has tried to work with Mike on giving more than one-sentence answers during interviews, with limited success. The words trickle out, haltingly, with a shy smile. Mack is proud that Mike's the only freshman who made varsity on his high school team, especially after he was benched by Aliviado during last year's state tournament for Junior Little League, the Little League division for the next age category up. Playing on the larger diamond, the 13-year-olds from Ewa Beach, competing against teams of mostly 14s, lost in the title game.

It was the last time the boys would play together as a team, as their high schools want them to be available for football practice in August. Aliviado had been hoping to get one more summer out of them to make a run at another national title, but he understands. Hard as he worked them in practice, he also encouraged the boys to play football, to build the toughness that would make them better in baseball. He never believed in specializing in one sport when you're young—"Too much pressure for kids," he says. Now they are well-rounded athletes in demand by school coaches in other sports.

It happens. Sometimes for the better.

• • •

The 2006 Little League World Series was the last under the six-year, $8.4 million contract with ESPN and ABC. It was replaced by an eight-year, $30.1 million contract with the same media group, which gained the rights to use the content on any of its 15 multimedia platforms. With all that new cash, Little League was able to provide a few benefits to all the local chapters around the world: lower charter fees, 80 free background checks of potential coaches, and the promise of a customized online coaching education program at no charge. The money helps Little League do more for its members than perhaps any organization in youth sports.

To the rest of the sporting public, the most visible outgrowth of the new deal was a series of public-service announcements that began to air on ESPN in 2007 encouraging sign-ups at local leagues. This was appropriate, because sign-ups are youth baseball's most visible challenge. Even in, of all places, Ewa Beach.

When the boys from West O'ahu won it all, predictions were made by Little League administrators that registration in the district would skyrocket. One area coach said he couldn't imagine any kid watching the World Series drama and not "say they don't want a chance at the same thing." But two years later, the only growth was at the T-ball level, and that's attributable mostly to more young families moving into the emergent town. The number of Little League teams for those between ages 9 and 12 has actually shrunk. And there aren't enough interested teenagers to create a team beyond that level. Aliviado's crew was it.

Around the state, it's a similar story: a slight dip in teams and players.

Why that is, everyone has a theory. Lacrosse is rising. Video games beckon. New coaches. New administrators. But really, it's a mystery to locals. They just know that an awesome meteor called the Ewa Beach All-Stars once passed among the satellites, and everyone stood still for a moment in time, eyes to the sky.

A community transfixed more than transformed.

AGE 13

THE MAN

Bryan, Texas

Thirteen is the age at which kids start to fall away from sports in droves. As newly minted teens, they begin to assert their independence from parents and make more of their own choices in terms of how they're going to spend their nonschool hours. In general, too, the metabolisms of mammals slow down as puberty sets in, and humans are no exception. But most critically, the athletic system in many towns isn't set up to accommodate kids who want to keep playing sports for sport's sake. Recreational leagues fold, handing off the responsibility for our kid's athletic life to middle schools with their one-school, one-team structure, assuming there's even money in the school budget available for sports. Travel teams get more expensive, more exclusive, more time-consuming. Coaches start to work really hard at identifying the strong and eliminating the weak. Keeping the base of the participation pyramid as wide as possible during these years is the primary challenge facing any community that appreciates the need to keep its kids active.

At the tippy-top of that pyramid, meanwhile, a different set of hazards emerges. They are no less daunting and far more mind-bending.

It's a spring morning in 2006. J-Mychal Reese has taken a seat in the first row of his Language Arts class, next to the encyclopedias lined against the cinder-block wall of room 718 at Sam Rayburn Middle School. His hairless chin is just a few feet from the purple blouse of his teacher Melody Kapchinski—close enough that she can hear his whispered answers. He sits up front because he was raised right, and kids who are raised right don't hide, not here in Texas prairie country, not when you're the son of a son of a career soldier. These days, hiding would be impossible for J-Mychal, anyway. So even as he slouches sideways in his desk chair, tedium twisting his body until his thin neck is parallel to the floor, he still mumbles, "Yes, ma'am," follows instructions, and keeps chitchat to a minimum.

This morning's reading is a story about a Mexican immigrant who wants to return home a millionaire. His plan is to buy a run-down house, fix it up, and sell it at a sizable profit. But he is old and tired and needs a grandson's help to realize his dream. At the mention of the word "dream," Kapchinski pauses. In her experience, sixth-graders don't always comprehend its intended meaning. Most of her students are creatures of the moment, barely capable of visualizing a life two hours from now, much less two decades hence.

"Is it a daydream?" she says, looking to the class for a response. No one speaks up.

"Is it an actual dream?" she asks. More silence.

J-Mychal breaks in with a plain, declarative, "No." He knows all about dreams. And he knows that his dream no longer belongs to the realm of kid fantasy. His is stoked, shaped, and monetized in a way his peers can't imagine. Rated the top sixth-grade basketball player in the U.S., he has been studying this very lesson for three years now.

Although still a boy, J-Mychal Reese has long been certified as The Man.

• • •

In Bryan—a family-oriented municipality of 66,000 an hour and a half northwest of Houston that's still home to folks who remember when it wasn't even on the map—the mayor saw enough evidence of J-Mychal's Man-hood to draw up a formal proclamation. A framed copy of the official document adorns a shelf in J-Mychal's bedroom, among the plastic trophies, Michael Jordan posters, and AAU team jerseys above his bed:

> *WHEREAS: J-Mychal Reese, a Bowen Elementary School fifth-grader, has become a basketball phenomenon whose legend continues to grow from his days on the Bryan Little Dribblers National Championship Runner-Up team ...*
>
> *WHEREAS: When J-Mychal completed fourth grade he was individually ranked 1st in Texas and 2nd in the nation for AAU Boys Basketball Class of 2012 ...*
>
> *WHEREAS: Reese was one of a select few fifth graders invited to the Adidas Junior Phenom Camp in San Diego, which included the top 80 sixth graders ...*
>
> *WHEREAS: He is currently individually 1st in the state and 1st in the nation for AAU Boy's Basketball Class of 2012; and he was selected as a finalist from among 600,000 entrants for the Jr. NBA National Team ...*
>
> *NOW, THEREFORE, I, Ernie Wentrcek, as Mayor of the City of Bryan, Texas, and acting on behalf of the Bryan City Council, do hereby proclaim the date of March 8, 2005, as:*
>
> *J-MYCHAL REESE DAY*

Some more historical perspective is in order here. LeBron James never had a day named after him when he was a boy. (Still hasn't.) Before he entered high school, he neither attended a sneaker-company camp nor was asked to play on a NBA selection team. Not a single newspaper profile was written on him until his freshman year in high school. It wasn't because he was an ordinary ballplayer before then—his budding skills were apparent to anyone who saw him play. It was just that elementary and middle school kids weren't being sorted by scouting services back then.

Rankings change everything. At the very least they changed J-Mychal's childhood. One day in 2003, he is at the 9-and-under AAU nationals in

Memphis, Tenn., slapping at an undersize ball in the shadow of Graceland. The next day his dad, John, is getting a call from a pal who says J-Mychal has been listed by the online service Hoop Scoop as the second-best fourth grader in America. John had no idea such a list even existed. It seemed absurd and counterproductive at first. After all, these are just little kids, trying to learn a team game—basketball isn't swimming or tennis, sports based on individual merit. But John would come to embrace the rankings, as they seemed to motivate his son. The next summer at nationals, prince J-Mychal pointed at the reigning king, all 4-foot-11 of him, and told one of his coaches quietly, "He's not No. 1 after this tournament." Then he led the Houston Jaguars to the championship and secured the top rank for himself.

That rank went on a résumé which was sent to the NBA, which flew him to Denver for a youth exhibition game during the 2005 All-Star Weekend. Celebrity was building up fast now. To promote the Jr. NBA (a low-wattage partnership between the league and local organizations nationwide that sponsor youth leagues), the little lefty starred in a commercial with Steve Nash, who told the camera, "J-Mychal Reese? I named my dog after him." Next came ink in newspapers, fanfare on the web, and airtime on local TV. One anchor remarked glibly, "J-Mychal could become an NBA superstar. Instead of MJ, I guess we can call him JM."

His father drew the son's unusual name from Mychal Thompson, the first overall pick of the Trail Blazers in the 1978 draft. But it's often just J-Mike now, predicted greatness deserving a more elegant reference than to a rebounding power forward from the 1980s. The shorter version could surely come in handy at autograph sessions. After one tournament game this spring, it took an excruciating 45 minutes to satisfy all the children and adults who lined up. But three years of requests hasn't gotten J-Mychal to pen his name in any way other than how it appears on his schoolwork.

"You got LeBron, O.J., and J-Mike," bellows Roger Brown, who introduces himself as the GM of Reese's AAU team. Brown and the other parents gather on the plastic, pull-out bleachers of a high school gym where the team is playing a game in the Kingwood Classic, a 650-team, all-age-groups tournament that has taken over the courts of north Houston on a muggy weekend in April. Across town, celebrated prep star O.J. Mayo is making the Reebok people nervous, breaking from his regular Ohio team to play with a Nike-affiliated club from Miami for a couple of days. Here in this gym, J-Mike is mostly making the other coach jittery, snaring a defensive rebound between two opponents, slicing through two more on the dribble with a nifty spin move at halfcourt, and concluding the one-man break with a running 10-footer that crawls over the outstretched left hand of a Ben Wallace look-alike. The last victim isn't pleased and knocks J-Mike to the floor. But the 5-9, 135-pound guard hops back up, acting as if he didn't notice the blow. It's nothing he hasn't absorbed time and again from players he's never met before. "Every time I touch the ball, they're in my face," he says. The next day, he gets the same treatment in a game against Team Melo, the Baltimore-based scrappers subsidized by NBA star Carmelo Anthony. The coach has heard about J-Mike's lofty rank, so he orders up double-teams and excessively physical tactics that lead to flagrant fouls. J-Mike glares at his opponent and sticks out his tongue as he walks to the free throw line to complete a three-point play. "Be cool, J-Mike!" yells one mother on his team in the packed gym. "Tell him you ain't from the ghetto!"

J-Mike keeps his poise just enough, deflecting the aggression, letting others implode. Team Melo's wound-up coach gets tossed for lunging at the ref. "Melo's not going to be happy when he hears about this," the embarrassed coach moans in the hallway, where he's been banished until the final buzzer.

Later, when we're alone, J-Mike tells me he wishes players weren't ranked until high school, after their bodies and psyches have had more time to develop. But I have to pry this opinion out of him—it's not his style to complain. And he does enjoy being challenged. That's why his father, John, lets him practice with the Bryan High School team he coaches, and why the Reeses have accepted an invitation for an upcoming trip to France to join a team that will represent the U.S. against top European teams. "I'm looking for him to get pushed, shoved, manhandled," John says. To withstand the beatings, John recently hired a $90-an-hour personal trainer to build strength in J-Mike's reed-thin legs.

Basketball always has been one of the cheapest sports to play. All you need is a court and a ball, or maybe just a court and a friend with a ball. But as with every other youth sport, the economic barriers to the highest levels of competition have grown exponentially over the past decade. With all the private instruction, tournament fees, and travel costs, John figures he will invest $90,000 in his son's game before college—just about enough to buy four years of in-state tuition twice over. Not that college is the ultimate goal. For J-Mike, who's been dribbling a ball since he was in diapers, it's NBA all the way. "People ask if we're putting too much pressure on him," John says. "Well, if a kid comes to you and says he wants to be a doctor, do you tell him he's not smart enough? Or that it's too expensive? Do you shoot that dream down? Or do you try to help him attain it?" Once, as father and son analyzed game video, John was so critical, it caused J-Mike to ask, "Do I do anything right?" Most of the time, though, it's the kid who pushes Dad for guidance, gym time, travel. The old man always complies.

John's own father was an Army sergeant who taught him how to make a bed so crisp, a quarter could pogo on the sheets. But he had neither the time nor resources to put the bounce into the basketball career of his youngest son, who topped out as a workmanlike 6-3 guard at Division II Angelo State in Texas. That won't happen with John's younger son, who already is better than his brother, Jerron, a high school junior.

• • •

Predicting the future of a sixth-grade basketball star is in some ways even more difficult an exercise than with Little League World Series heroes. Given the advantage of height in hoops, scientists say basketball is up there with weight lifting and rowing as a sport for which we should be most patient in identifying elite talent. Dwyane Wade, the 2006 NBA Finals MVP, rode the bench of his Chicago high school team until adding four inches before his junior year. Carmelo Anthony didn't make varsity until his growth spurt arrived. All-Star center Dwight Howard was 6-1 going into high school. Most famously, Michael Jordan was 5-9 when he was cut from his team as a sophomore. They ended up at 6-4, 6-8, 6-11, and 6-6, respectively.

Clark Francis gets it. "I really don't want to go out and watch younger players," says the guru, who goes out there and watches them anyway as Hoop Scoop's publisher. "But that's where the game is going. Three or four years ago, AAU coaches wouldn't be seen dead going to seventh- or eighth-grade games. Now they have to do it to keep up. It's big business." The push began with the rise of LeBron James, who by wearing Adidas kicks brought the German company scads of publicity before signing with Nike (and the Cleveland Cavaliers) out of high school. But the U.S. system of basketball development was already organized in a manner that would lead inevitably in this direction. Clubs, moreso than schools with their often restrictive eligibility and geographic-boundary rules, have the ability to aggregate elite talent—from all over a city, state, sometimes even the nation—so college scouts can do most of their evaluation of prospects on the summer circuit. The club scene is largely devoid of regulation, and coaches aren't always qualified to coach, but it's cost-effective for scouts to be able to see most of the top players in one place, such as the Kingwood tournament.

Plus, basketball recruiting is a high-stakes game: A star player is worth about $1 million annually to his athletic department while he's still in college.

The Europeans, too, rely on clubs to deliver the next generation of athlete-entertainers. But those clubs aren't underwritten by corporations looking to sell sneakers and they don't cater to the needs of colleges. Rather, they are run by companies aspiring to develop players who can graduate to their own pro teams. Take Benetton Treviso, the Italian powerhouse owned by the clothing firm. At the top of its club structure is the first division team, made up of adults who compete in the Euroleague before television audiences and raucous hometown crowds; players who competed for that squad early in their careers include Toni Kukoc, who would go on to win three NBA championships with the Chicago Bulls, and Andrea Bargnani, the first overall pick in the 2006 NBA draft. Beneath the first unit are age-group teams down through the 13-and-under level, and, below that, a so-called "minibasket" program at 38 town centers that serves 1,800 kids down to age 6.

Benetton pays for everything: gyms, uniforms, travel, balls, coaches. There's a strength coach on staff who teaches proper lifting technique to players once they reach their teens (at first just to get them used to the motions—weights are added later). There's a psychologist to help families manage expectations for their sons. There are administrators who push the club's teaching philosophy down to volunteer coaches in the minibasket program, which costs the club $60,000 a year. "It's a professional approach to their youth activity," says Maurizio Gherardini, who ran the club from 1992 until 2006 when he joined the NBA's Toronto Raptors as assistant general manager. "Once the kid gets started at a young age, he has the model of the first team as a guide."

The club doesn't cut kids until it begins to form select teams at the 13-and-under level, at which point players become bound to the club in exchange for being trained. They can only jump to another club with the consent of Benetton. Around age 16, the best talent might get a professional contract and begin training full-time. Still, the club's emphasis is on addressing weaknesses in a player's game, not exploiting his strengths. With the 6-foot-10 Bargnani, for instance, Benetton Treviso surrounded him with other big men, so that he could work on his perimeter game.

"We didn't care about winning championships at the youth level," Gherardini says. "We wanted to build players. We wanted to build men."

Well-groomed prospects emerge from U.S. gyms, too, of course. One of the best in recent years was Kevin Durant, the long-armed forward for the Seattle SuperSonics. Raised in the Washington, D.C., area, Durant trained like a Euro from age 11, with an emphasis on long-term development. He was taught three basic moves—a pull-up jump shot, a two-dribble jumper, and a baseline drive—that became the foundation of his game. He did crab walks and duck walks, for movement skills. He ran 100 laps at a time, for conditioning. He played on the wing, to round out his skill set, and was made to diagram mechanics in pencil. But credit for all of this goes to one youth coach who took a personal interest in the kid and happened to pull all the right levers. Durant survived the U.S. system more than he benefited from it, bouncing between at least five clubs and teams (AAU and high school) during his prep years.

In the U.S., high schools look to win high school championships above all else—developing prospects is inevitably a secondary concern. And the elite-leaning AAU clubs in charge of the summer scene cannot be as patient as European clubs in identifying and developing talent. If it doesn't look like the pipeline is stocked with rising stars, sneaker-company money might dry up. It's a scarce resource, available to less than one percent of the more than 24,000 boys' and girls' travel teams in the country. So coaches have got to do what it takes to stay visible, which means acquiring early bloomers who can help push your team deep into national tournaments and jockeying for individual player rankings. Most of the $7 to $10 million a year that athletic apparel companies drop on grassroots basketball—chump change in a $16 billion industry—gets directed to teams made up of those athletes closest to signing with colleges, sophomores and juniors. But some cash and gear trickle down to teams of younger players that make a splash.

MYTH NO. 13
Grassroots hoops has gotten too professional.

THE TRUTH
The problem is it lacks a professional approach.

And there's the inestimable status that comes with an official shoe company association. Remember the Basketball Town Pharaohs (see Age 8) who beat the Maryland Heat at the third-grade AAU nationals in Memphis? A year later, they were Team California, having parlayed their success into a deal for half-off discounts on swanky uniforms and shoes made by a major company. "We now get to walk into the gym as Adidas," coach Rod Greene told me, proudly.

That link helps entice new players. But players can just as quickly bolt for another club. And often they do, sometimes even within the same tournament (rarely, though, at tourneys sponsored by the AAU, which, more than some organizations, tries to check such behavior).

So that is why coach Greene, scout Francis, and the rest of the basketball-industrial complex find their way each August to the Adidas Jr. Phenom Camp at Alliant International University in the arid hills north of San Diego. Introduced in 2004, it's not a teaching camp so much as a place for kids to put on a show. The lure is, in the parlance of grassroots ball, *exposure*—to the sneaker reps who fund select travel programs, to the 14 college coaches the camp owner claims are in attendance, and to the reputation guru, who leans against a railing, pen in mouth, player guide held like an open Bible in a preacher's hand. Francis' eyes dart from the guide to the red-and-white jerseys of the sixth-graders, who, like chattel, are numbered 1 through 104 and dealt onto Adidas-affiliated college "teams." J-Mike runs the wing for "Virginia Tech." Advantage, Hokies.

J-Mike is a "grade exception," a term used by the AAU for a player who is a year older than the average student in his class. Having a child repeat a grade has become an increasingly common strategy for parents who think their kid might have a future in basketball. It's a way to gain a physical and mental advantage and a leg up in the recruiting game. O.J. Mayo repeated sixth grade; by seventh grade he was No. 1 in his class, a ranking that held until late in high school, when he signed to play college ball at USC. J-Mike, who turned 13 during sixth grade, got held back before first grade. (A role player on J-Mike's AAU team, D.J. Griggs, would do it in 2006, dropping down and successfully capturing the attention of Francis at Jr. Phenom. While competing against smaller campers, Griggs showed himself to be a "big-time athlete with the versatility to play inside and outside," and a player "whose upside is nothing short of spectacular," Francis would swoon on Hoop Scoop.)

Then there's the center on J-Mike's AAU team, Jon Allen, who is more "man exception" than grade exception. Jon went through puberty at age 5, due to a rare quirk in the family genes. He has towered over other kids his age for years and now stands 6-2, a foot and a half taller than some of the other players at Jr. Phenom. He has been dunking since fifth grade. That's the year he joined J-Mike's team—he lives one town over in College Station—and helped it to a national title. His height has raised him to No. 2 in the class of 2012, in Francis' estimation. But what Francis doesn't appear to have considered is that Allen may not grow another inch. Allen males usually do all their growing before high school. Jon privately dreams of the NBA, which peers presume is in his future based on his rank. His 5-11 father, Jud, once a preteen star, now built like a wrestler, supports him but harbors no expectation that his son will play even in college.

The most important player on Jon and J-Mike's AAU team might be L.J. Rose, its skinny point guard. L.J., who is not a grade exception, has a court presence that belies his 12 years. At halftime of games, while the other players shoot around, his coaches talk alone with him, confident their floor general will implement the desired changes and get players in the right spots. His leadership and sublime passing were essential to the Jaguars winning the past two national championships. Yet his annual rank fell from 9th last year to 25th. He is loath to question the judgment of adults but wonders: *Have I slipped?* Scrape beneath the thinnest of protective emotional shells that boys his age have, and he'll admit that it hurts, seeing opponents he trumps, even teammates who play behind him, fly past him in the rankings—and not understanding why. "It doesn't feel right," he says. "It feels like politics." His father Lynden—a lawyer who once captained the University of Houston basketball team all the way to the 1982 Final Four—assures the son that it's just because they don't go to the Jr. Phenom camps.

Francis himself is childless, but he does have a dog. "I'm not hurting anybody," he says, "or maybe I am hurting some people because they can't handle the rankings. But that's not really my responsibility." His job is to rank 'em; it's the parents' job to raise 'em.

Francis does acknowledge the futility of trying to rank 225 sixth graders in order each year. He has never seen most of them play and doesn't go to nationals, relying instead on reports from an assistant and AAU coaches who inevitably rate their own players highly. Some parents and coaches eager to get their kids slotted will ask 20 friends to call and recommend the player, or they'll simply disguise their own voice and lobby several times. Sometimes, the process reveals its flaws. When Francis ranked fourth graders for the first time, the year J-Mike debuted at No. 2, the wrong Indianapolis Ferrell brother was put atop the rankings—second-grader Kaleb instead of Kevin. Asked about this, Francis shrugs and suggests he cannot be expected to deliver a quality product at the elementary school ages; he calls even his fifth-grade rankings "a joke."

The short, heavyset guru has stopped ranking fourth graders and has thought about raising the bar higher, closer to the high school level on which he first built his reputation a quarter century ago. But the money is just too good for this superfan–turned–scout whose passion for the game took its current form after he got cut from his own high school team. "It's like anything else," he says. "Are people going to buy your stuff? It's capitalism at its best." Information about middle school boys and girls drives most of his 1,000 subscriptions (at $499 a year). In what has become a hot industry replete with corporate buyouts worth tens of millions of dollars, none of the other recruiting services—and there are dozens—trolls that low with as much detail.

The perception is that once a kid is on the list, it's hard to fall off, that Francis just shuffles the names each year. Not true. He adds names, especially if they show up at the Jr. Phenom Camp. It's the rare event at which he actually gets to eyeball his subjects. He promotes the camp on his website, and in return, the camp organizer, Joe Keller, picks up his travel costs and lists him on camp literature as "scouting service director," figuring the advertised presence of Hoop Scoop will stoke sign-ups. This two-man game draws more than 330 rising sixth-, seventh-, and eighth-graders for the weekend, at $400 a head. Parents who have flown in from as far away as New York rail about having to shell out daily fees for parking and admission and $20 for a bare-bones camp guide, but they're not about to pass up the opportunity for their kid to wear the word "Phenom" on his chest. It's a can't-miss come-on that will soon allow Keller to spin off dozens of regional camps. "It's easy with all these egotistical parents," he says.

A leaden brow and unblinking eyes give Keller the severe visage of a quick-draw gunslinger in some Wild West movie. But it took the patience of a gardener to bring exposure camps to the middle school hoops scene. He dreamed up the idea 10 years earlier while attending ABCD Camp in Teaneck, New Jersey, where many of the top high school–age players gathered each summer between 1984 and 2006. While there had been basketball camps for decades, ABCD was among the new breed, specifically tailored to connecting buyers (colleges, NBA teams) with sellers (players, parents). It was a dynamite business solution for its time, especially for the buyers, given the value of seeing the sellers battle it out under one roof without actually having to pay to get them there. The tab was picked up by parents and, to an extent, the athletic apparel companies, eager as they were to find the next endorser-king.

The owner of ABCD Camp was Sonny Vaccaro, who pioneered the art of delivering future stars to shoe companies. A big, loquacious man who greets even acquaintances with hugs, he signed Jordan while working for Nike in the 1980s and, after he switched companies in '92, Kobe Bryant for Adidas. He is a legend in the industry, an American original whom James Gandolfini of *Sopranos*-fame would later agree to play in a film on the youth basketball trade. Thus, he was the rainmaker Keller decided to approach with his idea of a camp for middle schoolers, which, after all, seemed ripe—shoe companies had just fought over LeBron while he was still in high school. Vaccaro, who was in the process of defecting to Reebok, invited Keller to his house in Calabasas, Calif. Over salad and a chicken dish, they kicked around the concept. Vaccaro offered encouragement but not a long-term commitment.

Adidas got wind of the meeting and called two days later. Soon, Keller had a five-year sponsorship deal with Vaccaro's former employer for free gear and use of the Adidas name. He could hardly believe his good fortune. All his life he had considered himself a hustler, a guy who could sell anything to anybody, but there had been no real payoff. He had held a series of odd jobs in his 20s after quitting college, which he had really only attended to play baseball. He had been a foreman in a decorative ironworks shop for a couple of years. His basketball credentials were limited: He had helped coach a SoCal AAU team that featured future NBA players Tyson Chandler and Josh Childress. Now he was sitting on a potential gold mine. He knew that even before one wealthy father offered him $5,000 to make sure his child got picked for the camp's all-star game on the final day of the first girls' Jr. Phenom in 2005. (Keller says he rejected the bribe: "If word got out, my integrity would have been shot.")

Vaccaro calls Keller's camp series the most successful for-profit venture he has seen in four decades of following the industry. But he isn't eager to have its founder compared to him. At least with ABCD, a true invitational camp that did not charge entry fees, most players are within a couple years of being able to sign with colleges. "I'm not demeaning Joe because he's been brilliant as a businessperson," says Vaccaro, who in 2007 would shut down ABCD and retire from grassroots basketball. "But it doesn't serve the purpose of what we're talking about, which is uncovering the very few kids who should be described as phenoms." He drills down to the meaning of the word, a young person who has demonstrated extraordinary promise. "The word's being too loosely applied here," he says. "Parents think that by putting their child in a Phenom camp, he is a phenom. Then when they find out he is *not* a phenom, their world crumbles."

That's not likely to happen with Jon Allen's tanned, mustachioed father. He puzzles at the wisdom of parents spending so much money to expose, rather than protect, their children. Of course, he knows how the game is played. Much as Jon wants to be here, Jud knows a camp like this needs his son more than Jon needs the camp. The kid's presence can be a marketing tool; names can be made with a successful challenge to the No. 2. So Jud takes a series of recruiting calls from people affiliated with the camp and ends up getting what he says is a free trip for him and his son to lovely San Diego, paid for by "someone"—he doesn't know who. Jud took care of the camp registration fee, but other key costs were gratis; he says he and Jon just showed up at their local airport, then the camp hotel, and they were taken care of. (Keller says he wasn't the benefactor and doesn't know who was.) It wasn't the first thing that Jon received under strange circumstances. In previous years, boxes of Adidas kicks had mysteriously showed up at his home. Right size, right team color. No note. No return address.

In the view of the NCAA, athletes aren't directly recruitable—face-to-face or by phone—until after their sophomore year of high school. But that's just what the rules say. "These kids *are* recruited," Francis says. "They are recruited for AAU. They are recruited for middle school. They will get recruited for high school. They'll get recruited again by AAU at the high school level, when they change teams. They'll be recruited four or five times before a college coach ever calls."

It may be a fine education in salesmanship, but not so much in basketball.

• • •

J-Mike got his first how-do-you-do letter from a college coach in the summer after fourth grade, from Arizona's Lute Olson. That's one year sooner than Demetrius Walker received his first valentine from a coach. But when the full treatment arrived for Walker, it was breathtaking. By the end of eighth grade, his third straight year atop his class rankings, he had a crate of envelopes from some of the most prominent college programs in the nation. His favorite mailing: a handwritten note from Duke's Mike Krzyzewski. Walker wondered how many other kids received the same letter, but he felt enough of a connection to approach the legendary coach at a tournament a few months later and say hello. Coach K remembered who Walker was with some prompting by Keller, his AAU coach.

"Mind if I take a picture with you?" Demetrius asked Coach K.

The photo would become the screensaver on his mother's phone. Thanks to the No. 1 rank he had carried through middle school, Walker, three years ahead of J-Mike, was becoming perhaps the most celebrated eighth grader in basketball history. He entertained comparisons to LeBron. At tournaments, little kids knocked on his hotel room door in the middle of the night, asking for headbands. Even *Sports Illustrated* ran a profile, teasing readers with the cover line, "Meet Demetrius Walker. He's 14 years old. You're going to hear from him."

Or maybe not. Just a year and a half later, he is 29th in his class and, in the estimation of Francis, lucky to be rated that high. "If his name wasn't Demetrius Walker, he'd probably be 100," he says. Why the sudden plunge? Everyone has their own notion of what happened in the summer of 2005, when by Walker's admission he played poorly in tournaments. Walker: "I rolled my left ankle," limiting his fabled hops. Keller: "He thought he was the best. It was so easy for him he got bored." Francis: "He couldn't handle the pressure."

I find Walker at the Phenom 150, another one of Keller's new, gotta-be-there camps—this one's for boys entering ninth and tenth grades. It is populated by many of the same players Walker dominated two years ago at Jr. Phenom on the same Alliant International courts. Only now, his rivals smell blood. It has nothing to do with his ankle, which has had nearly a year to heal. More critically, his growth hormone has gone on hiatus. In middle school, Walker was a 6-3 man-child who dominated the paint with quick hands and three-sixty dunks. He's still 6-3. His rivals, however, shot up in size. So his layups are no longer uncontested. He gets pushed to the perimeter, where a jumper he never needed before has a ways to go before it's even D1 caliber.

He sweats and waits. He's tries find encouragement in his family tree. "Mom is six-feet," he says, as if reading from a résumé. "Dad is six-feet, 6-1. Dad's brothers are 6-6, 6-7, 6-4, and 6-3. My mom's brother is six-feet. My great grandmother is 6-2, and my great grandfather is 6-3." So far, the highlight of his year was a visit to a doctor's office. He had to find out if he had any growth left in his bones, so he had himself evaluated, like a French soccer prospect. "They examined my knees," he says. I don't know if it was an MRI or an X-ray exam, but I seen some space and I was like"—he exhales in relief—"that's all I need."

The chance, maybe, to live up to his name.

Possibly. But physical maturation experts tell me that hand, not knee, X-rays offer the most accurate reads after the age of 5.

As Walker's mother does with her son, John Reese tells his boy not to get stuck on being The Man. That MJ, whose image adorns the cover of J-Mike's school notebook, wasn't No. 1 at this age or even when he entered the NBA. (He was the third player drafted in 1984.) That in a nation of two million sixth-grade boys, surely more rivals will emerge. "What if some kid doesn't have the money to go to nationals or camps where these kids get ranked?" John says. He recognizes that fighting for a ranking can undermine team-play mentality, as Francis is more likely to notice shots made than picks set in his limited time evaluating players.

J-Mike's mother worries more about the social perils of being The Man. Already, Celeste says, "People don't look at him as being a regular 13-year-old kid who plays Nintendo and hangs out with his buddies." Her fear is reasonable, if Walker's experience is any guide. He has had fun with the fame and the autographs, as they make him feel special. But he also misses his privacy, the anonymity that comes with a more normal childhood. As his local celebrity grew, Walker passed up opportunities to hang out with friends at the mall or movie theater, where people scrutinized his every move. "I just became a homebody," he says. So now friends think he's big-timing them.

J-Mike's buddies are not from the neighborhood but from all over southeast Texas—the No. 2, 11, 16, and 25 ranked players in the country. They're his AAU teammates, some of whom live two hours away because that's how it works in elite grassroots hoops. There are no leagues and no home courts. In essence, these are all-star exhibition teams, like low-level Harlem Globetrotters, except in this case the players live too far apart to practice together more than occasionally.

When they gather for tournaments, it's great fun. Stone-faced on the court and respectfully quiet around adults, J-Mike unleashes a bust-up smile at the all-kid tables of restaurants in distant cities. He likes his teammates so much that when his dad was offered a plum high school job in Dallas, J-Mike told him, "You can move but I'm staying. I'll find another family to live with here." But the day may come when J-Mike outgrows even this team, the two-time defending national champions. "Gotta keep the big picture in mind," John Reese sighs. The group is now called the 12-and-under Texas Ambassadors, the core of it having been recruited away from the Jaguars program. But the Ambassadors' 16s have invited J-Mike to play up with them. And in California, plans are being made to gather the nation's top middle schoolers on one team to compete in a half-dozen tournaments on both coasts. Team Phenom, as it is called, will be bankrolled by Keller, who in a year could look to include J-Mike in his backcourt. "I like to shock the world when I do things," the Adidas subcontractor says.

Linzy Davis can play that game. A prominent AAU coach affiliated with Nike, Davis makes an offer that cannot be refused: a chance for J-Mike to compete in France in what Davis calls the "Junior World Championship" for 13-and-unders. He can do some *real* globetrotting—and bring Jon and L.J., too. They will combine with select members of Davis' AAU team from Georgia, where he sells hospital supplies and runs a basketball recruiting magazine, to represent the United States in Europe. Davis has been bringing 19-and-under teams made up of select players to northern France for years for a summer tournament. This will be his first trip to the continent with a younger squad, and it's a gambit for all.

• • •

I meet Davis in the quaint town of Ardres in northern France, where J-Mike and his teammates, in swooshed-up USA jerseys, join a modest pretournament parade celebrating the cultures of the assembled teams. Behind the marching band, the 47-year-old Davis greets me with the firm handshake of a corporate climber, and an expression of mission. "The biggest challenge I've had with the 19s is with the McDonalds All-Americans," he says. "They think they've already arrived, that they're already great." He tells me his goal is to save the youngsters on J-Mike's team by introducing them early to European clubs that at times have run fundamentals clinics on his older teams, just as NBA select teams have gotten schooled in the Olympics and World Championships.

But this trip is primarily about, frankly, recruiting. Davis doesn't officially represent the swoosh, but he sees himself as an emissary. "What the shoe companies are finding is if you don't get the kid by middle school, you're never going to get him," he says. LeBron switched his allegiance from Adidas to Nike when he hit the NBA, but others remain loyal to their AAU brand, and at a discount. "The reason for the relationship is so I don't have to pay as much for a guy," he says. "When negotiation time arrives, Adidas is already going to know that he's a Nike guy. I may not have to offer $7 million a year in a bidding war; I can offer him two." So Davis, bottom line, is in no position to alienate these sixth-graders. Their affections are critical. Davis must please the kids, not the other way around.

How to do that? From his experience with American players, Davis assumes that each boy will need to get his points to feel good about this trip.

His stats. His status. Oh, and maybe championship rings.

Turns out, the only entitlement that won't come easily while in France are the actual rings, which will have to be ordered later. The Henri Seux International Tournament, or "world championship" as Davis has sold it, includes only one approximation of a national select team—the one representing the U.S. The rest are random club teams from towns in Ireland, Switzerland, Montenegro, France, and elsewhere on the continent. There are no rankings or shoe money to consolidate the largest and most talented boys in those countries; these are local kids with formative skills but not much size. The Americans win their first game amid a flurry of blocked shots and uncontested layups, overwhelming a Slovenian team whose best player bears a facial resemblance (minus the beard and horns) to Mr. Tumnus in the movie *Chronicles of Narnia: The Lion, the Witch, and the Wardrobe.* Final score in the truncated, 12-minute game: 66-2. Everyone gets their points.

The kids on the other teams don't look demoralized—they seem just happy to be here, like they're on holiday. Which makes sense. National championships in some European countries don't even begin around age 14, so they bring few expectations to an event like this. But their coaches grumble about the thick crop of dark hair on the U.S. center's legs, and they approach tournament officials.

Big Jon flashes his passport ID, and gets to keep playing.

In the wooden barn of the Ardres club, beneath ads for a local *boulangerie* and *patisserie,* the blowouts resume. The Euros get swallowed by the full-court traps and shock-and-awe force of the taller, faster Americans. A prepubescent Ardres boy has such trouble inbounding the ball over Big Jon that his pass hits the low-slung rafters.

Courtside as he awaits the next game, Geneva coach Michael Brooks winces beneath a faded baseball cap. With leads like that, "they should be working on their weaknesses, not their strengths," says the former NBA player and U.S. national team captain, who finished out his career in Europe two decades ago, liked the less-hurried lifestyle there, and stayed. "Work your system. Take outside shots." Just wait, he says, arching a weary eyebrow. Some of these Euros, if not here then elsewhere, will someday grow tall. The best of them will go into full-time training at age 16, focus on development in a manner the AAU and high school system cannot match, and come to play the way NBA coaches prefer. Even George Raveling, Nike's director of global basketball, would echo as much in 2006, predicting that foreign players will comprise half of the NBA by 2010. All of that concern would cause Nike and Adidas the next year to create more skills-based summer programming for the most highly ranked U.S. prospects. But the basic structure of American hoops, compromised as it is by its rewarding of early results and reputations, would remain in place.

"Physically, the Americans are much more advanced," Brooks says. "But how far will natural physical talent take you? At some point you must learn what to do when you cannot jump over that guy anymore. In America, people are so anxious to get to the highest level they don't take the time to learn to play correctly—the way we once learned it from coaches like John Wooden. Now everybody wants to go for the steal so they can do a fantastic dunk. It's all one-on-one. In Europe, it's three, four passes, pick. They play for the other guy.

"To me, America will always be *the* basketball power. But we are slowly losing the edge because the Europeans are catching up to us, and quickly." He waves dismissively toward the court, and says. "You can't judge a European basketball player on this. Judge on what happens later. These here are kids."

After the fourth annihilation of the day, the American boys plop down in the spectator seats above the court and gaze out at two Euro teams that just began the next game. I find my way to the perimeter of the pack, and ask several of them if they learned anything today that might explain how the Old World could produce such rising NBA stars as Dirk Nowitzki, who the following year would become the first Euro voted league MVP, and Tony Parker, who would become the continent's first finals MVP after leading San Antonio to its fourth title in a decade. Most of the boys shrug, stumped. It's baffling, given today's results.

J-Mike, though, feels it. He sets down his concession-stand fries and surveys the scene, puzzling out the illusion. With the supersize Americans out of the way, the ball movement, quick cuts, and screens—the foundation of Euro hoops—has finally emerged. "They pass a lot," he concludes, speaking softly. He seems intrigued, which is encouraging but probably shouldn't surprise anyone who has seen him run the court with the Ambassadors. Like any coach's kid, he appreciates the team game and can play it. When he's asked to do so.

Perhaps American basketball's No. 1 sixth-grader has been underestimated.

• • •

"What is the definition of accomplishment?" Back in room 718, with one final question, Ms. Kapchinski wraps up the reading about the immigrant who hopes to be a millionaire. It's a tricky question; she wants not the dictionary answer but what the word means to each of her students. She wants drawings, too. A Latino boy in glasses scratches his noggin. A blonde girl fiddles with one of her large hoop earrings.

J-Mike, pencil dangling in his left hand, puts his head down and starts to write.

In his current situation, predictions of success are easy to confuse with success itself. Yet he can't relax: The challenge with being No. 1 in sixth grade is that there's only one direction J-Mike can go from there. And he has seven years to endure. Seven more years until David Stern can call his name. Seven years of scouts and sycophants, provocateurs and profiteers, rivals and reporters, all dialed into his premature rank. Seven years of stratospheric expectations, on top of the three he has already put in, a slog no kid in hoops history has been asked to endure. When MJ was this age, he played football and baseball and nobody cared.

J-Mike hands his work sheet to Kapchinski. On it he has scrawled, "To play in the NBA." His drawing is of a finish line.

AGE 14

GAME ON

Miami, Florida

In the spring of 2007, the U.S. Supreme Court felt compelled to review the matter of adults sucking up to middle school students with athletic promise. The justices agreed to review relatively few cases that year. Those that made the cut dealt with such important issues as global warming, tobacco advertising, abortion, racketeering, and faith-based funding—not to mention "BONG HITS 4 JESUS" (a banner held up by an Alaska student at a public event). But the men and women in black robes found room in their schedule to consider the case of the *Tennessee Secondary School Athletic Association vs. Brentwood Academy*, a lawsuit that had been bouncing around the federal court system for a decade.

Brentwood is a small, rich, private school in Nashville with a habit of collecting state championships in football. The TSSAA is Tennessee's governing body for high school sports, an organization steered by principals and coaches from large public schools who don't much like losing their top athletes to Brentwood and their well-funded ilk. The Brentwood coach wrote to some eighth-graders who had committed to the school encouraging them to show up for spring practice. He signed the letter, "Your Coach." The TSSAA called that recruiting and banned Brentwood from the playoffs for two years. Brentwood argued that it was free speech and hardly a violation of the rule—every state has one—

forbidding high schools from recruiting students for athletic purposes. So off to court the two sides went, spending an estimated $5 million in legal fees combined as the dispute made its journey through the appeals process. Along the way, the Clinton administration took one side (Brentwood), and the Bushies the other (TSSAA).

The outcome threatened to change the shape of high school sports itself. If a state's athletic association cannot keep a private school from openly recruiting a rising star, what's next? Formal athletic scholarships that could get more kids like Vonn Fe'ao out of underperforming public schools? The national high school rankings in some sports are already populated with many private schools, including boarding schools loaded with international talent. If still more energy and talent shifts in their direction, the public schools would be left to compete for what? Second-tier championships? Intrinsic rewards? The mind reels when contemplating an open market on preteen athletes.

The TSSAA lost five out of six court battles in its march to Washington. But in the Supremes the defenders of the status quo found a group with which they could harmonize. The vote was 9-0 against Brentwood. To John Paul Stevens—the oldest member of the court at age 87—who wrote the court's opinion, nothing less than the purity of prep sports was at stake. "In our view," he declared, "the dangers of undue influence and overreaching that exist when a lawyer chases an ambulance are also present when a high school coach contacts an eighth grader." The most ancient of Supremes warned that "hard-sell tactics directed at middle-school students could lead to exploitation, distort competition between high school teams, and foster an environment in which athletics are prized more highly than academics."

Fine sentiment. Except that all those hazards can be found already on the landscape of big-time high school sports, largely unchecked by state high school associations which lack the resources to root out violations.

For some public schools, the poaching of athletes is the least of today's challenges.

• • •

The No. 2 ranked high school football team in the nation coming into the 2007 season was Miami Northwestern Senior High. On a comfortably warm Friday night in late August, about 4,000 of its fans fill the stands behind the Bulls sideline at Traz Powell Stadium—a cold, concrete structure that comes to life at the sight of the Northwestern action heroes bursting through a smoke-filled tunnel at the edge of the end zone, like birds released from a box. Tonight's crowd is here for a preseason game. Regular season games often draw twice as many paying customers, capacity at Traz Powell, and sometimes more than 20,000, in which case games have been moved to the Orange Bowl.

Larry Williams, a chrome-domed former track athlete from the 1970s who now serves as president of the Northwestern alumni association, explains to me that these gatherings are all about the community. He's referring to Liberty City, the proud, struggling heart of black Miami that has little else to rally around. "A game is almost like a holiday," he says. "Alcoholics sober up. Crime goes down. Everybody's at the game, and those that aren't want to know what's going on. It's a blue-and-gold love that can't be replaced."

Nor is it a love that can be ignored. "When you come to Miami Northwestern, we expect you to win," he says. "That's just the way of life. I mean, you go to Notre Dame, they expect you to win. At the University of Texas, they expect you to win. University of Miami, they expect you to win." He delivers this news in the direct, even tones of the accountant that he is in his non-Northwestern life, as if relaying word of the tax bill that you didn't fully expect.

"There's nothing wrong with having high expectations," he shrugs.

Truth is, high school football is of great importance in many American cities and towns. This year, the Bulls just have more pure talent than perhaps any team in the country, with at least half a dozen seniors projected to receive Division I scholarships. They have size, with some lineman tipping 300 pounds on the scales. They have speed, with wideouts on both ends who can make opposing defenders look like they are moving in slow motion. They have skill, the kind that gets the teachers and lawyers and drug dealers at Traz Powell chattering about who's headed to the NFL someday. And they have a chance at securing national bragging rights, as a made-for-TV matchup against the preseason No. 1 team in the *USA Today* rankings, Southlake Carroll of the Dallas area, is scheduled for September 15 in north Texas.

Unfortunately, the Bulls also have an indictment that messed up summer workouts and nearly led to the cancellation of the season.

JUSTICE INTERCEPTED:
THE ALL-CONSUMING POWER OF FOOTBALL

That's the title a grand jury gave to its final report on a series of events that unfolded the previous fall as the Bulls pursued a state championship. The only person hit with criminal charges was the principal at the time, but evidence unearthed during the investigation by the State Attorney's office led to the dismissal of the head coach and raised serious questions about whether high school sports glory has grown so important to adults that taxpayer-funded schools can no longer live up to their oath to serve and protect students—both athletes and non-athletes.

"Society has a way of demonstrating its true priorities and character when confronted with crisis," the grand jury wrote in the introduction of its report. "So do microcosms of society, such as a school system. When confronted with a crisis, the people who make up these systems either rise to the occasion and act for the greater good or act in ways that are deceitful, selfish, and ultimately destructive to all involved. The latter occurred here."

The trouble started in September of 2006 with a sex crime that involved the star running back, Antwain Easterling. The solidly built, 5-foot-11 senior had moves that captured the attention of the nation's top collegiate programs. He also caught the eye of a petite, socially awkward freshman, a clarinet-playing member of the band who was looking to fit in at her new, football-centric school. After one game they got to talking, and she agreed to have sexual intercourse with him in a school bathroom. He was almost 19; she had just turned 14. In Florida, that's a third-degree felony because of the gap in their ages—the idea being that a child so much younger than their partner doesn't have the judgment necessary to make such a decision responsibly.

Happens all the time, teammates of Easterling say. Sometimes even in school bathrooms.

But it was the cover-up that really shredded reputations.

When school officials learn about a possible crime on school grounds, they are supposed to report the information to police. In this case, the principal and 20 other officials would hear about the incident over the next two months and do nothing about it. That group included guidance counselors, teachers, administrative staff, the school psychologist, and head coach Roland Smith—who according to Easterling also told him not to tell anyone about the incident, that it was "nobody else's business." (Smith denies saying this.) Word of the sex crime wouldn't reach police until December 5, nearly two months after the girl and her mother had informed school officials about the encounter. Police were alerted only after the mother, while getting coffee at a donut shop, bumped into an officer assigned to the school and asked how the criminal investigation was going—only to be told that there was no investigation.

Two days later, Easterling was taken in for questioning. He initially denied having had sex with the girl, then was fed a hamburger and French fries ... and confessed. (Note to CIA: Why resort to waterboarding when there's fast food?)

Despite the full-bellied admission of guilt, Easterling was allowed to suit up for the state title game at nearby Dolphin Stadium. Emerging from the tunnel before the game, he received an ovation from the crowd of 24,368 that was so robust, school administrator Debra Davis recalls, "You would have thought you was at the NFL Super Bowl." Then he ran for 157 yards and a touchdown as the Bulls crushed their Orlando-area opponent, Lake Brantley, 34-14.

In trying to make up his mind about whether to suspend Easterling for that game, principal Dwight Bernard was torn. Easterling had been kicked out of Northwestern previously after a knife was found in his book bag, only to return in time for his junior season. Knowing that Easterling was eligible to sign with a college program in a couple months,

Bernard asked Davis, "Will we be ruining his career?" The same question was not being asked about the girl, who, in her own way, had arrived at Northwestern as a rough-hewn gem with sparkling potential: She was an honors student, classified as gifted, with a sensitivity for the pain of others that was reflected in her writing.

Her mother gave me a copy of one of her daughter's poems that had been selected for inclusion in a national student publication before her eighth-grade year. The girl had titled it "Tearful Hopes," a portion of which reads:

Why must this world be a slayer of my hopes?
Why must life have its ups and downs and slopes?
Why must I see the ones I love die?
Why must I watch my mother cry?
For my granddad with cancer who doesn't have time
to live
My grandma with cancer then you dare to tell me
be positive
But now that I look down at my scattered hopes I've
learned to go back to my past
Everything shapes my life that makes who I am going to
be so I'll work on my present as long as I'm alive
So when my hopes crumble I'll iron them back out
When I reach a goal in life I'll help other realize what
high hopes are about

Clearly, the girl brought some personal issues to Northwestern, and she had sought counseling in the past to deal with them. But since the bathroom encounter with Easterling—which quickly became fodder for school gossips—her behavior had turned increasingly erratic. She stopped taking her attention deficit disorder medication, began skipping class, and agreed to have sex with more partners she barely knew, both on and off campus. Her mother tried to get her transferred to another school. No room elsewhere, she was told.

Twice in the ensuing months, the girl attempted suicide. Once with a knife, once with pills. Eventually she was placed in a 24-hour psychiatric facility. "She blames herself for everything that happened," her mother told me, sobbing. "Everything."

Northwestern players blame her, too. They lost their popular head coach; Roland Smith and most of his staff were dismissed by Miami-Dade County Public Schools Superintendent Rudy Crew after the grand jury's report was released in June. When I meet with the captains and stars of the 2007 team at a preseason practice, I ask if they have any sympathy for the girl, given her downward spiral.

Sitting on metal bleachers next to the practice field, all five of them pause to collect their thoughts beneath the afternoon sun. I've asked them to be honest. Finally, Terrell Killings, a 6-foot-4, 300-pound offensive guard and one of the best students on the team, weighs in. "To what she's done to the program? No," he says, emphatically. "I have sympathy for her situation, that her parents probably don't instill love in her. But at the same time, she has single-handedly took part in destroying one of the greatest programs, probably, in this country's history."

Killings' father was the athletic director during the scandal, so the fallout was especially wrenching for him. But his comment also shows how allied the players are to their former coach, who some of them saw as a father figure and others viewed as a conduit to their NCAA and NFL dreams. "I feel that throughout the course of the season, we was unbeaten, 15 and 0," receiver Tommy Streeter says. "But that 14-year-old beat us in this situation."

Defensive lineman Marcus Forston scrunches his nose, trying to reconcile his humanity with his sketchy knowledge of the events. "You know, right now, today," he says in a deep bass, "I'm still praying for her, even though I know she was wrong. She's going through a mental institution so we should pray for her ... Even though she was wrong."

Big Marcus feels compelled to make that point, twice. I'm left to wonder why.

It's as if Bulls football needs to be protected above all else.

• • •

Nationally, children begin playing tackle football later than they do any other major team sport, often around age 11. Another crop comes along at 14 and 15 when bodies are needed to fill out high school teams. Jayvee coaches get the kids who couldn't make travel teams in other sports or the fat kids looking for ways to use their girth or the ones whose parents made them wait on football to preserve joints and brains. In most places, it's a sport in which kids can afford to hold off until the teenage years, as size and basic athleticism trump technique.

Patience isn't the pattern in Liberty City, where football is seen as a way out of a community that has endured more than its share of social dysfunction over the decades—from drugs to violence to racism. Built half a century ago as a tool with which to enforce segregation, it's basically a city within a city, walled off to the motorists whizzing by on I-95 on their way to some downtown skyscraper or South Beach nightclub. Tourists and suburbanites don't see the entrenched poverty. The piles of random trash that boys walk past on their way to football practice. The teenage dropouts on cracked sidewalks wearing "WE ALL WE GOT!" T-shirts. The lack of investment by corporate America, even when it comes to the placement of chain stores and restaurants.

I order at the lone Burger King in Liberty City. They're out of burgers, I'm told.

"Football is going to be my meal ticket," Forston says. "It's going to get me to college so I can get my degree and do better things in life." He recently told University of Miami coach Randy Shannon, who grew up in Liberty City too, that he wants to be a Hurricane.

Shannon's personal journey serves as inspiration. His father was murdered when he was 3. Two brothers and a sister, crack addicts, died of AIDS. And he still emerged with a college degree and a bright future. As Terrell Killings says, "At the end of the day, it's not about football. It's about getting these kids into college so that they can lead better lives."

At Northwestern, the competition for starting spots is fierce. And some of those spots end up going to kids like Jacory Harris—the best quarterback in the state—who lives outside the district but has enrolled in the school's medical magnet program and thus qualifies to play for the Bulls. So parents in Liberty City are motivated to sign up their kids for football programs as early as age 4, pads and all. Most preschoolers have little clue how to play this rule-bound game, but volunteer coaches line them up to scrimmage anyway. In contact drills, their outsize helmets look like bobbleheads, shaking to and fro.

Luther Campbell runs one of these youth programs, Liberty City Optimist. It's based at Hadley Park, a tree-lined space a few blocks to the south of Northwestern. Hadley is an oasis, really, the kind of well-groomed, well-run park that urban municipalities like Baltimore desperately need and Liberty City has a surprising plethora of, thanks to the availability of cheap land and the civic recognition that kids need somewhere to go after school. Campbell meets me by the bleachers at the main field, where sometimes as many as a thousand people gather to watch Saturday afternoon games. Today, at dusk, it's just me and him and another brilliant South Florida sunset that paints the skies purple and orange above the west end of the park.

"You know those stories about Chinese swimmers and gymnasts in their sport schools? That's football in Miami," Campbell says in a voice made thin and raspy from two decades of throaty, call-and-response before hip-hop audiences around the world. "I mean, it's serious here. Some of these parents will actually try and sneak in their kids at 3 years old. So imagine the experience they have by the time they reach high school!"

Campbell, though not a great rapper, is a music pioneer of sorts. His forte, as front man for 2 Live Crew back in the 1980s, was the use of sexually explicit lyrics to drive polite society absolutely mad. Lyrics from *Nasty as They Wanna Be* at one concert got his group rung up on obscenity charges. Which only made the album's sales skyrocket. Campbell fought the prosecution on free-speech grounds, gathering the support of intellectuals and artists as the case worked its way up the court system. The biggest difference between his case and that of Brentwood Academy is that, ultimately, he won. The Supreme Court declined to review the case, effectively upholding an appellate court's decision in his group's favor.

So, to recap:

Suck my asshole = protected speech.

Your Coach = unprotected speech.

There are constitutional principles in play, of course, which can explain such an apparent incongruity. But for the black Hugh Hefner, as Campbell refers to himself, the bottom line is that fame, or at least infamy, brought him lots of money. And some of that money he used to co-found Liberty City Optimist.

His teams found success and, by the mid-90s, the Warriors were winning Pop Warner national championships. Suddenly the community had something to rally around—youth football—which inspired the creation of rival programs around town. Now there are about a dozen such programs in Liberty City, many of them accommodating more than 200 boys; Liberty City Optimist serves 575 kids through age 15 and has a waiting list. Several of these programs belong to an association Campbell recently created, the National Youth Football League, after breaking away from Pop Warner. (Campbell says he didn't like its costly national championships, at which teams were spending about $30,000 each pursuing kiddie Super Bowls at the Disney World complex, where accommodations are safe but relatively expensive. The NYFL holds its title games at local stadiums as most of its teams come from South Florida, where Pop Warner is now trying to hold onto its base by offering to defray the travel costs of needy teams.)

Campbell is as responsible as anyone for the rise of football in Miami, a city now known for its production of football talent. Several of his players have gone on to the NFL, including receivers Chad Johnson and Antonio Bryant. "Lots of players came through here," he says. He'll be watching some of them in Dallas in a few weeks, when Northwestern plays in its biggest game ever, as he's a big fan of the Bulls.

At the same time, the Easterling episode bothers him. Which perhaps is saying something, given his business-related embrace of sexual adventure. He leans toward me so that I know he's sincere. "I feel more for the little girl than I feel for anyone," he says. "When this whole thing started, all I was thinking about was this little girl being in a bathroom after some 18-year-old guy did what he did to her. And I think about my daughters. I got daughters, and a lot of other people got daughters.

"Now, the coach ain't off the hook either. He need to go address that behavior with that kid. I don't care whether it's Antwain Easterling or Eric Dickerson or Michael Vick. You, head coach, need to be man enough to discipline that kid. You got to be able to step up and say, 'Look, you're not playing, buddy.' "

I suggest that perhaps that's easier said than done. Gambling on Bulls games is an open secret in the community, and some folks you just don't want to upset. After one loss early in his tenure, Smith had his car vandalized. "That's the job Mr. Smith took," Campbell says, unswayed. "When you take that job, you take on all of that pressure to win. You know you're putting your family, your car, and everything else in jeopardy."

• • •

Wanda Jenkins doesn't have much to lose, except her son.

That would be 14-year-old Jerrill, who stands at a crossroads. He's one of the best players on Campbell's most senior team at Liberty City Optimist, the 160-pounders. His teammates call him the Hummer, because as a running back he's hard to take down. He has big feet and big hands and runs with what his mother recognizes as inner anger. He's had the need to work out that aggression since he was a little boy, when Wanda used to sprint alongside him at Warrior games, shouting "Go! Go! Go! Go!" in his ear hole all the way to the end zone, which made Campbell laugh.

She's been the team mom for years, the rare parent who stays for every practice. Everybody asks the wide-faced woman in reading glasses and hoop earrings, "Why you always at Jerrill's practices?" And she tells them, "Because I wasn't there for my other kids, and I don't want to make the same mistake with him." She was a junkie for years, unable to cope with a sexual crime against a daughter by a man she knew. She's been clean ever since Jerrill was 3.

Climbing out of financial hell also has been hard. She has a steady job as a hospital technician. She's fixing her credit. She gradually upgraded her mode of transportation—from an '88 Acura Legend to a '99 Ford Taurus to, just this year, a white '07 Chevy Malibu, warranty and all. But home is still a small rental in what is known as the Pork N' Beans projects, a sprawling patch of triplexes reminiscent of Army barracks. Even in pastel colors they look dingy, a fact not lost on Jerrill, the last of her four children and the only one still living with her. For six years he has been asking— regularly, gently—when they'll be able to move to a place with air conditioning or with wiring for high-speed Internet or just without cockroaches. It's embarrassing to live here, in the poorest hood in the poorest part of Miami, a city that celebrates fast money.

"Doing my best," she tells him.

In the meantime, he's forbidden from playing outside. Even if there is a big, blue, sporty Northwestern Bull painted on the liquor store across the road.

"I'm not going to let the streets take him over," Wanda says while scrubbing Jerrill's cleats on the couch in the dimly lit living/family/dining room. "That's why I keep him in sports: baseball, basketball, football. We don't stop."

But keeping a kid off the streets is merely a temporary reprieve. Giving Jerrill the academic and behavioral tools to transcend his environment is the next, crucial step in any move toward the American Dream. And that hasn't always happened when football players have been turned over to Northwestern, where Jerrill plans to try out for the Bulls next year as a sophomore.

His Optimist coaches tell me Jerrill could be the next Antwain Easterling.

Which isn't a comforting notion to Wanda. "When I was going to school there, if someone on the football team did something wrong they would have gotten in trouble," she says. "Now they holding kids up here"—she lifts her hand above her head—"and they let them slide. I just can't understand the Easterling thing. It was so dumb." She shakes her pony-tailed head. "The coaches need to show Jerrill the way to go and to be more productive in school. Look at what's all around here."

Easterling graduated and got his athletic scholarship. But he barely made it, signing with the University of Southern Mississippi after the scandal broke and the premier schools backed off. Then he had to go to summer school to secure his NCAA eligibility, cutting it so close that he had to sit out his first college game. And it's not clear if he learned any lesson from the felony conviction that a judge agreed to wipe from his record if he went to counseling and stayed out of criminal court. Two months later, in March of his senior year, he was still playing fast and loose with his future when police found him in a car with marijuana. Fortunately for Easterling, the misdemeanor wasn't serious enough to cause him further legal trouble. And he had signed a month earlier with Southern Miss, a program with a history of giving "second chances" to blue-chippers acquainted with handcuffs.

Even so, by the end of freshman season, Easterling's future at Southern Miss was in doubt. After getting suspended indefinitely by his coach for an undisclosed violation of team rules, the hotshot running back threatened to quit the Golden Eagles, yelling to a reporter after practice, "Make sure you hear this—I'm leaving." His coaches were left scrambling again, trying to find a reason to keep him on the team. They found one, and Easterling agreed to stay. But the coach was fired a few days later for not winning enough, and Easterling again was suspended indefinitely.

Smith, the Bulls' former coach, is proud of his record of sending players to college. "I've been about kids all my life," says the onetime University of Miami cornerback, who himself grew up in Pork N' Beans. He gave me a list of 63 Bulls who advanced to the college level during his eight years at Northwestern. About a third of them went to big-time programs like Florida State or Mississippi. Another third went to historically black colleges. The rest went to small four-year colleges or junior colleges.

The graduation rate of those players won't be final for several years, as some on the list, like Easterling, have just landed on college campuses. But Demeka Breedlove-Mays would be surprised if many of them find success. She was raised in Liberty City, too, and went on to be a language arts teacher for five years at Northwestern, where her innovative work with disadvantaged students won her, out of a pool of 20,000 candidates, the 2005 Miami-Dade County Teacher of the Year award. So when the bright, young educator agrees to speak with me on the record—no easy decision for someone from the neighborhood—I listen, gratefully.

"I love Northwestern football like anyone else," Breedlove-Mays says, realizing old friends are going to call her a hater for the impolitic critique she's about to deliver from her new home of Atlanta. "I am a fan and an alumnus of the school. I loved many of the football players that I had as students. What I did not like about the program was that many of my football students would return after graduating and would be disappointed.

"If they make it to the college level, more than likely they don't have basic skills to survive. And they have not matured in a way that would help them survive, because at Northwestern they had been treated as privileged kids. Unfortunately, a lot of them drop out their freshman or sophomore year of college. Those who actually stay on and get their degrees are few and far between."

Breedlove-Mays' observation undermines the justification most often served up by most adults, and parroted by many kids, for distressed communities having a serious emotional investment in big-time school sports: Access to a college education. The colleges themselves are complicit in this charade. Often coaches are given waivers by the admissions office that allow highly coveted athletes to enter the university with academic credentials well below those of the average applicant. Well-funded and well-staffed tutoring operations paid for by athletic departments are often in place to flood the under-prepared jock with assistance and to steer him to the right courses. But frequently it still doesn't work out. Which perhaps should come as no surprise when it happens to former Bulls, whose team GPA last year was just 2.3.

Killings has one of the top GPAs on the team, a 4.3 that's getting him recruiting attention from schools as elite as Duke. But the former AD's son is an anomaly. More common have been players such as Taurean Charles, who when he was at Northwestern uttered some of those bromides about college sports being his "meal ticket." A Showtime documentary, *Year of the Bull*, followed him through 2001, a turbulent year at Northwestern, where he was one of the nation's top defensive linemen. The film captures his struggle to balance academics with local fame and the demands of his coaches, one of whom knocks him to the ground when Charles is reluctant to practice with an injured neck. The film concludes with him at the University of Florida as a freshman.

By his sophomore year, Charles was dismissed from the Gators. He lost his scholarship after hitting a female friend, getting into a fight at a fraternity, and struggling with his grades. As for the Northwestern coach who attacked him, self-described father figure Horace Morris, the postscript isn't any better: He left the Northwestern staff after the documentary's release to take an administrative position at another Dade County public school ... where he was arrested for allegedly forcing a 13-year-old girl to give him oral sex. (Morris pleaded not guilty to the felony crime.)

Breedlove-Mays doesn't condone the actions of Morris and Charles. But she sees their failings as evidence of a school board that's more invested in the making of action heroes than civic heroes.

"Northwestern has been a failing school since 2000, okay?" she says, referring to the grades handed out by the state of Florida based on comprehensive assessment tests. "They've received Fs and Ds every year. Only 12 or 13 percent of students read at or above their grade level. What we're seeing is academic achievement taking a backseat to athletic achievement.

"These kids believe football is the way out. Until the district and school show that there is another way out, there's going to continue to be this problem."

• • •

Rivals of the mighty Bulls—which effectively mean teams in every state, given the heightened focus on national rankings—might want to check themselves before lifting their nose at Northwestern. The Bulls have the spotlight, the athletes, and more social problems to deal with than most. But in high schools generally, Friday night lights are associated with bad behavior. A recent survey of high school students that included 5,275 athletes in 14 sports found that football players were the team members most often involved in dubious acts, both on and off the field.

They were at the top of the list among athletes who concede that in the past year they had: bullied, teased, or taunted someone (75%); hit a person in anger (70%); cheated on a test in school (72%); and used racial insults or slurs (56%). Football players were also near the top among athletes who admit to having: stolen something from a store (33%); cheated or bent the rules to win (47%); drunk alcohol (54%); and used performance-enhancing drugs (6%).

Many were prepared to sacrifice ethics for the sake of winning. About half said it would be okay for their coach to prepare them for a game with the aid of an opponent's playbook that had been sent to him anonymously. Almost as many (43%) would fake an injury to get a free timeout late in the game if the coach asked him to do so. And three-quarters of the football players said they were fine with a lineman deliberately inflicting pain on an opposing player in order to intimidate him.

Pep rally, anyone?

The results of the survey, conducted by the Josephson Institute of Ethics and released in 2007, perhaps do not bode well for the future of the nation, given that football is the sport played by the most high school students (1.1 million). Conduct tolerated and sometimes promoted in high school football could encourage young men to engage in dishonest and dangerous practices as they move into adulthood.

But sociologists also know that sport, in and of itself, is neutral as a vehicle for character development. No child gets "saved" or "ruined" by a sport, contrary to the clichés commonly thrown around. Behavior is shaped by the institutions involved and the people who organize the activity. Indeed, it's a theme that one prominent Northwestern booster, the Reverend Richard Dunn, used in making his plea to keep the Bulls' 2007 season from being cancelled: "Football is neither moral nor immoral."

That's what the former Bull lineman told superintendent Rudy Crew, who agreed to meet with community leaders after the grand jury indictment came down in June. Crew was trying to figure out how to move forward at Northwestern, and he was angry. Since news of the scandal broke, the leader of the nation's fourth-largest school district had met several times with the victim. He found her to be a "beautiful, highly intelligent, extraordinary young lady with tremendous insights for a 14-year-old," precisely the kind of student he wanted to support in his effort to improve the academic standing of the county's urban schools. He also found her to be "very, very pained and tortured," and it galled him that she was not protected at Northwestern, a school that taxpayers had spent $79 million on for new buildings a decade earlier in the hope of generating leaders for the city.

"We all failed this girl," Rev. Dunn says. Whatever he may have felt, however, his job in talking to Crew was to salvage the upcoming season, including the much-anticipated Dallas game pitting the top two teams in the country. "Football has been the one common denominator in bringing this community together. We can't agree on anything else. This team is bigger than the school."

Crew saw the football crowd as a bunch of old jocks living vicariously through his students. A former high school player himself who grew up in Poughkeepsie, N.Y., he felt that the alumni association had undermined the leadership of the school—Northwestern was on its *fifth* principal in *two* years—by causing divisiveness among the faculty. They certainly marginalized Dwight Bernard, who Crew had hired specifically because he was not a jock and had promised to push academic achievement. Bernard may have tried, but, in doing so, he largely left the football juggernaut alone, unwilling to antagonize its flock.

"What you hear about is their football team," Crew told prosecutors behind closed doors in May when he gave his sworn statement in the Bernard case. "And I may be a vote of one, but I am tired of hearing about it."

An outsider to Miami's incestuous school bureaucracy, Crew was brought in as a reformer willing to take tough stands. In his previous role as chancellor of New York City's public schools, he antagonized his boss, Rudy Giuliani, by opposing the equally pugnacious mayor's proposals for school vouchers, and it cost him his job. Like Bernard, Crew knew he had to bear in mind the priorities of the Northwestern alumni, who exercised a less direct form of power than Giuliani. Bulls boosters seemed to be everywhere in Miami, in churches and law offices, on the school board and even on his own staff. Back in December of 2006 when the case broke, Crew had thought about suspending Easterling before the state title game, but declined, fearing a lawsuit.

In July, when he announced his response to the grand jury report, gold and blue shirts filled the school board auditorium. Among the crowd of 200 were alums who had flown in from other states, aware that Crew had already removed Bernard from the principal's office and given him a desk job downtown. Crew found the show of force kind of sad, as PTA meetings at Northwestern are sparsely attended. But he wasn't going to call off the season, in part because that would have felt like he was punishing the players who had done nothing wrong. He did announce that he was removing their head coach and most of the assistants, however. To which many of the alums and players responded by walking out in mid-speech. "Where ya'll going?" Crew said, startled by the sudden exodus.

MYTH NO. 14
Playing sports builds character.

THE TRUTH
It depends on who runs, and who surrounds, the team.

Marcus Forston was one of the few players who stayed behind, and he apologized for his teammates' behavior.

• • •

So the job of making Northwestern a safe and productive place for boys like Jerrill Jenkins, as well as for the next 14-year-old girl who arrives at the school with both gifts and personal challenges, now falls to a quiet, persistent storm who goes by the name of Charles Hankerson, the current principal, the man tapped by Crew to replace the ineffectual Bernard.

As with any hurricane, Hankerson has one good eye. His right. The other one works but the eyelid droops to half-mast due to a childhood disease. It made him easy to underestimate as a high school and college basketball player. Now it gives him the countenance of a grizzled combat veteran wholly uninterested in any bullshit you may happen to be shoveling, a trait that comes in handy when trying to refocus a school on its mission to educate.

A few days after Crew's announcement, Hankerson has his lieutenants gather the varsity and jayvee teams in the school auditorium. The players are quietly sitting shoulder-to-shoulder, 15 rows deep, when the tall, straight-backed boss strides briskly into the room, all business.

"Body punches. You've just been hit with your first," he says of losing their dismissed coaches, who have yet to be replaced. "The mark of a true man is how you respond. You have a choice ... " He asks if the men the players had so much affection for would want the team to move forward—then supplies his own answer. "The easiest thing for you to do now is quit going to class. Lose discipline. Not work as hard. The manly thing to do is work twice as hard, be twice as committed.

"The focus is changing here. The names are changing. But the program remains the same."

The kids don't know much about the new guy, who took over after their last game. Some know he's a former hoops coach who had some success at a nearby high school. Some have heard he's a turnaround specialist who, as principal, had upgraded another struggling school to a C grade. A few might know he was like them once, a Miami kid who took charge of his future, earned his stripes, and now plays a little golf on weekends. They probably don't realize that he easily could get a cushier gig than Northwestern, yet he took the job anyway because he feels a calling—like this is where he's needed most.

But everyone gets the message: Mr. Hankerson is taking back the hallways. He loosens his belt, unzips his fly, and yanks his trousers halfway down his butt. Eyes pop at the sight of this dignified African-American man striking a ghetto pose.

"The first one I see like this," he says, "you ain't playing no more. Y'all want to be real? I'm being real. I'm not into fads and trends. I'm telling you straight up: I'm holding you to a higher standard. I won't let you think of yourself as anything less than quality young men.

"I realize I'm going to have to lose a few of you along the way."

Minutes later, a player's hand goes up. He's still thinking about the dress code.

"Um, you want our shirts tucked in every day of the week?"

"Every day."

A low groan rises from his audience. It's going to be like this every step of the way as he attempts to flip the culture at Northwestern, where football players are held in such regard that teachers have used them to clear the hallways. Lure them into the classrooms and other kids follow.

Hankerson wants to get Northwestern to a C grade or better on the state assessment test—by next year. To help end the hallway chaos, he's brought in a security specialist and scores of new cameras to watch the bathrooms and doors. With Crew's support, he's creating an academic rescue program for ninth-graders to get as many of them as possible on a college prep track. There will be weekly checks of each student's academic progress. He's gotten several colleges in the Miami area to set up recruiting offices on campus, where they'll also work with students. For the athletes, there will be additional, mandatory tutoring sessions before practice. And each must sign a behavior contract that bans them from sports—all sports—for the year if they reach six days of suspension. Just one fight will trigger such a penalty.

A century after Luther Gulick foisted interscholastic sports on the New York City school system that Crew would later oversee, it's not at all clear the marriage is still good for large public schools. The state of Florida has an abundance of such schools now due to population growth and budget constraints, and its teams in many sports are nationally ranked. But the traditional one-team, one-school structure of competition has left many students without participation opportunities in an era of rising obesity rates. Northwestern might be an athletic powerhouse, but it's a fitness also-ran: Most of its students fail the state physical fitness test, no great surprise given that only 20 percent of its 2,509 students play on school teams. And for all the trophies earned by Bulls teams, the school remains a dropout factory, with only half of its entering freshman graduating four years later. Florida's public high schools have some of the worst student retention rates in the country.

In some ways, football is a bright spot on that grim landscape. Rosters are relatively large at many schools; at Northwestern 70 varsity and

50 jayvee players suit up. Add the band, cheerleaders, and other support groups and football can create bonds and lift the spirits of hundreds. But the sport comes with significant costs, too. Equipment is expensive. Games require hiring dozens of police officers or other security to keep the peace. Northwestern had to buy specially-printed tickets just to thwart counterfeiters. Generally speaking the coaches aren't paid much—less than $5,000 a year for the head coach and $1,700 for assistants. Despite that, Northwestern spent $383,214 on football during the 2006-07 school year, between apparel, food, awards, ambulance services, disbursements to opposing schools, fees to sanctioning bodies, U-Haul trucks, Avis rental cars, a spring game two counties away, and other costs. The Bulls even stayed in a hotel the night before the state title game at nearby Dolphin Stadium, just like big-time college teams do.

For its other 16 athletic teams, the school spent just $77,279 combined.

There's also a hidden health cost that comes with sanctioning an increasingly violent game: knee, shoulder, back, and neck injuries that can linger for a lifetime. Doctors only now are starting to comprehend the full amount of damage to the brain that can occur. Football accounts for nearly two-thirds of the estimated 62,816 mild traumatic brain injuries incurred in high school sports annually, according to an article in *The Journal of the American Medical Association*. Another study found that catastrophic head injuries were three times as prevalent among high school football players as college players, and that "an unacceptably high percentage of high school players were playing with residual symptoms from a prior head injury." Football's macho culture encourages kids to stay on the field after getting a concussion, risking what is known as second-impact syndrome, which can leave lasting damage. Since 1997, at least 50 players nationwide on the high school level or below have been killed or have sustained serious head injuries. No big surprise, given the hazards of a 280-pound senior lineman pulverizing freshman tailbacks half their size. Some pediatricians now tell parents that it's not a sport they recommend kids play.

Steroids use among teenagers in general has fallen in recent years, but high school football players have grown so large and fast that in 2007 the state of Florida felt compelled to begin steroids testing. The legislature allocated $100,000 for the effort, enough to screen only a few hundred athletes—not much of a deterrent. And it's more money allocated to schools that isn't being spent on books.

A reasoned argument could be made that football has become a bad fit for public schools. But Hankerson knows the game isn't going the way of boxing any time soon—and he isn't about to make that argument anyway. Because he's an ex-athlete and a pragmatist who appreciates the potential of any sport in achieving his larger mission. Football matters to the would-be lions arrayed before him, so he'll use it as a prod to encourage helpful behavior. At games, he'll be on the sideline supporting them. But he won't hesitate to get in the face of anyone who showboats after scoring a touchdown.

"Someone has to say that we don't win at all costs," Hankerson says to me in his office, his ever-present walkie-talkie laid on the desk. "I guess that's me."

Hankerson isn't entirely alone. Lots of adults in the community are pulling for him. They are the Wanda Jenkinses of Liberty City, the silent majority who want Northwestern football to represent opportunity—a real opportunity. Even some boosters, like Rev. Dunn, are ready to line up behind the principal with principle. But there are also agitators, like the guy who called Hankerson in his office and threatened him, claiming to know which Miami school Hankerson's 15-year-old son attends.

That night, at an alumni association meeting, a seething Hankerson let it be known he will not tolerate such intimidation. "My son— With my son, I draw line."

Alumni association president Larry Williams responded by insisting no one in his group would have done that.

Hankerson wants to ignore the football-centric alumni, a group that he's kicking off the sideline at games. But he can't. They're still around, the fans and speculators and drunks, watching practice every day in their lawn chairs quite sure that the program still belongs to them. They underwrite Northwestern football with all those tickets purchased. For all the money the school spent on the Bulls last season, the program still turned a profit—bringing in $452,225, leaving nearly $70,000 that was used to pay for other sports and activities. Should there be another awful scandal, Hankerson and Crew might have the authority to call off the season ... but it would cause financial chaos. And civic mutiny.

The community wants that Dallas game—the one that's drawn such interest that an off-shore sports book is now taking wagers. It wants that No. 1 *USA Today* ranking. It wants Randy Shannon visiting Liberty City homes. It wants all the spoils that come with a high school football dynasty. As Luther Campbell told me in no uncertain terms, fans are expecting an undefeated season. Every year.

"This monster," Hankerson calls it. He says it's nothing he can tame on his own. "But *we* can."

We?

"We," he says, "is ESPN. We are the scouting services. We are the college coaches. We are the parents. We are the students. We are everyone who has the tendency to dream the big dream of the NBA and the NFL. I say let's first concentrate on graduating high school. Secondly, let's concentrate on graduating from college. And then if that other stuff happens, then that's extra."

Hankerson buys some credibility in the community with the hiring of Billy Rolle. Liberty City knows him as the coach who led the Bulls to their last state title, back in '98, before moving to another county school and winning a state title there. Hankerson likes him for a different reason: Rolle's a lot like him, an understated but firm leader who's on board with the idea that Northwestern football cannot be the pinnacle of a child's existence. Chill Will, as Rolle is known thanks to his cool demeanor, comes from a family of educators, as well as an extended Bahamian-immigrant clan that includes NFL cornerbacks Antrel and Samari Rolle.

Pedigree does not make the outcome of a football game any easier to control. All that Rolle and Hankerson can do, really, is guide a group of players that anyone, not just a Bulls fan, would want to cheer for. To attempt to deliver on the great promise of youth and school sports as envisioned by its founders more than a hundred years ago.

But seeing their approach validated on the big stage sure would be sweet.

• • •

In mid-September, the Northwestern Bulls board a plane bound for Texas. They are very excited—and very nervous. For 48 of the 55 players, it is the first time in their lives they have flown anywhere. When they get to their Dallas hotel, they find copies in their rooms of a local magazine with the headline: "Why You Should Hate Southlake: Because the Kids Are Smarter, Stronger, and Better Looking Than Yours. And They Prove it Every Friday." On the cover is a posed shot of quarterback Riley Dodge, arms folded in a green letterman's jacket, collar up, chin (and nose) held high. He is flanked by a pair of newly mature girls—a curly-haired blonde on his left, a shiny brunette on his right—both with superiority etched into their smiles.

Southlake, as the article explains, is one of the wealthiest cities in north Texas. The rapidly growing town of 25,000 is a destination community for upwardly mobile families, whose children attend a high school that sends 97 percent of its students to college. A dozen seniors on last year's football team got Division I athletic scholarships, six times as many as Northwestern. While the Bulls must share Traz Powell with other district schools, the Southlake Carroll football team has its own $15 million, 11,500-seat stadium with luxury seating that was featured in *The Wall Street Journal* for its creature comforts. The Dragons also have a 45,500-square-foot, indoor practice facility. Many of the athletes live in McMansions, and everyone shops at the massive, perfectly planned Town Square, designed by the same architect who laid out the Texas Rangers' ballpark. There's a Lane Bryant and a Cheesecake Factory, a lovely fountain and gazebo, and so much more. Southlake is new and clean and loaded—and almost exclusively white. The only black starter on the team is running back Tré Newton, son of retired Dallas Cowboys lineman and convicted marijuana dealer Nate Newton.

Ever since the game between the state champions of Florida and Texas was scheduled, the Bulls have been called thugs. Not by the Southlake players, but by fans on Internet message boards aware of the

Easterling saga and eager to mix it up. To the Bulls, the magazine piece feels like piling on. So does a front-page *USA Today* article that highlights the Perfect City vs. Liberty City contrasts—like the fact that most kids from the latter qualify for reduced-price lunches (it's one percent at Southlake). The Bulls are reminded that they stand on the wrong side of the growing divide between rich and poor in America, and that hurts. But there's no lashing out. Forston tells a *Miami Herald* reporter, "We may be from less fortunate families, but that's something we can't control. The only thing we can control is the next generation."

Big, steady Marcus calls the game "a business trip," which it is, as all expenses are being paid by the Dallas-based marketing company that organized the game and sold it to ESPN. Hankerson folds in an educational component, taking the team to the Sixth Floor Museum to learn about John F. Kennedy's assassination.

Nike is outfitting each team in special uniforms for this game, hyped as the Super Bowl of high school ball, the national championship in September. As if the racial distinctions weren't apparent enough, the Dragons are dressed all in white—white shirts, white pants, white socks, white shoes, white helmets. The all-black Bulls are in black from the shoulder pads down. Hankerson has approached Nike about doing something else for the school, perhaps an annual $5,000 academic scholarship open to all students. (He would eventually get it.)

A revved-up crowd of 31,896 is on hand at Gerald R. Ford Stadium, which is better able to accommodate the demand for tickets to the game. It's the home field of Southern Methodist University, whose football team was once among the nation's best but has never recovered from a 1980s scandal related to improper payments to players by boosters which shuttered the program for two years. Today, a sea of green-and-white shirts and painted faces injects some spirit into an old house, in anticipation of only the third match-up of national No. 1 and No. 2 teams in the last quarter century.

Southlake strikes first, with a touchdown pass from Riley Dodge. The quarterback may have a cowboy name but there's nothing freelance about his football or that of his team. The son of the former coach, he directs a pro-style offense that moves with speed and precision, a scheme the kids in Southlake start learning in seventh grade. He's got D1-caliber receivers on both sides and a member of the jockocracy, Newton, who's bound for the University of Texas, behind him. The Dragons, who have won 49 consecutive games, offer a formidable challenge to the Bulls, who only two months earlier were organizing summer practices on their own because they didn't have a coach.

Still, Chill Will and his players keep their composure, confident in their capacity to respond. Tall, spidery receiver Tommy Streeter hauls in a pass over the safeties' heads to even the score at 7. He doesn't celebrate. He barely smiles. All business.

The TV announcers dutifully mention this has been a turbulent year at Northwestern, even pulling up a full-screen graphic with a timeline of the sex crime and its cover-up. Eerily, the Bulls fumble on the next play; a defender scoops up the ball and rambles in for a score. It's now 14-7, Southlake.

On the ensuing kick, an overeager Bull takes the ball deep in the end zone, fumbles, and tries to run it out. It's foolishness. The 4,000 or so Northwestern fans gasp. "When he did that, I about threw up," says Campbell, who's sitting near a guy holding a sign that reads, FREE LUNCH SECTION. On the sideline, Rolle wipes his brow after the miscue, brushing away the sudden surge of sweat. He'll do that a lot in the first half.

The Bulls aren't accustomed to making comebacks. They had outscored their opponents 317-0 during one seven-game stretch the previous year. On the other hand, in their lives away from the field many of them have been playing from behind since they were born. Speedy linebacker Sean Spence anticipates a throw over the middle by Dodge. The interception sets up another TD pass to Streeter, who kneels on the sideline with teammates and prays.

The Bulls are starting to look like the better team. They're driving again. On a slant route, Streeter gets separated from the ball just as it arrives, the kind of violent hit that can cause a concussion. The Dragons safety who delivered the clean, jaw-rattling blow swaggers away, waving his hand provocatively. Again, the Bulls don't take the bait.

They just score. On the very next play. On another perfect pass from reed-thin QB Jacory Harris, whom Rolle has entrusted with calling the plays and running the offense. This time, his receiver ends up in the embrace of Hankerson, who has positioned himself next to the end zone on the Northwestern sideline. There the principal is more a party to the action than a participant in it. But now the action has come to him—Aldarius Johnson catches a difficult, over-the-shoulder ball that leaves player standing right in front of school boss. Hankerson, in black polo shirt and baseball cap, smiles broadly and wraps his long arms around Johnson's helmet. Johnson hugs Hankerson around the waist, briefly.

With the extra point, Northwestern goes up 21-14. Southlake musters a little rally, but from there on out the game really belongs to the Bulls. They're the team that plays smarter. They're the team that makes fewer critical errors. They're the team that finds their poise. They're the team that makes the right adjustments.

The sideline reporter pulls Hankerson aside, and asks about Northwestern in the aftermath of the affair that laid bare the hazards of adults looking to children for their entertainment. *We're moving on,* Hankerson basically says, citing the school's new academic policies and sparkling 93 percent attendance rate. *We're playing smarter. Making fewer critical errors. Finding our poise. Making the right adjustments.* "We have told them they are somebody," he says hopefully, "that they matter and they can dream like all other students in this country."

The last seconds wind down. In the warm, crystalline night air of north Texas, Campbell beams through gapped teeth. Not because the Bulls stuck it to the big, bad, rich school—he found Southlake fans nothing but eager to show they're not snobs—but because his boys won without living down to *their* own reputation. "They made us proud," he says later. They will continue to do so. Not only will the Bulls go on to win every game, their second consecutive state title, and the mythical national championship, but not one player this season will earn a suspension. And the team GPA will rise to 2.9, up more than a half a grade point. Thirteen seniors will earn Division I athletic scholarships, twice as many as had been expected, with eight of them joining Shannon at the University of Miami. It's a remarkable haul for any program, and it was made possible by the improved grades of onetime borderline students who no longer were just good athletes. It's not deliverance, for the players or their community, but it's something. On the Saturday after signing day in early February, the entire team would get a parade through the blighted, excited neighborhoods surrounding the school.

Back in Liberty City on the night of the catalytic Southlake game, a delirious Wanda Jenkins is watching on TV and ready to get this party started. She's seen enough already to break into song, the alma mater of a school about which she's hopeful again. Like the team members he expects to join next season, Jerrill is learning. He'll soon get honored by Hankerson as Student of the Month for his test scores and effort. Her son, *her son*—the quiet, wanting boy who was always scared to raise his hand in class and who in the coming years is going to be either exploited or enriched for his ability to run with a leather ball.

The final scoreboard in Dallas reads, 29-21, Miami Northwestern. Game over.

Or maybe, against all odds, it's game on.

EPILOGUE

NEXT

Palo Alto, California

As a journalist and father, I've been riding the runaway train that is youth sports for the better part of five years now. I have seen some wild and wonderful things on my journey, and have had the opportunity to pick the brains of an incredible range of people, from the brilliant to the bizarre. Only once was I left totally speechless. It was near the end of my conversation with Jack Welch, who, after we had talked for 20 minutes, expressed his appreciation for what he called the "valuable and important" challenge of achieving the trifecta of excellence, character-development, and broad-based participation in children's sports. Abruptly, truly curious, he asked me what I would do to get more kids moving without sacrificing the ethic of meritocracy that he treasures.

I wasn't expecting it. The classic structure of the interviewer-interviewee relationship is that the latter dispenses the information while the former collects it. Yet here was one of the world's great corporate managers—now a consultant who is paid millions by Fortune 500 companies for his opinions—turning the tables and pressing me for solutions. In that moment, I understood why he was such an effective leader: He didn't pretend to know it all. He eagerly sought the perspective of others. I also realized what it must have felt like to have been one of the people who reported directly to Welch ... and who hadn't prepared for the meeting. I mumbled a few words about how, uh, you know, I hadn't figured that out yet.

"Well," he said, "you gotta come up with a recommendation."

So, here we are. The epilogue. My take on how to move forward.

I should start by admitting that I'm still not sure I have answers. But I do have a few ideas to pass along.

Some of the most potent of those are embodied by people who can be found at the annual National Youth Sports Awards, held each spring at Stanford University. Contrary to what the name may suggest, the event has nothing to do with celebrating the best child athletes of the past year. Sponsored by the Positive Coaching Alliance, the ceremony identifies a handful of coaches and administrators—adults—who are particularly successful at creating environments that promote the desired trifecta. Phil Jackson for many years has been spokesman for the national nonprofit. In 2006 the group's founder, Jim Thompson, asked me to serve as emcee of that year's award dinner. The people I meet that night make me proud to be an American, and their stories serve to remind me that youth sport, indeed, is the most important institution in all sports.

One of the honorees is Tal Bayer, accepting an award on behalf of the Hyde Leadership Public Charter School in Washington, D.C. Young, bald, and white, Bayer looks like Brian Urlacher's less chiseled cousin. But football isn't his game, rugby is, and, as coach of Hyde's team, he has used the sport to transform the lives of kids in the troubled neighborhoods from which the school draws its students. Since 2002 when the school's first graduating class passed through, all of his seniors—more than 85 of them so far—have been accepted to four-year universities. You don't have to live in an inner city to appreciate how astounding that achievement is, sending every kid to college every year. Bayer entices kids to take up the old world game by challenging their emerging manhood ("You tough enough to play football *without* pads?"), but he keeps them in the fold by forging a team culture that is in no way organized around the principle of delivering star athletes. Ultimately, Hyde produces its fair share of elites—two of Bayer's players have gone on to compete for U.S. national teams, on which black faces are rare. But it's all about building citizens and leaders. This is was what Teddy Roosevelt had in mind a century ago.

Much of the credit belongs with Hyde's educational philosophy. Sports are not an extra-curricular activity, as they are at most schools. They are "co-curricular," meaning that they're built into set of courses that students take. Every teenage student must play a sport—half of the 90 male students of that age choose rugby—and they receive grades based strictly on effort, attitude, and accountability. Teammates participate in the grading process, and each student must get a passing mark in order to graduate. Both players and coaches sign behavior contracts, and anyone can call a "concern meeting" about anyone else on the team who is struggling—as the whole team is held responsible when one of them fails to meet expectations. At out-of-town retreats in the wilderness, kids learn communication and empathy skills. Back on the field, they knock the snot out of surprised opponents, as Hyde is the only all African-American team in the nation. It's more than a touch fitting that they've received support from the embassy of New Zealand, whose famed national rugby team is called the All Blacks.

Hyde's success is instructive. The U.S. educational system, from the middle schools on up, needs either to bring athletics into the mainstream of its teaching culture or to get out of the enterprise entirely. Because as an add-on it's no longer working in many places. Whacking budgets for teams and intramurals and reducing time allotments for physical education and recess does not constitute a commitment to use athletics as a tool in developing children. As a society we've come to expect that city recreation departments will provide the opportunities until kids get to middle school. But middle schools have dropped the relay baton. At some schools, the youngest students aren't even allowed to try out for teams. Then when they get to high school, they're more likely than ever to get coached by someone with no educational credentials. I'm not saying that an outsider cannot provide a quality experience for a kid; my sons would be lucky to be coached by the real estate agent in charge of my town's varsity basketball team. But it does mean that you're less likely to get someone like Bayer, who has received extensive training in methods that can instill character.

Rugby athletes at Hyde aren't the only ones to advance to college campuses. But Bayer's job is made easier by the fact that his sport is played through clubs, not the NCAA, at the university level. No kid is hunting for athletic scholarships—because colleges aren't offering them. "They learn to develop an appreciation for what the sport is, not because it might be their ticket out or because they'll be in the media," Bayer says. "When we first get these kids, it's all about them. But we break them down and get them to feel they're playing for the school and for each other. They come to take pride in just wearing that high crest on their jersey, and I don't ever want to lose that aspect. If we had college scouts to deal with, the environment might change." In other sports—NCAA sports—parents obsess about athletic grants, unaware that there's far more financial aid available for academic achievers and those in need. And it's real financial aid, not a series of one-year, pay-for-play contracts that the coach is under no obligation to renew.

The NCAA presents itself as the guardian of all school-based amateur sports in this country. Closer to the truth, the NCAA is the guardian of spectator sports within a school context. Since a couple of those sports (basketball and football) spin off huge profits and serve as marketing vehicles for universities, one of the functions of the NCAA, as a cartel, is to control costs wherever possible for its members. That means justifying the athletic grant-in-aid, which from day one has been used as a tool to prevent students from negotiating deals commensurate with their athletic value to a college program. It's the best salary cap in sports, and so the NCAA has great interest in having its revenue-producing athletes gain at least some access to a real education, even if that's not why they're really on campus.

The NCAA's point man on the education question is Kevin Lennon, its vice president for member services. He's the behind-the-scenes author of the latest NCAA initiative to boost graduation rates in its money sports, the first-ever penalty system for teams with low academic success rates. Lennon is the son of a former Notre Dame coach and a true believer in the nobility of the athletic scholarship. At the same time, in his personal life he's been taken aback by the downstream impact of parents and kids chasing potential distant payoffs.

I catch up with him in New York at a sports business conference. "My daughter is in competitive gymnastics, and she's a fourth grader," says Lennon, who like all NCAA staffers lives in the Indianapolis area. "She's in a 16-hour-a-week commitment right now, but if she goes to the next level it will be a 20-hour week—for a fifth grader." Parents are willing to roll with it because they see a scholarship waiting. Lennon finds himself trying to educate parents on the remote odds facing their cartwheeling kids, urging them to relax, but his message gets lost in the ambition. "I asked [the program director] if my daughter could do what I'd call the B plan, where she does half these hours but stays at the same level, and doesn't score as high, but we get a little more family time. The answer was no. You are either all in, or you are all out."

Nine-year-old girls melting down under the wrath of coaches. Ten-year-old boys on travel soccer teams getting worshipped by adults because they can score goals. Lennon has seen the excesses in youth sports. "The worst thing to do is watch your kid umpire," he says. "It's harder than watching them play the game because everybody is on this poor guy." His teenage son started calling games when he was in elementary school, an age at which kids are now recruited as officials because not enough adults want to take the abuse. "My wife and I sit in the outfield now when he's umpiring because even my behavior got a little bit questionable," he says. "After the game I would go to the coach and say, 'How do you feel about bullying an 11-year-old? I mean, do you feel good about yourself? This is just you and me here now, buddy.' And some of these people acted like they had no idea what they did wrong. Or they said my son gets paid $25 per game"—to absorb the belligerence.

A lot of the youth sports incidents that escalate into violence occur in a similar manner. It's often not some knucklehead trying to start a fight. It's a good guy, like Lennon, getting outraged at the treatment of children, confronting the problem at its visible source ... and things get out of hand. It's an impulsive form of vigilante justice.

The athletic scholarship, of course, isn't the only factor driving bad behavior on community playing fields. But it lends a financial rationale to the premature creation of travel and other select teams that now dominate the youth sports landscape. It's the big tease—the ever-escalating, if still largely inaccessible, $1.5 billion pot that shifts the motivation to play sports from intrinsic rewards to extrinsic ones.

"If you went back and looked at American higher education, it's an interesting question as to whether we would have set up college sports the same way," Lennon says. "But the bottom line is, we're not going to disband."

Nor should the NCAA disband. But if education truly is the mission of college sports, then there is no good reason these titles need to be pursued by (under-) paid mercenaries hired and fired by the athletic department. Do away with the so-called athletic scholarship and base all aid on financial need or academic merit—and all of a sudden the AAU has a tough time getting signups for its third-grade national championships. The parents of fifth-graders feel less compelled to join that year-round travel baseball team. A sprawling industry built upon the sale of pans to those prospecting for gold surely will resist this proposal, but it would serve the interest of the greater public.

I'd recommend that NCAA members agree to go a step further and do away with special admissions for recruited athletes. Let the student get accepted to college without a coach's all-powerful help, just as the Hyde rugby players have to. Right now, if a university with a Division I program wants a blue-chipper, the only hurdle for that athlete is to clear the NCAA minimum standard, which isn't all that rigorous. It's based on a sliding scale that combines their high school GPA and standardized test score: a 2.3 GPA requires a 900 on the SAT, while a 3.0 GPA lets the prospect qualify with no more than a 620 SAT. As long as parents know that their kid can get into a place like Florida or Harvard with academic credentials vastly inferior to those of other entering freshmen, they will be encouraged to sign them up for exposure camps instead of Kaplan courses.

Some people will argue that if we make athletes meet regular admissions standards, then kids from less advantaged school districts will lose access to a college education. Not true. Some will step up their game academically, realizing that they can't wait until late in high school, as

Carmelo Anthony did, to get their grades in order. Others can go to community colleges and non-NCAA four-year colleges where the curriculum is better tailored to students with lesser academic credentials. None of these athletes would be denied an *educational* opportunity; the NBA or NFL dreamer who can't get into a BCS school simply would have to find his *athletic* opportunity in other, less ideal places.

If a player has that rare talent to make it to the pros, the scouts will find him. Just as the NFL did with Eric Swann, who played for a semi-pro team after high school and still became the sixth overall draft pick in 1991. Just as the NBA does every year, scouring the globe for prospects. In fact, if the NCAA stopped going out of its way to hoard most elite athletic talent of a certain age, the pro leagues would be forced to take control of their player pipelines. They would have to invest in the grooming of its next generation of stars, just like the European clubs do, instead of using colleges and high schools as de facto farm clubs.

This would be an excellent development. Imagine David Stern requiring every NBA, National Basketball Development League, and WNBA club to offer age-group teams at the teenage levels—from U-20 down through U-14. Players would be drawn exclusively from the local area and region, so disruptions to a kid's education and family life would be minimized. A prospect like J-Mychal Reese would get trained by youth coaches affiliated with the San Antonio Spurs, for instance, and use existing facilities. Games would be played but the priority would be on skill development as clubs would be looking to produce talent that eventually could help its NBA team. These clubs later would receive a discount on draft day for—or perhaps first dibs on—any prospect that came up through its system. The best kids could still choose to play on their high school teams, if they still found it to be a challenge. But the elite-vs.-participation pathways would become more defined, allowing schools to focus more narrowly on broad-based access to sports, and their educational mission.

Such a model would be harder to create in football due to the size of teams and inefficiency in identifying talent during the teenage years. But it certainly can work in other sports. Major League Soccer is already moving in this direction, having mandated that all clubs in 2007 start to create age-group developmental teams. Homegrown players who train with the club for two years as amateurs can sign a professional contract with that club and avoid the league draft. Or if that's not in the cards they can go to college.

Lennon, for one, isn't hostile to making room for the European club model.

"I think there is a sense that the maturity level of our international students is perhaps a bit higher," he says. "What produces that, I don't know. I'm sure some of it is cultural. My gut tells me that in some other countries the academics expectations, even for the quality athletes, may be higher. If you are a Tony Parker, even if you are learning basketball a different way than our domestic high school kids do, you are still putting in your time with your studies.

"Better skill development while at the same time advancing the academic preparation: If you could do both those things, now you have a winner."

But Lennon is just a NCAA staffer, talking off the cuff. Any move to strip college athletes of both their special advantages and economic restrictions—to treat them like regular students—would have to start with his bosses, the presidents and chancellors of the member universities.

• • •

The other honoree at the National Youth Sports Awards who struck me as having a particularly compelling angle was Robert Fukuda, one of those people who make others smile because *he* always seems to be smiling. A big man, with a wide face, little to no neck, and an Army-grade buzz cut that makes his black hair stand on end, he moves with the economy of a judo champion. Which he was in high school and college. These days, he is executive director of the U.S. Judo Federation, the largest and oldest organization in the sport.

It's not the USOC-appointed national governing body for judo. And Fukuda is just fine with that.

"We have not applied to be the NGB and quite honestly we don't want to be," he says. "We are a grassroots organization. We like just having people exposed to judo, to do it, and to have fun. If you become the NGB your focus has to be on the very top, the elite—especially now with the way the USOC is. More than ever they want to see medal production. If you don't meet your high performance goals that year, they cut your support. We don't think that approach best serves people in the community."

After assisting as a technical official and advisor at the 1996 Atlanta Olympics, Fukuda moved from the Bay Area to Fruitland, Idaho. It's a town of 4,250 along the Oregon border that was known for its apples and prunes until cheaply-priced, imported fruit shrank the orchards, eliminating jobs and forcing many families to move an hour away to Boise. Already the head of the national federation, he opened a dojo (the Western Idaho Judo Institute) and laid down a code that was based on long-term growth, not short-term results.

Judo, despite its zen-like vibe, can be rather impatient in the crowning of champions. It was the first martial art to become an Olympic sport, in 1964, and for decades its various and competing organizations have been handing out hardware for national champions down to the age of 8. One of the main groups—not Fukuda's—now goes down to age 5, which trumps even the new "diaper division" at the Callaway World Golf Championships. For a child in judo, the quickest route to the podium is to focus on the ways to grip the *judogi*, or uniform, of one's opponent, so that he or she can be thrown to the ground. Fukuda rejects this method of teaching with his youngest students, instead focusing on posture, body awareness, and the other fundamentals of judo.

"The places that try to turn 7- to 10-year-olds into champions teach advanced skills," says Fukuda, who won't even take sign-ups for kids under the age of 7. "Kids pick up those skills quickly and they become great junior champions. But they get used to winning right away, and the foundation isn't there. As they get older, they get beat and beat badly by kids they used to thrash, which gets very hard to take psychologically. The parents start to go crazy, and the kid usually ends up leaving the sport. That's not a good experience for anyone in the family."

As with Bayer, Fukuda produces more than his fair share of the eventual top talent. The U.S. national roster in recent years has featured three college-age students who came up through his club, not bad for a little dojo of 25 in rural Idaho. But success on the mat is just a byproduct of his program, which he designs as a means of developing character. Trash talk and personal fouls lead to instant disqualification—as well as a discussion with Fukuda about how sports ethics relate to the world of coworkers, social authorities, and business competitors the athletes will soon face. Fukuda does not assume that lessons learned on the mat about discipline, humility, sacrifice, and respect are necessarily going to transfer to domains outside of sports. So he connects the dots for them, using the Socratic method. (*Would you do that to your friend?*) "I think kids today," he says to me, "have to be clued in more than kids in the past." The world, and the lives of children, are more complicated now.

Fukuda also talks to the kid's benefactors about expectations. "A lot of it is, you have to train the parents," he says. "I tell them that if you want to teach your child how to attack problems and interact with other children, then this place is okay. But if you want to just win matches, go elsewhere. When you tell it straight to parents, it's like an awakening. They're like, 'Oh, that makes a lot more sense.' Those families often end up being the ones who stay the longest in the program."

Take the lesson and run with it: Organize your local sports program around the needs of kids, not adults. If Fukuda can lay down such a set of principles in a business which he depends on to pay his food bills, everyday parents should be emboldened to do the same in their community programs. Most non-profit groups that offer soccer, baseball, basketball, and other sports opportunities are run by volunteer boards. Those boards are often dominated by the most motivated sports parents—the dad, for instance, who wants to create tournament teams at ever-younger ages because he's ready to compete and/or he wants to give his kid a leg up on peers. The voice of the more moderate parent—the silent majority, I would argue—gets lost because few of them bother to vote in elections. So, show up. Run for the board or, better yet, the town recreation committe that controls access to public fields and gyms. Create a mission statement that gives more than lip service to the goal of broad-based participation. Mandate equal playing time through age 12. Promote loosely structured play, with age-appropriate doses of skill instruction. Ban games on Mother's Day and tournaments on holiday weekends. Post signs on the sidelines telling parents that it's fine to cheer, but keep it upbeat and leave the coaching to the coaches.

Agitate. Build coalitions. Democracy in action is a beautiful thing. In 2005, the same year a New Haven-area softball coach was pounded into submission by an angry parent with an aluminum bat, a fourth-grade teacher and high school track coach named Rick Collins formed the Connecticut Youth Sports Initiative, a grassroots effort to reform youth sports in the state. For a couple of years he wrote (for free) monthly columns that were published in local community newspapers. Thousands of e-mails poured in, meetings of concerned parents and coaches were held, and a movement was born. He approached his own town council to adopt a simple set of core values that encourages youth sports programs to serve the needs of all kids, with annual reviews by the city's recreation department. There was pushback, naturally, but he got a dialogue started.

In his columns, Collins swung for the fences: a prohibition on all travel teams until seventh grade. I'm not sure a one-size-fits-all measure would work everywhere. Some towns and the interest in some sports are small enough that travel teams have to be formed a year or two earlier, just to find competition. Even Steve Keener, the Little League president who rails against the influence of travel teams, has had his son enrolled in a travel hockey program since age 9 because not enough Williamsport kids play the game to support an in-city league. But any town thinking about adding select teams for the prepubescent set needs to ask itself: Are we discouraging broad-based participation? It's not just a matter of whether kids are going to be cut during tryouts, but whether energy and resources could get sucked out of the recreational league. Travel teams, with their cool uniforms and adult-confirmed status, ghettoize the critical American institution of rec ball, and no child wants to feel second-class. Social acceptance is everything to kids of this age.

There's no reason rec ball has to stunt the development of talent, at least through the elementary school years. With trained coaches and a focus on fun and fundamentals, junior jet will come along just fine. He might even turn out to be a better athlete, as he's less likely to get slotted into one position for the sake of winning early, and more likely to be exposed to other sports where he can pick up transferable skills. If he's a star in soccer and role player in basketball, that's OK, too—empathy makes for a better team player. Of course, without travel teams that prematurely weed out his peers, he also eventually may have more rivals for those coveted spots on his lone high school team in a given sport.

That is the true benefit for any kid of early travel teams: The elimination of future competition. Which also doesn't make for good public policy.

One could even argue that it should qualify as illegal discrimination. Most town-based travel teams are affiliated with a national governing body, such as U.S. Soccer, that's recognized by the U.S. Olympic Committee. The Ted Stevens Olympic and Amateur Sports Act applies to NGBs and its members and protects the opportunity of "any amateur athlete," all the way down to the youth level, to "participate in amateur athletic competition." It doesn't guarantee every child a spot on his town travel or high school basketball team, of course. But, like other federal civil rights laws, the Sports Act prohibits discrimination based on, among other criteria, age. If kids born in the early part of the year statistically are far more likely to gain travel team spots than their later-born peers—just a few months' physical growth can make a huge difference at the youth level—does that constitute a pattern of age discrimination? What about the 12-year-old who looks 10 and must beat out peers the size of 15-year-olds if there's no rec team for him to play on? "No one's looking out for the late bloomer," says growth and maturation expert Robert Malina. "We've got to keep that kid active."

Early childhood should be a protected zone. Kids should be able to grow into their bodies and psyches before we start sorting out the presumed laggards. I'm not advocating the filing of lawsuits by parents upset that little Suzie got cut from her U8 travel soccer team, but Congress should bolster the Sports Act to require the USOC and the NGBs to prioritize broad-based participation above all else at the youth level. That means monitoring attrition rates and setting annual goals. It means disbursing USOC funds to NGBs based primarily on progress at the grassroots level, not by Olympic medal count. It means funding scientific sports research relevant to child athletes and disseminating the results. It means restricting the use of USOC-controlled Olympic marks, such as the name Junior Olympics, to organizations that agree not to hold national championships before the teenage years. It means supporting community groups with coaching education that can be distributed cheaply and effectively over the Internet. It means helping the USOC do all this with some funding, which in turn will create real accountability. It means tasking a government agency, perhaps the Department of Health and Human Services, to ensure the USOC is acting in a manner that promotes public health.

It means putting an era defined by George Steinbrenner into the history books.

Fear not, parents of early bloomers. There still will be venues for the next Tiger and Earl Woods. Across sports, private clubs and businesses will continue to step up to meet the needs of the most ambitious kids and parents, and ideally the pro leagues will invest in channels that groom those prospects who eventually flash true potential. But when NGBs are involved, and especially when taxpayer-funded facilities are being used, the needs of the public at large will prevail. So, in turn, will the most precocious child athletes, who, if they really need more of a challenge in fourth grade, can—and should be allowed to—play up in the rec leagues with the sixth graders.

Many of the solutions we seek can be found right at home, in our local communities. But small ball isn't the only answer: We must look outward, too, if indeed the nation is going to both promote physical activity *and* regain its place as the most admired sports power on the world stage.

For an outline of the ultimate participation-performance solution, we must drive three miles off the Stanford campus, to an old aluminum barn where a stopwatch and familiar voice await.

• • •

Bee-eeeeeep ...

It's the same recorded, metronomic sound I heard on the basketball court at the Australian Institute of Sport.

Bee-eeeeeep ...

Only now I'm back at the Spartan headquarters of Sports Potential, and I'm doing the sweating, huffing back and forth between cones set up on the asphalt.

Bee-eeeeeep ...

This is the endurance shuttle run. It's the last of the 30 tests and analyses the sports scientists here have put me through with the goal of recommending sports that I might enjoy based on my physical, physiological, and psychological characteristics. It's the same program Tehuna Mahoni submitted to, and Steve Spinner, the CEO, has agreed to put me through it so that I can get a personal feel for the experience.

I finish the run, my time gets punched into the handheld computer, and 15 seconds later the results are displayed on a laptop. At number four is a sport I'm not surprised to see up high: Tennis, a game I naturally gravitated to when I was a kid, and still play. There's also volleyball, golf, and baseball (pitcher)—all sports that have been part of my life at some point. But at the very top is one I had never even thought of: Fencing. *Fencing?* I click on the associated bar graph.

A line chart is displayed that compares my traits to those of elite fencers. Mine are in blue, theirs in green. My body type is nearly a perfect match, our respective lines moving together across 18 category points like arm-locked tango dancers. My test results sync up well, too, with the only real differences in hand speed (I'm slower) and abdominal strength (I'm stronger, shockingly). I am intrigued.

Actually, I'm sold. I resolve to someday channel my inner Zorro.

It's easy to imagine a talent identification tool like this one being used to help adults get and stay active. It's even easier to imagine it being integrated into the mainstream of physical education classes at middle schools and high schools, as a once-a-year assessment to help spot options at a time when participation opportunities in sports are shrinking rapidly. Clubs would be notified of potential prospects in the area, as would school-based coaches, and connections could be made. Here and there in a nation of 300 million, surely, great champions will emerge in sports that we—and some kids—didn't think we had any chance to compete in.

But imagination alone isn't enough to float a win-win solution. A year after I underwent my test, Sports Potential ran out of venture capital and ceased operations. I'm not surprised. Talent ID in sports is an idea that precedes the market. It's the cell phone in 1988, Google in 1998, solar power in 2008.

But its time will come. Because it's predicated on a simple and powerful notion: That we all can be good at something. And that we want to be good at something. But the tool must be offered broadly, not just in the couple dozen or so health clubs where Sports Potential was able to set up shop and offer $175 assessments. The key is to get it into the schools and make it free. Spinner tried, but he was stymied by the educational system's triple-whammy of bureaucracy, budgets, and aversion to innovation.

At the time this book was heading to print, Spinner and his board were in discussions to donate his brainchild—$5 million worth of custom software, databases, everything—to either the International Olympic Committee or, preferably, the USOC. It's where such a tool truly belongs, as the USOC has the political connections and self-interest to get Talent ID introduced into schools. "All you need is a government or corporate grant, and you're in good shape," says Spinner, who contends that, in a non-profit mode where entire PE classes get screened, the cost per test could be driven down to as little as $10. Since the product is already built out, expenses are limited, mostly in bringing in trained testers.

I would suggest that the powers-that-be seize this opportunity. The school system—even more than travel teams, even more than the convenient villain that is video gaming—is responsible for teens dropping out of sports. The traditional one-team, one-school model works with smaller schools such as Hyde, but not at the larger institutions in the era of No Child Left Behind. There should be a companion mandate called No Child Athlete Left Behind, and if schools aren't going to restore opportunities, perhaps by allowing the creation of two or more varsity squads to represent a school where there's student interest (why *not* have A and B teams?), then they need to work better with local clubs that can. This type of collaboration is especially important in cities like Baltimore, with its endowment of swimming, lacrosse, and other programs in nearby suburbs.

"Every major city has programs in which underprivileged kids can participate," Spinner says. "Some of them are desperate, too—these programs are looking for inner city kids. It's not a matter of them having a limit of how many they can support with scholarships; they just want kids. Go into the New York Fencing Club, for instance." He's referring to the Manhattan club that has produced several Olympians, young African-Americans whose fees were picked up by a local foundation. "It's beautiful," he says. "It's all these minority kids fencing."

The Centers for Disease Control recommends that schools "link students to community physical activity programs" and that "exercise prescriptions" be tailored to kids' needs and interests. A well-considered Talent ID program that works with area clubs would help achieve those goals. The USOC has reason to embrace this model, as well. Its 2001 survey of past Olympians found that most of their training opportunities came through private and community-based programs, not high schools and colleges. The report concluded that it "would appear that the future of Olympic sport organization within the United States would favor a highly developed club system." Not the random, unchecked mish-mash we have right now.

Back in 2005, I had the chance to speak with Peter Davis, an Australian Institute of Sport alum who had gone on to become chief of coaching and sports science for the USOC. His ominous words have stuck with me.

"Come Beijing, we're going to be in big trouble," he told me shortly before returning home to take a top position with the Australia's rugby association. "The game's not over yet, but we cannot be competitive if we continue to rely on random kids getting into the right sport. Talent identification *can* work in this country, if it's targeted and regionalized. If it's a winter sport, for instance, do it in Minnesota and Maine, not Los Angeles.

"For 15 years, we've been sitting back. What China's doing will make us sit up and take notice." But the goal shouldn't be chasing the Chinese, with their highly elitist, politically-driven sports schools for the very young. The goal should be treating athletic participation as a human right, in the same way that every child has a right to an education. The mission is sport for all.

• • •

Obviously, any true commitment to broad-based participation begins with infrastructure. Fields. Gyms. Rec centers. Fund 'em, or pay the price later.

Which brings us to the final item for the to-do list: Financial relief for youth coaches.

Those who volunteer to organize teams often spend more time around a child than any adult outside of the home or school. They are rewarded for their efforts with that warm-'n'-fuzzy feeling of helping a kid, and maybe a gift card to Dunkin' Donuts. We need to further sweeten the pot. Programs are having trouble recruiting coaches, no surprise in an era when Americans are working harder than ever at their day jobs—and running a team can take up a hundred hours or more over the course of a season. Government (state and/or federal) should offer a modest income tax credit of, say, a few hundred dollars for anyone who volunteers as a head coach in a certified program. That would encourage more parents to step forward and, just as importantly, promote the training of coaches, the critical agents in whether a child decides to sign up again the following year. Right now it's hard to lay down any expectations for coaches, as their time is all pro bono.

Given the public costs of obesity, the grassroots, not the fatted-calf pro leagues, should be getting the tax breaks. As is, corporations that buy luxury boxes and seats get to write off those costs as (wink-wink) business expenses. Player salaries get amortized, as if they were furniture or buildings. Tighten up on those rules and more than enough money flows into the treasury to support relief for the three million or so youth coaches around the country. Heck, just ending the use of tax-free bonds for the construction of pro stadiums would go a long ways toward offsetting the budgetary loss involved. But that's just me talking.

Maybe someone else can explain why the public at large is better served by putting a couple million more dollars into Jerry Jones' pocket.

• • •

Evolution is not the same thing as progress. Charles Darwin knew as much. Events happen, rules change, mutations occur. The modern era has delivered the *Tigerwoodus Amongus*, a compelling species that now can be found in gyms, on grass, anywhere kids sports are played. It is a force to be reckoned with, both inspiring parents and prompting them to orchestrate the play of children at early ages so that they don't perish from the sports habitat prematurely. But sometimes it's better just to give them the space and tools and let nature take its course.

Cole enjoys his travel soccer team. But he likes skateboarding even more. He and his neighborhood friends spend many hours in our driveway, or, in the winter, our garage bay, perfecting complicated tricks that my eye has trouble following. He flips and twists the board in all sorts of directions, sometimes landing with his feet on top of it, sometimes not. He gets frustrated, but only for a moment; and he never gets discouraged. He keeps working at it and working at it and working at it, jumping and sweating and bruising—and learning. *Ollies. Kickflips. Varial kickflips. 180 heelflips. Fakie bigspins. Axle stalls.* He keeps adding to his repertoire, and when he does, he wants to tell me all about it. Or have me videotape it. And then he hops on YouTube and clicks around for new ideas and inspiration. And heads outside to experiment some more. It's a highly creative process that I can imagine will bear rewards if, as he gets older, he can transfer this method to other environments—including today's knowledge-based workplace, where innovation and initiative drive the global economy. A couple of times, I've found myself wondering: How good might he be at soccer or one of the other sports he's been signed up for since he was young if he was this passionate about improving his technique? But maybe that's the point: There are no sign-ups. Skateboarding is all his own. It's an adult-free zone, except when he wants to make it otherwise. All we've done is buy him boards and shoes.

We're still looking for a sport for Anna, now 9. The bullet train to high school that is travel soccer blew past her before she had a chance to spot it, and she doesn't seem much interested in team games anymore. But over the winter, she found her friends on the gentle slopes of a nearby hill, and took to skiing. And just the other day, she summoned Cole and I up to what we call the toy room, a play space above the garage filled with puzzles, costumes, games, and music CDs. At the bottom of the ball bin she had found a rainbow-colored streamer with a baton attached to the end, like the ones rhythmic gymnasts use. She cleared the floor, dialed up one of her favorite songs on the room's boom box, and lowered her head theatrically, awaiting the first note. As the melody kicked in, Anna swirled the baton just above the olive carpet, locating the soul of the song. The next three minutes was like watching Audrey Hepburn for the first time in *Breakfast at Tiffany's*: a revelation. Anna twirled, leaped, dove, and juked athletically, all the while painting the air with graceful strokes that required both improvisation and calculation. Cole and I looked at each other as if to say, where has *she* been hiding? It would be premature to say that Anna had found her rhythm, gymnastically. But it was a reminder that there is a sport out there for her, if she can be engaged on her own terms.

As for Kellen, still young enough that he calls himself Della because he hasn't nailed all the consonants, we found him hanging from the top of one of our garage doors one afternoon. My wife had clicked the automatic opener, Kellen grabbed the handle out of curiosity and then held on for dear life as it rose ... and rose ... and rose. Christine didn't notice until Anna summoned her from the kitchen with a terrified shriek at the sight of her baby brother dangling nine feet in the air. "Hold on Kellen!" Christine yelled, flying down the mud room stairs. And hold on he did. When she retrieved him, and set him down on the driveway, she asked what was running through his mind while way up high.

"Della strong!" he said, shiny with pride. A talent was IDed, I suppose.

But Kellen's one of those kids who won't need any guidance. He's already obsessed with sports. In fact, the copycat just stuck his brother's protective cup in his shorts and headed into the backyard. The boy who must always be moving wants to practice some with his mini-lacrosse stick and a tennis ball. All by himself, if necessary.

That's all I could want for any of my kids with these games we play. To choose on their own to get out there. Because when that occurs, everything else falls into place.

ACKNOWLEDGMENTS

A few years ago I climbed Mount Rainier, outside Seattle. It was a great experience, two literally breathtaking days in the thin air and on the melting ice bridges of the most glaciated peak in the continental U.S. And when I was done, I swore I'd never do anything like that again. It was that taxing. Then I decided to write this book, which just goes to show how quickly I forget valuable lessons. At times *Game On* felt like some foolhardy attempt to scale Mount Everest. In the hope that by looking across many games and regions the true shape of modern youth sports would emerge, I interviewed hundreds of sources in two dozen states and on three continents, burying myself in an avalanche of notes and studies. One does not rise above such density without the aid of others, so I want to thank the many Sherpa who showed me the way and lightened my load.

At the front of this alpine conga line is my remarkable wife, Christine, who was more than understanding of my need to spend most weekends, most nights, and most vacation time attacking this project. She shouldered much of the responsibility in our home without complaint and urged me on with her trademark enthusiasm. A debt of gratitude also is owed to Cole, Anna, and Kellen, who pried me from behind my basement desk with invitations to ride bikes, kick balls, and wrestle. They also helped give me the confidence to write about the needs of children in sports by allowing me to observe them in play.

I am grateful to all of the families who let me into their homes and minds as they navigate the uncertain terrain of youth sports: The parents who more often than not saw sports as a means to help their children become champions in life, and the kids themselves, who tolerated my nosy questions about their hopes, fears, and dilemmas. Helping me fill in the blanks were many experts in child and athlete development who gave freely of their time: Dan Gould, Colleen Hacker, Jay Coakley, Alicia McConnell, Istvan Balyi, Crystal Branta, and Marty Ewing, among others. Robert Malina, whose research-based perspective needs to be promoted, was especially helpful in cutting through the myths that surround youth sports.

I'm not the first person to appreciate the social importance of doing sports right at the grassroots level. Jim Thompson at the Positive Coaching Alliance inspired me. Bob Bigelow challenged me. Dan Doyle encouraged me. Steve Spinner intrigued me. Tom McMillen emboldened me. Mike May at the Sporting Goods Manufacturers Association gave me valuable, revealing data. Dean Mitchell of Rep. Mike McIntyre's office unearthed key testimony from Congressional archives.

This project got started with an expression of interest from my agent, Scott Waxman, who envisioned *Game On* as not so much a sports book as a window into contemporary American life. Gary Hoenig, GM of ESPN Publishing, signed off on the project, and *ESPN The Magazine* editors Gary Belsky, Neil Fine, and Chad Millman were more than generous in carving out time for me to finish the manuscript. ESPN Books chief Chris Raymond came up with the winning title. Bill Vourvoulias, the editor, was a writer's dream to work with, improving my copy throughout without imposing his own voice. Working alongside Bill is a cadre of pros: John Glenn, Jessica Welke, Ellie Siefert, Sandy DeShong, and Steve Horne and his crew. Darrell Trimble checked facts, and Zach Benabid transcribed interviews. I also appreciate the support of folks up the ladder at ESPN, including Keith Clinkscales, John Walsh, and John Skipper. On the TV side, Vince Doria, Ronnie Forchheimer, and Tim Hays let me pursue related pieces for *Outside the Lines*, as did Bob Wallace, Andy Tennant, Robert Abbott, Julie Anderson, and Kristin Huckshorn for *E:60*. At ESPN.com and *The Magazine*, respectively, Kevin Ball and Sue Hovey skillfully edited related articles. And Andrew Hetherington scored what would become the book's metaphorical cover shot by enticing my son Kellen, who was just 1 at the time, to play with toy balls before the lens for what seemed like hours (which explains the full diaper).

Friends, colleagues, and family offered up keen advice and reminded me of the importance of the project. Four deserve special mention: Jim Jordano, Ernie Nadel, Lesley Pacey, and Sue Blethen.

I'd also like to thank Howard Schnellenberger, whom I've never met. He doesn't know it, but he got me into this business. Back when he was the University of Miami's football coach, he boarded a National Airlines jet to Tampa. My mother, Marcia, a flight attendant, recognized him and bumped him up to first class. They got to talking. Mom, as moms tend to do, bragged about her 16-year-old son who wrote about sports for his high school paper. "Sometimes we hire kids like that," Schnellenberger said, and next thing you know, I'm passing out stat sheets in the Orange Bowl press box. There, *Miami Herald* writer Jim Martz took an interest and helped me get a part-time job with the paper. Seeing my first byline in the rack at 7-Eleven sealed the deal. And so here I am, forever grateful to anyone who has helped me along the way. It's a long list that includes Bill Dwyer, Bob Silver, Cathy Henkel, Craig Lazarus, Bob Ley, Sandy Padwe, and many others.

If my mother encouraged me to write, my father taught me to appreciate sports in its purest form. As a kid, he was the fastest boy in his class, the one who could always turn a corner with a football tucked under his arm. But an accident at age 14 changed everything. He was riding on the back of a friend's motor scooter when it clipped the protruding exhaust pipe of a car, lopping off his right foot just above the ankle. Miraculously, doctors were able to reattach the appendage, but that was the end of my father's participation in sports as a teenager; he would spend the next few years in rehab, learning to walk again on a cobbled-together leg that was half an inch shorter than the other. A trauma like that can focus the mind. When he became a father, the sole message L. Thomas Farrey ever gave his only son when it came to sports was to have fun. To enjoy the simple pleasure of moving around vigorously on one's own two feet. I grew up throwing balls with him between the trees in the front yard of our home. On the tennis court, my gimpy dad enjoyed hitting the ball into the corners, just to see me run. I came to take great pleasure in the challenge of chasing down the most hopeless of returns. Three decades later, tennis is one of the sports I still play.

In time, a life was shaped. I became a participant, then a fan, then a chronicler of American sports. All of which led to the making of this book, one that surely chose me as much as I chose it. My thanks go out to anyone who might give the words contained within some consideration. The truth is that, for me, they just had to be written. As homage, if nothing else, to the lessons that I haven't forgotten.

Tom Farrey
Burlington, Conn., May 2008

FURTHER READING

For practical advice on how to create a youth sports culture that serves the needs of children, a fine place to start is Jim Thompson's 86-page handbook, *Positive Coaching in a Nutshell* (Warde Publishers, 2008), with its bite-size tips, tools, and techniques. His theories get a deeper treatment in *The Double-Goal Coach* (HarperCollins, 2003).

Parents looking for pointers on how to navigate the realm of youth sports—from when to introduce children to travel teams to how to manage college recruiters—have a choice of several rich resources, among them Dan Doyle's *The Encyclopedia of Sports Parenting* (Hall of Fame Press, 2008) and Rick Wolff's *The Sports Parenting Edge* (Running Press, 2003). Much-needed medical perspective comes in the form of Dr. Paul Stricker's *Sports Success Rx!: Your Child's Prescription for the Best Experience*, published in 2006 by the American Academy of Pediatrics.

In 2001, former NBA player Bob Bigelow issued a critique of the modern youth sports culture in *Just Let the Kids Play* (Health Communications, Inc.), co-written with Tom Moroney and Linda Hall. It sparked enough discussion that Bigelow now travels around the country lecturing on the topic. Regan McMahon's *Revolution in the Bleachers: How Parents Can Take Back Family Life in a World Gone Crazy Over Youth Sports* (Gotham Books, 2007) updates these issues, with special attention given to girls' sports. Former AAU coach Bruce Svare offers up some spot-on solutions—several of which agree with those proposed in the epilogue of my book—in *Reforming Sports Before the Clock Runs Out* (Sports Reform Press, 2004).

Among books that explore the culture of a single sport, Buzz Bissinger's *Friday Night Lights: A Town, a Team and a Dream* (HarperCollins, 1990) remains the gold standard. But it's also worth reading Charles Euchner's *Little League, Big Dreams* (Sourcebooks, 2006) and Robert Andrew Powell's *We Own This Game: A Season in the Adult World of Youth Football* (Grove, 2004).

Prescriptive advice for how to teach skills in specific sports is plentiful, but two books stand out for me: *Coaching Youth Baseball the Ripken Way* (Human Kinetics, 2007), by Hall of Famer Cal Ripken and his brother Billy, and *Cross Over: The New Model of Youth Basketball Development*, self-published by Brian McCormick.

Researchers and journalists might want to consider for their libraries *Sports in Society: Issues and Controversies* (McGraw-Hill, 2007), by sociologist Jay Coakley; it's a textbook, but it's a remarkably thorough resource on a range of topics that include, but are not limited to, children and sports.

To understand the history and challenges of the school-based team system I recommend three myth-shattering books: *Air Ball: American Education's Failed Experiment with Elite Athletics* (University Press of Mississippi, 2006), by John Gerdy; *The Game of Life: College Sports and Educational Values* (Princeton University Press, 2001), by James L. Shulman and William G. Bowen; and *Unsportsmanlike Conduct: Exploiting College Athletes* (University of Michigan Press, 1995), by former NCAA chief Walter Byers.

More resources on the topics of youth sports and athlete development are available through my website, tomfarrey.com, which will be updated as further research in these fields is published.

APPENDICES

APPENDIX A: WHY BOYS AND GIRLS PLAY SPORTS

In 1989, about 8,000 kids involved in school and nonschool sports programs were asked by Michigan State researchers about their motives for playing youth sports.

Reasons for participating in school sports

Boys	*Girls*
1. To have fun	1. To have fun
2. To improve my skills	2. To stay in shape
3. For the excitement of competition	3. To get exercise
4. To do something I'm good at	4. To improve my skills
5. To stay in shape	5. To do something I'm good at
6. For the challenge of competition	6. To be part of a team
7. To be part of a team	7. For the excitement of competition
8. To win	8. To learn new skills
9. To go to a higher level of competition	9. For team spirit
10. To get exercise	10. For the challenge of competition

Reasons for participating in nonschool sports

Boys	*Girls*
1. To have fun	1. To have fun
2. To do something I'm good at	2. To stay in shape
3. To improve my skills	3. To get exercise
4. For the excitement of competition	4. To improve my skills
5. To stay in shape	5. To do something I'm good at
6. For the challenge of competition	6. To learn new skills
7. To get exercise	7. For the excitement of competition
8. To learn new skills	8. To play as part of a team
9. To play as part of a team	9. To make new friends
10. To go to a higher level of competition	10. For the challenge of competition

Source: Martha Ewing and Vern Seefeldt, "Participation and Attrition Patterns in American Agency-Sponsored and Interscholastic Sports," Sporting Goods Manufacturers Association, 1989.

APPENDIX B: THE ODDS OF PLAYING COLLEGE SPORTS

The probability of a high school athlete going on to play in college, both in Division I and all levels, broken down by sport and sex.

SPORT	D1 TEAMS	ODDS OF MAKING D1	ALL TEAMS	ODDS OF MAKING ANY
Men				
Rowing	24	1 in 2	59	1 in 1
Fencing	21	1 in 5	36	1 in 3
Gymnastics	17	1 in 8	19	1 in 7
Rifle	22	1 in 15	35	1 in 9
Ice hockey	58	1 in 22	133	1 in 9
Lacrosse	56	1 in 28	214	1 in 9
Swimming	141	1 in 30	381	1 in 14
Water polo	21	1 in 33	46	1 in 18
Football	234	1 in 42	614	1 in 18
Div. 1-A football	117	1 in 77		
Skiing	14	1 in 47	35	1 in 21
Baseball	286	1 in 48	873	1 in 17
X-Country	299	1 in 48	865	1 in 18
Golf	289	1 in 53	762	1 in 20
Track	261	1 in 56	656	1 in 24
Tennis	265	1 in 59	742	1 in 21
Soccer	197	1 in 67	737	1 in 19
Wrestling	86	1 in 100	224	1 in 42
Basketball	326	1 in 111	1,000	1 in 35
Volleyball	22	1 in 111	79	1 in 37
Women				
Rowing	85	2 in 1	141	3 in 1
Equestrian	13	1 in 2	39	1 in 1
Fencing	27	1 in 4	45	1 in 2
Rifle	27	1 in 4	36	1 in 4
Ice hockey	29	1 in 11	74	1 in 4
Gymnastics	63	1 in 16	85	1 in 12
Lacrosse	80	1 in 26	264	1 in 9
Water polo	31	1 in 26	61	1 in 15
Swimming/diving	188	1 in 30	489	1 in 14
Golf	228	1 in 31	483	1 in 16
X-Country	321	1 in 33	940	1 in 14
Field hockey	77	1 in 37	257	1 in 11
Skiing	16	1 in 39	39	1 in 19
Soccer	301	1 in 42	913	1 in 15
Track	295	1 in 42	704	1 in 22
Tennis	309	1 in 62	876	1 in 20
Softball	264	1 in 72	911	1 in 23
Bowling	28	1 in 83	45	1 in 50
Volleyball	311	1 in 91	982	1 in 29
Basketball	323	1 in 100	1,025	1 in 31

SOURCE NOTES

On the following pages is a select list of notes. The full version—several dozen pages of references, resources and details—can be found at the *Game On* link at www.tomfarrey.com.

Introduction

16 **nearly all of the 100 sports and activities measured** The SGMA publishes annual reports estimating national participation levels across a variety of sports. Between 1987 and 2006, the SGMA derived its estimates from surveys conducted by New York-based American Sports Data, a key provider of sports participation information to a variety of companies in several industries. In 2007, SMGA partnered with a new company, Synovate, whose survey employed a different questionnaire type (online instead of mail-based) and methodology, and had a higher household response volume (60,169 compared with 14,076). In that report, Synovate suggested that between 2000 and 2006 there were total participation drops among children and adults in baseball, basketball, hockey, softball, wrestling, and gymnastics. But no estimates are provided prior to 2000 in any sport, and SGMA advises against comparing the Synovate numbers with the American Sports Data figures, which differ slightly in places while still showing the same overall pattern—that total participation is down in many sports. As a result, when discussing SGMA numbers in the book, I cite findings from the American Sports Data surveys except where noted, as those reports are the only ones that track participation levels going back to the 1980s. Mike May, SGMA spokesman, told me that using figures and conclusions from those reports would be appropriate in terms of understanding long-term, historical trends.

Age 1

32 **the odds of a child's eventually making a living as an athlete** Author's estimate based on data supplied or distributed by the Census Bureau, the National Federation of High School Associations, the NCAA, and other college sports associations and professional leagues.

41 **a 2001 study of U.S. Olympic champions** "The Development of Psychological Talent in U.S. Olympic Champions," a report funded by the U.S. Olympic Committee and authored by Dan Gould.

Age 2

46 **the parent's desire to make the child's life better** All italicized passages in this chapter are taken from *Training a Tiger*.

48 **They learned to read as early as possible** Description of Puritan methods is drawn from *Huck's Raft: A History of American Childhood*, by Steven Mintz (Belknap/Harvard University Press, 2004).

49 **the benefits of early, supervised learning in golf** Ericsson's essay on the hourly commitment required by elite athletes was published in *Optimising Performance in Golf*, Patrick R. Thomas, ed. (Australian Academic Press, 2001).

55 **the transmission of nerve signals to the muscles** Much of the description of neural development is drawn from the second edition of *Growth, Maturation, and Physical Activity*, by Robert Malina, Claude Bouchard, and Oded Bar-Or, (Human Kinetics, 2004).

58 **first gaining proficiency on simpler maneuvers** Support for the green-to-tee method can be found in *Total Golf: A Behavioral Approach to Lowering Your Score and Getting More Out of Your Game*, by Thomas C. Simek and Richard M. O'Brien (Doubleday, 1981).

Age 3

69 **Nathan, a bespectacled boy in a Red Sox sweatshirt** Mark and Nathan's last name has been changed by the author due to information included about sexual offenders living near their home.

70 **a close friend who has been arrested in the past year** From the "Governor's Prevention Initiative for Youth Survey 2000," a report issued by the Governor's Prevention Partnership, a public-private initiative dedicated to the health and safety of children in Connecticut.

71 **function of the endocrine and immune systems** Health benefits of physical activity drawn from Healthy Youth!, a website sponsored by the National Center for Chronic Disease Prevention and Health Promotion, and "Physical Activity and Health, a Report of the Surgeon General," 1996.

athletes are more likely than nonathletes to attend college From Deven Carlson et al., "What Is the Status of High School Athletes Eight Years After Their Senior Year?" a 2005 report by the National Center for Education Statistics.

95 percent of their highest-ranking executives Various studies linking sports and academic or professional achievement can be found on the National Federation of High Schools website (www.nfhs.org).

74 **one semester of P.E. and one semester of health** Interview with Leonard Corto, athletic director for the Consolidated School District of New Britain and district coordinator for physical education, athletics, health, and safety.

those who attend a daily class has dropped to 33 percent These figures come from the National Youth Risk Behavior Survey, which monitors behaviors that contribute to the leading causes of death, disability, and social problems among the young. The 33 percent number is for high school students in 2005.

14 percent of schools reduced physical education time From "From the Capital to the Classroom: Year 4 of the No Child Left Behind Act," a March 2006 survey of schools conducted by the Center on Education Policy.

75 **among those that received any of the roughly $70 million** The SGMA's 2005 "State of the Industry" report lists the annual federal government support for the Physical Education for Progress (PEP) bill: $5 million in 2001, $50 million in 2002, $60 million in 2003, $69 million in 2004, and $74 million in 2005. The program received $67 million in 2006, bringing total PEP allocations to that point to $325 million. The "fun fitness" initiative referenced is run by PE4Life, a grant recipient that works with schools.

the average preteen absorbs 7,600 food commercials a year "Food for Thought: Television Food Advertising to Children in the United States," a Kaiser Family Foundation report published March 2007.

79 **a dramatic rise in corpulence** A survey of developed countries titled "Organization for Economic Co-Operation and Development Health Data 2006," places the U.S. at the top of the list in obesity rates.

80 **restrictions on team membership in high school** "Youth Sports: An Overview," by Martha Ewing and Vern Seefeldt, *President's Council for Physical Fitness and Sports Research Digest*, 1997.

81 **15 percent of its Gross Domestic Product (GDP) on health care** From the CDC report "Health, United States 2005."

82 **fitness habits of a child's parents play a key role** From the American Academy of Pediatrics policy statement "Prevention of Pediatric Overweight and Obesity," August 2003.

83 **one-quarter of all basketball shoes sold** Interview with Matt Powell of SportsOneSource, a research firm that focuses on the athletic footwear industry.

Age 4

89 **One study of Portuguese prospects** "Height, Mass, and Skeletal Maturity of Elite Portuguese Soccer Players Aged 11-16 Years," Robert M. Malina et al., *Journal of Sports Sciences*, 2000.

The pattern of skewed birth date distributions "The Relative Age Effect in Soccer: A Match-Related Perspective," R. Vaeyens et al., *Journal of Sports Sciences*, July 2005.

92 **"We should be modeling our programs on that"** From "Wayne Gretzky-Style 'Field Sense' May Be Teachable," Jennifer Kahn, *Wired*, May 22, 2007.

95 **Here's how Balyi describes the phases** From "Long-Term Athlete Development: Trainability in Childhood and Adolescence," by Istvan Balyi and Ann Hamilton. The article can be found in its entirety at: www.sportdevelopment.org.uk/bayli20041.pdf.

98 **to ... keep kids from committing to other sports** "Preschoolers Starting Sports Lessons," by Jeannine Stein, *Los Angeles Times*, June 5, 2007.

children do not fully develop these skills until 12 Jay Coakley, *Sports in Society: Issues and Controversies*, (McGraw-Hill, 2006).

99 **a paradigm-shifting, 70-page document** "Best Practices for Coaching Soccer in the United States," available at: www.ussoccer.com.

103 **more than doubled over the past two decades** Some of the information in this paragraph is drawn from "Soccer in the USA 2002-2003," published by the U.S. Soccer Foundation, and from a 2006 FIFA survey, "The Big Count."

most kids quit the game in ... their teenage years "Insight 2006: U.S. Trends in Team Sports," a SGMA report. It shows that 29.8 percent of 6-year-olds play outdoor soccer, rising to 34.3 percent at age 9, then falling to 19.3 percent by age 13 and 7.4 percent by age 18.

Age 5

105 **a short neck, bony cheeks, and deep-set, blue eyes** Information on John F. "Jack" Welch and his years at General Electric is drawn from interviews and from secondary sources. Among the books consulted were Welch's 2001 autobiography, written with John A. Byrne, *Jack: Straight from the Gut*, and *Winning*, co-written with his second wife, Suzy Welch.

108 **Youth sport is, like organized sports itself** D. Stanley Eitzen and George H. Sage, *Sociology of North American Sport*, (WCB/McGraw-Hill, 1997, sixth ed.).

110 **the "Muscular Christianity" movement** Background on Muscular Christianity is drawn from several sources, including Andrew W. Miracle Jr. and C. Roger Rees, *Lessons of the Locker Room* (Prometheus Books, 1994); and Mintz, *Huck's Raft*.

112 **"effectively control the play of a large number of children"** Luther Gulick, *A Philosophy of Play* (Charles Scribner's Sons, 1920), p. 12.

113 **a hearty endorsement of the PSAL** J. Thomas Jable, "The Public Schools Athletic League of New York City: Organized Athletics for City Schoolchildren, 1903-14," as reproduced and condensed in Chapter 12 of *The American Sporting Experience: A Historical Anthology of Sport in America*, by Steven A. Reiss (Leisure Press, 1984).

115 **when [children] are allowed to create their own games** Coakley, *Sports in Society: Issues and Controversies*, p. 132.

121 **A 1958 article** "Promoting Health, Teamwork and Sportsmanship: Little League Keeps Getting Bigger and Bigger," Dana Mozley, *The Sporting News*, August 20, 1958.

Age 6

128 **the pot had passed $1 billion** The totals on athletic scholarships were provided to the author by NCAA spokesman Erik Christiansen in a series of e-mails. Here's how much aid was distributed in Division I and II in selected years:

1992-93: $377 million to 86,411 athletes (or $4,362.87 per person)
1996-97: $649 million to 97,789 athletes ($6,636.74)
2000-01: $1.05 billion to 111,436 athletes ($9,422.45)
2003-04: $1.4 billion to 123,000 athletes ($11,382.11)

payouts had reached $1.5 billion NCAA president Myles Brand, from a letter dated Nov. 13, 2006, to Rep. William Thomas, then-chairman of the House Ways and Means Committee.

129 **the maximum value of a typical scholarship** Estimate by author using data presented by the College Board in its 2006 publication *Trends in College Pricing*.

130 **For football players it's 45 hours a week** "Hours Needed for Football Shocks NCAA," by Mike Knobler, *Atlanta Journal-Constitution*, Jan. 12, 2008.

annual operating revenues for all NCAA divisions From Brand's letter to Rep. Thomas. He wrote that of the $7.8 billion in total annual operative revenues for all NCAA divisions, $4.2 billion is generated from "athletics sources such as ticket revenues, contributions, and the like. The remaining $3.6 billion are funds allocated by the institution, state, or other governmental entities for the benefit of student-athletes."

only $12 million of the $109 million in revenues 2006-07 figures submitted to the U.S. Department of Education as required by the Equity in Athletics Disclosure Act.

131 **there are only 3,541 pros** The number of Italian club professional players (sixth most in the world) is drawn from FIFA's "The Big Count."

3,700 freshmen each year will receive formal commitments Author's estimate based on the 2003-04 NCAA Gender Equity Report.

135 **only 5,068 females under age 20 were registered** From "USA Hockey Female Registration Report, 1990-91 to 2004-05."

By 2000, two out of five high school girls played sports Calculated by the Women's Sports Foundation based on National Federation of State High School Associations and U.S. Department of Education statistics. For boys, the figure has remained constant at one in two since the signing of Title IX.

On the D1 level, there are now about 700 athletes on 34 teams As of Dec. 2007, according to the NCAA sports sponsorship database, available at: web1.ncaa.org/onlineDir/exec/sponsorship. There were 5 more teams than in 2005, the basis for the figures for the college odds chart in Appendix B.

Age 7

138 **the square-faced girl tending the net today** Amanda Reilly's name and those of other members of her family are pseudonyms. All other names in the chapter are unchanged.

145 **drawn from households with incomes of at least $100,000** From "Sports Participa-

tion in America: Ice Hockey," a 2006 report published by the SGMA.

146 **only four percent of kids from disadvantaged backgrounds** From "Who Reports Participation in Varsity Intercollegiate Athletics and 4-Year Colleges?" a Dec. 1996 survey and report by the National Center for Educational Statistics.

just under two-thirds of the athletes they recruited William G. Bowen and Sarah A. Levin, *Reclaiming the Game: College Sports and Educational Values* (Princeton University Press, 2003), p. 70.

147 **devote 260 days a year to your team** Robert A. McCormick and Amy Christian McCormick, "The Myth of the Student-Athlete: The College Athlete as Employee," *Washington Law Review*, February 2006, p. 103.

148 **cooperation and access were the cornerstones of its five precepts** Jable, *The American Sporting Experience*, p. 232.

149 **girls ... in strenuous sports** From *Gaining Ground: A Progress Report on Women in Sports*, SGMA, 1998, as reported by the Women's Sports Foundation.

They are less likely to get pregnant, smoke, or use illicit drugs Information drawn from the 2001 Women's Sports Foundation report "Health Risks and the Teen Athlete."

152 **no legal definition of amateurism** In an e-mail interview, Gary Roberts, Tulane law professor and the faculty athletics representative to the NCAA, said amateurism is "not a legally significant or defined term" under U.S. law. "The NCAA is free to define amateurism any way it chooses," writes Roberts, who served as president of the Sports Lawyers Association from 1995 to '97. "It could certainly allow students to sign endorsement deals or sign with an agent and still be an amateur."

more than 8,000 ... athletes from foreign countries From "1999-2000—2005-2006 NCAA Student-Athlete Race and Ethnicity Report," an NCAA publication.

156 **there are fewer women ... playing basketball now** From the SGMA's "U.S. Trends in Team Sports." There were 11 million girls and women of all ages playing basketball in 1987, 12.9 million in 2000, and 10 million in 2005. Among both sexes, frequent players (those who play at least 52 times a year) have fallen from a peak of 10.2 million in 1993 to 7 million in 2005. The total number of players has dropped from its peak of 45 million in 1997 to 32 million. Since 1998, players who said basketball was their favorite sport dropped from 26 to 21 percent. The number of first-year-players has slowed most dramatically, from 6.5 million in the '90s to 3.7 million in 2005.

Age 8

159 **one count found 21 such groups in ... baseball alone** "A Lot to Play For," Brad Townsend, *Dallas Morning News*, July 24, 2005.

167 **He had bought it for the family of King** AAU President Bobby Dodd, in an e-mail interview, wrote that in 1999 he did buy the house in question, but that "I did not buy a house for Travis King. I did purchase a home that my granddaughters live in." Dodd, who does not have children, considers King's children to be family.

173 **"focus on enjoyment rather than competition"** From "Active Healthy Living: Prevention of Childhood Obesity Through Increased Physical Activity," a 2006 AAP policy statement.

175 **only one received a payout** Klinkhammer says he was shown claim figures by the AAU's insurance broker, Jim Foy, at a risk-assessment seminar in the early 1990s. Foy declined to confirm or deny any figures he may have shown Klinkhammer but suggested that

Klinkhammer's recall might not be accurate. "I sit there and explain insurance to people, and they don't understand," Foy said. Foy declined to provide an average monetary payout on AAU claims but called the organization's policy the best in youth sports for coaches and athletes. "Insurance costs are far more than people think," he said. "Just because we don't pay a claim doesn't mean we don't spend a lot of money figuring out if we should pay a claim."

175 **The AAU terminated his contract in 2005** Dodd says the AAU ended its contract with MYSA because "we didn't want them using our mailing list to promote other events. Klinkhammer runs good program. I wouldn't say anything negative about him. But the AAU district wanted to take it over again instead of having it run by an outside group." Klinkhammer denies that he was using the AAU's mailing list to promote other events and says the AAU ended the relationship because it demanded that MYSA work exclusively with Dodd's organization.

176 **35 percent of all overnight stays that Americans make** "Youth Sports Have Sweet Smell of Money," by Lya Wodraska, *The Salt Lake Tribune*, October 23, 2005.

his club received money over a longer period The information on the crimes committed by Sweeney and his relationship with Dodd are drawn mostly from three sources: Dodd's interview with the author; a transcript of the minutes from a Feb. 16, 2005, AAU Executive Committee meeting in Orlando; and reporting by Alan Schmadtke of the *Orlando Sentinel*, including his Dec. 7, 2003, article, "Longtime AAU Relationship: Leader Dodd has Long History with Sweeney, Despite Latter's Misdeeds."

177 **"We call that bad character"** Dodd, in an e-mail interview, responded: "I expressed to several people, after the fact, that if the situation of sponsorship from an association were to come up again that I would be a club member that would not recommend it. I do not recall discussing this with Dan at the time of my visit. Perhaps I did."

178 **Williams runs a summer league** The Boo Williams Summer League Ltd., based in the Hampton Roads area of Virginia, was given $65,000 in cash and $50,000 in noncash items by Nike in 2004, according to the league's federal tax filing. The organization sponsors 140 AAU and summer-league teams for kids between the ages of 10 and 19, with revenues of $914,000 and expenses of $845,000.

179 **granting those tournaments to Dodd's personal AAU club** Williams says Dodd's YOMCA club pays an annual fee to cohost the 8-and-under and 13-and-under national boys' championships. Williams declined to say how much. He said no other groups have bid on the event, but that the committee would consider any bid. The tournament was first granted to Dodd's club about a decade ago, when Ron Crawford was chair of the basketball committee. He said he generally preferred to keep national championship tournaments in one city, and that Dodd runs a good tournament, so it has stayed in Memphis. "Some people say the bid process is not fair," Crawford said. "But I want those kids to have a great experience and that comes from experienced officials."

180 **a tax filing signed and provided to me by Dodd** The document referred to is an AAU 990 form that covered the 12-month period leading up to Aug. 31, 2005.

Age 9

187 **The Amateur Sports Act of 1978** Updated in 1998, it was renamed the Ted Stevens Olympic and Amateur Sports Act, to reflect, among other changes, the fact that amateurism is no longer a requirement for competing in most international sports.

192 **only the elite performers accorded a share of the spotlight** "Youth Sports in America: An

Overview," by Vern D. Seefeldt and Martha Ewing. The paper was a condensation of materials contained in a monograph, *The Role of Organized Sport in Education and Health of American Children and Youth*, commissioned by the Carnegie Corporation of New York in 1996.

195 **a roadmap for anyone or any organization** "The Path to Excellence" can be found at www.usolympicteam.com/excellence/Olympian_Report.pdf. The 2003 follow-up, "Reflections on Success," is at www.usolympicteam.com/ReflectionsonSucces.pdf.

198 **With untrained coaches, the attrition rate was 26 percent** Drawn from a 1992 study by University of Washington professors Ron Smith and Frank Smoll. A summary of this and related studies can be found in a paper by the Institute for the Study of Youth Sports: ed-web3.educ.msu.edu/ysi/project/CriticalIssuesYouthSports.pdf.

199 **survey results presented to the American College of Sports Medicine** Robert Rohloff, a Milwaukee-based pediatrician, led an anonymous survey of 376 parents of youngsters ages 3 to 22 involved in organized sports, the majority in elementary and middle school.

200 **insurance premiums for the NBA stars ... in the Athens Olympics** The cost of insuring the NBA contracts of players was in "the mid-six figures," according to USA Basketball spokesman Craig Miller. Other figures derived from the body's federal tax filings.

201 **there is no such program** Miller said discussions about requiring coaches' education have not been well received by affiliates, due to "self-interest. None of them are going to say, 'Hey, USA Basketball, take $10 from our fees and create a program.'" Unlike soccer, swimming, and some other federations, USA Basketball does not receive a cut of youth memberships.

Age 10

208 **Ten is the age at which the average future U.S. Olympian** Sports in which Olympians first found local competitive success at that age include ice hockey, gymnastics, alpine skiing, and figure skating. See "The Path to Excellence," p. 19.

210 **serves as chief pathologist for seven Australian hospitals** As in the rest of the book, the present tense here describes the time at which the chapter was being reported, in this case Dec. 2004. In Aug. 2006, after moving from Melbourne to Brisbane, Venter resigned from Genetic Technologies to focus on his pathology job with the Mater Health Services.

212 **30 individual teams or athletes in all** "Aussies Rule the World," by Alex Murdoch, *The Courier-Mail*, Nov. 9, 2007.

215 **Australian Sports Commission ... now receives $205 million** Most of the financial figures regarding Australian government investment in sports are provided by Peter Logue, Australian Sports Commission spokesman. Like the USOC, Australia's Olympic Committee itself receives no government support. However, with the AIS driving research and elite athlete development and the ASC overseeing the nation's sports activity, the Olympic Committee plays a much less critical role in that country than does the USOC in the U.S.

221 **Meet the next Ole Einar Bjørndalen** Norway's Bjørndalen is the dominant athlete in the biathlon, having won five Olympic gold medals.

after a decade of knocking skulls The information about the gene APOE and harm suffered by boxers and pro football players is drawn from academic studies in 1997 and 2000 led by Dr. Barry Jordan of New York Hospital-Cornell University Medical College.

224 **The AAU pays their expenses, keeping a small fee** Information on the President's Challenge was provided by Jeff McClaine, Associate Director of the program.

226 **fascinated with the mortal machinery of athletes** Information about Naismith comes

from *Big Game, Small World*, by Alexander Wolff (Warner Books, 2002).

229 **the CTSA report card he unveils** "2005 Youth Sports National Report Card," by the Citizenship Through Sports Alliance.

Age 11

234 **the Orioles moved into ... Camden Yards with a sweetheart lease** During the term of the 30-year lease, the Orioles pay rent based on a complicated sharing arrangement taking into account admissions, concessions, novelty, parking, advertising, and other revenues, according to the Maryland Stadium Authority. In addition, the Authority and the city share the 10 percent statewide admissions and amusement tax (8 percent goes to the Authority, 2 percent to the city). The city pays the Authority $1 million annually for the length of the lease.

worth more than twice what Angelos paid for it *Forbes* valued the Orioles at $395 million in its rankings of franchise values, "Business of Baseball," April 19, 2007.

236 **the hunt for national championships for little kids was taking hold** In contrast to funding for rec centers, city money has been made available since the 1980s for youth travel teams qualifying for regional and national tournaments through a contractual arrangement with the company that runs the municipal golf courses. The contract spins off about $400,000 a year for travel teams in all sports.

Corey Jones Jones' name has been changed by the author to protect his identity due to the disclosure of his illegal drug activity.

239 **insisted that he learn to play every position** Background on Babe Ruth's childhood and his years at St. Mary's is drawn from: *Babe: The Legend Comes to Life*, Robert W. Creamer (Simon & Schuster, 1974); *Young Babe Ruth:His Early Life and Baseball Career, from the Memoirs of a Xaverian Brother*, Brother Gilbert (McFarland and Co. Publishers, 1999); and exhibits at the Babe Ruth Birthplace and Museum in Baltimore.

242 **a 47-page analysis** "Baltimore's Camden Yards Ballparks," by Bruce W. Hamilton and Peter Kahn, Nov. 1996. Kahn was Hamilton's graduate assistant. The report is available at: www.econ.jhu.edu/people/Hamilton/Camden.pdf.

spun off $7.6 million in local sales taxes "The Impact of Oriole Park at Camden Yards on Maryland's Economy," a report compiled by Towson University on behalf of the Maryland Stadium Authority, April 2007. Available at: www.mdstad.com/pdf/OriolePark.pdf.

245 **they stayed with the foundation** Figures for the Orioles' support of local baseball were provided by club spokesperson Monica Pence. The Baltimore Orioles Foundation tax filings mentioned are for 2003 through 2005.

the Ravens provided $1 million in charity to local organizations Figures on Ravens contributions were provided by community relations director Melanie LeGrande. The $1 million in program services to the community figure is according to the 2005 tax filing of the Ravens All-Community Team Foundation.

as much as the city of Baltimore spent The city allotted $12.1 million for all recreational services in 2006, according to the city's Recreation and Parks division fiscal budget. Items covered by that amount include the operation of recreation centers and playgrounds, all pools, specialized facilities for soccer and ice skating, programs for senior citizens and the handicapped, plus providing SAT training for students.

246 **at a cost of more than $20 billion** Author's estimate of stadiums and arenas built, renovated, or approved since 1992, from an analysis of two sources: the Marquette Univer-

sity Law School Sports Facility Reports (available at law.marquette.edu) and the League of Fans (see www.leagueoffans.org/mlbstadiums1990.html).

247 **the nation is now wildcatting for youth sports** The Gulf of Mexico Energy Security Act of 2006, which allows expansion of off-shore oil and gas drilling in the eastern Gulf, sets aside 12.5 percent of royalty revenues for the Land and Water Conservation Fund—which has helped to create more than 40,000 athletic and playing fields, 12,000 hiking trails, 5,000 campgrounds, 10,000 swimming and boating facilities, and 600 hunting and nature areas in addition to hundreds of state parks in every state in the nation—beginning in 2016 potentially could deliver $100 million a year, according to the National Recreation and Park Association.

The last check written to any city under the act was in 2003 Administered by the National Park Service of the Department of the Interior, the Urban Park and Recreation Recovery program was established in 1978, with an authorization of $725 million to provide matching grants and technical assistance to economically distressed cities and counties. Since then, a total of approximately 1,500 grants totaling more than $270 million have been paid. Baltimore has received $4.6 million of that money.

Baltimore gets some state assistance for its parks The 2006 recreation and parks budget for Baltimore was $29.1 million, of which $172,775 came from the state and $4.2 million came from a motor vehicle tax, according to the city budget. Nothing from federal sources.

248 **no other ethnic group has lost more sports participants** From "United States High School Sophomores: A Twenty-Two Year Comparison, 1980–2002," a September 2006 report by the National Center for Education Statistics. In 1980, 57.1 percent of African-American high school sophomores competed in sports. By 1990 that figure had fallen to 51.4 percent, and by 2002 it had dropped to 48.8. Among whites, the percentage remained relatively stable during that same period (from 54.4 to 53.8 percent). Hispanics and Asians also experienced a drop-off in participation rates, though not as steep as African-Americans. The report can be found at: nces.ed.gov/pubs2006/2006327.pdf.

Age 12

258 **dropped from 2.6 to 2.3 million over the past decade** Annual Little League participation figures are available at: www.littleleague.org/about/aroundtheworld.asp.

259 **according to annual surveys** "Sports Participation in America: Participation Trends in 103 Fitness, Sports, Outdoor, and Recreation Activities," SGMA's 2006 report and others from previous years.

265 **"We can't start asking how many nights he slept there"** Keener says the document submitted to Little League Baseball shows that custody of Vonn was transferred to Pativaine Scanlan after a Jan. 12, 2005, hearing in family court. The reasons for the transfer are not listed on the document. The attorney who submitted the paperwork on behalf of the Fe'aos, Craig Kugisaki, did not return phone calls, and Heather and Sese Fe'ao, Vonn's parents, could not be reached. Layton Aliviado said that he didn't know how to reach them either. Vonn did not return a phone message requesting an interview with his parents.

the father of one boy killed a neighbor "Man Accused of Killing Neighbor Over Little League Dispute," by Chris Park, *The Morning Call* (Allentown, Pa.), June 1, 2007.

269 **Reynolds, the color analyst** Harold Reynolds would later lose his job with ESPN due to an allegation of sexual harassment, stemming from an incident he claims was just a hug. He now works for MLB.com and is suing ESPN over his dismissal.

271 **he suggested that the tournament he created be abolished** Stotz's founding Little League, his battles with the board, and his eventual departure from the organization are drawn from several sources, including an interview with Karen Stotz Myers and *Play Ball! The Story of Little League Baseball*, by Lance and Robin Van Auken (Penn State Press, 2001).

274 **one Little League chapter just added webcasts of games** Houston's West University Little League installed cameras in 2005.

275 **teams ran out of quality pitchers** The injuries to Rancho Buena Vista players were reported by Charles Euchner in *Little League, Big Dreams: Inside the Hope, the Hype, and the Glory of the Greatest World Series Ever Played* (Sourcebooks, 2006).

276 **500 percent more likely to injure their elbows** The findings of Glenn Fleisig, research director of the American Sports Medicine Institute. He summarized his research on Little League's website in March 2006. Viewable at: www.littleleague.org/askll/06marsession.asp.

quietly backed down two years later on the advice of lawyers Little League's "dual participation" rule was challenged by the American Softball Association in March 1992 over a teen who wanted to play on two teams at the same time, according to LLB president Steve Keener. The case was resolved out of court in February 1994.

280 **Don Turley, manager of the Spring team, would say to a reporter** From "Too Much, Too Soon," by Mark Zeigler and Ed Graney, Copley News Service, Aug. 26, 2005.

he didn't mention Little League when filling out a questionnaire "The Winner," S.L. Price, *Sports Illustrated*, Apr. 16, 2007.

Age 13

291 **worth about $1 million annually to his athletic department** Estimate provided to *The Indianapolis Star* by Robert Brown, a professor of economics at Cal State-San Marcos.

292 **Durant survived the U.S. system more than he benefited from it** Background on Durant comes largely from two sources: "Kevin Durant: The Kid Who Could Be King," a May 24, 2007, article by Percy Allen of *The Seattle Times*, and "Durant on Durant," an as-told-to piece compiled by Elena Bergeron in the July 2, 2007 edition of *ESPN The Magazine*.

293 **the $7 to $10 million a year** Estimate provided by Sonny Vaccaro, a founder of the summer-basketball industry who has worked for Nike, Adidas, and Reebok.

303 **foreign players will comprise half of the NBA by 2010** Raveling was quoted in a *USA Today* article by Greg Boeck on April 21, 2006, "Team-First, Back-to-Basics Foreigners Changing NBA."

Age 14

310 **the principal and 20 other officials would hear about the incident** Information about the events surrounding the crime, including its handling by school officials, is drawn from multiple sources, including author interviews and a review of more than 1,000 pages of testimony and other documents that were part of the State Attorney's case against former Miami Northwestern principal Dwight Bernard. Bernard pleaded not guilty to the charge of official misconduct, a felony. At the time this book went to press, his trial was pending.

who ... told him not to tell anyone about the incident Part of Easterling's statement to prosecutors, according to a transcript of his sworn statement. When asked by the author about this claim, Smith denied Easterling's account.

313 **children begin playing tackle football ... around age 11** The SGMA's "U.S. Trends in Team Sports," 2006. Among major team sports, tackle football has the oldest peak age

(15) in terms of total participation. However, the sport loses more than half of its participants between the start and end of high school as freshman and jayvee options evaporate: from 570,000 players at age 15, to 400,000 at 16, to 230,000 by age 18.

315 **its costly national championships** Football programs from poor areas around the country have struggled with the cost of sending teams to the Pop Warner Super Bowl. In order to participate in the December event, teams were required to stay at Disney hotels and buy tickets to other parks within Walt Disney World, according to a Jan. 7, 2007, *Boston Globe* report by Bob Hohler. Pop Warner, which has held its championships there since 1997, is the rare organization that imposes these requirements on teams playing at the complex.

320 **arrested for allegedly forcing a 13-year-old girl to give him oral sex** Miami-Dade police officials allege that Morris took a student into his office at the Jan Mann Opportunity School and forced her to perform oral sex, according to a report filed Sept. 15, 2005. At the time this book when to press, his trial was pending.

322 **precisely the kind of student he wanted to support** Crew's views are drawn from an interview with the author and from his statement to the State Attorney's office.

326 **For its other 16 athletic teams, the school spent just $77,279 combined** Financial data for the 2006-07 school year drawn from the school's annual ledger, as supplied in response to a public records request.

injuries that can linger for a lifetime These injuries occur in other sports, too, just not with as much frequency. Football has the highest injury rate of all high school sports—4.36 per 1,000 practices and games ("athletic exposures"), according to the Centers for Disease Control. The overall injury rate for all sports is 2.44 per 1,000 athletic exposures.

playing with residual symptoms from a prior head injury "High School Players Shrug Off Concussions, Raising Risks," by Alan Schwarz, *The New York Times*, Sept. 15, 2007. The study cited in the article was led by Barry P. Boden of the Orthopaedic Center in Rockville, Md., and its results were published in *The American Journal of Sports Medicine*.

Steroids use among teenagers ... has fallen The University of Michigan's Monitoring the Future study shows that the percentage of 12- to 17-year-olds who have tried steroids declined by 45 percent between 2001 and 2007. The survey looks at use among all students, not just athletes.

Epilogue

349 **tailored to kids' needs and interests** "Guidelines for School and Community Programs to Promote Lifelong Physical Activity Among Young People," CDC recommendations, March 7, 1997. Available at: www.cdc.gov/mmwr/preview/mmwrhtml/00046823.htm.

Appendices

361 **The probability of a high school athlete going on to play in college** High school participation numbers used are drawn from a 2005-06 report by the National Federation of State High School Associations. College rates are for the 2004-05 year and are drawn from the NCAA's "Sports Sponsorship and Participation Rates Report: 1981-82 to 2004-05." Figures do not account for roster slots that may go to foreign students. All percentages are rounded to tenths.

Women: Rowing As a sport, rowing is a statistical anomaly. Participants often compete on the club level during high school. Colleges tend to have large women's teams, in part to offset large rosters of football players on the men's side. As a result, there are more women on NCAA-sponsored crew teams than there are on high school squads.

INDEX

C

ABOUT THE AUTHOR

TOM FARREY is an investigative journalist whose work has been recognized for excellence in print, on television, and online. A correspondent with ESPN's prime-time newsmagazine *E:60*, he also has reported on air for ESPN's *Outside the Lines* and *SportsCenter*, as well as ESPN.com and *ESPN The Magazine*, where he is a senior writer. He joined ESPN in 1996, after eight years with *The Seattle Times*. In 2007, he was one of seven journalists selected among the 100 Most Influential Sports Educators in America by the Institute for International Sport at the University of Rhode Island. His reports have won many honors, including two Emmy awards for Outstanding Sports Journalism.

Farrey lives in Connecticut with his wife, Christine, and their three children, Cole, Anna, and Kellen. This is his first book.